The Government

and the Economy, 1783–1861

EDITED BY

CARTER GOODRICH
University of Pittsburgh

THE BOBBS-MERRILL COMPANY, INC.

A Subsidiary of Howard W. Sams & Co., Inc.

PUBLISHERS • INDIANAPOLIS • NEW YORK • KANSAS CITY

IN MEMORY OF MY FATHER
CHARLES LYMAN GOODRICH
AND OF MY WIFE'S GRANDMOTHER
FLORENCE PERRY VILLERS
WHO SHARED WITH US RECOLLECTIONS OF
AMERICAN LIFE IN NEW ENGLAND VILLAGES
AND IN NEW YORK CITY, WHICH CARRIED
BACK INTO THE PERIOD OF THIS BOOK.

FOREWORD

It is only natural that a generation which confronts the problem of economic growth in today's underdeveloped nations should look back to the American experience as a new nation and be tempted to contrast today's "national planning" with the "individualism" of early America. Yet, as Carter Goodrich pointed out in an address to the Economic History Association a decade ago, "it is not quite true that the United States just 'growed' like Topsy."

As a glance at the major headings of this volume will suggest, American governments, from the winning of Independence to the outbreak of the Civil War, promoted transportation, encouraged manufactures, protected commerce, and regulated various phases of the economy. The state and federal governments did not engage in central planning nor in a massive amount of public enterprise, yet, as Professor Goodrich concludes in his Introduction, they "took deliberate action to promote industrialization and economic growth" even if "on a largely pragmatic basis."

This anthology illustrates and will enable others to test this thesis. It is testimony to the way in which a generation of scholars has reversed a cherished popular myth, as well as to the way in which scholarship can be enriched by present-day comparisons. The documents are chosen from a wide range of usually inaccessible materials—reports by government agencies, state papers, speeches in state legislatures and Congress, executive messages, memorials, and laws. The selections and the introductions that set each in its context are informed by years of research by Professor Goodrich and a host of scholars, a number of whom he has guided or stimulated. The book also testifies to Professor Goodrich's years of practical experience, ranging from his service in the 1940's as Chairman of the governing body of the International Labor Organization, to the economic missions for the United Nations in the 1950's that took him to the Middle East, South America, and Southeast Asia.

This book is one of a series whose aim is to provide the essential primary sources of the American experience, especially of American thought. The series, when completed, will constitute a documentary library of American history, filling a need long felt among scholars, students, libraries, and general readers for authoritative collections of original materials. Some volumes will illuminate the thought of significant individuals, such as James Madison or Louis Brandeis; some will deal with movements, such as the Antifederalists or the Populists; others will be organized around special themes, such as Puritan political thought, or American Catholic thought on social questions. Many volumes will take up the large number of subjects traditionally studied in American history for which, surprisingly, there are no documentary anthologies; others will pioneer in introducing contemporary subjects of increasing importance. The series aspires to maintain the high standards demanded of contemporary editing, providing authentic texts, intelligently and unobtrusively edited. It will also have the distinction of presenting pieces of substantial length which give the full character and flavor of the original. The series will be the most comprehensive and authoritative of its kind.

Alfred Young
Leonard W. Levy

CONTENTS

Part Two: The Encouragement of Western Settlement

Part Three: The Encouragement of Manufactures

Part Six: The Facilitation of Corporate Enterprise

Part Seven: The Development of Human Capacities

Part Eight: The Utilization of the Working Force

SLAVERY

FREE LABOR

IMMIGRATION

INTRODUCTION

The Economic Functions of
American Governments

This book of contemporary documents examines the economic functions of American governments in the period between 1783 and 1861. The United States that emerged from the Revolution was a nation of farmers and planters with an active minority of merchants. Agriculture and commerce continued to advance, but the decades immediately preceding the Civil War also laid the firm foundations of the nation's greatness as an industrial power. In the light of the present-day efforts of the developing nations to industrialize, it is of particular interest to ask what was the role of government in promoting the industrialization of the United States.

The traditional answer has been that the role was very small indeed and that American economic development was the work of private enterprise subject only to the minimum of government aid or interference. A recent economic history of the period by Douglass North brings new support to this viewpoint. North argues that, at least for the years between 1815 and 1860, economic growth can be explained for the most part by the responses of individuals to market forces with relatively little need to take into account the decisions of governments.[1] On the other hand, Guy Stevens Callender called attention to

---

[1] Douglass C. North, *Economic Growth of the United States, 1790–1860* (Englewood Cliffs, N.J.: Prentice-Hall, 1961), especially pp. 66–67.

a "remarkable movement toward state enterprise here in America, where of all places in the world we should least expect it."[2]

Callender's principal reference was to governmental measures to promote the construction of the means of transport—roads, river improvements, canals, and railroads. This activity was indeed extensive and it was undertaken by governments at every level—national, state, and local. Part One below suggests something of the range of projects and agencies and the variety of relationships between governmental and private enterprise. In spite of the comprehensive plan for national action proposed by Albert Gallatin (Document 1), the federal role turned out to be a relatively minor one; but almost every state took part in the movement, as well as ambitious merchant cities like Baltimore and Philadelphia and a large number of other local governments. During the period, governmental sources contributed over seventy per cent of the total investment in canals and, though the figures are less complete, perhaps thirty per cent of the investment in railroads.

In this field, governmental activity was plainly intended to promote economic development, even if the phrase was not then in use. Contemporary proponents found justification for it in the same arguments that are now used to support the expenditures of modern governments in providing various forms of social overhead capital before it would be profitable for private enterprise to supply them. The Army Engineers in 1823 drew a distinction between two types of improvement. Some, which serve settled areas, should be judged "like all commercial speculations" by their rate of return. Others, however,

---

2 Guy Stevens Callender, "The Early Transportation and Banking Enterprises of the States," 1902, reprinted in J. T. Lambie and R. V. Clemence, eds., *Economic Change in America* (Harrisburg, Pa.: The Stackpole Co., 1954), pp. 522–559. See especially pp. 522–524.

should be viewed "with reference to general, rather than individual advantage":

> The revenue from a canal may be much less than that on ordinary investments, and yet benefits amount to much more, as regards national economy and advantage. On this hypothesis, the defect of revenue is amply compensated, as regards the nation, by the greater facility and speed of transportation, thereby making the articles conveyed less costly, the circulation of capital more rapid, and a larger proportion of the labour of men and animals disposable for the other branches of industry; and also, by opening extensive regions to a market, which, without this cheap mode of conveyance, would be inaccessible.[3]

Projects undertaken or supported by public authorities were in general of the second type, on which substantial traffic and revenue could be expected only if and when the improvement itself stimulated economic activity in what had been largely an undeveloped area. The main purpose, then, was developmental, "the revenue," as the Engineers said, "being a secondary object."

Under these circumstances, it is not surprising that a consolidated balance sheet of the various governments concerned, if one could be made, would show that they spent more on internal improvements than they ever received in direct returns. Some of the undertakings were poorly conceived, and some of the public or mixed enterprises were seriously mismanaged; and Pennsylvania's state works (Document 5) provide one of a number of illustrations of programs begun with enthusiasm

---

[3] "Report of the United States Army Engineers on the Morris Canal," cited by H. Jerome Cranmer in Carter Goodrich, ed., *Canals and Economic Development* (New York: Columbia University Press, 1961), p. 157. From this Professor Cranmer draws the distinction between *exploitative* improvements, which could earn early profits because they exploited existing trade opportunities, and *developmental* improvements. See also Gallatin's argument in Document 1.

and abandoned in disgust. Still others, however, were conspicuously successful. The Erie Canal, a state enterprise that did so much to open the West and create a national market, represents one of the great breakthroughs in American economic history. It is, moreover, difficult to believe that the railroad network could have reached Chicago, St. Louis, and beyond by 1861 if the Baltimore and Ohio and Pennsylvania Railroads had not been helped over the barrier of the Appalachian Mountains by substantial amounts of municipal investment. On balance it seems clear that the net effect of government promotion in this period was to give a significant impetus to the economic growth of the country.

Both developmental purpose and developmental effect are also to be found in government policies concerning the land. Here the principal concern was the transfer of the vast public domain into private hands; and the principal agency was the federal government, which owned by far the greatest part of it, although certain of the states, such as Georgia (Document 8) and Texas faced a similar problem and handled it in somewhat similar ways. The two great alternatives of policy were either to treat the public domain as a great fiscal resource and therefore sell it in the way and at the pace that would yield the largest revenue, or on the other hand to dispose of the land in the way that would do most to promote the settlement of the West. The struggle was a complex one and, as Part Two shows, gave rise to great debate; but it was the second alternative that prevailed. In Document 6 Senator William H. Seward defines the best and highest interest of the people of the United States with respect to this domain:

> It is not to derive from it the highest amount of current revenue; it is not to accumulate in our coffers the highest and greatest amount of avails in the sales of the public lands which is available. But it is to bring them into cultivation and settlement in the shortest space of time and under the most favorable auspices.

The objective of rapid settlement was generally although not always taken for granted in the American debates. A contemporary Englishman, Edward Gibbon Wakefield, erected an entire theory of colonization on his judgment that the United States offered a bad example of excessive and wasteful dispersion of settlement; but national expansion and the creation of new states seem to have appeared desirable ends to most Americans and certainly to almost all the spokesmen for the West. Belief in this objective provided support for grants of land to railroad corporations as well as for measures making the land available on easier terms to actual settlers.

The objective of settlement "under the most favorable auspices" raised a different issue. "It should be the policy of republics," so Thomas Hart Benton told the Senate, "to multiply their freeholders," who should, as he said, be thought of as more precious to a nation than rubies (Document 10). Few of his colleagues matched his rhetoric, but the objective of encouraging settlement on the basis of the family farm won increasing recognition in the debates and in the legislation. At the end of the period only the presidential veto of James Buchanan (Document 13) prevented the adoption of a Homestead Act.

The effectiveness of legislative measures in determining the actual occupation of the land should not be exaggerated. Even when the intent of the measure was to favor the small working farmer, in practice he often had to purchase at a somewhat higher price from a "speculator" who had obtained title before him. On the other hand, a quite different qualification is suggested by the successful assertion of "squatter's rights" reported in the Senate debates (Document 11). Given the nature of the western land and its adaptability to growing corn and wheat, it might be argued that it would have been difficult to devise legislation to keep the small farmer *off* the land, just as it would have been difficult to devise legislation to put the small farmer *on* the land of the sheepruns of Australia, where the "squatter" was a large holder rather than a small one, or on the Argentine pampas in the great days of the cattle industry. Nevertheless it remains significant that so large a legislative effort was devoted to promoting the rapid settlement of the West and that part of it was consciously directed toward fostering a particular type of social structure.

The actions for the encouragement of manufactures may also be regarded as deliberately promotive in purpose. The writings of Alexander Hamilton and Friedrich List placed the case for protection on national grounds, arguing that manufacturing would make fuller use of the capacities of the people and that infant industries in the difficult period of transition needed "the incitement and patronage of government" (Documents 15, 17). It was, however, only after the forcing period of the Embargo and the War of 1812 had brought about considerable growth of manufacturing that the infant industries had attained substantial interests to protect and influence to exert. Major controversy over the tariff began at this time; and in its later course, as Documents 18 and 19 suggest, it is much easier to observe the play of conflicting business, local, and regional interests than it is to detect the working out of any rational scheme of national priorities. Nor is it possible to assess with confidence the effects of protection on industrial development. The notable advance in the 1850's, perhaps the most decisive decade in American manufacturing history, took place under protection but also under tariff rates that were lower than in the decades that preceded and followed it. Given the resources of the country and the attitudes of its people, it may perhaps be suggested, as in the case of western settlement, that it would have been hard to devise legislation that would have prevented the development of the United States into a great manufacturing nation.[4]

In the quite different field of education, governmental deci-

---

[4] American scholars have been inclined to follow the view of the late Professor Taussig, the greatest authority on American tariff history, that the effect of protection on American industrial development was a rela-

sions seem to have had an important effect on the development of the economy. One of the interesting recent tendencies in the thinking of American economists is the new emphasis on, or rediscovery of, the importance of education as a factor in economic development. In this the direct contribution of the federal government was very limited; and George Washington's dream of a national university, for which his will provided a bequest (Document 37), failed to materialize. State governments, however, in some cases aided by federal land grants, spent considerable sums of money in assisting colleges and academies and in creating state universities. Moreover, extensive programs of public school education were carried on by the cooperation of state and local authorities—in Massachusetts, where Horace Mann was the leader and spokesman (Document 39), and in many other states, although less extensively in the South than in the North. Contemporary foreign observers, such as those who attended the New York Industrial Exhibition in 1853 (Document 40), testified that the United States led the world in its provisions for public education and found in them one explanation for the nation's rapid industrial progress.

All these represented governmental decisions relating to economic development that historians cannot properly ignore. Our sense of their importance has been heightened by recent studies of the previously neglected activities of state and local authorities, particularly those of the Handlins on Massachusetts, Hartz on Pennsylvania, Heath on Georgia, and Primm on Missouri.[5]

---

tively minor one. Frank W. Taussig, *Some Aspects of the Tariff Question* (Cambridge: Harvard University Press, 1915), and *The Tariff History of the United States*, 7th ed. (New York: G. P. Putnam's Sons, 1923). Perhaps the time has now come, with the availability of new quantitative methods and materials, to attempt a reappraisal of the question, examining the growth of competing industries in other countries as well as that of American industry.

[5] See Bibliographical Note below. These and a number of other books referred to in the Note were sponsored by the Committee (now Council) on Research in Economic History.

A renewed appreciation of "the effect of education upon worldly fortunes" has also increased our sense of the economic importance of the government activity of the time, again at the state and local levels. Examining the role of government from a somewhat different point of view, Henry W. Broude has analyzed certain types of government expenditures, particularly in the West, "which may have resulted, though only as a by-product, in positive contributions to development."[6]

American governmental efforts to promote development went much further than any that had been undertaken in the earlier industrial revolution in Great Britain, where most of the canals and all the railroads were built by private capital. In this comparison the American "movement toward state enterprise," broadly defined, does indeed appear "remarkable." On the other hand, the promotive actions of American governments were considerably less extensive than the tasks attempted by governments in many of the developing nations of today. If the Part headings of this book are taken as a checklist of economic functions frequently performed by governments, the limits and the specialized nature of American action become at once apparent.

This is true even in transportation, where the volume of public investment and its strategic importance were so great. Government promotion was almost entirely limited in practice and intention to projects believed to be "developmental" rather than "exploitative"; it increasingly took the form of participation with private enterprise rather than of public works; and leadership in these jointly supported projects came more often from the private than from the public side. Sometimes, indeed, this was a matter of deliberate policy; and a committee of Virginia legislators, for example, based their proposals on the

---

[6] In H. G. J. Aitken, ed., *The State and Economic Growth* (New York: Social Science Research Council, 1959), reprinted in H. N. Scheiber, ed., *United States Economic History: Selected Readings* (New York: Alfred A. Knopf, 1964), pp. 114–135, especially p. 124.

belief that these works would be carried on more economically "if their management be left to the individuals who subscribe to their stock with a view to private gain" (Document 3).

In the case of land policy, the importance of the decisions regarding the disposition of the public domain should not obscure a recognition of how much was *not* decided by government. The public authorities did not attempt "land reform" in the controversial modern sense of taking land away from large holders for distribution to smaller ones, although the more extreme "land reformers" of the day did try unsuccessfully to obtain legislation to prevent the formation of large holdings. Governments did not give direct guidance to the process of colonization, or adopt programs of soil conservation; and they did little to improve the techniques of agriculture. State legislatures gave encouragement to voluntary agricultural societies that were attempting to make agriculture more scientific, but a proposal for federal land grants to the states for the development of agricultural colleges was vetoed at the end of the period (Document 37). Governments at various levels helped provide the means by which the farmer could get his produce to market. The federal government might pass the public land "cheaply and easily" into his hands. Once on the land, however, which crops he raised and how he raised them were his own responsibility.

In the case of manufacturing, except for small and early state programs like that of New York (Document 16), government encouragement was confined to tariff protection. The other measures proposed by Alexander Hamilton for federal action —subsidies, prizes, loans, and direct governmental efforts to import machines and skilled workmen—were never adopted.

The protection of foreign commerce was considered an important reason for the adoption of the Constitution, but the economic measures undertaken for this end aroused relatively little controversy within the country. What became the prevailing policy was stated by George Washington in his Farewell Address:

> . . . our commercial policy should hold an equal and impartial hand, neither seeking nor granting exclusive favors or preferences; consulting the natural course of things; diffusing and diversifying by gentle means the streams of commerce, but forcing nothing.[7]

Documents 21 and 22 suggest the difficulty of carrying out this principle in a world of special privileges. Aside from the negotiation of commercial treaties, which came increasingly to embody the principle of freedom of navigation on a most favored nation basis, the government provided for American commerce the protection of the navy and the services of consular officials. Foreign trade as well as western settlement profited from expeditions of exploration carried on by the army or the navy, and the opening of Japan by Commodore Perry (Document 24) provided a spectacular case of the promotive activity of government. But it was not government initiative that carried American trade to all corners of the world, and what the self-confident merchant marine of the period wished most from government was support in obtaining the opportunity to compete with the ships of other nations on equal terms.

Government activity in the field of money and credit was a matter of greater complexity and much greater controversy. The first Congress, at a time when the country's banking system was in its very beginnings, chartered a large national bank and subscribed to its stock as an agency of public benefit, although placing its management, on Alexander Hamilton's recommendation, entirely in private hands. The second Bank of the United States, founded in 1816 with still larger capital and a minority of government nominees on its board of direc-

---

[7] J. D. Richardson, *A Compilation of the Messages and Papers of the Presidents, 1789–1903* (New York: Bureau of National Literature and Art, 1897–1920), vol. I, p. 223; September 17, 1796.

tors, assumed so great a responsibility for the leadership and stability of the financial system that certain modern writers have treated it as an early example of a central bank. But this innovation in national influence over the provision of credit came to an abrupt end in the "Bank War" of the 1830's in which Andrew Jackson was the victor and Daniel Webster one of his most eloquent opponents (Documents 27 and 28). For the rest of the period, the federal government made no attempt to regulate banking directly, treating it in general, in Jackson's words, like any other business.

Action by state governments took various forms. As Document 29 indicates, some of the southern states created banks intended to give special attention to the needs of planters and farmers. Several western states refused to charter any banks at all, and a number of state governments established publicly owned or publicly directed institutions. Private banks under state charters often operated under little restriction; and James K. Polk and many others accused them of "fraud upon the note-holders" when the notes they issued depreciated in value (Document 31). It was only slowly that certain states began to devise systems, like those referred to in Document 30, to bring greater uniformity to the circulating medium.

The record, then, shows great variations from time to time within the period and from jurisdiction to jurisdiction. Government action ran the gamut from bold innovation to an almost complete disclaimer of responsibility for the provision of credit. A clearer contrast with the programs of present-day developing nations appears with respect to the supply of investment capital. Hamilton believed in the importance of attracting foreign investment and attempted to provide a favorable climate for it, while leaders like Jackson and Benton regarded it with deep distrust. The national government borrowed for war purposes and the Louisiana Purchase but never for development. A number of the states did borrow abroad for internal improvements and other developmental purposes, once New York had showed them the way, and some of them defaulted on their obligations. There was, however, no concerted effort toward "developmental" banking or the channeling of investment through government agencies into private industry. There was no Development Bank, no Agricultural Bank or Agricultural Credit Corporation—except to the limited degree that certain of the southern banks were attempts to serve such purposes, no Industrial Bank, no *Corporación de Fomento* as in a number of Latin American countries to stimulate local enterprise, no *Nacional Financiera* as in Mexico to mobilize the nation's capital. Perhaps no such agencies were needed; some contemporary observers as well as some modern writers believed that too much rather than too little credit was being put at the disposal of American entrepreneurs. The absence of such institutions, however, marks one limit of the responsibility accepted by American governments for the promotion of development.

Economic activity was subject to a number of regulations and restrictions, particularly at the state and local levels. Statutes governing the operation of ferries and bridges and taverns continued in force from colonial times and were sometimes extended. The assize of bread, fixing its price and weight, survived or was revived in certain cases. Inspection was required for articles of export such as tobacco from the southern states or fish from New England (Document 32). More novel types of regulation grew up with the new forms of economic activity, such as the attempts to regulate banking; and the charters of railroads, like those of the earlier turnpikes, typically contained provisions setting maximum charges or maximum rates of return. Yet restrictions of the older type were decreasing in importance and the newer types of regulation were still in early stages of development.

More characteristic of the time was the permissive role of government in facilitating the growth of the business corporation. At the beginning of the period, the right to use the corporate device was given only in exceptional cases and by a

grant of special privileges that were to be justified only on the
ground of some unusual service to the public. These grants,
moreover, were often regarded with suspicion and hostility.
The Governor of New York declared in 1812 that it was "a
question worthy of our serious meditation whether corporations . . . have not already been multiplied to a dangerous and
alarming extent."[8] Yet, by the end of the period they had
multiplied many times more, and the corporation had become
the generally accepted form for the conduct of business of
substantial size. Incorporation under the regulation of general
statutes had begun to take the place of the special acts. The
process was of great importance in favoring the development
of large-scale enterprise and what Daniel Webster described,
perhaps to a doubting audience, as "the application of capital
for the benefit of all." The national government played no part
in bringing about this change except when, as in Document 34,
cases affecting the privileges of corporations reached the federal courts. The new laws were the work of state legislatures
but perhaps they should be thought of rather as adaptations to
changing business practice than as acts of governmental innovation. To one contemporary observer, they represented the
removal of futile and unnecessary restraints that had attempted
to keep men "from promoting their own interests" (Document 36).

With respect to labor and the working force, what most
strikes the modern observer is the lack of regulation or government action. Even regarding the institution of slavery, which
was soon afterward to be brought to an end by war and
governmental decision, the bitter controversies over national
policy were mainly concerned with the extension of the system
to new areas. The federal government claimed no right to interfere with its working in the original slave areas. The states
themselves gave to the system the legal sanction and setting of

[8] Daniel D. Tompkins, New York *Assembly Journal*, 1812, p. 8.

slave codes—Georgia's is an example (Document 41)—but in practice left the day-to-day management of the working force almost entirely to the discretion of the individual slaveowner.

Except as provisions for education affected the capacities of the workers, governments also did little to regulate the conditions of free labor. Some states adopted restrictions on child labor in factories in order to correct conditions such as those described by a Pennsylvania committee in Document 44. Toward the end of the period, rather ineffectual laws prescribing the ten-hour day were adopted in several jurisdictions. Hospitals and other philanthropic institutions were supported by public authorities. Poor relief continued from colonial times as a governmental function, mainly on the local level; but from time to time its traditional bounds had to be stretched to meet the problems of urban unemployment or to care for the immigrant population arriving in such ports as New York and New Orleans.[9]

Labor conditions were also regulated in some cases by the action of the trade unions, which developed strength at an early date in some of the older skilled city trades although very little in the factories of the new industrialism. Their organization encountered government restrictions in the form of prosecution as conspiracies under the common law, and most of the early cases went against them. The unions of the time did not ask for direct governmental encouragement and would certainly not have received it if they had. Instead, their spokesmen defended their collective action in what now seem surprisingly individualistic terms. What Caesar Rodney demanded

---

[9] Benjamin J. Klebaner, "Poverty and Its Relief in American Thought, 1815–1861," *Social Service Review*, XXXVIII (1964), 382–399. "It is a proud boast of Louisiana," said Governor T. B. Robertson, "that she clothes and feeds more naked and hungry foreigners and strangers than any other country in the world." Louisiana *House Journal*, 1824–1825, p. 5. See also Document 47.

unsuccessfully for Philadelphia cordwainers in 1806 and what Chief Justice Lemuel Shaw granted to Boston shoemakers in 1842 (Document 45) was the right to be let alone to bargain like other competitors in a free market.

There was even less governmental action with respect to the great additions to the working force that came from abroad. Some political leaders, like Andrew Johnson, praised the contributions of immigrants to the American economy. Others, like the authors of a Congressional Report of 1856 (Document 47), denounced "foreign criminals and paupers" as the principal cause of the nation's ills. One eastern state, New York, imposed a tax on ships bringing immigrants to help pay for the additional social services that their arrival would occasion. One western state, Wisconsin, conducted for two years a modest campaign to attract immigrants to its own lands (Document 46). It was, as M. L. Hansen said, commerce that bridged the Atlantic,[10] and immigrants came as the result of innumerable individual decisions rather than as a result of governmental attempts to encourage or discourage the movement. Within our period neither national nor state governments adopted policies either of selective immigration, as Hamilton had suggested (Document 15), or of assisted immigration, as in certain other countries, or of restricted immigration, as in the present century.

The Parts that have been reviewed deal with the economic functions performed by governments and therefore with public expenditures rather than with public revenues. Yet the difficulties of raising revenue and the common reluctance to impose taxes set limits on what functions governments could perform and affected the choice of the methods employed. This was particularly obvious in the activities intended to promote devel-

---

[10] M. L. Hansen, *The Atlantic Migration, 1607–1860* (Cambridge: Harvard University Press, 1941), ch. 8, "Commerce Bridges the Atlantic."

opment. For example, Hamilton argued, and many economists would agree, that subsidies and premiums would in some respects be more efficient instruments for encouraging manufactures than the protective tariff; but congressional choice of the latter method could hardly fail to be influenced by the fact that it operated by bringing money into the treasury, whereas the former would operate by paying money out. Similarly, aid to railroads through land grants had the great attraction of appearing to be costless, since what was given away was a currently unproductive asset, although a well-conceived program of loans might have been a more effective method of promoting railroad construction.[11] More broadly, the general practice of using government resources to supplement private funds rather than of building the improvements as public works was based partly, although by no means entirely, on the fact that it made a lesser demand on the public treasury.

The desire to keep down expenditures and taxes would of course be natural for any government at any time, but there were also factors making the feeling particularly strong in the period under consideration. Jefferson's ideal of "economy in the public expense, that labor be lightly burdened,"[12] was widely shared, and Americans often congratulated themselves that they were not as highly taxed as the subjects of European monarchies. Methods of taxation, moreover, were not highly developed. "It is evident from the state of the country," wrote Hamilton in *The Federalist,* "from the habits of the people, from the experience we have had on the point itself, that it is impracticable to raise any considerable sum by direct taxation." "The genius of the people," he added, "will ill brook the in-

---

11 Carter Goodrich, *Government Promotion of American Canals and Railroads, 1800–1890* (New York: Columbia University Press, 1960), pp. 201–203.

12 First Inaugural Address, March 4, 1801, in Richardson, *Messages and Papers of the Presidents,* vol. I, p. 323.

quisitive and peremptory spirit of excise laws."[13] Under the Constitution, the federal government could not impose direct taxes except in proportion to the population of the states as counted for purposes of representation, and it used the power only on a few occasions. Hamilton's second sentence found somewhat ironic confirmation when one of the excise taxes in his own fiscal program brought on the Whiskey Rebellion of Western Pennsylvania farmers who were dependent on the distilleries for a market for their grain. In practice, the principal sources of federal revenue were customs duties, as Hamilton had foreseen, and for part of the period the proceeds from the sale of the public lands. At times these sources provided more income than was needed and, since it seemed inexpedient to reduce or eliminate the customs duties that also served the purpose of protection, federal surpluses sometimes became embarrassing. It was in anticipation of such a surplus that the frugal Jeffersonian, Albert Gallatin, produced his twenty million dollar program of internal improvements; he ceased to advocate the program when the surplus failed to materialize.

By the time of the major federal surpluses, the principal responsibility for internal improvements had shifted to the states and it was their sources of revenue that became the crucial issue. While local governments rested mainly on the property tax, as they always had, many of the state governments had only what seem very rudimentary or almost accidental sources of support, deriving their income from special taxes such as that on auctions, from sales of lands, from the windfall distribution of the federal Surplus Revenue in 1837, and from bonuses on bank charters or dividends from their investments in bank stocks. The state of Pennsylvania, according to Gallatin, was able out of such dividends "to defray . . . all the ex-

---

[13] "Publius" (Alexander Hamilton), in No. XII of the Federalist papers, 1787, in Harold C. Syrett, ed., *The Papers of Alexander Hamilton*, vol. IV (New York: Columbia University Press, 1962), pp. 348–349.

penses of government without any direct tax during the forty ensuing years" after the establishment of the Bank of Pennsylvania in 1793 "and till the adoption of the system of internal improvement, which required new resources."[14] These new resources for improvements, both for the states and cities, came almost entirely from borrowing. In the unfavorable phase of the business cycle, when further loans could not be obtained, programs were often abandoned, leaving some of the works unfinished. Much of the borrowing, moreover, was done without making adequate provisions for repayment. The city of Baltimore, which levied a railroad tax every year for forty years, was one of the few notable exceptions. Pennsylvania was among the states that defaulted on their interest payments, but it was able to extricate itself from financial difficulty after only a few years of sharply increased taxation.[15]

Internal improvement, said its enemies, is "another name for eternal taxation."[16] What individual and corporate effort may have gained by the lightness of the tax burden must therefore be weighed against the limitations that the deficiencies of the fiscal system placed on the promotive activities of government.

The documents will convey the spirit of the time better than any introduction to them. Some of them express exultation over what can be accomplished by the government of a free people; others display the greatest scorn for the ineptness and corruption of public agencies. Some were written in the heat of controversy and others are matter-of-fact discussions of ways and means. It will be necessary in each case to ask who makes the statement, and when, and what were the consequences in future action.

---

[14] Quoted in Bray Hammond, *Banks and Politics in America* (Princeton: Princeton University Press, 1957), p. 165.

[15] Harvey H. Segal, *Canal Cycles, 1834–1861,* unpublished Ph.D. dissertation, Columbia University, 1956, pp. 191–192. See also Document 5.

[16] Goodrich, *Government Promotion,* p. 276.

If the comparison is with the developing nations, the obvious point of similarity is that American governments also took deliberate action to promote industrialization and economic growth. They did so on a largely pragmatic basis, with little attention to ideological considerations, and with little centralized planning. Their measures, I believe, had on balance a significant positive effect on development; but their impact would have been still greater if they had been better coordinated and carried on by more effective government instruments. It is important to note that American governments were ready to withdraw from promotive activity as soon as it appeared that private enterprise was able to take over the responsibility.[17] It was in any case confidently assumed that individuals would seize the opportunities provided through governmental initiative, that settlers would find their way to the areas opened up by a canal or a railroad, and that if the land was made available they would know what to do with it. If American governments helped to provide what in many of the developing countries is called the "infrastructure," they did so in the belief that individuals and corporate enterprise would be eager to build the superstructure upon it.

If the comparison is with the functions of American governments today, what is most apparent is the difference in the direction of government activity. Promotive action has by no means ceased, as is evident in the billions spent on roadbuilding and in the way commercial aviation has emerged and atomic energy is beginning to emerge from the nursery of military research. Emphasis, however, has shifted to a vast network of regulation, to welfare measures for which the period of the present volume provides little precedent, and to attempts to stabilize the economy more sophisticated than those which

---

[17] *Ibid.*, ch. 8. For a similar tendency in other countries in the process of development, see H. G. J. Aitken, ed., *The State and Economic Growth, passim.*

Alexander J. Dallas and Nicholas Biddle had in mind. Together with the imperative demands of a modern defense establishment, these governmental activities now require a much larger fraction of the national income. Yet one significant element of continuity remains. It is still the deep-seated preference of the American people to employ the powers of government to influence the economy at strategic points needing special attention rather than to attempt its operation in detail.

BIBLIOGRAPHICAL NOTE

The book is a collection of documents of the period from 1783 to 1861, some of them readily accessible, others more difficult to locate. Further exploration in the materials must depend on the investigator's ingenuity and industry and on the nature of his specific inquiry, but the footnotes to the documents will indicate some of the types of sources that may be used. They include the messages of the Presidents (available in the first five volumes of James D. Richardson, *A Compilation of the Messages and Papers of the Presidents, 1789–1903* [New York: Bureau of National Literature and Art, 1897–1912], the proceedings of Congress under their various titles, other documents of the national government (collected for the early years in *American State Papers*), legislative proceedings and executive documents of the states, statutes and law reports, collections of the writings and correspondence of conspicuous figures, reports of foreign observers, and contemporary pamphlets and periodicals.

The brief bibliography given below is confined to secondary sources and the documentary collections of Callender and Commons. The items under the heading "General" deal with the subject matter of all or most of the chapters of the book, the others mainly with that of a single chapter. Critical reviews of literature in the field are contained in:

LIVELY, ROBERT A. "The American System, a Review Article," *Business History Review*, XXIX (March 1955), 81–96.

GOODRICH, CARTER. "Recent Contributions to Economic History: the United States, 1789–1960," *Journal of Economic History*, XIX (March 1959), 25–43.

Additional references will be found in most of the books cited below, and particularly in the three volumes of *The Economic History of the United States.*

GENERAL

BROUDE, HENRY W. Ch. 1 in *The State and Economic Growth,* Hugh G. J. Aitken, ed. New York: Social Science Research Council, 1959. Reprinted in *United States Economic History: Selected Readings,* Harry N. Scheiber, ed. New York: Alfred A. Knopf, 1964. Pp. 114–135.

BRUCHEY, STUART. *The Roots of American Economic Growth, 1607–1861: An Essay in Social Causation.* New York: Harper & Row, 1965.

CALLENDER, GUY STEVENS, ed. *Selections from the Economic History of the United States, 1765–1860.* Boston: Ginn & Co., 1909. Reprinted, New York: A. M. Kelley, 1965.

DORFMAN, JOSEPH. *The Economic Mind in American Civilization.* Vols. I & II, *1606–1865.* New York: The Viking Press, 1946.

GATES, PAUL W. *The Farmer's Age: Agriculture, 1815–1860.* New York: Holt, Rinehart and Winston, 1960. Vol. III of *The Economic History of the United States.*

HANDLIN, OSCAR, and MARY FLUG HANDLIN. *Commonwealth: A Study of the Role of Government in the American Economy: Massachusetts, 1774–1861.* New York: New York University Press, 1947.

HARTZ, LOUIS. *Economic Policy and Democratic Thought: Pennsylvania, 1776–1860.* Cambridge: Harvard University Press, 1948.

HEATH, MILTON SYDNEY. *Constructive Liberalism: The Role of the State in Economic Development in Georgia to 1860.* Cambridge: Harvard University Press, 1954.

HOFSTADTER, RICHARD. *The American Political Tradition, and the Men Who Made It.* New York: Alfred A. Knopf, 1948.

HURST, JAMES WILLARD. *Law and the Conditions of Freedom in the Nineteenth-Century United States.* Madison: University of Wisconsin Press, 1956. Parts I and II.

NASH, GERALD D. *State Government and Economic Development: A History of Administrative Policies in California, 1849–1933.* Berkeley and Los Angeles: University of California Press, 1964. Introduction and Part I.

NETTELS, CURTIS P. *The Emergence of a National Economy, 1775–1815.* New York: Holt, Rinehart and Winston, 1962. Vol. II of *The Economic History of the United States.*

NORTH, DOUGLASS C. *Economic Growth of the United States, 1790–1860.* Englewood Cliffs, N.J.: Prentice-Hall, Inc., 1961.

PRIMM, JAMES NEAL. *Economic Policy in the Development of a Western State: Missouri, 1820–1860.* Cambridge: Harvard University Press, 1954.

TAYLOR, GEORGE ROGERS. *The Transportation Revolution, 1815–1860.* New York: Rinehart, 1951. Vol. IV of *The Economic History of the United States.*

SPECIAL

CADMAN, JOHN W., JR. *The Corporation in New Jersey: Business and Politics, 1791–1875.* Cambridge: Harvard University Press, 1949.

CALLENDER, GUY STEVENS. "The Early Transportation and Banking Enterprises of the States in Relation to the Growth of Corporations," *Quarterly Journal of Economics,* XVII (1902), 111–162. Reprinted in *Economic Change in America,* Joseph T. Lambie and Richard V. Clemence, eds. Harrisburg: The Stackpole Co., 1954. Pp. 522–559.

COMMONS, JOHN R. *et al.,* eds. *A Documentary History of American Industrial Society.* 11 vols. Cleveland: A. H. Clark Co., 1910, 1911. Esp. vols. III and IV, "Labor Conspiracy Cases," John R. Commons and Eugene A. Gilmore, eds. Reprinted, New York: Russell & Russell, 1958.

FOGEL, ROBERT W. *The Union Pacific Railroad: A Case in Premature Enterprise.* Baltimore: The Johns Hopkins Press, 1960. Chs. 1 and 2.

GOETZMANN, WILLIAM H. *Army Exploration in the American West, 1803–1863.* New Haven: Yale University Press, 1959.

GOODRICH, CARTER. *Government Promotion of American Canals and Railroads, 1800–1890.* New York: Columbia University Press, 1960.

GOODRICH, CARTER, JULIUS RUBIN, H. JEROME CRANMER, and HARVEY H. SEGAL. *Canals and American Economic Development.* New York: Columbia University Press, 1961.

HAMMOND, BRAY. *Banks and Politics in America, from the Revolution to the Civil War.* Princeton: Princeton University Press, 1957.

HANSEN, MARCUS LEE. *The Atlantic Migration, 1607–1860: A History of the Continuing Settlement of the United States.* Cambridge: Harvard University Press, 1941.

HEATH, MILTON S. "Public Railroad Construction and the Development of Private Enterprise in the South Before 1861," *Journal of Economic History,* X (1950), 40–53.

HIBBARD, BENJAMIN HORACE. *A History of the Public Land Policies.* New York: Macmillan, 1924. Reprinted, New York: Peter Smith, 1939.

HILL, FOREST G. *Roads, Rails and Waters: The Army Engineers and Early Transportation.* Norman: University of Oklahoma Press, 1957.

KIRKLAND, EDWARD C. *Men, Cities and Transportation: A Study in New England History, 1820–1900.* 2 vols. Cambridge: Harvard University Press, 1948.

MILLER, NATHAN. *The Enterprise of a Free People: Aspects of Economic Development in New York State During the Canal Period, 1792–1938.* Ithaca: Cornell University Press, 1956.

REDLICH, FRITZ. *The Molding of American Banking: Men and Ideas.* New York: Hafner Publishing Co. Part I, *1781–1840,* 1947; Part II, *1840–1910,* 1951.

SMITH, WALTER B. *Economic Aspects of the Second Bank of the United States.* Cambridge: Harvard University Press, 1953.

TAUSSIG, FRANK W. *The Tariff History of the United States.* 7th ed. New York: G. P. Putnam's Sons, 1923.

WARE, NORMAN. *The Industrial Worker, 1840–1860: The Reaction of American Industrial Society to the Advance of the Industrial Revolution.* New York: Houghton Mifflin, 1924. Reprinted, Gloucester, Mass.: Peter Smith, 1959.

EDITOR'S NOTE

A number of recent works have contributed greatly to our understanding of the role of governments in American economic development. Their authors will know where I found clues to the location of many of the documents. Joseph Dorfman, David Montgomery, and Julius Rubin have suggested specific selections.

A work of this sort could hardly be done without use of the magnificent resources of the New York Public Library and the Library of Congress. For particular courtesies, I am under obligation to Mr. Harold C. Whitford of the Economic Division of the New York Public Library and to Miss Ruth Salisbury and Miss Hazel Johnson of the University of Pittsburgh Libraries.

The source of each of the readings is indicated in a footnote to the first page on which the reading appears. In most cases it has been necessary to cut the document, often substantially, to prepare it for use in this volume, but none has been in any way rewritten. In order to save space, these elisions have been indicated in a somewhat unorthodox manner. Ellipses at the end of a paragraph are used for any omission from one sentence to several paragraphs or pages. Where they cannot be added (e.g., to ends of charts or headings), three centered dots are used. Ellipses at the beginning of a paragraph indicate that the preceding part of that particular paragraph has been omitted. A few obvious typographical errors in the originals have been corrected; the format of tables has been somewhat modernized; and the typography makes no attempt to imitate that of the period or to reproduce the elegant calligraphy of Nicholas Biddle's copying clerk. Spelling and punctuation are left unchanged, even where a group of backcountry Georgia lawmakers in haste and anger broke the rules of their own day as well as of ours.

CARTER GOODRICH

University of Pittsburgh
May 10, 1965

The Government

and the Economy, 1783-1861

PART ONE

THE PROMOTION

OF TRANSPORT

1. Albert Gallatin: A Plan for National Action

Of all activities of American governments during the period, those most clearly and deliberately intended to promote economic development were the efforts to improve the facilities of transportation. "Internal improvements"—river improvements, the construction of roads, canals, and, later, of railroads—were major objectives of policy. The most comprehensive program for action by the national government was contained in a report by Albert Gallatin, Secretary of the Treasury under President Jefferson, which is one of the greatest planning documents in American history.

The Report was based, as it says, on the "great geographical features of the country." The major objects to be sought were better communications along the seaboard and, still more important, connections between the seaboard and the interior. With respect to the former, a protected coastal navigation could be obtained by cutting less than a hundred miles of canal through four "necks of land." Communications with the West could be established by taking advantage of four points at which the headwaters of eastern and western rivers were close together and of the breach in the mountain wall provided by the Hudson and Mohawk rivers. These were great national objects; and Gallatin argued that they deserved and required the support of the "General Government," which might be given either by constructing the improvements as public works or by subscriptions to the stock of improvement companies. The cost should be met by a ten-year program of federal expenditures, based on anticipated budget surpluses of twenty million dollars.

All four of Gallatin's "necks of land" were eventually cut by canals. The Erie Canal and the New York Central Railroad exploited the Hudson-Mohawk opening, and the Pennsylvania, Baltimore and Ohio, and Chesapeake and Ohio railroads crossed the Appalachians by way of three of Gallatin's four pairs of rivers. Yet very little of all this, as later selections will show, was to be done by the federal government; and the course of future development followed the lines of Gallatin's geography much more closely than it followed his recommendations for public policy.[1]

The selection that follows gives Gallatin's proposals in their full geographic detail. It omits most of the passages describing the improvements that had already been carried out or projected in the United States. These included the Middlesex Canal between Boston and Lowell, "the greatest work of the kind which has been completed in the United States"; the less successful canal connecting the Santee River with the harbor of Charleston; the works in progress on the Mohawk River, on the Potomac in which George Washington held so strong an interest (Document 36), on the James River, and many others. Gallatin also reported progress in road-building, particularly in the eastern and middle states; and he described the Lancaster Road, "the first extensive turnpike that was com-

---

[1] For a map and table comparing Gallatin's proposals with actual construction, see Goodrich, *Government Promotion of American Canals and Railroads, 1800–1890* (New York: Columbia University Press, 1960), pp. 33–35.

pleted in the United States," as "the first link of the great Western communication from Philadelphia." In many cases the account ends with the statement that the project has been suspended or abandoned for lack of funds; and the cumulative effect of these reports, based on data presented in an appendix of nearly two hundred folio pages, is to reinforce the Secretary's argument for national action.

THE SECRETARY OF THE TREASURY, IN OBEDIENCE TO THE

RESOLUTION OF THE SENATE OF THE 2D MARCH, 1807,

RESPECTFULLY SUBMITS THE FOLLOWING REPORT ON

ROADS AND CANALS:

The general utility of artificial roads and canals is at this time so universally admitted, as hardly to require any additional proofs. It is sufficiently evident that, whenever the annual expense of transportation on a certain route, in its natural state, exceeds the interest on the capital employed in improving the communication, and the annual expense of transportation (exclusively of the tolls,) by the improved route, the difference is an annual additional income to the nation. Nor does in that case the general result vary, although the tolls may not have been fixed at a rate sufficient to pay to the undertakers the interest on the capital laid out. They, indeed, when that happens, lose; but the community is nevertheless benefited by the undertaking. The general gain is not confined to the difference between the expense of the transportation of those articles which had been formerly conveyed by that route, but many which were brought to market by other channels will then find a new and more advantageous direction; and those which on

---

From "Report on Roads and Canals," 10th Congress, 1st Session, Document No. 250, *American State Papers, Miscellaneous,* vol. I, pp. 724–741; pp. 742–921 are Appendix pages.

account of their distance or weight could not be transported in any manner whatever, will acquire a value, and become a clear addition to the national wealth. Those and many other advantages have become so obvious, that in countries possessed of a large capital, where property is sufficiently secure to induce individuals to lay out that capital on permanent undertakings, and where a compact population creates an extensive commercial intercourse, within short distances, those improvements may often, in ordinary cases, be left to individual exertion, without any direct aid from Government.

There are, however, some circumstances, which, whilst they render the facility of communications throughout the United States an object of primary importance, naturally check the application of private capital and enterprise to improvements on a large scale.

The price of labor is not considered as a formidable obstacle, because whatever it may be, it equally affects the expense of transportation, which is saved by the improvement, and that of effecting the improvement itself. The want of practical knowledge is no longer felt; and the occasional influence of mistaken local interests, in sometimes thwarting or giving an improper direction to public improvements, arises from the nature of man, and is common to all countries. The great demand for capital in the United States, and the extent of territory compared with the population, are, it is believed, the true causes which prevent new undertakings, and render those already accomplished less profitable than had been expected.

1. Notwithstanding the great increase of capital during the last fifteen years, the objects for which it is required continue to be more numerous, and its application is generally more profitable than in Europe. A small portion therefore is applied to objects which offer only the prospect of remote and moderate profit. And it also happens that a less sum being subscribed at first than is actually requisite for completing the work, this

proceeds slowly; the capital applied remains unproductive for a much longer time than was necessary, and the interest accruing during that period becomes, in fact, an injurious addition to the real expense of the undertaking.

2. The present population of the United States, compared with the extent of territory over which it is spread, does not, except in the vicinity of the seaports, admit that extensive commercial intercourse within short distances which, in England and some other countries, forms the principal support of artificial roads and canals. With a few exceptions, canals particularly cannot, in America, be undertaken with a view solely to the intercourse between the two extremes of, and along the intermediate ground which they occupy. It is necessary, in order to be productive, that the canal should open a communication with a natural extensive navigation which will flow through that new channel. It follows that whenever that navigation requires to be improved, or when it might at some distance be connected by another canal to another navigation, the first canal will remain comparatively unproductive until the other improvements are effected, until the other canal is also completed. Thus the intended canal between the Chesapeake and Delaware, will be deprived of the additional benefit arising from the intercourse between New York and the Chesapeake, until an inland navigation shall have been opened between the Delaware and New York. Thus the expensive canals completed around the falls of Potomac will become more and more productive in proportion to the improvement, first, of the navigation of the upper branches of the river, and then of its communication with the Western waters. Some works already executed are unprofitable; many more remain unattempted, because their ultimate productiveness depends on other improvements, too extensive or too distant to be embraced by the same individuals.

The General Government can alone remove these obstacles.

With resources amply sufficient for the completion of every practicable improvement, it will always supply the capital wanted for any work which it may undertake, as fast as the work itself can progress; avoiding thereby the ruinous loss of interest on a dormant capital, and reducing the real expense to its lowest rate.

With these resources, and embracing the whole Union, it will complete on any given line all the improvements, however distant, which may be necessary to render the whole productive, and eminently beneficial.

The early and efficient aid of the *Federal* Government is recommended by still more important considerations. The inconveniences, complaints, and perhaps dangers, which may result from a vast extent of territory, can no otherwise be radically removed or prevented than by opening speedy and easy communications through all its parts. Good roads and canals will shorten distances, facilitate commercial and personal intercourse, and unite, by a still more intimate community of interests, the most remote quarters of the United States. No other single operation, within the power of Government, can more effectually tend to strengthen and perpetuate that Union which secures external independence, domestic peace, and internal liberty.

With that view of the subject the facts respecting canals, which have been collected in pursuance of the resolution of the Senate, have been arranged under the following heads:

1. Great canals, from north to south, along the Atlantic seacoast.

2. Communications between the Atlantic and Western waters.

3. Communications between the Atlantic waters, and those of the great lakes, and river St. Lawrence.

4. Interior canals.

GREAT CANALS ALONG THE ATLANTIC SEACOAST

The map of the United States will show that they possess a tide water inland navigation, secure from storms and enemies; and which, from Massachusetts to the southern extremity of Georgia, is principally, if not solely, interrupted by four necks of land. These are, the isthmus of Barnstable; that part of New Jersey which extends from the Raritan to the Delaware; the peninsula between the Delaware and the Chesapeake; and that low and marshy tract which divides the Chesapeake from Albemarle sound. It is ascertained that a navigation for sea vessels, drawing eight feet of water, may be effected across the three last; and a canal is also believed to be practicable, not, perhaps, across the isthmus of Barnstable, but from the harbor of Boston to that of Rhode Island. The Massachusetts canal would be about twenty-six, the New Jersey about twenty-eight, and each of the two southern about twenty-two miles in length, making altogether less than one hundred miles.

Should this great work, the expense of which, as will hereafter be shown, is estimated at about three millions of dollars, be accomplished, a sea vessel entering the first canal in the harbor of Boston would, through the bay of Rhode Island, Long Island sound, and the harbor of New York, reach Brunswick on the Raritan; thence pass through the second canal to Trenton on the Delaware, down that river to Christiana or Newcastle, and through the third canal to Elk river and the Chesapeake; whence, sailing down that bay and up Elizabeth river, it would, through the fourth canal, enter the Albemarle sound, and by Pamlico, Core, and Bogue sounds, reach Beaufort and Swansborough in North Carolina. From the last mentioned place, the island navigation, through Stumpy and Toomer's sounds, is continued with a diminished draught of water, and by cutting two low and narrow necks, not exceeding three miles together, to Cape Fear river; and thence by an open but short and direct run along the coast is reached that chain of islands between which and the main the inland navigation is continued to St. Mary's along the coast of South Carolina and Georgia. It is unnecessary to add any comments on the utility of the work, in peace or war, for the transportation of merchandise, or the conveyance of persons. . . .

I. Massachusetts Canal

1. Sandwich isthmus between Barnstable bay on the north, and Buzzard's bay on the south, had first attracted the public attention. Surveys and levels were taken, for the purpose of ascertaining the practicability of opening a cross cut to be supplied by the sea itself, from the mouth of Back river in Buzzard's bay, to the mouth of Scusset river in Barnstable bay.

The distance was found to exceed seven miles; the elevation of the highest intermediate ground is forty feet above low water mark in Barnstable bay; the depth of water at the mouth of Black river does not, at low water, exceed seven feet and a half; and the channel to that spot through Buzzard's bay is obstructed by shoals. The tide which rises but three feet and a half in that bay, rises three hours and a half later, and more than eighteen feet in that of Barnstable. The shore on which that formidable tide would operate, is an open beach, without any harbor or shelter whatever. Independent of other obstacles, it was apprehended that the same natural causes which had formed the isthmus, might fill the canal, or make a bar at its entrance; and the project seems to have been abandoned.

2. The ground was also examined between Barnstable harbor on the north, and Hyanus harbor on the south, at some distance east of Sandwich. The breadth of the peninsula does not exceed here four miles and a half, and there would be a harbor at each end of the canal. The same difference exists in the tides which rise four feet in Hyanus, and sixteen feet in Barnstable harbor. The entrance of this is obstructed by shoals; but the great obstacle to a cross cut is the elevation of the intermediate

ground, estimated at eighty feet above tide water. Navigable ponds on that high ground might, perhaps, form part of a lock canal, and supply the remainder with water. But a canal, frozen in winter, would not have effected the great object in view, which was to enable vessels from sea to proceed in winter from Martha's Vineyard to Boston, without sailing around Cape Cod. Although the difficulty of the navigation from Boston to Barnstable diminishes the utility of this communication, as one of the great links in this line of inland navigation, it may be resorted to should that which will be next mentioned prove impracticable for sea vessels.

3. The attention of the Legislature of Massachusetts, under whose authority the grounds at Sandwich and Barnstable had been examined, has lately been turned to a direct communication between Weymouth landing, within the harbor of Boston and Taunton river, which empties into the bay of Rhode Island. A favorable report has been made during the last session, of which a copy has lately been obtained. The distance from tide water to tide water is twenty-six miles by one route, and twenty-three and a quarter miles by another. The highest intermediate ground is one hundred and thirty-three feet above tide water, but may be reduced ten feet by digging to that depth the length of a mile. Two ponds known by the name of Weymouth and Cranberry, the largest and least elevated of which covers five hundred acres, and is fourteen feet higher than the summit of the proposed canal, will supply the upper locks with water by feeders four miles long. Whether the quantity of water contained in those ponds, and estimated equal to a daily supply of 450,000 cubic feet, will be sufficient for a sloop navigation, and whether any other ponds or streams may be brought in aid, does not seem to be fully ascertained. After descending twenty feet towards Weymouth, and seventy towards Taunton, an ample supply for the lower locks will be derived from other large ponds, the principal of which are known by the names of Braintree and Nippinitic. The expense

may, on a supposition that the route is partly through a rocky soil, be estimated as follows:

Digging twenty-six miles, at $30,000 a mile,	$780,000 00
Lockage two hundred and sixty feet, at $1,250 a foot,	325,000 00
Feeders, purchase of land, &c.	145,000 00
	1,250,000 00

II. New Jersey Canal

A company was incorporated some years ago by the Legislature of New Jersey for opening a canal between the Raritan and Delaware. Acting under the erroneous opinion that the navigation of small rivers might be improved and used as a canal, the company intended to have united, by a cross cut of one mile, the Assampink or Trenton creek with Stony brook, a branch of Millstone river, and to have descended Trenton creek to the Delaware and Stony brook, and Millstone river to the Raritan. The capital, which was inadequate, was not paid; but their survey of the intended route has shown the practicability of a canal for sea vessels on a proper plan. The distance from Brunswick to Trenton is twenty-six miles; and the only obstacle on the way is the "sand hills," some distance west of Brunswick. These may, it is said, be avoided by a deviation which would not increase the distance more than two miles; and they may, at all events, be perforated as has been done by the turnpike company, who have opened a road on a straight line between the two towns without having in any place an angle of ascent of more than three degrees. The highest intermediate ground between Assampink and Stony brook is only fifty feet above tide water; and it is suggested that the summit level may be taken seven feet lower, cutting seven miles through a level meadow between the confluence of the Assampink and Shippetankin creeks and Rowley's mill, near the confluence of Stony brook and Millstone river. . . .

The expenses may be estimated as follows:

Digging twenty-eight miles, at $20,000 per mile,	$560,000 00
Lockage, one hundred feet (probably less,) at $1,250 per foot,	125,000 00
Feeders, purchase of land and water rights,	115,000 00
	800,000 00

III. Delaware and Chesapeake Canal

A company incorporated by the States of Delaware and Maryland for opening this canal has commenced its operations; now suspended for want of funds.

The canal will commence at Welsh point, on Elk river, an arm of the Chesapeake, and terminate at a distance of twenty-two miles on Christiana creek, a branch of the Delaware. At low water the depth of water in Christiana is nine feet, and in Elk twelve feet, within one hundred feet from the shore. The tide rises four feet in both rivers. The canal might, without increasing the distance, be conducted to Newcastle on the Delaware itself, instead of ending on Christiana creek.

The highest intermediate ground over which the canal will be carried on a level of thirteen miles in length, is seventy-four feet above tide water, the descent being effected by nine locks on each side. The digging is generally easy; no expensive aqueducts or bridges, nor any other obstacle but those which have already been overcome in digging the feeder through a very rocky soil. . . .

The present annual carriage across the peninsula, which would be drawn through the canal, is estimated at forty-two thousand tons, exclusively of passengers. This will be greatly increased by the facility which the canal itself will afford to the commercial intercourse between the two bays, and to the conveyance of articles now carried through other channels, or too heavy for transportation at the present expense of carriage. The coals wanted for Philadelphia, and which, brought down from the sources of the Susquehannah and Potomac, but principally from the vicinity of Richmond, would naturally pass through the canal, have been alone estimated at more than one hundred thousand tons a year. The annual carriage of all articles may, in the present state of population, be fairly estimated at one hundred and fifty thousand tons, and the direct annual saving to the community at $300,000; being at the rate of two dollars a ton for the difference between land and water carriage across the peninsula, after paying the tolls. These, at the rate of fifty cents a ton, will give to the undertakers a revenue of $75,000, leaving, after a deduction of $10,000 for annual repairs, and of $10,000 more for attendance and contingencies, a nett income of $55,000.

The expenses of the whole work are estimated as follows:

Digging twenty-two miles,
    at $20,000 a mile, $440,000 00
Eighteen locks, at $10,000 each,   180,000 00
    (The whole lockage, being one hundred
    and forty-eight feet, would, at $1250
    a foot, amount to $185,000 00.)
Feeder, (nearly completed) reservoirs,
    lock at the feeder, purchase of water
    rights and land, including a debt
    of _____ dollars, due by the
    company,   230,000 00

                                       $850,0000 00

The interest on which sum at 6 per cent is $51,000. . . .

IV. Chesapeake and Albemarle

. . .

A company incorporated by the States of Virginia and North Carolina, for opening a canal through the Dismal Swamp, has made considerable progress in the work.

The canal extends twenty-two miles in length from Deep creek, a branch of the south branch of Elizabeth river, seven miles above Norfolk to Joyce's creek, a branch of Pasquotank river, a northern arm of Albemarle sound. Vessels drawing eight to nine feet water may ascend both creeks to each extremity of the canal.

The intervening ground along the eastern margin of the Dismal Swamp is almost level; the rise towards the middle not exceeding two feet above the two extremities, which are only eighteen feet and nine inches above tide water. The digging is very easy; the only obstacles arise from the stumps and roots of trees, and are nearly overcome; and a single aqueduct, or rather culvert, over a small run emptying into the Northwest river, is necessary. . . .

It must, in order to become a national object, be capable of receiving vessels which navigate Albemarle sound, and for that purpose be restored to its first intended dimensions, or rather be widened and deepened on the plan adopted for the Chesapeake and Delaware canal. The expense would be as follows:

Digging, viz.: deepening to 8 feet,
     preserving the same level the whole way,
     and widening to a proper breadth,
     22 miles, at eight thousand dollars
     a mile, $176,000 00
Four stone locks, at ten thousand dollars,   40,000 00
Feeder to Lake Drummond, aqueduct,
     and contingencies,   34,000 00
                                                           _____
                                                            $250,000 00

• • •

The following table is a recapitulation of the distance to be cut on the whole line, and of the estimated expense:

CANALS	DIRECTION	DISTANCE	LOCKAGE	EXPENSE
		MILES	FEET	
Massachusetts canal	Weymouth to Taunton	26	260	$1,250,000 00
New Jersey canal	Brunswick to Trenton	28	100	800,000 00
Delaware and Chesapeake canal	Christiana to Elk	22	148	750,000 00
Chesapeake and Albemarle canal	Eliz. river to Pasquotank	22	40	250,000 00
Total		98	548	$3,050,000 00

COMMUNICATIONS BETWEEN THE ATLANTIC AND WESTERN WATERS

The Appalachian mountains, to use an ancient generic denomination, extend in a direction west of south, from the 42d to the 34th degree of north latitude, approaching the sea, and even washed by the tide in the State of New York, and thence in their southerly course gradually receding from the sea-shore. Viewed as a whole, their breadth may be estimated at one hundred and ten miles, and they consist of a succession of parallel ridges, following nearly the direction of the seacoast, irregularly intersected by rivers, and divided by narrow valleys. The ridge which divides the Atlantic rivers from the western waters, generally known by the name of Allegany, preserves throughout a nearly equal distance of two hundred and fifty miles from the Atlantic Ocean, and a nearly uniform elevation of three-thousand feet above the level of the sea.

Those mountains may, however, be perhaps considered as consisting of two principal chains; between these lies the fertile limestone valley, which, although occasionally interrupted by transversal ridges, and, in one place, by the dividing or Allegany ridge, may be traced from Newburgh and Esopus on the Hudson river to Knoxville on the Tennessee.

The eastern and narrowest chain is the Blue Ridge of Virginia, which, in its northeast course, traverses, under various names, the States of Maryland, Pennsylvania, and New Jersey, forms the high lands broken at West Point by the tide of the Hudson, and then uniting with the Green mountains, assumes a northerly direction, and divides the waters of the Hudson and Lake Champlain from those of Connecticut river. On the borders of Virginia and North Carolina, the Blue Ridge is united by an inferior mountain with the great western chain, and thence, to its southern extremity, becomes the principal or dividing mountain, discharging eastwardly the rivers Roanoke, Pedee, Santee, and Savannah into the Atlantic Ocean; southwardly, the Chatahoochee and the Alabama into the Gulf of Mexico; and westwardly, the New river and the Tennessee. The New river, taking a northwardly course, breaks through all the ridges of the great western chain, and, at a short distance beyond it, unites, under the name of Kanhawa, with the Ohio. The Tennessee pursues at first a southwest direction between the two chains, until having reached, and in a westwardly course turned, the southern extremity of the great western chain, it assumes a northwardly direction, and joins its waters with those of the Ohio, a few miles above the confluence of that river with the Mississippi.

The western chain, much broader, and generally more elevated, is known under the name of Cumberland and Gauley mountains, from its southern extremity near the great bend of the Tennessee river, until it becomes in Virginia the principal or dividing mountain; thence, in its northerly course, towards the State of New York, it discharges westwardly the Green

Briar river, which, by its junction with the New river, forms the Kanhawa, and the rivers Monongahela and Allegany, which, from their confluence at Pittsburg, assume the name of Ohio. Eastwardly it pours into the Atlantic Ocean James river, the Potomac, and the Susquehannah. From the northernmost and less elevated spurs of the chain, the Genesee flows into Lake Ontario; and in that quarter, the northerly branches of the Susquehannah seem to take their source from amongst inferior ridges, and, in their course to the Chesapeake, to break through all the mountains. From the Susquehannah the principal chain assumes a more eastwardly direction, and washed on the north by the lateral valley of the river Mohawk, whilst it gives rise southwardly to the Delaware, it terminates under the name of Catskill mountain, in view of the tide water of the Hudson.

This description has been introduced for the double purpose of pointing out all the rivers which can afford the means of communication, and of showing the impracticability, in the present state of science, of effecting a canal navigation across the mountains.

The most elevated lock canal, of which a correct description has been given, is that of Languedoc; and the highest ground over which it is carried is only six hundred feet above the sea. It is not believed that any canal has been undertaken, or at least completed in England, of an elevation exceeding four hundred and thirty feet above the waters united by it. The Allegany mountain is generally, and from observations made in several places, about three thousand feet above the level of the sea. The precise height of the dividing ridge was ascertained by the commissioners who laid out the United States road from Cumberland on the Potomac, to Brownsville on the Mononga-hela, at two thousand two hundred and sixty feet above the first, and at two thousand one hundred and fifty feet above the last river. Cumberland, from the levels taken by the Potomac company, is itself seven hundred and thirty-five feet above tide water. Although some more advantageous and less elevated places may be found, particularly amongst the ridges which divide some of the upper branches of the Susquehannah from the corresponding streams emptying into the river Allegany, there is none which is not of an elevation much beyond what has ever been overcome by canals in any other country. The impracticability arises from the principle of lock navigation, which, in order to effect the ascent, requires a greater supply of water in proportion to the height to be ascended, whilst the supply of water becomes less in the same proportion. Nor does the chain of mountains, through the whole extent where it divides the Atlantic from the western rivers, afford a single pond, lake, or natural reservoir. It may be added, as a general feature of American geography, that except in the swamps along the southern seacoast, no lake is to be found in the United States south of 41° north latitude; and that almost every river north of 42° issues from a lake or pond.

The works necessary in order to facilitate the communications from the sea-ports across the mountains to the western waters, must, therefore, consist either of artificial roads extending the whole way from tide water to the nearest and most convenient navigable western waters; or of improvements in the navigation of the leading Atlantic rivers, to the highest practicable points, connected by artificial roads across the mountains, with the nearest points from which a permanent navigation can be relied on down the western rivers.

The principal considerations in selecting proper directions for those communications are the distance from the navigable western waters, both to tide water, and to the nearest navigable Atlantic river, and the extent of navigation, either natural or susceptible of improvement, which may be afforded by the rivers; distance alone is mentioned, so far as relates to roads, because the mountains, however insuperable for canals, offer no important impediment to land communications. So far from

being an insurmountable barrier to commercial intercourse between the two great sections of the Union, it is now ascertained
that those mountains may, almost in every direction, be crossed
by artificial roads as permanent, as easy, and less expensive
than similar works in the lower country; for Congress having,
contrary to current opinion, directed that the road from Cumberland to Brownsville should be laid out so that its ascent
should not in any place exceed an angle of five degrees with
the horizon, no difficulty has been experienced in effecting the
object without cutting through hills; and, although the road
thus laid out be, in a distance of seventy-two miles, two or
three miles shorter than that heretofore in use.

Although the distance from the sea to the principal dividing
mountain, through its whole length, between the western
sources of the Susquehannah and those of the Savannah, be
nearly the same, yet the Atlantic bays penetrating the coast at
different depths and in different directions, the distance from
the sea-ports to the nearest western navigable waters varies
considerably. Taken in straight lines from each port to the
nearest branch, beyond all the mountains of each of the four
great western rivers, they may be stated as follows:

From Philadelphia to the confluence of Conemaugh
    and Loyalhannon, branches of the Allegany,   miles, 220
From the city of Washington to the confluence of
    the rivers Monongahela and Cheat,   150
From Richmond to Morris's on the Kanhawa,
    below all the falls of that river,   210
From Savannah or Charleston to any navigable branch
    of the Tennessee, the distance exceeds   300

The distance from the same western points to the upper
navigation of the corresponding Atlantic rivers cannot be stated
with precision, as the upper points, to which the navigation of
these rivers may be improved, are not yet ascertained. The

shortest portage between the waters of the Potomac and those of the Monongahela, in their natural state, from West Point on the Potomac to Cheat river below the falls, is about fifty miles in a straight line; but, in order to secure a tolerable navigation, particularly on the Potomac, the route from Cumberland to Brownsville (Red Stone Old Fort) has been preferred, and the distance by the road lately laid out is seventy-two miles. The portage between the north fork of the Juniata, a branch of the Susquehannah, and the corresponding waters of the river Allegany is somewhat shorter. That between Pattonborough, on James river, and the falls of the Kanhawa, exceeds one hundred miles.

The most prominent, though not perhaps the most insuperable obstacle in the navigation of the Atlantic rivers, consists in their lower falls, which are ascribed to a presumed continuous granite ridge, rising about one hundred and thirty feet above tide water. That ridge from New York to James river inclusively arrests the ascent of the tide; the falls of every river within that space being precisely at the head of the tide; pursuing thence southwardly a direction nearly parallel to the mountains, it recedes from the sea, leaving in each southern river an extent of good navigation between the tide and the falls. Other falls of less magnitude are found at the gaps of the Blue Ridge, through which the rivers have forced their passage. Higher up, the rapidity of the northern rivers, which penetrates through the inferior ridges of the great western chain, increases as they approach the dividing or Allegany mountain, and their sources being nearly at the same elevation, their rapidity increases in proportion to the shortness of their course. For that reason the navigation of the Susquehannah, above the Blue Ridge, is better than that of the Potomac, which affords, as has been stated, the shortest communication from tide water to the nearest western river. The levels of the last mentioned river having been taken by the Potomac company, the general result is annexed, as giving a more correct idea of the navigation of the Atlantic rivers than could be conveyed in any other manner:

	DISTANCE		FALL	RATE OF FALL
From the mouth of Savage river down to Cumberland,	31	miles	445 feet	14½ feet per mile
Thence to the Blue ridge,	130½	do.	490 do.	4 do.
Harper's Ferry or Shenandoah Falls,	5½	do.	43 do.	
Thence to Great Falls,	40	do.	39 do.	do.
Great and Little Falls to tide water,	12	do.	143 do.	
Total	219	miles	1,160 feet	

• • •

The navigation of the Kanhawa and of the eastern branches of the Tennessee, Monongahela, and Allegany, in their course through the mountains, may at a future period be improved. But, from the foot of the mountains, all those rivers, and particularly the Ohio, flow with a much gentler current than the Atlantic rivers, a circumstance easily accounted for when it is recollected that Brownsville, on the Monongahela, and at a distance of two thousand miles by water from the sea, is only one hundred and fifteen feet more elevated than Cumberland, on the Potomac; whilst this river, with all its meanders, reaches tide water within less than two hundred miles. All those rivers at the annual melting of the snows rise to the height of more than forty feet, affording from the upper points to which they are navigable a safe navigation to the sea for any ship that can pass over the bar at the mouth of the Mississippi. As early as the year 1793, a schooner built on the Monongahela, between Brownsville and Pittsburg, reached New Orleans by that extraordinary inland navigation, and arrived safely at Philadelphia. This first essay stimulated the spirit of enterprise so conspicuous in the American character, and numerous vessels, from one hundred to three hundred and fifty tons burden, are now annually built at several shipyards on the Ohio, even as high up as Pittsburg, and bringing down to New Orleans the produce of the upper country consumed there, carry to Europe and to the Atlantic ports of the United States the cotton, the sugar, and the tobacco of Louisiana and of the States of Tennessee and Kentucky.

That branch of national industry gives value to the immense forests of the Ohio and of its numerous branches, and will soon make a considerable, and perhaps necessary accession to the shipping of the United States, and has a tendency to diminish the price of freights from New Orleans to the other American and to foreign ports. The importance of this last consideration will be duly felt, if the magnitude of the exports of which New Orleans is destined to be the emporium, be contrasted with the probable amount of its importations; for such are the labor, time, and expense necessary to ascend the rapid stream of the Mississippi, (and the nature of its banks, annually overflowed on a breadth of several miles, precludes the possibility of towing paths,) that, whilst the greater part of the produce of the immense country, watered by that river and its tributary streams, must necessarily be exported through its channel, the importations of a considerable portion of that country will continue to be supplied from the Atlantic seaports, by water and land communications, susceptible of considerable improvement; and thus, unless another outlet be found for a portion of the exports, or unless the upper country can supply vessels, those exports must necessarily pay a double freight.

The only impediments to that navigation are on the Tennessee, "the Muscle shoals," of which no particular account has been received, and on the Ohio, the falls of Louisville. Ordinary boats can with difficulty pass these in summer, and the navigation is, even during the freshets, dangerous for the large vessels. The attention of the Legislature of Kentucky, and of the inhabitants of the Western country, generally, has, therefore, been particularly drawn to the opening of a canal at that place. A company has been lately incorporated by the State of Kentucky for that purpose, with a capital which may amount to $500,000, but a small portion of which has yet been subscribed. The expense, however, is estimated at a sum less than the nominal capital.

The proposed canal would be near two miles in length, and must be dug, in some places, to a depth of twenty-seven, but generally about sixteen feet. The breadth at the bottom being twenty feet, with the necessary slope, would make it, generally, sixty-eight feet wide at top, and, in particular places, not less than one hundred. The fall at low water is about twenty-two feet, and would require three locks, of dimensions sufficient to pass ships of four hundred tons, and drawing fourteen feet of water. The greatest expense will be that of digging, and removing the earth, which may be estimated at four hundred thousand cubic yards, and, according to the representation made of the nature of the ground, will not probably cost more than $200,000. To this may be added $100,000 for the locks and other necessary works, making, altogether, $300,000. The greatest difficulty seems to be the protection of the locks and canals against the rise of the river, which sometimes overflows the whole ground through which the canal must be opened.

The expense of the improvements suggested in the communications between the Atlantic and Western waters may be stated as follows:

1st. Four artificial roads from the four great Western rivers, the Allegany, Monongahela, Kanhawa, and Tennessee, to the nearest corresponding Atlantic rivers, the Susquehannah or Juniata, the Potomac, James river, and either the Santee or Savannah, leaving to the several States the continuation of those roads eastwardly to the nearest seaports. Those roads should unite on each river

points from which a permanent and safe navigation downwards could, except during the driest
season, be relied on; and will, therefore, on each
route, be estimated at one hundred miles, making, altogether, four hundred miles, which at
$7,000 a mile, the material being generally on
the spot, would cost $2,800,000
2dly. The improvement of the navigation of the
four Atlantic rivers, from tide water to the highest practicable point, effected, principally, by
canals around the falls wherever practicable, and
by locks wherever necessary. The most expensive
of these would be the proposed canal from Columbia, on the Susquehannah, either to tide
water or to the Delaware and Chesapeake canal;
and, considering how much has been effected already, and may still be done on the other rivers,
by the several incorporated companies, it is believed that every useful improvement might be
completed by a public expenditure not exceeding   1,500,000
3dly. The canal at the falls of the Ohio, estimated at   300,000
                                                     ——————
                                                     $4,600,000

Although a canal navigation, uniting the Atlantic and Western waters in a direct course across the mountains, appears
impracticable, yet those mountains may be turned either on
the north, by means of the Mohawk valley and of Lake Ontario, or on the south, through Georgia and the Mississippi
Territory. The first communication will be noticed under the
head of "the river St. Lawrence and Great Lakes." Of the
second it will be sufficient to observe that the country lying
between the sources of the rivers Chatahoochee and Mobile,
and the Gulf of Mexico, is an inclined plane, regularly de-

scending towards the sea, and that, by following the proper levels, it presents no natural obstacle to the opening of a canal, fed by the waters of the two last-mentioned rivers, and extending from the tide water on the coast of Georgia to the Mississippi. The distance, in a direct line, is about five hundred and fifty miles, and, to be overcome, requires only time, perseverance, and labor. When it is recollected that such an undertaking would discharge the Mississippi into the Atlantic, the remarks already made on the trade of that river, and other obvious considerations, will sufficiently point out its immense importance. Nor should the plan, on account of its magnitude, be thought chimerical; for the elevation and other natural obstacles of intervening ground, or want of a sufficient supply of water, and not distance, are the only insuperable impediments to an artificial navigation.

This work, which is presented, not as an immediate, but as a distant object, worthy of consideration, would probably require ten millions of dollars and thirty years for its completion. The annual sales of the public lands in the Mississippi Territory, which are estimated at fifty millions of acres, would, after paying the debt due to the State of Georgia, afford sufficient funds; and the increased value of the residue would alone more than compensate the expense.

It is proper to add that an inland navigation, even for open boats, already exists from New Orleans, by the canal Carondelet, to the lake Pontchartrain, thence, between the coast and the adjacent islands, to the bay of Mobile, and up its two principal rivers, the Alabama and the Tombigbee, to the head of the tide, within the acknowledged boundaries of the United States. The current of these two rivers being much less rapid than that of the Mississippi, they have long been contemplated, particularly the Tombigbee, as affording a better communication to the ascending or returning trade from New Orleans to the waters of the Tennessee, from which they are separated by short portages.

COMMUNICATIONS BETWEEN THE ATLANTIC RIVERS

AND THE RIVER ST. LAWRENCE AND GREAT LAKES

Vessels ascend the river St. Lawrence from the sea to Montreal. The river Sorel discharges at some distance below that town the waters of Lake George and Lake Champlain, which penetrate southwardly within the United States. From Montreal to Lake Ontario, the ascent of the river St. Lawrence is estimated at about two hundred feet. From the eastern extremity of Lake Ontario, an inland navigation for vessels of more than one hundred tons burthen, is continued for more than one thousand miles, through Lakes Erie, St. Clair, and Huron, to the western and southern extremities of Lake Michigan, without any other interruption than that of the falls and rapids of Niagara, between Lake Erie and Lake Ontario. The descent from Fort Schlosser to Devil's Hole, a distance of four miles, which includes the perpendicular falls of Niagara, has, by correct measurement, been ascertained at three hundred and seventy-five feet. The whole fall from Lake Erie to Lake Ontario is estimated at four hundred and fifty feet, making the elevation of Lake Erie above tide-water six hundred and fifty feet.

Lake Superior, the largest of those inland seas, communicates with the northern extremity of Lake Huron, by the river and rapids of St. Mary's. The fall of these is not ascertained; but it is said that a small canal has been opened around the most difficult part by the Northwest Fur Company.

Five of the Atlantic rivers approach the waters of the St. Lawrence; viz: The Penobscot, Kennebeck, Connecticut, the North or Hudson river, and the Tioga branch of the Susquehannah. This last river will afford a useful communication with the rivers Seneca and Genesee, which empty into Lake Ontario. The length of the portage has not been precisely stated; and the general navigation of the Susquehannah has already been noticed. It may, however, be observed, that it is the only Atlantic river whose sources approach both the Western waters and those of the St. Lawrence.

The three Eastern rivers afford convenient communications with the province of Lower Canada, but not with that extensive inland navigation which penetrates through the United States, within two hundred miles of the Mississippi. No statement has been received of any improvement having yet been made on the Penobscot or Kennebeck; and a very imperfect account has been obtained of some short canals opened around the several falls of the river Connecticut. One at Bellows' Falls, in the State of Vermont, has been particularly mentioned, and is the highest improvement on the river.

What is called the North river is a narrow and long bay, which in its northwardly course from the harbor of New York breaks through or turns all the mountains, affording a tide navigation for vessels of eighty tons to Albany and Troy, one hundred and sixty miles above New York. This peculiarity distinguishes the North river from all the other bays and rivers of the United States. The tide in no other ascends higher than the granite ridge, or comes within thirty miles of the Blue Ridge, or Eastern chain of mountains. In the North river it breaks through the Blue Ridge at West Point, and ascends above the Eastern termination of the Catskill, or great Western chain.

A few miles above Troy, and the head of the tide, the Hudson from the north, and the Mohawk from the west, unite their waters, and form the North river. The Hudson, in its course upwards, approaches the waters of Lake Champlain, and the Mohawk those of Lake Ontario.

I. Hudson and Champlain, or Northern Navigation

• • •

The distance in a straight line from Waterford to Skeensborough is fifty miles; and the expense of opening a permanent boat navigation on a proper plan through the whole line is, from imperfect materials, estimated at about $800,000. This communication would divert to a port of the United States the trade of one-half of the State of Vermont, and of a part of that of New York, which is now principally carried through the channel of the St. Lawrence, and of the province of Canada.

II. *Mohawk and Ontario, or Western Navigation*

. . .

The elevation of the summit level between the Mohawk and the waters of Lake Ontario, being only three hundred and ninety feet above the tide water at Troy, and one hundred and ninety feet above Lake Ontario, a canal navigation is practicable the whole distance. Whether this should be attempted for a sloop or boat navigation, must depend principally, if not altogether, on the supply of water. It is stated that the canal from the summit level to Troy must necessarily follow the valley of the Mohawk, and perhaps occasionally enter and cross the river. Calculated for a boat navigation the expense may be estimated as follows:

Mr. Weston estimated the expense of a canal, from Lansing mills to tide water at Troy, around the Cohoes falls, at $ 250,000

The distance from the summit level to Lansing mill is 120 miles, and to Lake Ontario, deducting the twenty miles occupied by Lake Oneida, forty miles, together one hundred and sixty miles of canal, digging of which, at $8000 a mile, is 1,280,000

The fall from the summit level to Lansing mills is two hundred and fifty feet, and to Lake Ontario, one hundred and ninety feet, together four hundred and forty feet lock-

age, which will require fifty-five locks of
eight feet lift each. These at $7,500, the
cost of the stone locks erected by the company at the Little Falls, will cost about   420,000
Feeders and aqueducts may be estimated at   250,000
                                                ─────────

Making altogether two millions two hundred
    thousand dollars, $2,200,000

It is not believed that a sloop navigation, if practicable, could
be effected for a less sum than five millions of dollars. . . .

III. Niagara

The fall from Lake Erie to Lake Ontario has already been
stated at four hundred and fifty feet. A company had also
been incorporated by the State of New York for the purpose of
opening a canal at this place; but it does not appear that any
thing ever was attempted after the survey had been made. The
intention seems to have been to open a canal navigation for
boats only from Fort Schlosser to Devil's Hole; the lake itself
and Giles's creek would have supplied the water, and the expense was estimated at four hundred and thirty-seven thousand dollars.

It is, however, evident that the canal, in order to be as
eminently useful as the nature of the undertaking seems to require, should be on such scale as to admit vessels which can
navigate both lakes. Considering the distance which in that
case must be extended to about ten miles, and the lockage of
four hundred and fifty feet, it is not believed that the expense
can be estimated at less than one million of dollars.

The works necessary to effect water communications between
the tide water of the North river, the St. Lawrence, and all

the lakes, (Lake Superior only excepted,) are, therefore, estimated at four millions of dollars, viz:

Northern navigation to Lake Champlain,	$800,000
Western navigation to Lake Ontario,	2,200,000
Falls of Niagara for a sloop navigation,	1,000,000
	$4,000,000

... Their utility will not be confined to the extensive navigation of the lakes themselves: for the mountains being completely turned when arrived into Lake Erie, the ridge which separates the waters emptying into that and into Lake Michigan, from the northern branches of the Ohio, and from the waters of the Mississippi, is of a moderate elevation, and is gradually depressed in its course westwardly. There is no doubt of the practicability of opening canals, at a future period, between several of those waters, either by selecting proper levels, or by means of short tunnels across favorable parts of the ridge. It will at present be sufficient to point out the principal communications now in use.

The distance from Lake Erie to Lake Chetoughe, an extensive and important and elevated reservoir which is the source of the Canowango, a branch of the Allegany, is seven miles by a continual ascent, the elevation of which is not ascertained.

From Presque Isle, on Lake Erie, to Le Bœuf, on French creek, another branch of the Allegany, the distance is sixteen miles, and a company is incorporated by the State of Pennsylvania for making an artificial road across that portage.

The navigation from Lake Chetoughe and from Le Bœuf to Pittsburg offers no impediment whenever the waters are high; and the greater part of the salt now consumed in the northwest counties of Pennsylvania, as far as Pittsburg, and some distance down the Ohio, is brought from the salt springs of New York by Oswego, through Lake Ontario; thence across the portage of Niagara to Lake Erie; and thence, by either of the two last mentioned portages, to the waters of the river Allegany.

The distance from the place where the Cayuga, a river emptying into Lake Erie, ceases to be navigable, to the navigable waters of the Muskingum, which empties into the Ohio one hundred and seventy miles below Pittsburg, is only six miles; and a company is said to be formed for the improvement of that communication.

Sandusky river and the Scioto take their sources in the same swamp. The navigation of the Miami of Lake Erie is interrupted by some falls; but its upper branches approach those of the Miami of the Ohio, and of the Wabash, and are stated as being nearly on the same level.

The Illinois river, which empties into the Mississippi above St. Louis, rises in a swamp, which, when the waters are high, affords a natural canoe navigation to the sources of Chicago creek, a short stream, which falls into Lake Michigan at its southern extremity.

Another communication generally used by the Indian traders is that from Green bay, also in Lake Michigan, to the Mississippi by Fox river and the Wisconsin. Nor is there any doubt that, if the inland navigation between the North river and the lakes was completely opened, the whole Indian trade either of the Mississippi by Lake Michigan, or of the northwest by Lake Superior, must necessarily centre in an Atlantic port of the United States—a consideration of minor importance as a commercial object, when compared with the other advantages of that great communication, but of great weight in its relation to the political intercourse of the United States with the Indians. . . .

TURNPIKE, OR ARTIFICIAL ROADS

A great number of artificial roads have been completed in the eastern and middle States, at an expense varying from less than $1,000 to $14,000 a mile. . . .

The greater progress made in the improvement of roads in the northern parts of the Union must be principally ascribed to a more compact population, which renders those improvements more necessary, and at the same time supplies with greater facility the means of effecting them. . . .

The same principles which have directed the arrangement adopted in this report in relation to canals, will also point out those roads which seem, in the first instance, to claim the patronage of the General Government.

Those which appear most necessary for the communications between the Atlantic and western rivers have already been mentioned under that head; and the improvement of the water communication between the North river and the great lakes ought to take the precedence of any other in that direction.

That road which, therefore, seems exclusively to claim public attention, is a great turnpike extending from Maine to Georgia in the general direction of the seacoast and main post road, passing through all the principal seaports. The general convenience and importance of such a work, are too obvious to require any comments; and the expense seems to be the primary object of consideration.

The distance will be roughly estimated at one thousand six hundred miles; and from what has been stated on the subject of roads generally, it may be inferred that the greater part of the road being intended almost exclusively for travelling, and not for transportation of heavy articles, the expense cannot exceed the rate of three thousand dollars a mile. For although some detached portions of the route being commercial roads, must be improved as such, and at a greater expense; an equivalent reduction in other parts will result from those portions which are already improved by private companies, and from the impossibility, for want of materials for an artificial stratum, of going in some places beyond what has been described as the first or cheapest species of turnpike. The whole expense may, therefore, be estimated at $4,800,000. A secondary object, but of more importance to Government than to individuals, would be the improvement, on a much less expensive scale, of certain portions of roads leading to some points on the extremes of the Union, intended principally for the purpose of accelerating the progress of the mail, and the prompt transmission of information of a public nature. The points contemplated are Detroit, St. Louis in Upper Louisiana, and New Orleans. The portions of road which, traversing a wilderness cannot be improved without the aid of the United States, are, from the Tuscarora branch of the Muskingum to Detroit; from Cincinnati, by Vincennes, to St. Louis; and from Nashville in Tennessee, or Athens in Georgia, to Natchez. The expense necessary to enable the mail and even stages to proceed at the rate of eighty miles a day, may, at the rate of about two hundred dollars a mile, including bridges over all the small streams, be estimated, for those three roads, at two hundred thousand dollars.

RECAPITULATION AND RESOURCES

The improvements which have been respectfully suggested as most important in order to facilitate the communication between the great geographical divisions of the United States, will now be recapitulated; and their expense compared with the resources applicable to that object.

I. From north to south, in a direction parallel
to the seacoast.
  1. Canals opening an inland navigation for
     sea vessels from Massachusetts to North
     Carolina, being more than two-thirds of

the Atlantic seacoast of the United States, and across all the principal capes, Cape Fear excepted, $3,000,000

2. A great turnpike road from Maine to Georgia along the whole extent of the Atlantic seacoast,   4,800,000

        $7,800,000

II. From east to west, forming communications across the mountains between the Atlantic and western rivers.

1. Improvement of the navigation of four great Atlantic rivers, including canals parallel to them,   1,500,000

2. Four firstrate turnpike roads from those rivers across the mountains, to the four corresponding western rivers,   2,800,000

3. Canal around the falls of the Ohio,   300,000

4. Improvement of roads to Detroit, St. Louis and New Orleans,   200,000

        4,800,000

III. In a northern and northwestwardly direction, forming inland navigations between the Atlantic seacoast, and the great lakes and the St. Lawrence.

1. Inland navigation between the North river and Lake Champlain,   800,000

2. Great inland navigation opened the whole way by canals from the North river to Lake Ontario,   2,200,000

3. Canal around the falls and rapids of Niagara, opening a sloop navigation from Lake Ontario to the upper lakes as far as the extremities of Lake Michigan,   1,000,000

        4,000,000

Making, together, $16,600,000

The great geographical features of the country have been solely adhered to in pointing out those lines of communication; and these appear to embrace all the great interests of the Union, and to be calculated to diffuse and increase the national wealth in a very general way, by opening an intercourse between the remotest extremes of the United States. Yet it must necessarily result from an adherence to that principle, that

those parts of the Atlantic States through which the great
western and northwest communications will be carried, must,
in addition to the general advantages in which they will participate, receive from those communications greater local and
immediate benefits than the Eastern and perhaps Southern
States. As the expense must be defrayed from the general funds
of the Union, justice, and, perhaps, policy not less than justice,
seems to require that a number of local improvements, sufficient to equalize the advantages, should also be undertaken
in those States, parts of States, or districts which are less immediately interested in those inland communications. Arithmetical precision cannot, indeed, be attained in objects of that
kind; nor would an apportionment of the moneys applied according to the population of each State be either just or practicable, since roads and particularly canals are often of greater
utility to the States which they unite, than to those through
which they pass. But a sufficient number of local improvements,
consisting either of roads or canals may, without any material
difficulty, be selected, so as to do substantial justice and give
general satisfaction. Without pretending to suggest what would
be the additional sum necessary for that object, it will, for the
sake of round numbers, be estimated at $3,400,000
   Which, added to the sum estimated for general
      improvements,   16,600,000

   Would make an aggregate of $20,000,000

An annual appropriation of two millions of dollars would accomplish all those great objects in ten years, and may, without
inconvenience, be supplied in time of peace by the existing
revenues and resources of the United States. This may be
exemplified in several ways.

   The annual appropriation, on account of the principal and
interest of the public debt, has, during the last six years,
amounted to eight millions of dollars. After the present year,

or, at furthest, after the ensuing year, the sum which, on account of the irredeemable nature of the remaining debt, may be applied to that object cannot, in any one year, exceed four million six hundred thousand dollars; leaving, therefore, from that source alone, an annual surplus of three million four hundred thousand dollars applicable to any other object.

From the 1st January, 1801, to the 1st January, 1809, a period of eight years, the United States shall have discharged about thirty-four millions of the principal of the old debt, or deducting the Louisiana debt incurred during the same period and not yet discharged, about twenty-three millions of dollars. They may, with equal facility, apply, in a period of ten years, a sum of twenty millions of dollars to internal improvements.

The annual permanent revenue of the United States, calculated on a state of general peace, and on the most moderate estimate, was, in a report made to Congress on the 6th day of December, 1806, computed for the years 1809, 1815, at fourteen millions of dollars. The annual expenses on the peace establishment, and including the four million six hundred thousand dollars on account of the debt, and four hundred thousand dollars for contingencies, do not exceed eight millions and a half, leaving an annual surplus of five millions and a half of dollars. To provide for the protection and defence of the country is undoubtedly the object to which the resources of the United States must, in the first instance, be applied, and to the exclusion of all others, if the times shall require it. But it is believed that, in times of peace, and to such period only are these remarks applicable; the surplus will be amply sufficient to defray the expenses of all the preparatory measures of a permanent nature which prudence may suggest, and to pay the sum destined for internal improvements. Three millions annually applied during the same period of ten years, would arm every man in the United States, fill the public arsenals and magazines, erect every battery and fortification which could be manned, and even, if thought eligible, build a navy.

That the whole surplus would be inadequate to the support of any considerable increase of the land or naval force kept in actual service in time of peace, will be readily admitted. But such a system is not contemplated; if ever adopted, the objects of this report must probably be abandoned; for it has not heretofore been found an easy task for any Government to indulge in that species of expense, which, leaving no trace behind it, adds nothing to the real strength of the country, and, at the same time, to provide for either its permanent defence or improvement.

It must not be omitted that the facility of communications constitutes, particularly in the United States, an important branch of national defence. Their extensive territory opposes a powerful obstacle to the progress of an enemy; but, on the other hand, the number of regular forces which may be raised, necessarily limited by the population, will, for many years, be inconsiderable when compared with that extent of territory. That defect cannot otherwise be supplied than by those great national improvements, which will afford the means of a rapid concentration of that regular force, and of a formidable body of militia on any given point.

Amongst the resources of the Union, there is one which, from its nature, seems more particularly applicable to internal improvements. Exclusively of Louisiana, the General Government possesses, in trust for the people of the United States, about one hundred millions of acres fit for cultivation, north of the river Ohio, and near fifty millions south of the State of Tennessee. For the disposition of these lands a plan has been adopted, calculated to enable every industrious citizen to become a freeholder, to secure indisputable titles to the purchasers, to obtain a national revenue, and, above all, to suppress monopoly. Its success has surpassed that of every former attempt, and exceeded the expectations of its authors. But a higher price than had usually been paid for waste lands by the first inhabitants of the frontier became an unavoidable ingredient of a system intended for general benefit, and was necessary, in order to prevent the public lands being engrossed by individuals possessing greater wealth, activity, and local advantages. It is believed that nothing could be more gratifying to the purchasers, and to the inhabitants of the Western States generally, or better calculated to remove popular objections, and to defeat insidious efforts, than the application of the proceeds of the sales to improvements conferring general advantages on the nation, and an immediate benefit on the purchasers and inhabitants themselves. It may be added, that the United States, considered merely as owners of the soil, are also deeply interested in the opening of those communications which must necessarily enhance the value of their property. Thus the opening an inland navigation from tide water to the great lakes, would immediately give to the great body of lands bordering on those lakes as great value as if they were situated at the distance of one hundred miles by land from the seacoast. And if the proceeds of the first ten millions of acres which may be sold were applied to such improvements, the United States would be amply repaid in the sale of the other ninety millions.

The annual appropriation of two millions of dollars drawn from the general revenues of the Union, which has been suggested, could operate to its full extent only in times of peace and under prosperous circumstances. The application of the proceeds of the sales of the public lands, might, perhaps, be made permanent until it had amounted to a certain sum, and until the most important improvements had been effected. The fund created by those improvements, the expense of which has been estimated at twenty millions of dollars, would afterwards become itself a perpetual resource for further improvements. Although some of those first communications should not become immediately productive; and although the same liberal policy, which dictated the measure, would consider them less as objects of revenue to Government, than of increased wealth and general convenience to the nation, yet they would all, sooner or later, acquire, as productive property, their par value. Whenever that had taken place in relation to any of them, the stock might be sold to individuals or companies, and the proceeds applied to a new improvement. And by persevering in that plan, a succession of improvements would be effected until every portion of the United States should enjoy all the advantages of inland navigation and improved roads, of which it was susceptible. To effect that great object, a disbursement of twenty millions of dollars, applied with more or less rapidity, according to the circumstances of the United States, would be amply sufficient.

The manner in which the public moneys may be applied to such objects remains to be considered.

It is evident that the United States cannot, under the constitution, open any road or canal, without the consent of the State through which such road or canal must pass. In order, therefore, to remove every impediment to a national plan of internal improvements, an amendment to the constitution was suggested by the Executive when the subject was recommended to the consideration of Congress. Until this be obtained, the assent of the States being necessary for each improvement, the modifications under which that assent may be given, will necessarily control the manner of applying the money. It may be, however, observed that in relation to the specific improvements which have been suggested, there is hardly any which is not either already authorized by the States respectively, or so immediately beneficial to them, as to render it highly probable that no material difficulty will be experienced in that respect.

The moneys may be applied in two different manners. The United States may, with the assent of the States, undertake some of the works at their sole expense, or they may subscribe a certain number of shares of the stock of companies incorporated for the purpose. Loans might also, in some instances, be made to such companies. The first mode would, perhaps, by effectually controlling local interests, give the most proper general direction to the work. Its details would probably be executed on a more economical plan by private companies. Both modes may, perhaps, be blended together so as to obtain the advantages pertaining to each. But the modifications of which the plan is susceptible must vary according to the nature of the work, and of the charters, and seem to belong to that class of details which are not the immediate subject of consideration.

At present the only work undertaken by the United States at their sole expense, and to which the assent of the States has been obtained, is the road from Cumberland to Brownsville; an appropriation may, for that purpose, be made at any time. In relation to all other works, the United States have nothing at this time in their power but to assist those already authorized, either by loans, or by becoming stockholders; and the last mode appears the most eligible. The only companies incorporated for effecting some of the improvements, considered in this report as of national and firstrate importance, which have applied for such assistance, are the Chesapeake and Delaware Canal, the Susquehannah Canal, and the Dismal Swamp companies; and authority might be given to subscribe a certain number of shares to each on condition that the plan of the work to be executed should be approved by the General Government. A subscription to the Ohio Canal, to the Pittsburg Road, and perhaps to some other objects not fully ascertained, is also practicable at this time. As an important basis of the general system, an immediate authority might also be given to take the surveys and levels of the routes of the most important roads and canals which are contemplated: a work always useful, and by which the practicability and expense of the undertakings would be ascertained with much more correctness than in this report. A moderate appropriation would be sufficient for those several objects.

In the selection of the objects submitted in obedience to the order of the Senate, as claiming, in the first instance, the aid of the General Government, general principles have been adhered to as best calculated to suppress every bias of partiality to particular objects. Yet some such bias, of which no individual is perfectly free, may, without being felt, have operated on this report. The National Legislature alone, embracing every local interest, and superior to every local consideration, is competent to the selection of such national objects. . . .

All which is most respectfully submitted.

ALBERT GALLATIN
Secretary of the Treasury
Treasury Department, April 4, 1808

2. Andrew Jackson:
The Objections to National Action

Gallatin's proposals rested on the financial basis of an expected surplus in the federal budget, but the Embargo and the War of 1812 soon proved this expectation unfounded. Even after the war, when the Treasury was again full and the demand for improvements stronger than ever, state and regional rivalries prevented the adoption of a comprehensive national program. New York State built the Erie Canal with its own means, after Congress refused federal aid; and other states, as well as ambitious cities like Baltimore, embarked on their own rival programs. "The National Legislature . . . embracing every local interest, and"—in Gallatin's optimistic or politic phrase—"superior to every local consideration," appeared unwilling or unable to carry out the invidious task of selecting the great national objects.

Even before Gallatin's Report, the government had begun

building the National Road, and appropriations for its extension were continued beyond Jackson's time—although ownership and administration were turned over to the several states. Between Gallatin and Jackson, the government made small subscriptions to the companies constructing canals between the Chesapeake and Delaware bays, between the Chesapeake and Albemarle Sound, and around the Falls of the Ohio, as well as a more substantial subscription to the Chesapeake and Ohio Canal Company. No more than this had come of the plan for concerted national action.

If Gallatin's Report is the classic expression of the argument in favor of a national program of internal improvements, President Jackson's Veto Message on the Maysville Road is often taken as the classic statement of the argument against such a program. There is, to be sure, one respect to which the two documents are not in opposition. The Maysville Road, to which Congress had proposed a subscription, formed no part of Gallatin's Plan and could scarcely have met his specifications as a great national object. A vigorous passage in the Message condemned the proposal precisely on the ground that it was purely a local project within a single state, the Washington, Paris, and Lexington of the company's title all being towns in Kentucky. Yet other parts of the Veto, as well as passages in the First Annual Message that preceded it and the Second Annual Message that followed, show a broader range of objections to a national program. To mix the funds of the federal government with those of private citizens through stock subscriptions was, he thought, unwise and improper. Until the national debt was paid off, federal money should not be appropriated for purposes of improvements. Moreover, even when a surplus became available, it would be better to distribute it to the states in proportion to their representation in Congress. Selection of projects by the national government would necessarily have the effect of favoring some states more than others, and the resulting ill-feeling would tend to weaken the bonds of union. This, he said, had been illustrated by "the difficulties which have hitherto attended appropriations for purposes of internal improvement."

After Jackson's veto, Congress appropriated no money for new improvements until after the Civil War, although federal aid through grants of land was to become important in the 1850's.

The selections are taken from the message on the Maysville Road, omitting most of the constitutional argument, and Jackson's Second Annual Message.

THE MAYSVILLE ROAD VETO

May 27, 1830

To the House of Representatives

GENTLEMEN: I have maturely considered the bill proposing to authorize "a subscription of stock in the Maysville, Washington, Paris, and Lexington Turnpike Road Company," and now return the same to the House of Representatives, in which it originated, with my objections to its passage.

Sincerely friendly to the improvement of our country by means of roads and canals, I regret that any difference of opinion in the mode of contributing to it should exist between us; and if in stating this difference I go beyond what the occasion may be deemed to call for, I hope to find an apology in the great importance of the subject, an unfeigned respect for the high source from which this branch of it has emanated, and an anxious wish to be correctly understood by my constituents in the discharge of all my duties. Diversity of sentiment among public functionaries actuated by the same general motives, on the character and tendency of particular measures, is an incident common to all Governments, and the more to be

From James D. Richardson, *A Compilation of the Messages and Papers of the Presidents, 1789–1903* (New York: Bureau of National Literature and Art, 1897–1920), vol. II, pp. 483–490, 493.

expected in one which, like ours, owes its existence to the freedom of opinion, and must be upheld by the same influence. Controlled as we thus are by a higher tribunal, before which our respective acts will be canvassed with the indulgence due to the imperfections of our nature, and with that intelligence and unbiased judgment which are the true correctives of error, all that our responsibility demands is that the public good should be the measure of our views, dictating alike their frank expression and honest maintenance.

In the message which was presented to Congress at the opening of its present session I endeavored to exhibit briefly my views upon the important and highly interesting subject to which our attention is now to be directed. I was desirous of presenting to the representatives of the several States in Congress assembled the inquiry whether some mode could not be devised which would reconcile the diversity of opinion concerning the powers of this Government over the subject of internal improvement, and the manner in which these powers, if conferred by the Constitution, ought to be exercised. The act which I am called upon to consider has, therefore, been passed with a knowledge of my views on this question, as these are expressed in the message referred to. In that document the following suggestions will be found:

> After the extinction of the public debt, it is not probable that any adjustment of the tariff upon principles satisfactory to the people of the Union will until a remote period, if ever, leave the Government without a considerable surplus in the Treasury beyond what may be required for its current service. As, then, the period approaches when the application of the revenue to the payment of debt will cease, the disposition of the surplus will present a subject for the serious deliberation of Congress; and it may be fortunate for the country that it is yet to be decided. Considered in connection with the difficulties which have heretofore attended appropriations for purposes of internal improvement, and with those which this experience tells us will certainly

arise whenever power over such subjects may be exercised by the General Government, it is hoped that it may lead to the adoption of some plan which will reconcile the diversified interests of the States and strengthen the bonds which unite them. Every member of the Union, in peace and in war, will be benefited by the improvement of inland navigation and the construction of highways in the several States. Let us, then, endeavor to attain this benefit in a mode which will be satisfactory to all. That hitherto adopted has by many of our fellow-citizens been deprecated as an infraction of the Constitution, while by others it has been viewed as inexpedient. All feel that it has been employed at the expense of harmony in the legislative councils.

And adverting to the constitutional power of Congress to make what I considered a proper disposition of the surplus revenue, I subjoined the following remarks:

> To avoid these evils it appears to me that the most safe, just, and federal disposition which could be made of the surplus revenue would be its apportionment among the several States according to their ratio of representation, and should this measure not be found warranted by the Constitution that it would be expedient to propose to the States an amendment authorizing it. . . .

The bill before me does not call for a more definite opinion upon the particular circumstances which will warrant appropriations of money by Congress to aid works of internal improvement, for although the extension of the power to apply money beyond that of carrying into effect the object for which it is appropriated has, as we have seen, been long claimed and exercised by the Federal Government, yet such grants have always been professedly under the control of the general principle that the works which might be thus aided should be "of a general, not local, national, not State," character. A disregard of this distinction would of necessity lead to the subversion of the federal system. That even this is an unsafe one, arbitrary in its nature, and liable, consequently, to great abuses, is too obvious to require the confirmation of experience. It is, how-

ever, sufficiently definite and imperative to my mind to forbid
my approbation of any bill having the character of the one
under consideration. I have given to its provisions all the reflection demanded by a just regard for the interests of those
of our fellow citizens who have desired its passage, and by the
respect which is due to a coordinate branch of the Government, but I am not able to view it in any other light than as
a measure of purely local character; or, if it can be considered national, that no further distinction between the appropriate duties of the General and State Governments need
be attempted, for there can be no local interest that may not
with equal propriety be denominated national. It has no connection with any established system of improvements; is exclusively within the limits of a State, starting at a point on
the Ohio River and running out 60 miles to an interior town,
and even as far as the State is interested conferring partial
instead of general advantages.

Considering the magnitude and importance of the power,
and the embarrassments to which, from the very nature of
the thing, its exercise must necessarily be subjected, the real
friends of internal improvement ought not to be willing to
confide it to accident and chance. What is properly *national*
in its character or otherwise is an inquiry which is often extremely difficult of solution. The appropriations of one year
for an object which is considered national may be rendered
nugatory by the refusal of a succeeding Congress to continue
the work on the ground that it is local. No aid can be derived
from the intervention of corporations. The question regards the
character of the work, not that of those by whom it is to be accomplished. Notwithstanding the union of the Government
with the corporation by whose immediate agency any work of
internal improvement is carried on, the inquiry will still remain, Is it national and conducive to the benefit of the whole,
or local and operating only to the advantage of a portion of
the Union?

But although I might not feel it to be my official duty to interpose the Executive veto to the passage of a bill appropriating money for the construction of such works as are authorized by the States and are national in their character, I do not wish to be understood as expressing an opinion that it is expedient at this time for the General Government to embark in a system of this kind; and anxious that my constituents should be possessed of my views on this as well as on all other subjects which they have committed to my discretion, I shall state them frankly and briefly. Besides many minor considerations, there are two prominent views of the subject which have made a deep impression upon my mind, which, I think, are well entitled to your serious attention, and will, I hope, be maturely weighed by the people.

From the official communication submitted to you it appears that if no adverse and unforseen contingency happens in our foreign relations and no unusual diversion be made of the funds set apart for the payment of the national debt we may look with confidence to its entire extinguishment in the short period of four years. The extent to which this pleasing anticipation is dependent upon the policy which may be pursued in relation to measures of the character of the one now under consideration must be obvious to all, and equally so that the events of the present session are well calculated to awaken public solicitude upon the subject. By the statement from the Treasury Department and those from the clerks of the Senate and House of Representatives, herewith submitted, it appears that the bills which have passed into laws, and those which in all probability will pass before the adjournment of Congress, anticipate appropriations which, with the ordinary expenditures for the support of Government, will exceed considerably the amount in the Treasury for the year 1830. Thus, whilst we are diminishing the revenue by a reduction of the duties on tea, coffee, and cocoa the appropriations for internal improvement are increasing beyond the available means of the Treasury. And if to this calculation be added the amounts contained in bills which are pending before the two Houses, it may be safely affirmed that $10,000,000 would not make up the excess over the Treasury receipts, unless the payment of the national debt be postponed and the means now pledged to that object applied to those enumerated in these bills. Without a well-regulated system of internal improvement this exhausting mode of appropriation is not likely to be avoided, and the plain consequence must be either a continuance of the national debt or a resort to additional taxes.

Although many of the States, with a laudable zeal and under the influence of an enlightened policy, are successfully applying their separate efforts to works of this character, the desire to enlist the aid of the General Government in the construction of such as from their nature ought to devolve upon it, and to which the means of the individual States are inadequate, is both rational and patriotic, and if that desire is not gratified now it does not follow that it never will be. The general intelligence and public spirit of the American people furnish a sure guaranty that at the proper time this policy will be made to prevail under circumstances more auspicious to its successful prosecution than those which now exist. But great as this object undoubtedly is, it is not the only one which demands the fostering care of the Government. The preservation and success of the republican principle rest with us. To elevate its character and extend its influence rank among our most important duties, and the best means to accomplish this desirable end are those which will rivet the attachment of our citizens to the Government of their choice by the comparative lightness of their public burthens and by the attraction which the superior success of its operations will present to the admiration and respect of the world. Through the favor of an overruling and indulgent Providence our country is blessed with general prosperity and our citizens exempted from the pressure of taxation, which other less favored portions of the human family are obliged to bear; yet it is true that many of the taxes collected from our citizens through the medium of imposts have for a considerable period been onerous. In many particulars these taxes have borne severely upon the laboring and less prosperous classes of the community, being imposed on the necessaries of life, and this, too, in cases where the burthen was not relieved by the consciousness that it would ultimately contribute to make us independent of foreign nations for articles of prime necessity by the encouragement of their growth and manufacture at home. They have been cheerfully borne because they were thought to be necessary to the support of Government and the payment of the debts unavoidably incurred in the acquisition and maintenance of our national rights and liberties. But have we a right to calculate on the same cheerful acquiescence when it is known that the necessity for their continuance would cease were it not for irregular, improvident, and unequal appropriations of the public funds? Will not the people demand, as they have a right to do, such a prudent system of expenditure as will pay the debts of the Union and authorize the reduction of every tax to as low a point as the wise observance of the necessity to protect that portion of our manufactures and labor whose prosperity is essential to our national safety and independence will allow? When the national debt is paid, the duties upon those articles which we do not raise may be repealed with safety, and still leave, I trust, without oppression to any section of the country, an accumulating surplus fund, which may be beneficially applied to some well-digested system of improvement.

Under this view the question as to the manner in which the Federal Government can or ought to embark in the construction of roads and canals, and the extent to which it may impose burthens on the people for these purposes, may be presented on its own merits, free of all disguise and of every embarrassment, except such as may arise from the Constitution itself. Assuming these suggestions to be correct, will not our constituents require the observance of a course by which they can be effected? Ought they not to require it? With the best disposition to aid, as far as I can conscientiously, in furtherance of works of internal improvement, my opinion is that the soundest views of national policy at this time point to such a course. Besides the avoidance of an evil influence upon the local concerns of the country, how solid is the advantage which the Government will reap from it in the elevation of its character! How gratifying the effect of presenting to the world the sublime spectacle of a Republic or more than 12,000,000 happy people, in the fifty-fourth year of her existence, after having passed through two protracted wars—the one for the acquisition and the other for the maintenance of liberty—free from debt and with all her immense resources unfettered! What a salutary influence would not such an exhibition exercise upon the cause of liberal principles and free government throughout the world! Would we not ourselves find in its effect an additional guaranty that our political institutions will be transmitted to the most remote posterity without decay? A course of policy destined to witness events like these can not be benefited by a legislation which tolerates a scramble for appropriations that have no relation to any general system of improvement, and whose good effects must of necessity be very limited. In the best view of these appropriations, the abuses to which they lead far exceed the good which they are capable of promoting. They may be resorted to as artful expedients to shift upon the Government the losses of unsuccessful private speculation, and thus, by ministering to personal ambition and self-aggrandizement, tend to sap the foundations of public virtue and taint the administration of the Government with a demoralizing influence. . . .

In presenting these opinions I have spoken with the freedom and candor which I thought the occasion for their expression called for, and now respectfully return the bill which has been under consideration for your further deliberation and judgment.

ANDREW JACKSON

SECOND ANNUAL MESSAGE

In speaking of direct appropriations I mean not to include a practice which has obtained to some extent and to which I have in one instance, in a different capacity, given my assent—that of subscribing to the stock of private associations. Positive experience and a more thorough consideration of the subject have convinced me of the impropriety as well as inexpediency of such investments. All improvements effected by the funds of the nation for general use should be open to the enjoyment of all our fellow-citizens, exempt from the payment of tolls or any imposition of that character. The practice of thus mingling the concerns of the Government with those of the States or of individuals is inconsistent with the object of its institution and highly impolitic. The successful operation of the federal system can only be preserved by confining it to the few and simple, but yet important, objects for which it was designed.

A different practice, if allowed to progress, would ultimately change the character of this Government by consolidating into one the General and State Governments, which were intended to be kept forever distinct. I can not perceive how bills authorizing such subscriptions can be otherwise regarded than as bills for revenue, and consequently subject to the rule in that

---

From Richardson, *Messages and Papers of the Presidents,* vol. II, pp. 509–514; December 6, 1830. The passage cited follows a paragraph in which the President explained that he would not have objected to a bill making "direct" appropriations for certain lighthouses.

respect prescribed by the Constitution. If the interest of the Government in private companies is subordinate to that of individuals, the management and control of a portion of the public funds is delegated to an authority unknown to the Constitution and beyond the supervision of our constituents; if superior, its officers and agents will be constantly exposed to imputations of favoritism and oppression. Direct prejudice to the public interest or an alienation of the affections and respect of portions of the people may, therefore, in addition to the general discredit resulting to the Government from embarking with its constituents in pecuniary stipulations, be looked for as the probable fruit of such associations. It is no answer to this objection to say that the extent of consequences like these can not be great from a limited and small number of investments, because experience in other matters teaches us—and we are not at liberty to disregard its admonitions—that unless an entire stop be put to them it will soon be impossible to prevent their accumulation until they are spread over the whole country and made to embrace many of the private and appropriate concerns of individuals.

The power which the General Government would acquire within the several States by becoming the principal stockholder in corporations, controlling every canal and each 60 or 100 miles of every important road, and giving a proportionate vote in all their elections, is almost inconceivable, and in my view dangerous to the liberties of the people.

The mode of aiding such works is also in its nature deceptive, and in many cases conducive to improvidence in the administration of the national funds. Appropriations will be obtained with much greater facility and granted with less security to the public interest when the measure is thus disguised than when definite and direct expenditures of money are asked for. The interests of the nation would doubtless be better served by avoiding all such indirect modes of aiding particular objects. In a government like ours more especially should all public acts be, as far as practicable, simple, undisguised, and intelligible, that they may become fit subjects for the approbation or animadversion of the people. The bill authorizing a subscription to the Louisville and Portland Canal affords a striking illustration of the difficulty of withholding additional appropriations for the same object when the first erroneous step has been taken by instituting a partnership between the Government and private companies. It proposes a third subscription on the part of the United States, when each preceding one was at the time regarded as the extent of the aid which Government was to render to that work; and the accompanying bill for light-houses, etc., contains an appropriation for a survey of the bed of the river, with a view to its improvement by removing the obstruction which the canal is designed to avoid. This improvement, if successful, would afford a free passage of the river and render the canal entirely useless. To such improvidence is the course of legislation subject in relation to internal improvements on local matters, even with the best intentions on the part of Congress.

Although the motives which have influenced me in this matter may be already sufficiently stated, I am, nevertheless, induced by its importance to add a few observations of a general character.

In my objections to the bills authorizing subscriptions to the Maysville and Rockville road companies I expressed my views fully in regard to the power of Congress to construct roads and canals within a State or to appropriate money for improvements of a local character. I at the same time intimated my belief that the right to make appropriations for such as were of a national character had been so generally acted upon and so long acquiesced in by the Federal and State Governments and the constituents of each as to justify its exercise on the ground of continued and uninterrupted usage, but that it was, nevertheless, highly expedient that appropriations even of that character should, with the exception made at the time, be deferred until the national debt is paid, and that in the meanwhile some general rule for the action of the Government in that respect ought to be established. . . .

Profoundly impressed with the importance of the subject, not merely as relates to the general prosperity of the country, but to the safety of the federal system, I can not avoid repeating my earnest hope that all good citizens who take a proper interest in the success and harmony of our admirable political institutions, and who are incapable of desiring to convert an opposite state of things into means for the gratification of personal ambition, will, laying aside minor considerations and discarding local prejudices, unite their honest exertions to establish some fixed general principle which shall be calculated to effect the greatest extent of public good in regard to the subject of internal improvement, and afford the least ground for sectional discontent.

The general grounds of my objection to local appropriations have been heretofore expressed, and I shall endeavor to avoid a repetition of what has been already urged—the importance of sustaining the State sovereignties as far as is consistent with the rightful action of the Federal Government, and of preserving the greatest attainable harmony between them. I will now only add an expression of my conviction—a conviction which every day's experience serves to confirm—that the political creed which inculcates the pursuit of those great objects as a paramount duty is the true faith, and one to which we are mainly indebted for the present success of the entire system, and to which we must alone look for its future stability.

That there are diversities in the interests of the different States which compose this extensive Confederacy must be admitted. Those diversities arising from situation, climate, population, and pursuits are doubtless, as it is natural they should be, greatly exaggerated by jealousies and that spirit of rivalry so inseparable from neighboring communities. These circumstances make it the duty of those who are intrusted with the management of its affairs to neutralize their effects as far as practicable by making the beneficial operation of the Federal Government as equal and equitable among the several States as can be done consistently with the great ends of its institution.

It is only necessary to refer to undoubted facts to see how far the past acts of the Government upon the subject under consideration have fallen short of this object. The expenditures heretofore made for internal improvements amount to upward of $5,000,000, and have been distributed in very unequal proportions amongst the States. The estimated expense of works of which surveys have been made, together with that of others projected and partially surveyed, amounts to more than $96,000,000.

That such improvements, on account of particular circumstances, may be more advantageously and beneficially made in some States than in others is doubtless true, but that they are of a character which should prevent an equitable distribution of the funds amongst the several States is not to be conceded. The want of this equitable distribution can not fail to prove a prolific source of irritation among the States.

We have it constantly before our eyes that professions of superior zeal in the cause of internal improvement and a disposition to lavish the public funds upon objects of this character are daily and earnestly put forth by aspirants to power as constituting the highest claims to the confidence of the people. Would it be strange, under such circumstances, and in times of great excitement, that grants of this description should find their motives in objects which may not accord with the public good? Those who have not had occasion to see and regret the indication of a sinister influence in these matters in past times have been more fortunate than myself in their observation of the course of public affairs. If to these evils be added the combinations and angry contentions to which such a course of things gives rise, with their baleful influences upon the legislation of Congress touching the leading and appropriate duties of the Federal Government, it was but doing justice to the character of our people to expect the severe condemnation of the past which the recent exhibitions of public sentiment has evinced.

Nothing short of a radical change in the action of the Government upon the subject can, in my opinion, remedy the evil. If, as it would be natural to expect, the States which have been least favored in past appropriations should insist on being redressed in those hereafter to be made, at the expense of the States which have so largely and disproportionately participated, we have, as matters now stand, but little security that the attempt would do more than change the inequality from one quarter to another.

Thus viewing the subject, I have heretofore felt it my duty to recommend the adoption of some plan for the distribution of the surplus funds, which may at any time remain in the Treasury after the national debt shall have been paid, among the States, in proportion to the number of their Representatives, to be applied by them to objects of internal improvement.

3. The Virginia Program of Mixed Enterprise

The combination of public and private funds in internal improvements, which Jackson condemned as an "impropriety" in the case of the federal government, formed the principal basis of the program of the state of Virginia. A fully developed rationale for a system of mixed enterprise was contained in a report to the House of Delegates by its Committee of Roads and Internal Navigation. After developing the case for government action in general terms and with special reference to

Virginia's geography and competitive position, the Report proceeded to its more novel discussion of the means of making such action most effective. Though admitting that some projects might have to be carried out by the state itself, the Committee argued that principal reliance should be placed on methods that would stimulate and "draw forth" private enterprise. The state would need to provide some expert direction, and it is a reflection of the conditions of the time that the proposed Board of Public Works could afford to hire an engineer while an individual undertaking presumably could not. The state should also provide part of the capital, but only in the amount, and on the terms, that would best serve to "elicit private wealth for public improvement." To this end there should be established a Fund for Internal Improvements, out of which the Board of Public Works should subscribe two-fifths of the stock of any improvement company receiving legislative approval. The state should then appoint two of the five members of the company's board of directors, giving it enough control—in the Committee's view—to prevent abuses, but leaving initiative and direction where they should be, in the hands of individual and local leadership.

The Committee's proposals were enacted into law, almost without change, and became the basis of Virginia's system of mixed enterprise. The Fund's original nest egg was later increased by substantial borrowing, and the one greatest undertaking, the attempt to achieve a route to the West by way of the James and Kanawha rivers, required a much larger amount of state support than the system contemplated. For the large number of smaller improvements, the standard proportion for the state's contribution was raised from two to three fifths of the whole, but this was not permitted to alter the rule that majority control should rest with the private stockholders. Both Board and Fund remained in full operation until the outbreak of the Civil War halted work on the still unfinished Chesapeake and Ohio Railroad.[1]

---

[1] Carter Goodrich, "The Virginia System of Mixed Enterprise: A Study of State Planning of Internal Improvements," *Political Science Quarterly*, LXIX (1949), 355–387.

MR. LEWIS (OF CAMPBELL,) FROM THE COMMITTEE OF ROADS
AND INTERNAL NAVIGATION, PRESENTED A REPORT,
WHICH WAS READ AS FOLLOWS:—

The Committee of Roads and Internal Navigation, to whom
was referred so much of the Governor's Message as relates to
Roads and Canals, have, according to order, had that subject
under consideration, and prepared the following report there-
upon, which they beg leave to submit to the House of Delegates:

Whatever difference of opinion may have, at any time, sub-
sisted, as to the expediency of controling the voluntary direction
of the wealth and labor of individuals by the application of
legal constraint, there never has existed a doubt, but that it is
the duty, as well as the interest of every good government, to
facilitate the necessary communication between its citizens.

Next to the enjoyment of civil liberty itself, it may be questioned whether the best organized government can assure to
those, for whose happiness all governments are instituted, a
greater blessing than an open, free and easy intercourse with
one another, by good roads, navigable rivers, and canals. Their
tendency, by extending the commerce, to promote the agriculture and manufactures of a nation, and thereby to augment
its wealth and population, is too obvious to require much illustration.

The planter and farmer realize their share of this benefit,
in the augmented value of their lands; the manufacturer and
the merchant, in the increased and diversified demand for
their industry and capital.

From "Report of the Committee of Roads and Internal Navigation,"
December 23, 1815, Virginia *Journal of the House of Delegates,* 1815–
1816, pp. 73–78. The Report is given here in full.

Nor, are the higher interests of society less indebted for their advancement to the multiplication and improvement of these channels of useful intercourse. They afford the means of exploring the natural resources of a country, and invite the genius of speculation to fit them for the uses of man. Lands too remote from market to tempt cultivation; forests, hitherto regarded as inaccessible; beds of minerals and fossils unknown or neglected, are brought within the reach of ordinary enterprize, and rendered subservient to the convenience and comfort of the Citizen, or to the defence and safety of the State.

They confer on an extended empire the promptitude and energy of action, which are considered peculiarly characteristic of one of narrow dimensions; since, without contracting the limits of its territory, they reduce the distance, and expedite the communication between the seat of its government and its remotest extremities.

Whether the public force is to be spread out for defence, or combined for attack, they alike contribute to the rapidity and to the vigor of its operations.

In a republic, especially, where public opinion exerts a controling influence, and public virtue should be the spring of all public action, they may be considered an important auxiliary, if not a necessary ingredient of political liberty. They tend to diffuse more equally the knowledge which experience acquires, and the leisure which wealth alone can purchase; they strengthen the cords of social union, and quicken that generous feeling of patriotism, which is ever ready to exclaim at the contemplation of an extended scene of public improvement, "I love my country, because she is worthy of my affection."

The duty, which is obligatory upon all governments, is peculiarly incumbent on one, whose territory, like that of Virginia, nature has done so much both to unite and to separate— to whom she has presented so many advantages to improve, and so many obstacles to overcome. No State in the Union is intersected by so many navigable rivers, nor divided by so many chains of lofty mountains: none, perhaps, abounds with such happy varieties of climate and soil, and so many resources for internal commerce. In her coal, iron, lead and salt, she is unrivalled. Her tobacco and grain command the highest prices abroad. The fertile banks of her rivers, and the moist vallies of her mountains yield abundant crops of flax and hemp. Her low-lands would supply her with cotton for her own consumption, and the fleeces of the flocks, which pasture on her hills, are not surpassed in quality. Notwithstanding these advantages, the principal part of her commerce, and almost the whole of her navigation, pass out of her hands to enrich the coffers of her neighbors. There is scarcely a village to the West of the Blue-Ridge, and very few above tide water, from the Roanoke to the Potomac, which derive any part of their supplies of manufactured commodities, either foreign or domestic, from the seaports of Virginia.

While many other States have been advancing in wealth and numbers, with a rapidity which has astonished themselves, the ancient dominion and elder sister of the Union has remained stationary.

A very large proportion of her western territory is yet unimproved, while a considerable part of her eastern has receded from its former opulence. How many sad spectacles do her low lands present, of wasted and deserted fields! of dwellings abandoned by their proprietors! of Churches in ruins! The genius of her ancient hospitality, benumbed by the cold touch of penury, spreads his scanty board in naked halls, or seeks a coarser, but more plenteous repast in the lonely cabins of the West. The fathers of the land are gone, where another outlet to the ocean turns their thoughts from the place of their nativity, and their affections from the haunts of their youth. Beyond the Allegany; an unexpected revolution threatens the Atlantic States in general, the accomplishment of which will create new interests and views in that flourishing and important section of America, and bar, forever, the hope of re-uniting it by commercial ties to the markets of the East.

If it be true, as your committee confidently believe, that in a connection between the Roanoke, the James, or the Potomac river, with the waters of the Kanawha or Ohio, this Commonwealth possesses the best means of arresting the progress of this revolution, it is a duty which she owes not only to herself, but to the Atlantic States, and to the Union at large, to call those means into action.

Independent of the minuter circumstances, in the natural course and volume of her rivers, and the breadth and elevation of the intervening mountains, which point out Virginia as the proper channel of this connection, the superior mildness of her climate to that of her northern sisters; her position on the Atlantic coast of the United States; and the capacious bay which serves as the common estuary of her rivers, assure to her very high claims to the emporium of this commerce.

The United States of America, restricted by the territory of England to the North, and of Spain to the South, describe an arch on the intervening ocean, of which Virginia is the centre, and should be the key-stone, sustaining the Western States upon its broad and lofty summit, and binding the Eastern and Southern in solid, just and fair proportion. First in asserting the Independence of America, this Commonwealth will not be the last in giving to that independence stability, by confirming the Union, upon which it rests.

Your Committee are far from intimating that the General Assembly of Virginia has been totally unmindful of those natural advantages, or wholly regardless of their improvement.

The Commonwealth required time to recover from the pecuniary losses which she sustained during the war of the Revolution.—It found her citizens laboring under very heavy private debts, and left her government encumbered with a public debt of much greater magnitude.

Yet, under circumstances so inauspicious, the statesmen of

that day, and especially the illustrious man to whom, under heaven, this nation was indebted for the establishment of its freedom, did not disdain to enquire into the humblest means of giving to that freedom, value. From his zealous exertions, sprung the Potomac and James River Canal Companies. To the first of these, the Commonwealth is indebted for a water communication of three hundred and thirty eight miles; and upon it, and the contemplated works on the Shenandoah, she relies for the farther improvement of a navigation of three hundred and ninety miles. She has shared with a sister State, the benefits of the labor already performed on this river; in that, which remains to be accomplished on the South Branch of the Potomac, the Cacapehon and the Shenandoah, she has an exclusive interest.

The James River Company have opened a navigation of three hundred miles.

The Appomattox and the Dismal Swamp Canals naturally followed into existence, those which were indebted for their origin, to the patriotism of General Washington. The former opened a navigation of one hundred miles. The latter was designed merely to connect waters already navigable; but, in its present use, and remote consequences, is not inferior in importance, to any public work within the Commonwealth.

The expence of the first of the preceding works, does not exceed fifteen hundred dollars per mile upon the navigation already opened; that of the second, is about twelve hundred; an average expence which will be annually diminished in the progress of future improvements on the branches of those rivers, as the principal obstructions to their navigation were removed, before their waters could be brought into partial use.

The actual cost of those public works, does not exceed one third of the expence usually attendant upon the structure of Turnpike roads; which, in the absence of navigation, are the only substitute for them. It is due to the latter, however, to remark, that the addition recently made to them of parallel iron rails, immoveably set in the earth, at proper intervals, for the wheels of waggons, has more than equalized the advantages of such roads, with the best ascending navigation which the rivers of Virginia afford above their principal falls; and that the additional cost, which this improvement occasions to the structure of the Turnpike, though great in itself, is inconsiderable, when compared with its effect in reducing the expence of land carriage.

The Turnpike roads of the Commonwealth, except a few short passes of particular mountains, and a road recently begun from Fredericksburg, towards the Blue Ridge, are confined principally to the county of Loudoun, the adjacent counties of Fairfax, Fauquier and Frederick, and to the vicinity of the seat of Government.

There is but one, to which the funds of the Commonwealth have contributed any aid.

All these public works are alike in one respect: they purpose to defray the expense of their first cost, and of their subsequent repairs, out of the tolls collected upon them; and these are equitably levied upon those who use them, in sums proportioned to the benefit which they respectively derive from such use. Where it is absolutely certain that such works can subsist upon this basis alone, the revenue of the Commonwealth, although it may expedite their progress, is not indispensably necessary to their creation.

Private wealth will, of itself, take the direction which personal interest prompts. But there are many such works essential to the prosperity of the Commonwealth; the persons immediately interested in which, have not capitals sufficient to commence their foundation, and there are many others of like utility, which, if completed, would require the lapse of many years to make them profitable to the individual subscribers to their stock. The population and commerce which infallibly follow their direction, spread out upon their borders and swell their tolls, cannot be expected to precede their existence.

Although almost all the Turnpike roads within the Commonwealth, have been made without any other Legislative aid, than their respective acts of incorporation; yet, it is probable, that neither Potomac nor James River could have been rendered navigable above tide water, with such assistance alone. Maryland and Virginia, subscribed more than one half of the capital stock of the former, and Virginia alone, more than one third of the latter. The tolls hitherto collected on the one, would not have justified a subscription to its stock, with a view to mere profit; and although those of the latter have, for some time, realized the most sanguine expectations of its friends, and its stock is eighty per cent. above par, yet the revenue of the Company, apart from the appreciation of its stock, would not nett to its members six per cent. per annum upon the sums which they have actually expended on that river, from the commencement of their labors to the present period. Your committee, however, confidently believe, that there is not an individual within the Commonwealth, alive to a sense of her true interests, who would have desired, for the sake of a higher profit to the treasury upon the stock of the public in either of those works, to withdraw the funds which were required for their completion, and permit those noble rivers to return to a state of nature. Those who reside near to their banks, have directly participated in the benefits thus afforded them, of a cheaper mode of transporting the productions of their labor to market; and those even, who antecedently possessed the superior advantages of tide water, or who were compelled by their distance from both, to resort to the common highways, in order to reach the same market, have greatly profited by those improvements of navigation, which augmenting the extent and value of that market, could not fail, proportionably, to enhance the price of their produce. So true, it is, that whatever contributes to increase the population and wealth of the towns, must contribute to the growth and improvement of the country. And this effect is wrought not solely on the vicinity of those towns—it is seen not merely in the wealth which glitters in their suburbs; but discovered in the augmentation of their means of consumption, and the enlargement of their commercial capitals.

In this necessary and reciprocal relation of commerce and agriculture, the country below tide water in Virginia, has an immediate and even local interest in the progress and perfection of all those public works, exclusive of its general interest, in whatever advances the growth and prosperity of the Commonwealth.

The inhabitants of the low lands will, therefore, partake of the benefit of every application of the public revenue to the improvement of the connexion between their market towns and the country above them. It should be peculiarly their policy, to turn the commerce to the west, from its northern direction, into the bosom of their own territory. In the efforts which are contemplated to improve the roads passing immediately through their own country, they have an interest more sensible to the eye, but less so to the understanding.

Although much has been done for the improvement of the interior of Virginia, more yet remains to be accomplished. Roanoke and its tributary streams, including the rivers Dan, Nottoway, Meherin and Blackwater; the head waters of James, Potomac and Shenandoah rivers; those of the Rappahannock, Matapony and Pamunky, on the east side of the Alleghany— The great Kanawha and its waters, including, along with Greenbrier, and New-River, Gauly and Elk; the little Kanawha, Middle Island, the Monongalia and the branches which swell its current before it leaves the boundary of Virginia, are all entitled to public consideration.

If nature has divided the territory of the Commonwealth by numerous chains of lofty mountains, it is only to incite the genius of man to climb them; and the period is not unattainable —nay, it rests with the Legislature, to determine whether it be remote, when the roads which cross those natural and formidable barriers, shall not be surpassed by those which run along their base.

The experiment of the United States to connect, by a national road, the waters of Potomac, with those of Ohio; and a comparison of the surface over which that highway has been already conducted, with the corresponding ranges of mountains to the South, assure your committee, that such a hope is not chimerical.

Should the General Assembly determine to patronize by the application of the public revenue all such works as are likely to be of great public utility, it becomes important to decide whether an improvement may not be made in the mode heretofore pursued, of extending to them that patronage.

Your Committee are fully satisfied that much loss has hitherto been sustained by all the canal companies which have been incorporated, for want of skill in their conduct. Their directors have served, it is true, without compensation. They have generally been public-spirited private gentlemen; but neither professional engineers, nor capable, from experience and observation, of guarding against the errors and frauds of agents who pretended to be so.

No single company could afford to purchase or could fully employ, in a country where few public works were begun, the services of a distinguished engineer; and yet, without the previous surveys, plans and estimates of such an officer, no very arduous public work could be confidently begun or successfully conducted. To supply the defect of such an officer, would be the obvious interest of the Commonwealth, who, if not sufficiently compensated by the general utility of his labours, might demand of each company, such an interest in its stock, as should be equivalent to the value of the service rendered to the company by such officer.

Whatever fund the Legislature may be inclined to appro-

priate to internal improvement, a difficulty must occur in settling the relative importance of its proper objects; and, if the
appropriation were also required to designate some particular
object, it would be often impracticable, from the variety of
opinions always existing in an Assembly representing many
local interests, to procure an union in the choice of any one.
The first of these difficulties may be obviated by organizing a
proper body to collect and prepare for the General Assembly,
the facts and information necessary to cast upon every application for a portion of the fund, light enough, to guide the
sound discretion of the Legislature in the selection of subjects.

And these facts will be entitled to the higher confidence, if
reported under the sanction of official responsibility.

To allay such local jealousies as might obstruct an agreement
in favor of any single object of internal improvement, the fund
may be previously consecrated and set apart for the accomplishment of all, by one appropriation. If the terms of its future
application to any, be at the same time prescribed, a like participation, in the benefit of the fund, will be assured to every
interest which it is calculated to promote; and the speedy enjoyment of that benefit will be secured to each by proportion-
ing the magnitude of the fund, so set apart, to the number and
importance of the objects, for which it is designed to provide.

It may be sound policy for the Commonwealth, in order to
accomplish some great commercial or political purpose, to
throw open to general use, without the charge of tolls, a particular canal or road; but, it can never be its interest, for many
reasons, to become the sole proprietor of all the public works
within its territory. Experience testifies that they will be more
economically made, and better repaired, if their management
be left to the individuals who subscribe to their stock with a
view to private gain, than if confided to public officers or
agents.—The Commonwealth should subscribe so much, to
their stock, and on such terms as will suffice to elicit individual

wealth for public improvement—and the control which she retains over the conduct of the individual subscribers, should extend no farther, than to prevent or correct such abuses upon the community at large, as might be apprehended from the too eager incentive of gain.

By yielding to the individual subscribers the profit of the State on its shares of the Stock of any Company, where required to secure such individuals against temporary loss, a much smaller subscription of public money will suffice to draw forth private enterprize.

The Commonwealth can never be a loser, if a public work judiciously begun, be finally perfected—and the public security against such loss, will be found in the discretion which the Legislature retains over the choice of the objects, for which its patronage is sought.

As the market rate of interest decreases in every commercial country, with the growth of its capital, the maximum profit of the stock of each company may be reduced, after the lapse of a limited period of time.

The least profit allowed by law should be great enough to create the hope of private advantage in those whose enterprize can have no other object; and that *minimum,* which the community have so much interest in reducing, may be safely fixed at a lower amount, in proportion as the magnitude and conditions of the public subscription afford to private adventurers, an indemnity against any ultimate loss.

The principles laid down in the preceding part of this Report, the committee have embodied in the Resolutions which are subjoined to it; but, they would not have performed their duty to the house, if, before they recommend the application to objects of internal improvement, of all the public stock of the Commonwealth, as well as of the premiums which may be hereafter received for the incorporation of new, the extension of the capitals, or the duration of the charters of the existing

Banks; they had not enquired into the actual state of the debts, and of the annual Revenue and Expenditure of the Commonwealth.

That enquiry has resolved itself into the establishment of the following propositions:

1st. That for fifteen years, prior to the commencement of the late war, the ordinary Revenue of the Commonwealth had not only been adequate to meet the ordinary expenditure charged upon it, but to enable the Commonwealth to arm from time to time, a large part of her Militia—to lay the foundation of her Literary Fund, to erect several very costly public edifices, and to complete the purchase of the Stock subscribed by the Commonwealth to the Bank of Virginia; objects, which occasioned a disbursement from the ordinary revenue of a sum, exceeding one million of dollars.

2dly. That since the commencement of that war, the revenue of the Commonwealth, more than doubled, by additional taxes, and farther augmented by considerable loans from the Banks, has not only sufficed for the ordinary peace expenditure, but enabled the Legislature to assume the State quota of the direct tax of 1814, and to apply to the defence of the United States, a sum exceeding eighteen hundred thousand dollars, exclusive of the interest paid upon those loans.

3dly. That the Commonwealth has at present a claim upon the United States of unquestionable justice, for more than seventeen hundred thousand dollars of the above amount, together with the interest on such portions of it, at least, as were obtained on loan, which claim, when satisfied, will furnish a sum competent to discharge all the debts of the Commonwealth, to provide for the expenditure of the current fiscal year; and to leave at the end of that year, a balance in the treasury of three hundred and fifty thousand dollars to be applied to any other object of internal interest.

4thly. That the present taxes may be reduced to the amount levied before the late war, provided the United States shall

reimburse the sums advanced for the defence of the Commonwealth; and, even, should the payment of those sums be withheld, which a just confidence in the good faith of the General
Government forbids your committee to expect, a repeal may
yet be effected of such portion of the war taxes, as are not
absolutely pledged for the payment of the interest, and the
redemption of the principal of the public debt.

From all which it evidently appears that the fund which it
is proposed to apply to the purposes of internal improvement,
may be spared from the revenue of the Commonwealth, without any embarrassment of her finances, any violation of her
engagements, or pressure upon her Citizens.

Should the appropriation recommended by the committee
receive the sanction of the Legislature, the Fund for Internal
Improvement, will consist of the following stock—

5547 shares of the Stock of the Bank of Virginia, on which a dividend is now received, and which computed at par is worth	$554,700 00
2400 Shares of the Stock of the Bank of Virginia, whereupon no dividend will accrue until after the 1st day of May 1818,	240,000 00
3334 Shares of the Stock of the Farmers' Bank of Virginia,	333,400 00
250 Shares of the Stock of the James River Company, also estimated at par,	50,000 00
125 Shares of the Stock of the Appomattox Company,	12,500 00
70 Shares of the Stock of the Dismal Swamp Canal Company,	17,500 00
70 Shares of the Stock of the Potomac Company,	31,111 11 1–9
100 Shares of the Stock of the Little River Turnpike Company,	10,000 00
Making a total value of	$1,249,211 11 1–9

Of which the sum of 938,100 dollars is now productive of
an annual revenue exceeding ninety-eight thousand dollars;
and two hundred and forty thousand dollars will become alike
productive after the first day of May 1818.

In the present state of the fund, the progress of the public works to which it may be expected to give rise, will be until the first day of May 1818, at the rate of 245,000 dollars per annum. After that period, it will be further augmented by the addition of sixty thousand dollars. So that the total value of the Internal Improvements of ten years will be $2,777,500; and this calculation is grounded on a supposition, that the portion of the stock which is now unproductive, will continue to be so; and that no augmentation of the fund will have been made by the creation of new Banks.

But your committee confidently anticipate a considerable increase of the fund from the premium of future charters, without impairing the productiveness of the stock of the existing Banks.

A very large proportion of the paper medium of Virginia is, at present, derived from the Banks of the District of Columbia, and of the adjacent States. A Banking Capital might be created which would supply that medium, and yielding to the state a premium in stock, of 600,000 dollars, would add to the revenue of the fund for Internal Improvement, at least fifty thousand dollars, to the annual disbursements for Internal Improvements $125,000, and to the total value of the works accomplished in the period of ten years, $1,125,000. Nor do your committee consider the expectation too sanguine, provided this fund receive the application which is here proposed, that the present Banking capital of the Commonwealth may be doubled in a period of ten years, and consequently, the revenue arising from that portion of the fund.

If the latter calculation be admitted to be correct, a continued application of this fund for a second period of ten years, will defray the costs of public works, of the value of $10,452,500, exclusive of any allowance whatever, for the dividends upon the shares acquired by the Commonwealth in the stock of any public work which may be hereafter commenced, and of any estimate of the value of such works, as shall owe their existence to the sale and re-investment of any part of the public stock.

Finally, your committee beg leave to subjoin, that, of the whole fund thus usefully applied, a very inconsiderable part, if any, will have been derived from the pockets of the people, by the imposition of taxes. If an allowance be made for the dividends on the state shares of the stock of the Bank of Virginia, down to the period at which the last instalment of the sum subscribed by the Commonwealth for that stock, was paid to the Bank, this amount will be found not to exceed the subsequent dividends on the state shares in the stock of both Banks.

The General Assembly has an absolute and unquestionable right to make any other disposition of this fund, which, to its wisdom, may seem best; but, your committee are assured that the institution of the Farmers' Bank of Virginia, and the unexampled premiums for Banking in this Commonwealth, are ascribable to the confident expectation of the Legislature and the people, that the profits of this novel though productive system of finance, were to be turned into the channel of public improvement. By giving to these premiums, this direction, the stock of the nation will be retributed for the reduction which they occasion of its amount, and the constraint which they put on its activity.

Be it therefore Resolved, 1. That a fund be created by law, to be denominated "The Fund for Internal Improvement," and to be exclusively applied to the purpose of rendering navigable the principal rivers; of more intimately connecting, by public highways, the Eastern and Western waters, and the market towns of the Commonwealth.

2. That this fund shall consist of the shares now held by the Commonwealth in the stock of the Little River Turnpike Company, of the Dismal Swamp, Appomattox, Potomac and James River Canal Companies; of the Bank of Virginia, and Farmers' Bank of Virginia, together with such dividends as may, from

time to time, accrue on such shares of stock, and such bonus or premiums as may be hereafter received for the incorporation of new, the augmentation of the capitals, or the extension of the Charters of the existing Banks.

3. That for the purpose of preserving and improving this fund, and of disbursing such portions of it as the General Assembly may hereafter direct to be applied to any object of internal improvement, it shall be vested in a corporate body, to be styled—The President and Board of Public Works.

4. That the Governor of the Commonwealth shall be ex-officio, President of the Board of Public Works; that the Board, a majority of the members of which, shall be competent to transact any business devolving on the Corporation, shall consist of the Treasurer, and the Attorney General for the time being, and of   Citizens of the Commonwealth; whereof   shall reside Westward of the Allegany Mountain,   between the Blue Ridge and Allegany, and the residue between the Blue Ridge and the sea coast.

5. The members of the Board shall be chosen annually by joint ballot of the two Houses of the General Assembly, and receive such compensation for their services as may be allowed by law.

6. That in the absence of the Governor, the Board may elect a President pro tempore, from their own body.

7. The President and Board of Public Works, shall have power to appoint a principal Engineer or Surveyor of Public Works, a Secretary and Treasurer, together with such other officers and assistants as they shall find necessary, each of whom shall receive for his services, such compensation as the President and Board of Public Works may allow, to be paid out of the Revenue of the Fund for Internal Improvement, and to be reimbursed the fund by an allowance to the Commonwealth of so much of the stock of any Canal or Turnpike Company, as shall constitute a reasonable compensation for the services rendered such company, by the Surveyor and his assistants.

8. That the President and Board of Public Works, shall be authorised to subscribe in behalf of the Commonwealth, to such public works as the General Assembly may, from time to time, agree to patronize, such portions of the revenue of the Fund for Internal Improvement as may be directed by law; but that no part of the Fund shall be subscribed towards the stock of any Canal or Turnpike Company, until three-fifths at least of the whole stock necessary to complete such Canal or Turnpike, shall have been otherwise subscribed, nor until, of the stock so subscribed, one-fifth part shall have been paid in by the respective subscribers, or the payment thereof effectually secured.

9. That the dividends upon the stock which may be subscribed by the President and Board of Public Works, shall go exclusively to other subscribers than the said President and Board, until such portion of the stock of those subscribers, shall have nett to them six per centum per annum, from the specified time of such payment.—That any increase of profit, after that nett income has been assured to those subscribers, shall belong exclusively to the Fund for Internal Improvement, until the nett annual income of the whole stock actually expended by any company shall reach six per centum per annum, after which, the President and Board of Public Works and the other subscribers to the Stock of the Company shall divide the nett profits on such stock, in proportion to their respective interests.

10. That whenever the nett income of any Company shall be found for two succeeding years, or upon an average of five succeeding years, to surpass fifteen per cent. per annum, the General Assembly may reduce the tolls from which such income is derived, so as to limit the nett revenue of the Company to that amount—*Provided,* that should the tolls for any two succeeding years fail to yield a nett income to the Company of ten per cent. per annum, the President and Board of Public Works, on satisfactory evidence being adduced thereof, may authorise the tolls to be augmented so as to assure to the Company such nett income; *And Provided also,* that after the

lapse of sixty years, the maximum profit of the Company may be reduced to twelve per cent.; and after the lapse of one hundred years, to ten per cent. per annum.

11. That the President and Board of Public Works, shall have power to vest in any productive fund, the unappropriated dividends accruing upon any of the stock committed to their charge, until the same shall be specially applied by law to some object of internal improvement: that they may from time to time, subject to the control of the General Assembly, sell the whole or any part of the shares held by the Commonwealth in the stock of any Canal or Turnpike Company, for the purpose of re-investing the proceeds of sale in the stock of some other similar public work.

12. That the President and Board of Public Works shall have power to appoint, in behalf of the Commonwealth, so many directors of every public work, as shall bear to the whole number of directors of such work, the proportion of the Commonwealth's shares of stock in such work, to the whole number of shares subscribed thereto.

13. That it shall be the duty of the President and Board of Public Works to keep a fair and accurate record of all their proceedings, to be at all times open to the inspection of the members of the General Assembly, and of the president, directors, and other officers of any company interested therein, that they shall report to the General Assembly at, or near the commencement of every annual session, the exact state of the Funds for Internal Improvement, the progress and condition, noting especially the nett income, of all the public works within the Commonwealth; the surveys, plans and estimated expense of such new works, as they may recommend to the patronage of the General Assembly, together with all other important information which it may be in their power to collect relative to the objects committed to their trust.

14. And lastly, *Resolved,* that the appropriations contained in these resolutions shall continue in force, until the first day

of January, 1900, except, at such times as the United States of America may be involved in war, when the Legislature may withdraw, during the period of actual hostilities, the whole or any part of the said fund for the purpose of defence, provided such withdrawal can be made without a breach of public faith.

4. New York: A Triumph of Public Enterprise

In the same month in which the Virginia House of Delegates received the report of its committee on internal improvements, a mass meeting of citizens in New York City launched what became the decisive campaign for the construction of the Erie Canal. The two programs stood in sharp contrast. Virginia undertook to provide support on equal terms to projects initiated by its citizens in various parts of the Commonwealth. New York at this period concentrated its effort on a single major undertaking.[1] Virginia adopted the method of mixed enterprise. New York built its canal as a public work.

The Erie Canal was begun in 1817 and its completion was celebrated in 1825. The historian of the occasion declared that the Canal Commissioners had "built the longest canal in the world in the least time, with the least experience, for the

---

[1] In making the same distinction, Professor Heath cites Georgia as the most notable case of concentration of state effort on a single strategic improvement, the Western and Atlantic Railroad, which achieved the crossing of the mountains and served as feeder to the lines built by private and local government enterprise. Milton S. Heath, *Constructive Liberalism: The Role of the State in Economic Development in Georgia to 1860* (Cambridge: Harvard University Press, 1954), p. 281. In later decades New York State spread its efforts over a larger number of improvements. It may be added that there were other states in which the internal improvement programs had neither the merit of evenhandedness nor that of effective concentration.

least money, and to the greatest public benefit."[2] Even in retrospect the statement requires little discount. A financial success almost from the start, the Canal cut the cost of moving freight from Buffalo to New York City to an eighth or a tenth of its previous amount and for the first time made possible a mass exchange of goods between the East and Middle West. It would be hard to think of any event in American transportation history that had a greater or more immediate effect on economic development.

The mass meeting of December, 1815, asked De Witt Clinton to draw up a memorial in support of the project. Clinton was the political organizer of the movement, was to be for years the leading spirit among the Canal Commissioners, and was Governor of the state at the time the Canal was completed. His Memorial and others like it were sent to the Legislature with more than a hundred thousand signatures, roughly a tenth of the state's total population.

The greater part of the Memorial is given below. The document paraphrases Gallatin's statement of the special advantages of the Mohawk-Hudson route to the West, but the Memorial's geography is bolder than that of the Report. Gallatin had contemplated two canals, one to Lake Ontario and the other around Niagara between Lakes Erie and Ontario. The Memorial chooses and defends the alternative of a single and much longer canal reaching all the way to Lake Erie.[3] Finally, it concludes with an admonition not to miss the great opportunity. "It remains," said Clinton, "for a free state to create a new era in history."[4]

---

[2] Noble E. Whitford, *History of the Canal System of the State of New York* (Albany: Brandon Printing Co., 1906), vol. I, p. 125. Its length, 363 miles, was much greater than that of any European canal, and was surpassed only by the Grand Canal of China.

[3] For a discussion of this choice, see Julius Rubin, "An Innovating Public Improvement: The Erie Canal," in Carter Goodrich, ed., *Canals and American Economic Development* (New York: Columbia University Press, 1961), ch. 1.

[4] This is the spirit reflected in the title of Nathan Miller, *The Enterprise of a Free People* (Ithaca: Cornell University Press, 1962).

DE WITT CLINTON: ERIE CANAL MEMORIAL

MEMORIAL OF THE CITIZENS OF NEW-YORK, IN FAVOUR OF
A CANAL NAVIGATION BETWEEN THE GREAT WESTERN LAKES
AND THE TIDE-WATERS OF THE HUDSON

To the Legislature of the State of New-York,
The memorial of the subscribers, in favour of a canal navigation between the great western lakes and the tide-waters of the Hudson, most respectfully represents:

That they approach the legislature with a solicitude proportioned to the importance of this great undertaking, and with a confidence founded on the enlightened public spirit of the constituted authorities. If, in presenting the various considerations which have induced them to make this appeal, they should occupy more time than is usual on common occasions, they must stand justified by the importance of the object. Connected as it is with the essential interests of our country, and calculated in its commencement to reflect honour on the state, and in its completion, to exalt it to an elevation of unparalleled prosperity; your memorialists are fully persuaded, that centuries may pass away before a subject is again presented so worthy of all your attention, and so deserving of all your patronage and support.

The improvement of the means of intercourse between different parts of the same country, has always been considered the first duty and the noblest employment of government. If it be important that the inhabitants of the same country should

From David Hosack, *Memoir of De Witt Clinton* (New York, 1829), pp. 406–421. The Memorial appeared first in the *New York Herald,* January 3, 1816.

be bound together by a community of interests, and a recipro-
cation of benefits; that agriculture should find a sale for its
productions; manufacturers a vent for their fabrics; and commerce a market for its commodities: it is your incumbent duty,
to open, facilitate, and improve internal navigation. The pre-
eminent advantages of canals have been established by the
unerring test of experience. They unite cheapness, celerity,
certainty, and safety, in the transportation of commodities. It is
calculated that the expense of transporting on a canal, amounts
to one cent a ton per mile, or one dollar a ton for one hundred
miles; while the usual cost by land conveyance, is one dollar
and sixty cents per hundred weight, or 32 dollars a ton for the
same distance. The celerity and certainty of this mode of transportation are evident. A loaded boat can be towed by one or
two horses at the rate of 30 miles a day. Hence, the seller or
buyer can calculate with sufficient precision on his sales or
purchases, the period of their arrival, the amount of their
avails, and the extent of their value. A vessel on a canal is
independent of winds, tides, and currents, and is not exposed
to the delays attending conveyances by land; and with regard
to safety, there can be no competition. The injuries to which
commodities are exposed when transported by land, and the
dangers to which they are liable when conveyed by natural
waters, are rarely experienced on canals. In the latter way,
comparatively speaking, no waste is incurred, no risk is encountered, and no insurance is required. Hence, it follows, that
canals operate upon the general interests of society, in the
same way that machines for saving labour do in manufactures;
they enable the farmer, the mechanic, and the merchant to
convey their commodities to market, and to receive a return,
at least thirty times cheaper than by roads. As to all the purposes of beneficial communication, they diminish the distance
between places, and therefore encourage the cultivation of the
most extensive and remote parts of the country. They create
new sources of internal trade, and augment the old channels,

for the more cheap the transportation, the more expanded will be its operation, and the greater the mass of the products of the country for sale, the greater will be the commercial exchange of returning merchandise, and the greater the encouragement to manufacturers, by the increased economy and comfort of living, together with the cheapness and abundance of raw materials; and canals are consequently advantageous to towns and villages, by destroying the monopoly of the adjacent country, and advantageous to the whole country; for though some rival commodities may be introduced into the old markets, yet many new markets will be opened by increasing population, enlarging old and erecting new towns, augmenting individual and aggregate wealth, and extending foreign commerce. . . .

The general arguments in favour of inland navigation, apply with peculiar force to the United States, and most emphatically to this state. A geographical view of the country will at once demonstrate the unexampled prosperity that will arise from our cultivating the advantages which nature has dispensed with so liberal a hand. A great chain of mountains passes through the United States, and divides them into eastern and western America. In various places, rivers break through these mountains, and are finally discharged into the ocean. To the west there is a collection of inland lakes, exceeding in its aggregate extent some of the most celebrated seas of the old world. Atlantic America, on account of the priority of its settlement, its vicinity to the ocean, and its favourable position for commerce, has many advantages. The western country, however, has a decided superiority in the fertility of its soil, the benignity of its climate, and the extent of its territory. To connect these great sections by inland navigation, to unite our Mediterranean seas with the ocean, is evidently an object of the first importance to the general prosperity. Nature has effected this in some measure; the St. Lawrence emanates from the lakes, and discharges itself into the ocean in a foreign territory. Some of the streams which flow into the Mississippi, originate near the great lakes, and pass round the chain of mountains. Some of the waters of this state which pass into Lake Ontario, approach the Mohawk; but our Hudson has decided advantages. It affords a tide navigation for vessels of eighty tons to Albany and Troy, 160 miles above New-York, and this peculiarity distinguishes it from all the other bays and rivers in the United States, &c.

The tide in no other ascends higher than the Granite Ridge, or within thirty miles of the Blue Ridge, or eastern chain of mountains. In the Hudson it breaks through the Blue Ridge, and ascends above the eastern termination of the Catskill, or great western chain; and there are no interposing mountains to prevent a communication between it and the great western lakes.

The importance of the Hudson River to the old settled parts of the state, may be observed in the immense wealth which is daily borne on its waters, in the flourishing villages and cities on its banks, and in the opulence and prosperity of all the country connected with it, either remotely or immediately. It may also be readily conceived, if we only suppose that by some awful physical calamity, some overwhelming convulsion of nature, this great river was exhausted of its waters; where then would be the abundance of our markets, the prosperity of our farmers, the wealth of our merchants? Our villages would become deserted, our flourishing cities would be converted into masses of mouldering ruins, and this state would be precipitated into poverty and insignificance. If a river or natural canal, navigable about 170 miles, has been productive of such signal benefits, what blessings might not be expected if it were extended 300 miles through the most fertile country in the universe, and united with the great seas of the west! The contemplated canal would be this extension; and viewed in reference only to the productions and consumptions of the state, would perhaps convey more riches on its waters than any other canal in the world. Connected with the Hudson, it might be considered as a navigable stream that extends 450 miles through a fruitful country, embracing a great population, and abounding with all the productions of industry; if we were to suppose all the rivers and canals in England and Wales, combined into one, and discharging into the ocean at a great city, after passing through the heart of that country, then we can form a distinct idea of the importance of the projected canal; but it indeed comprehends within its influence a greater extent of territory, which will in time embrace a greater population. If this work be so important when we confine our views to this state alone, how unspeakably beneficial must it appear, when we extend our contemplations to the great lakes, and the country affiliated with them? Waters extending 2000 miles from the beginning of the canal, and a country containing more territory than all Great Britain and Ireland, and at least as much as France.

While we do not pretend that all the trade of our western world will centre in any given place, nor would it be desirable if it were practicable, because we sincerely wish the prosperity of all the states; yet we contend that our natural advantages are so transcendant, that it is in our power to obtain the greater part, and put successful competition at defiance. As all the other communications are impeded by mountains, the only formidable rivals of New-York, for this great prize, are New-Orleans and Montreal, the former relying on the Mississippi, and the latter on the St. Lawrence.

In considering this subject, we will suppose the commencement of the canal somewhere near the outlet of Lake Erie.

The inducements for preferring one market to another, involve a variety of considerations: the principal are the cheapness and facility of transportation, and the goodness of the market. If a cultivator or manufacturer can convey his commodities with the same ease and expedition to New-York, and obtain a higher price for them than at Montreal or New-Orleans, and at the same time supply himself at a cheaper rate with such articles as he may want in return, he will undoubtedly prefer New-York. It ought also to be distinctly understood, that a difference in price may be equalized by a difference in the expense of conveyance, and that the vicinity of the market is at all times a consideration of great importance.

From Buffalo, at or near the supposed commencement of the canal, it is 450 miles to the city of New-York, and from that city to the ocean twenty miles. From Buffalo to Montreal 350 miles; from Montreal to the chops of the St. Lawrence, 450. From Buffalo to New-Orleans by the great lakes, and the Illinois River, 2,250 miles; from New-Orleans to the Gulf of Mexico 100. Hence, the distance from Buffalo to the ocean, by the way of New-York, is 470 miles; by Montreal 800; and by New-Orleans 2,350.

As the upper lakes have no important outlet but into Lake Erie, we are warranted in saying, that all their trade must be auxiliary to its trade, and that a favourable communication by water from Buffalo, will render New-York the great depot and warehouse of the western world. . . .

. . . Supposing a perfect equality of advantages as to the navigation of the lakes, yet from Buffalo, as the point of departure, there is no comparison of benefits. From that place, the voyager to Montreal has to encounter the inconveniences of a portage at the cataract of Niagara, to load and unload at least three times, to brave the tempests of Lake Ontario, and the rapids of the St. Lawrence.

In like manner the voyager to New-Orleans, has a portage between the Chicago and Illinois, an inconvenient navigation on the latter stream, besides the well-known obstacles and hazards of the Mississippi. And until the invention of steamboats, an ascending navigation was considered almost impracticable. This inconvenience is, however, still forcibly experienced on that river, as well as on the St. Lawrence, between Montreal and Lake Ontario.

The navigation from Lake Erie to Albany, can be completed in ten days with perfect safety on the canal; and from Albany to New-York, there is the best sloop navigation in the world.

From Buffalo to Albany, a ton of commodities could be conveyed on the intended canal, for three dollars, and from Albany to New-York, according to the present prices of sloop transportation, for $2 8 \%_{100}$, and the return cargoes would be the same.

We have not sufficient data upon which to predicate very accurate estimates with regard to Montreal and New-Orleans; but we have no hesitation in saying, that the descending conveyance to the former, would be four times the expense, and to the latter, at least ten times, and that the cost of the ascending transportation would be greatly enhanced. . . .

In addition to this, it may be stated, that the St. Lawrence is generally locked up by ice seven months in the year, during which time produce lies a dead weight on the hands of the owner; that the navigation from New-York to the ocean, is at all times easy, and seldom obstructed by ice, and that the passage from the Balize to New-Orleans is tedious; that perhaps one out of five of the western boatmen who descend the Mississippi, become victims to disease; and that many important articles of western production are injured or destroyed by the climate. New-York is, therefore, placed in a happy medium between the insalubrious heat of the Mississippi, and the severe cold of the St. Lawrence. She has also pre-eminent advantages, as to the goodness and extensiveness of her market. All the productions of the soil, and the fabrics of art, can command an adequate price, and foreign commodities can generally be procured at a lower rate. The trade of the Mississippi is already in the hands of her merchants, and although accidental and transient causes may have concurred to give Montreal an ascendency in some points, yet the superiority of New-York is founded in nature, and if improved by the wisdom of government, must always soar above competition.

Granting, however, that the rivals of New-York will command a considerable portion of the western trade, yet it must be obvious, from these united considerations, that she will engross more than sufficient to render her the greatest commercial city in the world. The whole line of canal will exhibit boats loaded with flour, pork, beef, pot and pearl ashes, flaxseed, wheat, barley, corn, hemp, wool, flax, iron, lead, copper, salt, gypsum, coal, tar, fur, peltry, ginseng, beeswax, cheese, butter, lard, staves, lumber, and the other valuable productions of our country; and also, with merchandise from all parts of the world. Great manufacturing establishments will spring up; agriculture will establish its granaries, and commerce its warehouses in all directions. Villages, towns, and cities, will line the banks of the canal, and the shores of the Hudson from Erie to New-York. "The wilderness and the solitary place will become glad, and the desert will rejoice and blossom as the rose."

While it is universally admitted that there ought to be a water communication between the great lakes and the tidewaters of the Hudson, a contrariety of opinion, greatly to be deplored, as tending to injure the whole undertaken, has risen with respect to the route that ought to be adopted. It is contended on the one side, that the canal should commence in the vicinity of the outlet of Lake Erie, and be carried in the most eligible direction across the country to the head-waters of the Mohawk River at Rome: from whence it should be continued along the valley of the Mohawk to the Hudson. It is, on the other side, insisted that it should be cut round the cataract of Niagara; that Lake Ontario should be navigated to the mouth of the Oswego River; that the navigation of that river, and Wood Creek, should be improved and pursued until the junction of the latter with the Mohawk at Rome. As to the expediency of a canal from Rome to the Hudson, there is no discrepance of opinion; the route from Rome to the great lakes constitutes the subject of controversy. . . .

An invincible argument in favour of the Erie Canal, is, that it would diffuse the blessings of internal navigation over the most fertile and populous parts of the state, and supply the whole community with salt, gypsum, and in all probability coal. Whereas, the Ontario route would accommodate but an inconsiderable part of our territory, and instead of being a great highway, leading directly to the object, it would be a circuitous by-road, inconvenient in all essential respects.

The most serious objection against the Ontario route, is, that it will inevitably enrich the territory of a foreign power, at the expense of the United States. If a canal is cut round the falls of Niagara, and no countervailing nor counteracting system is adopted in relation to Lake Erie, the commerce of the west is lost to us for ever. When a vessel once descends into Ontario, she will pursue the course ordained by nature. The British government are fully aware of this, and are now taking the most active measures to facilitate the passage down the St. Lawrence. . . .

But taking it for granted, that the Ontario route will bring the commerce of the west to New-York, yet the other ought to be preferred, on account of the superior facilities it affords.

In the first place, it is nearer. The distance from Buffalo to Rome, is less than 200 miles in the course of the intended canal; by Lake Ontario and Oswego, it is 232.

A loaded boat could pass from Buffalo to Rome by the Erie route, in less than seven days, and with entire safety. By the Ontario route, it will be perfectly uncertain, and not a little hazardous. After leaving the Niagara River, it would have to pass an inland sea to the extent of 127 miles, as boisterous and as dangerous as the Atlantic. . . .

If the fall from Lake Erie to Lake Ontario be 450 feet, as stated in Mr. Secretary Gallatin's report on canals, it will require at least 45 locks for a navigation round the cataract. Whether it would be practicable to accommodate all the vessels which the population and opulence of future times will create in those waters, with a passage through so many locks accumulated within a short distance, is a question well worthy of serious consideration. At all events, the demurrage must be frequent, vexatious, and expensive.

When we consider the immense expense which would attend the canal proposed on the Niagara River, a canal requiring so many locks, and passing through such difficult ground; when we view the Oswego River from its outlet at Oswego, to its origin in Oneida Lake, encumbered with dangerous rapids and falls, and flowing through a country almost impervious to canal operations; and when we contemplate the numerous embarrassments which are combined with the improvement of Wood Creek, we are prepared to believe that the expense of this route will not greatly fall short of the other.

It is, however, alleged, that it is not practicable to make this canal; and that if practicable, the expense will be enormous, and will far transcend the faculties of the state.

Lake Erie is elevated 541 feet above tide waters at Troy. The only higher ground between it and the Hudson is but a few miles from the lake; and this difficulty can be easily surmounted by deep cutting; of course no tunnel will be required. The rivers which cross the line of the canal, can be easily passed by aqueducts; on every summit level, plenty of water can be obtained; whenever there is a great rise or descent, locks can be erected, and the whole line will not require more than sixty-two; perhaps there is not an equal extent of country in the world, which presents fewer obstacles to the establishment of a canal. The liberality of nature has created the great ducts and arteries, and the ingenuity of art can easily provide the connecting veins. The general physiognomy of the country is champaign, and exhibits abundance of water; a gentle rising from the Hudson to the lake; a soil well adapted for such operations; no impassable hills, and no insurmountable waters. As to distance, it is not to be considered in relation to practicability. If a canal can be made for fifty miles, it can be made for three hundred, provided there is no essential variance in the face of the country; the only difference will be, that in the latter case, it will take more time, and consume more money.

But this opinion does not rest for its support upon mere speculation. Canals have been successfully cut through more embarrassing ground, in various parts of the United States; and even in part of the intended route from Schenectady to Rome, locks have been erected at the Little Falls, and at other places; and short canals have been made, and all these operations have taken place in the most difficult parts of the whole course of the contemplated Erie navigation. Mr. William Weston, one of the most celebrated civil engineers in Europe, who has super-intended canals in this state and Pennsylvania, and who is perfectly well acquainted with the country, has thus expressed his opinion on this subject: "Should your noble but stupendous plan of uniting Lake Erie with the Hudson, be carried into effect, you have to fear no rivalry. The commerce of the immense extent of country, bordering on the upper lakes, is yours for ever, and to such an incalculable amount as would baffle all conjecture to conceive. Its execution would confer immortal honour on the projectors and supporters, and would in its eventual consequences, render New-York the greatest commercial emporium in the world, with perhaps the exception at some distant day of New-Orleans, or some other depot at the mouth of the majestic Mississippi. From your perspicuous topographical description, and neat plan and profile of the route of the contemplated canal, I entertain little doubt of the practicability of the measure.". . .

From a deliberate consideration of these different estimates and actual expenditures, we are fully persuaded that this great work will not cost more than 20,000 dollars a mile, or six millions of dollars in the whole; but willing to make every possible allowance, and even conceding that it will cost double that sum, yet still we contend that there is nothing which ought to retard its execution. This canal cannot be made in a short time. It will be the work perhaps of ten or fifteen years.

The money will not be wanted at once. The expenditure, in order to be beneficial, ought not to exceed 500,000 dollars a year, and the work may be accomplished in two ways; either by companies incorporated for particular sections of the route, or by the state. If the first is resorted to, pecuniary sacrifices will still be necessary on the part of the public, and great care ought to be taken to guard against high tolls, which will certainly injure, if not ruin the whole enterprise.

If the state shall see fit to achieve this great work, there can be no difficulty in providing funds. Stock can be created and sold at an advanced price. The ways and means of paying the interest will be only required. After the first year, supposing an annual expenditure of 500,000 dollars, 30,000 dollars must be raised to pay an interest of six per cent; after the second year, 60,000, and so on. At this rate the interest will regularly increase with beneficial appropriation, and will be so little in amount that it may be raised in many shapes without being burdensome to the community. In all human probability, the augmented revenue proceeding from the public salt works, and the increased price of the state lands in consequence of this undertaking, will more than extinguish the interest of the debt contracted for that purpose. We should also take into view, the land already subscribed by individuals for this work, amounting to 106,632 acres. These donations, together with those which may be confidently anticipated, will exceed in value a million of dollars, and it will be at all times in the power of the state to raise a revenue from the imposition of transit duties, which may be so light as scarcely to be felt, and yet the income may be so great as in a short time to extinguish the debt, and this might take effect on the completion of every important section of the work.

If the legislature shall consider this important project in the same point of view, and shall unite with us in opinion, that the general prosperity is intimately and essentially involved in its prosecution, we are fully persuaded that now is the proper time for its commencement.—Delays are the refuge of weak minds, and to procrastinate on this occasion is to show a culpable inattention to the bounties of nature; a total insensibility to the blessings of Providence, and an inexcusable neglect of the interests of society. If it were intended to advance the views of individuals, or to foment the divisions of party; if it promoted the interests of a few, at the expense of the property of the many; if its benefits were limited as to place, or fugitive as to duration, then indeed it might be received with cold indifference, or treated with stern neglect; but the overflowing blessings from this great fountain of public good and national abundance, will be as extensive as our country, and as durable as time.

The considerations which now demand an immediate, and an undivided attention to this great object, are so obvious, so various, and so weighty, that we shall only attempt to glance at some of the most prominent.

In the first place, it must be evident that no period could be adopted in which the work can be prosecuted with less expense. Every day augments the value of the land through which the canal will pass; and when we consider the surplus hands which have been recently dismissed from the army into the walks of private industry, and the facility with which an addition can be procured to the mass of our active labour, in consequence of the convulsions of Europe, it must be obvious that this is now the time to make those indispensable acquisitions.

2. The longer this work is delayed, the greater will be the difficulty in surmounting the interests that will rise up in opposition to it. Expedients on a contracted scale have already been adopted for the facilitation of intercourse. Turnpikes, locks, and short canals have been resorted to, and in consequence of those establishments, villages have been laid out and towns have been contemplated. To prevent injurious speculation, to avert violent opposition, and to exhibit dignified im-

partiality and paternal affection to your fellow-citizens, it is proper that they should be notified at once of your intentions.

3. The experience of the late war has impressed every thinking man in the community, with the importance of this communication. The expenses of transportation frequently exceeded the original value of the article, and at all times operated with injurious pressure upon the finances of the nation. The money thus lost for the want of this communication, would perhaps have defrayed more than one half of its expense.

4. Events which are daily occuring on our frontiers, demonstrate the necessity of this work. Is it of importance that our honourable merchants should not be robbed of their legitimate profits; that the public revenues should not be seriously impaired by dishonest smuggling, and that the commerce of our cities should not be supplanted by the mercantile establishments of foreign countries? Then it is essential that this sovereign remedy for maladies so destructive and ruinous should be applied. It is with inconceivable regret we record the well known fact, that merchandize from Montreal, has been sold to an alarming extent on our borders for 15 per cent. below the New-York prices.

5. A measure of this kind will have a benign tendency in raising the value of the national domains, in expediting the sale, and enabling the payment. Our national debt may thus, in a short time be extinguished. Our taxes of course will be diminished, and a considerable portion of revenue may then be expended in great public improvements; in encouraging the arts and sciences; in patronising the operations of industry; in fostering the inventions of genius, and in diffusing the blessings of knowledge.

6. However serious the fears which have been entertained of a dismemberment of the Union by collisions between the north and the south, it is to be apprehended that the most imminent danger lies in another direction, and that a line of

separation may be eventually drawn between the Atlantic and the western states, unless they are cemented by a common, an ever-acting, and a powerful interest. The commerce of the ocean, and the trade of the lakes, passing through one channel, supplying the wants, increasing the wealth, and reciprocating the benefits of each great section of the empire, will form an imperishable cement of connexion, and an indissoluble bond of union. New-York is both Atlantic and western; and the only state in which this union of interests can be formed and perpetuated, and in which this great centripetal power can be energetically applied. Standing on this exalted eminence, with power to prevent a train of the most extensive and afflicting calamities that ever visited the world, (for such a train will inevitably follow a dissolution of the Union,) she will justly be considered an enemy to the human race, if she does not exert for this purpose the high faculties which the Almighty has put into her hands.

Lastly. It may be confidently asserted, that this canal, as to the extent of its route, as to the countries which it connects, and as to the consequences which it will produce, is without a parallel in the history of mankind. The union of the Baltic and the Euxine; of the Red Sea and the Mediterranean; of the Euxine and the Caspian; and of the Mediterranean and the Atlantic, has been projected or executed by the chiefs of powerful monarchies, and the splendour of the design has always attracted the admiration of the world. It remains for a free state to create a new era in history, and to erect a work more stupendous, more magnificent, and more beneficial than has hitherto been achieved by the human race. Character is as important to nations as to individuals, and the glory of a republic, founded on the promotion of the general good, is the common property of all its citizens.

We have thus discharged with frankness and plainness, and with every sentiment of respect, a great duty to ourselves, to our fellow-citizens, and to posterity, in presenting this subject to the fathers of the commonwealth. And may that Almighty Being in whose hands are the destinies of states and nations, enlighten your councils and invigorate your exertions in favour of the best interests of our beloved country.

5. Pennsylvania:
The Revulsion Against Public Works

Early enthusiasm for internal improvements was followed in a number of states by an equally strong revulsion against them. In Pennsylvania, as Professor Hartz has pointed out,[1] this reaction was marked in the year 1857 by the sale of the "Main Line" of the Public Works to the Pennsylvania Railroad and by the adoption of a constitutional amendment forbidding either the state or local governments to invest in the stock of improvement companies. By 1860 seventeen other states had adopted similar provisions against aiding companies by at least one of the three methods of loan, subscription, or donation, although most of them did not extend the prohibitions to local authorities. Five states, moreover, accepted self-denying ordinances, making it unconstitutional for them to construct public improvements.[2] These decisions reflected widespread disillusion with government support of improvements, and particularly with the failures and financial losses

---

[1] Louis Hartz, *Economic Policy and Democratic Thought: Pennsylvania, 1776–1860* (Cambridge: Harvard University Press, 1948), chs. 3 and 4.

[2] Carter Goodrich, "The Revulsion Against Internal Improvements," *Journal of Economic History*, X (1950), 145–169.

in the years following the crisis of 1837, although some states like Virginia were still expanding their programs and others would do so after the Civil War.

The spirit of revulsion is expressed by the committee on the sale of Pennsylvania's State Works. These consisted of a "Main Line" from Philadelphia to Pittsburgh and a number of "Branches," connected or unconnected. The system was started in what has been described as a "panic reaction" to the triumphant opening of the Erie Canal.[3] This was to be rivaled or surpassed by the Main Line. However, Pennsylvania's way to the West led across mountains rather than by a "water level route" like that of New York; and what was built was an "amphibious" system in four parts—a railroad from Philadelphia to the Susquehannah, canals in the middle and western sections, and between them a crossing of the Alleghenies by inclined planes, a technical marvel for the time but an economic anomaly. Even so, parts of the system carried considerable freight; but it could neither surpass the Erie nor earn a substantial return on its investment. Its financial failure was responsible, together with inadequate provisions for ordinary tax revenue, for temporary default on the state's obligations. In the month of the committee's report, moreover, the Pennsylvania Railroad, a product of private and municipal rather than state investment, reached Pittsburgh with a line of unbroken railroad and made the state's Portage Railroad entirely obsolete.

The committee's recommendation for the sale of the public works was based not only on their financial failure, which it summarized, but on broader grounds as well. "The objects of government," it said, "should be few and simple as possible." President Jackson's warnings in the Maysville Road Veto were still to the point. When "politics" and "trade" are mixed, the natural consequences are mismanagement, inefficiency, and corruption of the public morals.

---

[3] Julius Rubin, "An Imitative Public Improvement: The Pennsylvania Mainline," in Goodrich, ed., *Canals and American Economic Development,* ch. 2, especially p. 113.

MR. EVANS, FROM THE SELECT COMMITTEE TO WHICH WAS
REFERRED THAT PART OF THE MESSAGE OF THE GOVERNOR
WHICH RELATES TO THE SALE OF THE PUBLIC WORKS,
AND THE MEMORIAL OF THE BOARD OF TRADE OF
PHILADELPHIA, MAKE THE FOLLOWING REPORT:

That they have had the subject under consideration, and have
given it that careful attention which its magnitude demands.
They concur in many of the views contained in the message of
the Governor, as to the value of the public works as a means
of developing the resources and promoting the commerce of
the State, as well as of liquidating taxation and paying the
State debt. They also concur in his views as to the extravagance
in their cost and management, and the necessity and extreme
difficulty of obtaining reform. Keeping in view the careful suggestions of the Governor, in relation to the existing evils in the
management of the system and the necessity of reform, as well
as his arguments for and against divorcing it from the government, your committee, for reasons which they beg leave respectfully to submit in this report, recommend to the Legislature the sale of all the canals and railroads owned by the
Commonwealth, and have accompanied this report with a bill
for effecting that object.

It is not necessary to discuss in this paper the policy and
motives of the founders of this improvement system. Having
arrived at the conclusion that public opinion, correct policy and

From "Report of the Select Committee," February 4, 1854, Pennsylvania
Senate Journal, pp. 328–337. Much of the detail on the finances of the
system and state is omitted and some illustrations of the overestimate of
the cost of projects. What appears to be a double counting of some
$78,000 in the table under "Board of Canal Commissioners" would not
affect the general argument.

sound morals, justify and demand a sale, it will be more useful to point out the reasons by which this conclusion is arrived at. The public debt is estimated by the Governor at $40,272,-235 01. The annual interest upon this sum, at five per cent., is, in round numbers, two millions of dollars. The multifarious monetary transactions of the several departments of the government, complicate the State finances, and render it difficult or impossible for the tax-payer to understand them; but the sole problem, stripped of verbiage, for the Legislature and the people to solve, is, How shall this debt and interest be met and paid, with least burthen to the tax-payers? It is a debt resting upon the people, for the payment of which their houses, lands and tenements, and even their honor and good faith, are virtually mortgaged. This interest and debt provided for, all the other obligations of the Commonwealth would be met without tax upon real estate, and a surplus be left in the Treasury.

HOW THE SYSTEM AFFECTS PUBLIC MORALS

The system of public works exercises an influence more powerful upon the morals, and in some respects, upon the interests of the people, than the government itself. The officials and agents of the system, whose name is legion, extend to all parts of the Commonwealth,—a vast engine of political power, unknown to the Constitution, moved by a common impulse, and operating upon the public mind at any time they are so disposed, in State conventions, and at the ballot box, in solid column and with almost irresistable sway. But it is not as a dangerous political machine that it is viewed in its worst aspects, nor as an exhausting drain upon the public purse; its malign influences upon the morals of the community, are even more to be dreaded than all other evils, and powerfully co-operate in making it a festering disease upon the public. At every stage, complaints have been made of the extravagance, fraud and peculation in the conduct of the works, and the most honorable agents have been stigmatized with odium by an indignant public, smarting under the known abuses and heavy burthens they have generated. Attempts to reform, however loudly professed and honestly made, have been unavailing to eradicate evils inherent in the system. Economy, ever regarded as a cardinal virtue, in public as well as private agents, has too frequently been treated as a secondary consideration. Public servants, whose virtues have commended them to general esteem, have not been regarded as the most fitting instruments to discharge the peculiar duties expected of them.

That practices at war with all the established principles of political economy, have resulted in debt, taxation, extravagance, mortification and disappointment, is a misfortune, but cannot be a matter of astonishment to the people of Pennsylvania. Thousands have expected and predicted such a result from a system which has set at defiance all the laws which govern business men. Had the object of this anomalous system been to destroy and not to build up, the revenues and morals of the State, it could not have been more ingeniously devised; and therefore it is an extraordinary and unaccountable fact, that with a people so proverbial for practical intelligence it was ever sanctioned and has not long since been abandoned.

Your committee are fully aware that a proposition for a sale will encounter an energetic opposition. Where there are so many holding places of profit with ten expectants for every incumbent, each confident that his turn will come next, a formidable opposition may be expected. It is a great evil of the system that young men of gifted minds and correct impulses are seized with an ambition of serving in some subordinate position, and are thus taken from mechanical pursuits and the peaceful walks of private life they are so well fitted to adorn. The evil is contagious, spreading from man to man. Appointed to offices at a distance from home, thrown among strangers and surrounded with temptations, the habits of young men are endangered; and being selected for partisan zeal, they frequently exercise an improper influence upon local elections in which they may not be interested.

These considerations, affecting the public morals and the purity of elections, are all to be taken in connection with the question of revenue and taxation. The moral purity of the public in proportion to its value should be guarded. And who can estimate its value? It is beyond price. Pecuniary considerations are as dross in comparison.

The present Constitution deprived the Governor of the power of dispensing extensive patronage, because it was the fruitful source of corruption. The proposed sale is supported by the same argument. If patronage abused was a sufficient cause for changing the fundamental law, is it not equally so for a sale of the public works? Was abuse of patronage in the hands of the Executive to be compared with its abuse on the public works? A remedy is more imperative in the latter case than in the former.

POPULAR OPINION

The voice of the people sanctions a sale. At a popular election in 1844, a majority of more than twenty-one thousand voted for a sale of the main line, and on various occasions the Legislature has agitated the subject. Numerous memorials in favor of a sale, have come up from the people, without a remonstrance against it. The law of 1844, authorized the sale only of the main line, and unfortunately affixed a price beyond the market value of that work. It was offered at twenty millions, but there were no purchasers at that price. The policy of relinquishing to companies unprofitable lines, was adopted by the State, when the Erie extension and other works were transferred to companies, without pecuniary consideration, because they were deemed unprofitable investments for the State. And this policy has been sanctioned by the people; no citizen has ever proposed a resumption. The Erie extension was abandoned—also the Gettysburg railroad, after an expenditure on the one of $3,192,621, and on the other of $681,531 00. Acting upon the same policy, we propose, by a fair sale, to abandon all the works at fair prices, and to separate forever the State from similar investments, except under the most urgent State necessity. . . .

COST AND REVENUE OF EACH LINE

The following table, carefully prepared by the Auditor General, shows the cost, revenue, and expenditure upon each line from the commencement of the system, together with the interest paid:

LINES	COST	REVENUE	EXPENDITURES
Columbia and Philadelphia railway	$ 5,277,278 44	$ 9,020,278 39	$ 5,860,291 11
Eastern division of canal	1,737,285 22	2,932,571 14	862,938 08
Juniata division of canal	3,575,966 29	1,496,429 79	1,950,687 92
Allegheny Portage railway	2,708,672 12	3,520,407 84	4,014,788 86
Western division of canal	3,173,432 18	2,812,312 32	1,340,535 07
Main line	16,472,634 25	19,781,999 48	14,029,241 04
Delaware division of canal	1,454,936 63	2,746,650 25	1,223,301 06
Susquehanna division of canal	897,160 52	475,254 57	605,990 18
North Branch division of canal	1,598,379 35	1,374,258 87	799,775 24
West Branch division of canal	1,832,583 28	573,338 29	815,318 57
Lines in operation	22,255,694 03	24,951,501 46	17,473,626 09
French Creek division of canal	817,779 74	5,819 67	143,911 94
Beaver Division	519,364 92	38,312 29	210,360 00
Finished lines	23,592,838 69	24,995,633 42	17,827,898 03

LINES	COST	REVENUE	EXPENDITURES
Unfinished improvements	8,695,044 65		
Board of Canal Commissioners	78,962 39		78,962 39
Board of Appraisers	17,584 93		
Collectors, weighmasters and lock keepers			1,540,793 16
Exploratory surveys	157,837 11		
Sale of public property		346,387 05	
Patent rights, engravings, printing, &c			52,203 45
Totals	$32,542,267 77	$25,342,020 47	$19,499,857 03

Interest paid on internal improvement loans
  to Dec. 1, 1853 $35,157,796 13

TOTAL COST OF RAILROADS AND CANALS

The foregoing statement exhibits the original cost at $32,542,267 77
Interest paid upon the same   35,157,796 13
Expense of conducting works   19,499,857 03

Total expenditures on public works   87,199,920 93
Add floating debt, as per Governor's message   1,223,429 00
Appropriations required for North Branch canal   171,058 51
Allegheny Portage railroad   961,360 29

                                                                 $89,555,768 73

REVENUES AND EXPENDITURES
FROM 1830 TO 1854—24 YEARS

It also exhibits the revenue from 1830 to 1854, on all the
  lines at $25,342,020 47
  Do   expenditures   do   do   19,499,857 03

                                                                  $5,842,163 44

Making an average annual income for 24 years, of $243,423 47

• • •

MANAGEMENT OF THE WORKS

Whether it is wise for the State to hold on to works, and per-
severe in a system which has broken so many pledges and so
totally failed of just expectation, is a matter for the sober and
candid judgment of those who have to bear the burthens. Like
the unsuccessful gambler, the State has been lured on in the
hope of redeeming losses. We have not profitted by experience,
but from year to year have rushed blindly into new expenditures. Every failure has been followed by the most fallacious
calculations to induce further expenditure, and disappointed
hopes by increased confidence. In the Governor's message it is
stated that in 1852, the work to avoid the Allegheny inclined
planes was estimated to cost "the meagre sum of $591,350."
It declares that $650,000 have been spent since that time, and
that over six hundred thousand is still required. . . .

Every allegation of fraud and profligacy alleged against the
present system of management is more than admitted by the
last report of the Canal Board. Of the expense of managing the
Allegheny Portage road, in 1853, they say it "amounted to the
enormous sum of $492,252." In 1852, they say it "amounted to
$402,195. To this must be added, however, $54,332, which had
not been reported by the former Superintendent, but has since
been discovered!" Again they say: "could the Board assume
that the amount expended in 1852 was all legitimate, there
would be little difficulty, &c." "Although the Board have not
been able to detect any fraud, yet from the very careless
manner in which business has been hitherto transacted there, it
is readily perceived how easy it might be to practice extensive
frauds, and at the same time the officer be innocent of any corrupt motive. Take the article of wood for example, and it cannot be doubted but that the State has been imposed upon to a
large amount." "In consequence of these frauds," say the Board,
"they have adopted a plan which, in the item of wood, will save

the State twenty thousand dollars a year," adding that "a regard for truth and candor constrains the Board to express the opinion that at least forty thousand dollars have been paid out for wood, within the past two years, for which not one dollar's advantage has accrued to the Commonwealth."

Such is the confession in the report of the Canal Board. Could language more emphatically condemn a system, which, after twenty years experience admits of such abuse?

In what company or bank, or what railroad, except that of the State, could it be possible for *forty thousand dollars* to be expended not only without the knowledge of the accounting officers, but "without one dollar's advantage?" It is a matter of congratulation, that a reform, whereby twenty thousand dollars are saved in "the single item of wood," has been discovered even after twenty years experience! Upon a short road of thirty-six miles, every dollar expended should be rigidly accounted for without difficulty, and the whole system should be simple, accurate and energetic; but for the want of such a system, thousands have been squandered, forty thousand in a single item—and the Canal Board, alluding to such small items, frankly confess that "it is readily perceived how easy it might be to practice extensive frauds!" Who can tell the full extent of imposition on this and other lines, when it is admitted it is so easily practised? The efficient management of the Portage road was especially referred to by the Governor in his message, January 5, 1853, and of the Superintendent he took occasion to say, "certainly a more honest and devoted public servant could not be found than the gentleman who superintended the operation of this work for the past year." If under such an "honest and devoted" man these things occurred, what might not be feared if they were in hands of men less scrupulous, such as have sometimes crept into office!

The objects of government should be few and simple as possible. To mingle with it business, whether mercantile or mechanical, is inconsistent with its object, and may be carried to a dangerous extent; and is alike destructive of sound morals as it is of private enterprise. The separation of politics and trade, would do much to restore our government to its original purity, and would be hailed by every virtuous citizen as the dawn of a better and brighter day. Government bounty saps the moral energies of any people. The views of President Jackson, in vetoing appropriations for a national road, possess force in this connexion. "In the best view of these appropriations," says he, "the abuses to which they lead far exceed the good which they are capable of promoting. They may be resorted to as artful expedients, to shift upon the government the losses of unsuccessful private speculation, and thus, by ministering to personal ambition and self-aggrandizement, tend to sap the foundations of public virtue, and taint the administration of government with a demoralizing influence." In another place, he also says, they "promote a dangerous and mischievous influence upon elections," and thus favor "combinations to squander the treasure of the country upon a multitude of local objects, as fatal to just legislation as to the purity of public men."

The improvements of the State create a necessity for a vast number of officers to manage them. These officers, obeying the will of one common head, necessarily lose much of that independence which is the boast of the freeman; and power, which theoretically belongs to the people, becomes centralized in a few hands, who are bound together by the cohesive power of official patronage, and thus the people experience all the evils of a vast consolidated government. The officials, under the system, profit by its expenses, and the temptation to increase these expenses is therefore ever present.

The doctrine of rotation in office, and of rewarding partisan service, is justly deprecated by the Governor. A necessity for reform is felt by every patriotic citizen. This evil has been acknowledged and deplored for years; but, after the experience we have had, no one who is not blind to the power of party, ever expects to realize the fond anticipations he has indulged that it would be corrected. With no disposition to reflect upon any officer of the government, it will often happen that the Commissioners who manage the works, will not be duly qualified for their office, when selected merely for their partizan claims and availability. While the choice is the result of a political scramble, the adroit manœuverer will be most likely to gain the prize; and he, of course, will feel bound, in choosing his subordinates, to provide the best places for those to whom he is under the deepest obligations. This is not only natural but unavoidable, whatever party may be in the ascendant. If party success fluctuates frequently, as it is prone to do in a free country, the subordinates must change with every change of party, no matter what the nature of their office, or the skill and experience required for its due performance. In mere political stations these changes may be tolerated, though even there it is often injurious, but in positions which require the incumbent to know something, to be expert and faithful, it must be obvious that the services of such should be secure from arbitrary and wanton change. Political views and partizan dexterity, indispensable qualifications with the State, constitute no recommendation with a well organized company, where competency is the only pre-requisite in the selection of both managers and subordinates. In such a company, as with the farmer, the merchant, the banker or the mechanic, the skillful and faithful operative or agent, is cherished and retained as long as possible, instead of being recklessly dismissed for his opinions, to make room for some retainer of certain politics but of uncertain fitness for the place. The failure of our entire system of management, and the evils it entails upon the people, it must be admitted, are only legitimate consequences of the departure from sound business principles, if not a just judgment upon our political fanaticism and folly.

MANNER OF SALE AND THE PRICE

The remarks of the Governor upon this important subject have been taken into respectful consideration. The objections to making the State a joint stockholder in an incorporated company, are not altogether without foundation; and the plan should not be adopted unless indispensable to effect a sale. But would it not be better to retain one-fourth of the stock if by so doing three-fourths could be sold, than to defeat a sale altogether? The great object is to bring about a sale, and it should not be defeated by subordinate objections. Objections may be started to every plan; great sores are not to be cured without severe remedies. Almost any sale is better than no sale. Almost any price is preferable to continuing a system at a loss of morals and money. Our motto should be a total and complete emancipation from all the works; but if that be not possible, then even a part would be a happy deliverance.

We concur with the Governor that the price is an important consideration, and that whether a sale would be expedient or not depends somewhat upon whether the proceeds of the sale would yield more than the net profits of the works. But when we consider how difficult it is to estimate the profits for a series of years—the fallacy of all former calculations, and the active competition which is springing up along all the lines, and the imbecility of State management, it becomes rather a question of what we can get than what we will take, and is therefore sound policy to sell on the best terms possible. We also concur with the Executive that the buyer will expect to get the "best of the bargain." But it must not be inferred from this that the State will get the worst. If this were an objection against a sale, it would be equally so against all exchanges and mercantile transactions. No one buys or sells a house unless he has the "best of the bargain." It is the principle which governs the farmer, the merchant and the banker. Every buyer thinks he has made a bargain and the seller flatters himself with the same idea. And both may be right—each may have the "best of the bargain." Exchange is a mutual advantage. That the State in selling the public works would have the "best of the bargain," is beyond a doubt; and that in the hands of energetic and economical companies they would yield remunerative returns for the capital invested, is evident from the permanent character of those sources upon which they depend for business.

The improvements of the State naturally divide themselves into four divisions, as follows:

1. The main line from Philadelphia to Pittsburgh.
2. The Delaware division.
3. Susquehanna division and North Branch canal.
4. The West Branch canal.

Several plans may be stated for effecting a sale, which the committee propose for the deliberation of the Senate in the accompanying bill:

1. Empowering the Governor to advertise and receive proposals for each line separately, and to sell to the highest and best bidder—fixing a minimum price.

2. In case the minimum price is not offered, books to be opened and subscriptions received to the stock of each line— the capital stock, number of shares and price per share, being fixed in the bill.

3. In case no sale be effected as above, the Governor is authorized to receive proposals for leasing each line for a term of ten years, which shall be submitted to the next Legislature.

Your committee are fully aware of the impossibility of maturing any plan free from all objections, either in the price or the manner or terms of sale.—But they entertain a deep conviction that all these are subordinate in the eyes of the people, to the emancipation of the Commonwealth from the burthens of the present system.

Your committee, in framing bills, have ventured, not without much hesitation, in designating a minimum price upon each line, as follows:

Main line from Philadelphia to Pittsburgh	$12,000,000 00
Delaware division	2,500,000 00
West Branch division	500,000 00
North Branch canal and Susquehanna division	5,000,000 00

In fixing these prices, it must be admitted that they hold out to enterprising corporations an opportunity of investing capital to such an advantage, and with such prospect of realizing large profits as rarely occurs; and while it is barely possible that the State may suffer a disadvantage, all the probabilities are that it will save, in the interest of the capital liquidated, from fifty to one hundred per cent. more than experience has taught us to believe it would derive from the public works. Even at this price the public debt would be reduced to a little more than twenty millions of dollars—a sum which would be extinguished by the ordinary revenue of the government, and without increase of taxation, in a comparatively short period of time.

From an examination of the tables and calculations in this report, your committee believe, sober minded and prudent citizens must arrive at an opinion favorable to a divorce of the State, once and forever, from a business which especially belongs to incorporated companies and mercantile men. The union of trade and politics must ever be dangerous; they should be friends not allies. One is sure to corrupt the other. Governments should be restricted to purely political powers necessary to the existence of society. Extensive patronage is followed by demoralization and corruption—it vitiates the public taste and enervates society. Can our people, under the auspices of our happy form of government, hope to escape the vices which naturally flow from this patronage, and avoid the uniform fate of other nations? A grand system of improvements under the glowing tongue of eloquent advocates, is apt to fascinate the imagination and to lead to the most extravagant expectations. The picture of wealth and grandeur held up to the admiration of posterity, of cities and towns springing up as if by magic, and of extensive revenues flowing into the coffers of the State, are well calculated to inspire the confidence of even those whom bitter experience has taught a different lesson.

Can the Legislature longer hesitate, with the flattering prospects resulting from a sale, to authorize it? There is great force in the language of the memorial referred to the committee, where it is given as "the deliberate opinion of this board, that the Legislature can do no single act more conducive to the prosperity of the entire Commonwealth, than to provide by law for early sales at fair prices of the public works."

6. The Debate Over the First Railroad Land Grant

The federal government returned to the direct support of internal improvements in 1850 with an act granting some 3,750,000 acres of land for the construction of an intersectional railroad from the northern border of Illinois to the Gulf of Mexico at Mobile. The grant was to include alternative sections of land along the route in the public land states of Illinois, Mississippi, and Alabama or, where these lands were already in private ownership, an equivalent acreage away from the line. The alternate sections retained by the government were to be sold at a minimum price of $2.50 per acre rather than $1.25.

The measure was not wholly without precedent. In 1827 and 1828 the government had granted lands to Ohio and Indiana for the construction of roads, to Indiana for the Wabash Canal, and to Illinois for the important canal linking the Lakes with the Mississippi system. In three of these cases the grant consisted of alternate sections along the line of the improvement. After the Maysville Road veto, the government continued to make substantial grants of land to the public land states, but these were to be used entirely at their discretion and without particular limitation to objects. What the 1850 act returned to, therefore, was federal decision as to the route and nature of the improvement.

Senator Stephen A. Douglas of Illinois introduced in 1848 a railroad land grant measure applying only to his own state and the proposed Illinois Central Railroad, but failed to secure its adoption. In 1850 he encouraged Senator William R. King of Alabama to amend the bill by adding the Mobile and Ohio Railroad to carry the project to the Gulf. This made it possible for a Wisconsin Senator to describe it as "a great chain to unite the North and South," and for an Alabama Representative to declare that the measure was "calculated to perpetuate this glorious Confederacy." Even Jefferson Davis of Mississippi, although objecting to the terms on which land away from the line was to be granted, said that the proposed railroad had "all the characteristics of a useful public highway, because it is continually changing the latitude and therefore the products through which it passes."[1] On the basis of its national character, the bill received the necessary votes for passage.

Parts of the debate are given below. Senator Douglas argues for the measure on practical grounds. The government will gain as a prudent landlord and will get back all it gives away by charging double price for what remains. The prospective settler will also gain, since the construction of the railroad will make land that is now valueless worth more than the $2.50 he will have to pay. Senator William H. Seward of New York supports the measure on broader grounds as a project of great national importance and, in a sense, an extension of the program begun by his own state in building the Erie Canal. The

---

[1] *Congressional Globe*, 31st Congress, 1st Session, Part I, pp. 370, 853; Part II, p. 1437.

country needs such improvements before there is a sufficient accumulation of private capital to construct them. Some of the western states have bankrupted themselves in attempting to provide them. The solution is for the federal government, which holds the public lands within their borders, to use these resources for the purpose.

One of the leading opponents of the measure was Senator Andrew P. Butler of South Carolina, who argued that it proposed unconstitutional use of public property for private purposes. When the Illinois Central bill was introduced in 1848, Senator Butler declared that it struck him "as singular that the West, while it was young, asked no aid from the Government; but now that it has become strong, it seeks assistance."[2] His 1850 remarks elaborate the theme of regional favoritism, with the older states in the relation of a King Lear to their western children; and he wins the laughter of the Senate by remarking that the constitutional principles of his colleague from Alabama seem to have been greatly influenced by local patriotism.[3]

After the passage of the 1850 act, the gates were open for further land grants, most of them for undertakings that could hardly have qualified as great national thoroughfares. During the decade Michigan received 750,000 acres for the important project of the Soo Canal, and measures were passed offering aid to the public land states for no less than forty railroads, on which some 18,500,000 acres were ultimately granted. The federal government still confined its contribution to land and refused financial assistance; but in the next decade, after our period, this barrier was also to be breached. The national government added massive financial aid to a lordly land grant in order to secure the construction of the first railroad across the continent.

---

[2] *Congressional Globe,* 30th Congress, 1st Session, Appendix, p. 537.

[3] Another eastern opponent, Representative Thomas Fuller of Maine, declared that some easterners had cast what he called western votes on the issue because of financial interest in the proposed railroad. *Congressional Globe,* 32nd Congress, 1st Session, Appendix, pp. 386–390. This is from the speech that is quoted for another purpose in Document 9 below.

SPEECH OF SENATOR STEPHEN A. DOUGLAS

MR. DOUGLAS. One word, sir, in answer to the questions propounded by the Senator from Georgia. In reply to the honorable Senator's question, where is this power to be found, I refer him to the clause of the Constitution of the United States which says that Congress may prescribe rules for the disposition of the public lands, territories, and other property of the United States. The power to dispose of the public lands is given in so many words, and where a power is expressly given without any limitation, I apprehend that it is our duty to judge of the terms of sale. We have a right to sell upon credit or to sell for cash. We have a right to make any other disposition of the public lands which we may think proper, provided that disposition is in accordance with the nature of the trust. In other words, we may make any disposition of these public lands which tends to increase the trust fund. I do not argue the question of our right to donate, as we do not propose to donate. I do not deem it necessary, therefore, to answer that question. We propose to make a proper constitutional and legal disposition of the lands, in a mode that will benefit and increase the trust fund under our charge. The power is expressly given; there is no limitation upon it; but I confess that we are bound to exercise that power in a manner that is consistent with the trust placed in our hands. We must not diminish, but we should increase and improve that trust fund, and make it bring the largest amount that we can. Now, sir, suppose that you had a large section of the public lands entirely inundated, so that they were not worth a farthing per acre. Suppose the giving away of one-tenth portion of these lands would render the whole of them available and saleable; if you have not the power

From *Congressional Globe*, 31st Congress, 1st Session, May 1, 1850, p. 849.

to give away the one-tenth on condition that the other shall be rendered available, the whole is worth nothing—it is waste, entirely valueless: but by giving away a portion you render the remainder valuable, and thus gain considerably by it; would any one say that it was not wise, if it was his own individual property, to make that disposition, or a portion of it, in order to render the other available? And if wise in his own case, is it not wise and proper in our case, also, provided we are the trustees, as the Senator alleges? Clearly I think so. I think, therefore, that is a constitutional disposition of them, a legal disposition of them, which proposes to improve the trust fund and increase its value by this mode of disposing of the property.

But the Senator from Georgia asks me, where is the power to make the purchaser pay double price for the land? Sir, we do not propose to make him pay double price for the land. We have land that is comparatively valueless, if not entirely so, that will not sell at the present price, because, as at present situated, it is not worth it. You cannot get a dollar and a quarter per acre for it, because it is not worth a dollar and a quarter. But we propose now to give away half of it, on condition that the other half shall be rendered worth two and a half dollars per acre. And, after this improvement is made, the land being worth two and a half dollars per acre, the purchaser buys it for what it is worth. Is it any hardship on him to sell him land worth two and a half dollars per acre for two and a half dollars, in preference to compelling him to give one and a quarter dollars for land that is not worth it? It is no tax on the purchaser. If we compel him to pay more money, we give him better land; he gets an equivalent for his money, and therefore it is no tax. It is no more a tax to give ten dollars per acre for land worth that amount, than to give one dollar and a quarter per acre for land only worth one dollar and a quarter. Hence that objection vanishes in a moment. And I must remind the Senator that this point of hardship on the settler, compelling him to pay a double price for the land in question, is done at our own consent; and being so, is it not reasonable to suppose that we have been more likely to look into this question carefully and practically than those so far removed from the scene of action that they cannot have that personal knowledge? Is it probable that I or my colleague would be willing to impose such hardships on the people of our own State? We have put in this provision because we believe it is just to the Government to put it there; because we believe it is just to our own people to put it there. We know that the land is not now worth the Government price. We believe it will be worth double, if not treble, the Government price by the construction of this road. That being the case, it will be for the advantage of the settlers and purchasers, as well as for the advantage of the Government, that the value of the land should be increased, and the price increased also. . . .

SPEECH OF SENATOR WILLIAM H. SEWARD

MR. SEWARD. I have no trouble myself, Mr. President, about the constitutional power of the Government of the United States to make works of national improvement—to construct roads of any kind which shall serve for great national objects. I can conceive of no public improvements more obviously adapted to promote the welfare and prosperity of the country, which are more indispensable to the security of the United States, than a railroad from Lake Michigan to the junction of the Ohio and Mississippi rivers. That being so, I think that the Government of the United States has a discretion as to the manner in which it will accomplish, or aid in accomplishing, such an object, and as to the funds which shall be devoted to that purpose. Then the question before us, so far as the principle is concerned, resolves itself into this: whether, this being a work of such a national character, productive of na-

From *Congressional Globe*, 31st Congress, 1st Session, May 1, 1850, p. 851.

tional benefits, it is one which is entitled to special consideration on the part of Government now. I think it is entitled to very special consideration, which will appear from examining the particular condition of the new States, as contrasted with the old ones. The old States of Massachusetts, Connecticut, New York, Pennsylvania, Virginia, the Carolinas, and Georgia, were all the owners of the public domain with their limits. When it was desirable for them to construct public works, they were always able to appropriate public lands or funds arising from the sold lands, or at least the taxes derived from the lands within their limits. The consequence has been that all the old States, having themselves very considerable resources, have constructed, directly or indirectly, very important public thoroughfares, useful and beneficial to commerce, and particularly to travel, and to the wealth, prosperity, and advancement of the whole country. But they have never been made by mere individual, unassisted enterprise, unless they have been attended by very great delay and embarrassment. A great and extensive country like this has need of roads and canals earlier than there is an accumulation of private capital within the State to construct them; and so an examination of the history of the old States would show that the Government of the States has lent or given its aid, directly or indirectly, to assist individuals or corporations in the construction of these great public works which are now so productive, either to the State or to the individuals by whom, in associated companies, they are owned. . . .[1]

I regard this work, which is now under consideration here, as an extension of that system, and the whole as constituting a great national enterprise—a great national thoroughfare. With me, then, the question is, whether it is wise and expedient to

---

[1] Senator Seward goes on to refer to the internal improvement system of the state of New York, and particularly to the Erie Canal and the railroads to Lake Erie. [ED.]

devote the public lands for the accomplishment of this purpose; and if so, whether it is necessary for the public interest that this road should be made earlier than it would otherwise be by private capital. Now, if it be true, as I have said, that all the old States owning lands within their borders, and having unlimited power to tax, have still found it difficult and embarrassing to prosecute these improvements, then it seems to me the case of new States is essentially harder, and more difficult, and more entitled to the consideration of the Government; for it happens that these new States are founded upon territory belonging to the United States; the United States own the lands, and the government of the States cannot appropriate them. The Government of the United States owns the lands, and they cannot be taxed except so far as they are sold; and these new members of the Confederacy are tributaries to the Federal Government, deprived of the resources which the older States have enjoyed for the purpose of completing their public works. I think, therefore, that the Government owes it to itself, and to the States, to make liberal, and at the same time judicious appropriations, to extend its net-work of railroads and canals over these new regions, where the people and the government are unable to construct the work themselves. And, if there were any apparent fallacy in this argument, I think I should nevertheless be convinced of its soundness, by the fact, that all the new States which have undertaken to construct these necessary thoroughfares—necessary not only for themselves, but for the whole country—necessary for the welfare and prosperity, and even the existence of the Union— have all found themselves embarrassed and crippled, and many of them rendered bankrupt, by the attempt to accomplish objects which they were unable to accomplish, and which the Federal Government had ample power to carry into effect. It is thus that the character of the States has been affected. It is thus that the morality of the governments of the States has been impeached; and it has been done in the manner I have indicated, from the circumstance that it was devolved upon the governments of the States to make works of internal improvement, while the resources which were applicable to that object belonged altogether to the Federal Government.

. . . What, then, is the best and highest interests of the people of the United States in regard to this domain? It is not to derive from it the highest amount of current revenue; it is not to accumulate in our coffers the highest and greatest amount of avails in the sales of the public lands which is attainable. But it is to bring them into cultivation and settlement in the shortest space of time and under the most favorable auspices.

SPEECHES OF SENATOR ANDREW P. BUTLER

Mr. Butler. . . . Now, sir, I am very much inclined to think that the people who settle in Iowa, Wisconsin, Michigan, and those other States in the West, have gone there under the most favorable circumstances, to settle on the richest lands, and to avail themselves of the richest part of the globe. It is very well to talk about the neglect and indifference of the Government to the welfare of new settlers; but, in point of fact, no people were ever so favorably dealt with both by nature and by the laws. They take possession of the richest portion of the globe at a price which is hardly more than a nominal one; and they will have the sceptre, indeed they have already the sceptre, of Government in their hands in this country, and they receive freely of the treasure and resources of the common country to improve that which is of itself so preëminently valuable. They will have what they ask for now, sir. This bill will pass, as I

From *Congressional Globe*, 31st Congress, 1st Session, April 29 and May 2, 1850, pp. 850, 903.

have said. It is linked on to a great many bills to provide great public highways through influential States, and I am well assured that the plan will be accomplished; but I am not very willing that the Congress of the United States should be made the instrument of diverting the natural currents of trade and travel in favor of certain localities, by virtue of a merely incidental circumstance, such as that the public lands of the country lie exclusively in certain States. I shall vote against it in every shape into which you may put it. . . .

. . . It is not an equitable distribution of the common property of the States of which the Government of the United States is a mere trustee, and for whose benefit we are bound to administer them.

My friend from Alabama knows very well what he is about. He knows that he is carrying this road to Mobile through his own State; and, so far as it is likely to contribute to the advancement of his State, I am glad of it. But perhaps the old thirteen States will be like Lear, who made bountiful gifts to his children and was afterwards turned out of doors himself. I am opposed to the whole principle of using the public lands for building private roads; for this is essentially a private road, although it belongs to the State of Illinois; and that part of it I believe which is to pass through Alabama and Mississippi belongs to a company. Well, if it results in benefit to the public I do not object to it, but it is absolutely using public property for private purposes. Now my friend from Alabama used a pretty strong expression. He says that Congress, in the plenitude of its power, has a right to make any appropriation of money that may come within the purview of its policy. Now, I ask him if he would make an appropriation of land for the purpose of building a national highway from Washington to New Orleans? Sir, when I give away the public lands for the making of this or that road, I wish to have some good ground for doing so; and it becomes me, and every one else, in the exercise of our discretion in relation to this part of the public property, to inquire whether there are good grounds. If I were to make a public road I would make one from here to New Orleans, and gentlemen could easily get such a road. Now, let it be understood that we want such a road, and let us agree also with my friend from Alabama in his latitudinarian construction of this clause of the Constitution, and we can soon raise money enough to build it. There is no difficulty in getting the money upon his mode of calculation. I observe that the mode in which many gentlemen construe certain provisions of the Constitution greatly depends upon local patriotism. (*Laughter.*)

7. Captain Douglas Galton: Government Aid Without Government Interference

Captain Douglas Galton of the Royal Engineers came to observe the railways of the United States near the end of our period and reported on them to the Privy Council's Committee on Trade and Foreign Plantations. He wrote of Senator Douglas's Illinois Central Railroad as a notable recent achievement and of a transcontinental railroad as the next great step ahead. Regarding the latter he noted that the choice of possible routes had been somewhat narrowed by the explorations carried on by the Army,[1] and he urged Canada to enter the competition, perhaps using convict labor to carry a line across the Rocky Mountains.

The principal objective of the earlier railroads had been, as he points out, to connect the eastern seaboard with the interior. Of the four roads that had accomplished this, only the New York Central, with its "favourable gradients," had done so al-

[1] "Reports of Explorations and Surveys to Ascertain the Most Practical and Economical Route for a Railroad from the Mississippi River to the Pacific Ocean," 33rd Congress, 2nd Session, *House Documents No. 91.*

most entirely without public aid. The other three had reached "the fertile lands in the west" with funds drawn about equally from private and public sources, with state aid for the Erie and municipal subscriptions for the other two. But Captain Galton shared what had come to be general disillusion with most forms of public promotion. Popularly elected officials were not competent to run railroads and the combination of private and public management was "false in principle."

One form of public aid, however, seemed to him free from this objection—construction "by a company to whom lands have been granted, but which otherwise has not been interfered with." This method had been remarkably successful in promoting development. Under frontier conditions, "any amount of land is well applied which will induce a company to construct a railway." The federal land grant, in Captain Galton's opinion, was an admirable social invention embodying government assistance without government intervention, and it might well be adopted under comparable conditions in the British dominions.

Railway Department, Board of Trade, Whitehall
8th December 1856

MY LORDS,

In the course of a rapid journey which I made through the United States during the last autumn, I took every opportunity of observing the railway system of that country; and as it presents many points of interest connected more especially with the extension of railways in new countries, I have thought it desirable to lay before your Lordships the following short summary of the information which I gathered.

From Captain Douglas Galton, *Report to the Lords of the Committee of Privy Council for Trade and Foreign Plantations on the Railways of the United States* (London, 1857), pp. 3–8, 10, 27.

OUTLINE OF THE RAILWAY SYSTEM

OF THE UNITED STATES

The European communities at the period of the introduction of railways possessed a fixed population, fair means of internal communication, and a considerable trade, so that the elements existed for calculating beforehand the probable amount of traffic which a railway would obtain, and the probable profit to be realized; a large amount of capital was also available for their construction; and when first opened for traffic, European railways were placed in a tolerably complete state.

In America the conditions were quite different. There were, indeed, large cities situated on the sea coast, or inland on the rivers, which formed the chief highways, but the rest of the country was either sparsely settled, or uninhabited except by Indians; the means of communication were indifferent, and trade was consequently undeveloped; but the immigration which was continually flowing westward required extensive facilities for transport.

Capital was, however, scarce; and as in a new country it is impossible to foresee at the opening of a railway where the main centres of traffic will eventually be, it would have been a mere waste to invest more capital in the construction of a railway than would render it efficient for the work immediately before it; a further expenditure being incurred as the requirements of the traffic became gradually apparent.

It is also to be borne in mind that a railroad causes the absorption, not only of the capital actually required for its construction, but, of a very much larger amount, for developing the resources of the country through which it passes. This is very apparent at the present time on the prairies; there the fertile loam, of which they are composed, is unsuited to the construction of a common road; but railways are laid easily and cheaply, and their establishment is immediately followed by the settlement of the country. The Illinois Central Railway is an instance of this. When first opened three years ago, the station-houses were almost the only habitations on the line; now there is a large village at each station, surrounded by vast tracts of cultivated ground. When I passed along the line last autumn, sacks of corn covered every available spot round the stations, and the means of the company were scarcely adequate for removing them.

The different circumstances under which railways are constructed, and the different instrument required, in a new as compared with an old country, would render it almost impossible to form any fair comparison between the relative cost of railways in Europe and the United States, even if there were any reliable summary of the cost of American railways; but none exists. . . .

The railways of the United States appear to have been designed principally with the view of connecting the sea coast with the fertile lands in the west; but the range of the Alleghany Mountains rising in the north near Lake Ontario, and running nearly parallel to the coast, intersects every line of travel between the important commercial sea-board cities and the western districts.

The direct eastern and western traffic which traverses this range passes over four principal railway routes, viz.:—

1st. The New York Central Railway, which is a link in the communication from Boston to the West; this is connected with New York by the Hudson River Railroad, and is connected with western lines at Niagara and Buffalo. This line passes up the valley of the Mohawk, and has favourable gradients along its whole length.

2nd. The New York and Erie Railway, which, crossing the Alleghany Mountains near the head waters of the Susquehanna and Delaware, forms a connexion with western lines at Niagara and along the south shore of Lake Erie.

3rd. The Pennsylvania Central Railway, which runs from Philadelphia to Pittsburg, and there forms a connexion with the railways crossing the centre of Ohio.

4th. The Baltimore and Ohio Railway, from Baltimore to Wheeling, and thence to Columbus and Cincinnati.

It is not probable that, for the present, any other line will be carried across the Alleghany mountains, at least to the north of Baltimore. Hence the development of the Western States, and the projected railroads to the Pacific, will add to the important traffic which these several roads already possess. . . .

The great question, however, of railway extension from east to west, which now occupies the attention of the American public, is the construction of a railway to connect the Eastern States with the Pacific Ocean. Five routes have been proposed, but the most practicable are limited to the three following lines, viz.—

1st. From St. Paul's to Vancouver, near the parallel of 48°.
2nd. From Council Bluffs to Benicia, which is near to San Francisco, viâ the south-west pass, near the parallel of 42°.
3rd. From Fulton to San Pedro, near the parallel of 32°.

The following comparison of the routes is obtained from the Secretary of State's report to Congress on the subject, viz.:—

	Length *Miles*	Height of Summit Level or Passes *Feet*	Estimated Cost	Proportion of Arable Land through which they pass
1st.	1,864	6,044	£25,000,000	30 per cent.
2nd.	2,032	8,733	£23,000,000	35 "
3rd.	1,618	5,717	£17,000,000	45 "

The question of a means of communication across this continent is one which Great Britain should not leave to be solved by the United States alone.

It would be foreign to the object of this report to discuss

this question, but it will not be superfluous to observe that the large American population which is flocking year after year to the new territories in the United States which adjoin the British possessions, render it almost necessary, if further complications on the subject of the boundary are to be avoided, that the country should be colonized on the British side. Political, commercial, and military considerations make it desirable that Vancouver's Island should become an important colony and be connected by railway with Canada. The land between Lake Superior and the Red River is known to be fertile, and it is probable that this fertility extends far beyond; hence a private company might be induced by grants of land to construct that portion of the railway which would lie between Lake Superior and some point a short distance to the east of the Rocky Mountains. The main difficulty lies at the Rocky Mountains. This portion would, however, afford a good opportunity for employing convict labour; and the construction of docks and other public works at Vancouver would enable this colony to be continued as a penal settlement for some years to come.

The principal north and south route, not including the railways along the eastern coast, is the Illinois Central Railway. This Railway runs from Cairo at the confluence of the Mississippi and Ohio rivers to Chicago and Dubuque; and from its termini lines are projected to run northwards to Superior City and southwards to Mobile on the Gulf of Mexico.

Chicago is the chief focus of railway communication in the west, and may be called the offspring of the railway system. . . .

RAILWAY LEGISLATION

The necessity which communities in a new country feel for means of intercommunication led the Legislatures and the people of the several States to give as many inducements as possible to the construction of railways. The owners of the land had, generally speaking, no ties to the soil and regarded their farms as an investment to be materially benefited by the proximity of a railway; they therefore usually afforded every assistance to its progress. But occasionally, no doubt, they have exacted what was, in America, a high price for their land. American railway companies have, however, on the whole been subject to very much lower charges on this account than English railway companies.

Railways in the United States appear to have been constructed under four different arrangements:—

1st. By the State.

2nd. By a company to whose share capital, or mortgage debt, the State has contributed, retaining an interest in the line and some power of interference.

3rd. By a company to whom lands have been granted, but which otherwise has not been interfered with.

4th. By a company unassisted, and therefore not interfered with.

1st. The railways made by the State do not appear to have been successful. The officers who are appointed to manage them are chosen by universal suffrage, sometimes annually, sometimes triennially; they are elected rather for political reasons than for being specially qualified for the duty. State railways have consequently not proved remunerative, and they have generally been transferred to private companies.

In Pennsylvania the line between Philadelphia and Harrisburg is held by the State, which maintains the road and furnishes locomotive power. The cars for passengers and freight are supplied by any parties who will place them on the road, paying a specified toll and adhering to certain regulations. The management of and the returns from the line are not satisfactory under this system, and it is in contemplation to transfer the working of the line to the Pennsylvanian Central Railway Company, which forms a continuation of it.

2nd. The States and municipal corporations have, in several

instances, given assistance to railway companies. In most cases the State or the corporation of the town has reserved to itself the right of appointing directors in proportion to the amount contributed; but as these directors are generally elected by universal suffrage for short periods, they often desire to regulate the management of the railway more with reference to local political objects, than to its interests as a commercial speculation.

This arrangement is therefore false in principle, and combines two conflicting elements. If the railway is a commercial speculation, the management should be left to the Company; if, on the contrary, it is to be worked with a political object, the commercial element should be left out of view, and the line be wholly managed by the State.

When the State has advanced money to a railway company, the only sound principle upon which a power of interference should be reserved to the State would seem to be this: to take security that the money shall be properly applied to the work, to require publicity of the accounts of the company, and to lay down specific terms upon which the traffic is to be conducted; but to leave to the company full powers of management, subject to these conditions.

3rd. The mode by which the State induces a company to construct a railway by grants of land is one which deserves attention, as being especially applicable in many of our colonial possessions.

This system is resorted to in the Western States with a remarkable degree of success. In these States the fertility of the soil cannot be made available without means of communication, and any amount of land is well applied which will induce a company to construct a railway. In all new territories the land is surveyed in lots each containing a square mile. The railway company, to whom land is granted, is allowed to take, in addition to the actual land required for the line, a specified quantity in alternate lots on each side within a certain distance from the line. In case any of those lots which would naturally fall to the company should have been previously bought by individuals, the railway company selects other lots.

This system gives security to capitalists for their investment. It makes it the interest and the business of the company to publish the merits of the district, and, by offering facilities to the travelling public, to induce the settlement of the country; hence, the value of the alternate lots of land which are retained by the State is increased.

The State, in granting the land, generally reserves a percentage on the gross receipts of the company. On the Illinois Central Railway this amount is 7 per cent.

As the progress of this railway affords a striking illustration of the advantages of this method, it appears desirable to give a brief account of it.

The company was formed for the purpose of making a railway through Illinois from Cairo, at the confluence of the Ohio and Mississippi, to Dubuque on the Mississippi, with a branch line to Chicago. Its course lay chiefly through prairie land, only inhabited at a few points. On the 20th September 1850, Congress granted to the State of Illinois 2,595,000 acres of land to aid in the construction of the Illinois Central Railroad. The vacant lands, in alternate sections within 6 miles of the road, were conveyed by direct terms in the grant, and, in lieu of such portions as had been previously sold, selections were authorized to be made between 6 and 15 miles on each side of the road. The company was incorporated by the Legislature of the State of Illinois in 1851, and the grant conferred upon it. The company created a capital stock of 17,000,000 dollars, on which 25 per cent. has been paid; and, for the additional money required for the construction of the railway, they have raised 20,000,000 dollars by mortgage on the security of 2,345,000 acres of the land granted to them, and they have reserved 250,000 acres, the proceeds from which are to assist in paying the interest on this mortgage.

The ordinary price of new land in the States is one dollar per acre; the Company are selling the land at prices varying from

5 to 25 dollars per acre, which is paid for in five annual instalments with 3 per cent. interest. When the last instalment has been paid, commissioners appointed by the State grant a title to the purchasers of the land upon the railway company producing to them such a number of mortgage bonds cancelled as amount to the price they have received for the land.

This line runs for the greater part of its course through prairie land without trees, land, which with a small expenditure of labour, produces most luxuriant crops.

When the line was first opened the country was nearly uninhabited; stations were placed at every 8 or 10 miles, round which villages and in some cases towns have sprung up, and fields of corn and herds of cattle are now to be seen on every side. If well managed, this railway should prove most lucrative to the shareholders. It has already largely developed the resources of the State, and the per-centage which it pays to the Government will eventually relieve the State from taxation to a considerable extent.

4th. A large number of railways have been constructed without State assistance.

It is, therefore, desirable to describe here the arrangements under which railway companies are ordinarily incorporated.

In a majority of States general railroad laws have been passed, enabling corporations to be formed for making railways, the course of which is to be approved of by Railroad Commissioners or by some executive authority, due notice of the intended route being given in order that all persons affected may have an opportunity to object. Very large discretionary powers are left with the commissioners as regards crossing roads, streets, rivers, &c. But as a general rule the companies prefer special charters, which confer greater privileges. A projected railroad is sometimes opposed on grounds of public inconvenience, but I was informed that opposition by individuals on private grounds is unknown and would not be tolerated. . . .

The charter usually gives the company great latitude in the selection of its route. When, therefore, the charter is obtained, the company frequently selects the route upon which the land can be obtained on the most favourable terms. A large proportion of the share capital is frequently raised amongst persons on the line of railway, and most of the work is paid for in bonds issued often at a great depreciation: and a further floating debt is frequently incurred. From the report of the Railroad Commissioners of New York it would appear that the money raised for the construction of railways in that State may be divided into forty-seven per cent. by shares, forty-nine per cent. by mortgage bonds, and four per cent. by floating debt, unsecured. . . .

5th. Those general legislative provisions for securing the public interests, which appear principally to deserve notice, are, that the railway companies shall keep their lines in repair and open for public use, and that they shall supply sufficient accommodation, and transport merchandise and property without partiality, favour, or affection, and with all practicable dispatch. That a railway company is prohibited from exercising the calling of a banker, broker, or dealer in any article whatever. That in some States a government department is empowered to inquire minutely into the causes of railway accidents, to examine witnesses on oath, and to call for all necessary books, papers, &c., and to publish their reports.

6th. But it is with reference to the construction of railways in our own colonies that the American system deserves especial notice. The considerations which led to the adoption of, and the necessities which fostered, that system apply with equal force to railways in the colonies. It appears, therefore, desirable to call attention to some of the deductions which may be drawn from the consideration of this system.

a. A railway would appear to be the best road for arterial lines of communication in a new country.

b. In making railways in a new country, bearing in mind the high rate of interest which money commands, the outlay for construction should be as small as possible consistent with safety and economy of working; the object being to devote the money, to be spent, to extending the mileage and opening out the country, rather than to making very solid works or to obtaining high speeds.

   c. Railways made by the States in America have not proved successful, in consequence of the persons selected to manage them being chosen for political considerations.

   d. The encouragement given to private companies for the construction of railways in new states, by means of grants of land, has proved very successful. It has facilitated the rapid settlement of the country and the development of its resources. It has directly benefited the State by enhancing the price of the land retained by the State, as well as by the permanent reduction of the general taxation occasioned by the contribution of seven per cent. on the gross receipts of the railway reserved to the State in consideration of the grant of land. But the successful instances of this system are limited to localities where land is of a superior quality, and the climate favourable.

   I cannot close this report without expressing to your Lordships how much I am indebted for the information which I have obtained, to the invariable courtesy that I received from every person connected with railways in the United States and Canada, and to the great readiness with which they furnished me with all the particulars in their power.

I have the honour to be, &c.

Douglas Galton
Captain, Royal Engineers

*The Lords of the Committee
   of Privy Council for Trade and Foreign Plantations*

PART TWO

THE ENCOURAGEMENT OF

WESTERN SETTLEMENT

8. Georgia: A State Homestead Policy

The opening of the West to agricultural settlement was a major purpose and a major achievement of the efforts to promote the construction of internal improvements. It was also encouraged by a variety of other acts of government, whether or not this was their stated purpose. The advance of settlement profited from the results of governmental efforts in exploration, like that of Lewis and Clark, which was first described as "literary" in purpose,[1] and of many later expeditions conducted by army engineers. Pioneers could move westward by what was called a "mil-

---

[1] See Document 23 below.

itary road as readily as by any other;[2] and the settlers on each successive frontier demanded that the national government perform the services of protection from the Indians and their ultimate removal by negotiation or force.

Another major method of encouragement was to make public land available to the settler on easy terms. It was on this issue that the greatest debates over settlement policy took place not only in the Congress, which had the lion's share of the land to divide, but in a number of the state legislatures as well. Of the latter, Georgia provides an early example. When its boundaries were established, Georgia was left with much more territory beyond the boundaries of white settlement than most of the other original states, though it was land that would become available only in successive stages as the federal government performed its function of securing cessions from the Creek and Cherokee nations. Disposal of this land, as Professor Heath says, "constituted the leading business of the state during the first third of the nineteenth century."[3]

A substantial body of Creek land became available in 1802, and the basic decisions of policy were made in the following year and embodied in the law that is cited below. The objective of encouraging settlement was given precedence over the objective of revenue. Settlers were to be chosen by the device of a public lottery, in which a single man or a family of orphans had one chance or "draw" and a family or widow with at least one child had two chances. The winners in the lottery were entitled to take up lots of uniform size. Though the original law provided for sales at modest prices, varying with the quality of the land, an amendment adopted in the same year abolished all charges except a standard fee of four dollars per hundred acres. Fractional lands, however, which did not fit into the pattern of the uniform lots, were to be sold,

---

2 W. Turrentine Jackson, *Wagon Roads West* (Berkeley and Los Angeles: University of California Press, 1952).

3 Milton S. Heath, *Constructive Liberalism: The Role of the State in Economic Development in Georgia to 1860* (Cambridge: Harvard University Press, 1954), ch. 7, especially p. 145.

and special provision was made for laying out the town of Milledgeville. The same general principles were followed in a series of lottery acts through 1832. "Under this policy some 26,000,000 acres, or nearly three-fourths of the area of the state, were distributed among more than 100,000 individuals or families."[4]

The Georgia act of 1803 represented in spirit and purpose a close approximation to the national homestead act adopted nearly sixty years later, though the size of the lots—202½ and 490 acres—was larger than the federal quarter section of 160 acres. In a sense, then, this southern slave state may be thought of as having anticipated a program that the nation was later to adopt under the pressure of northern free-soil interests.

The Georgia experience also foreshadowed the national experience in a less important respect. Some of the eager winners in the lottery rushed to take up their plots in the newly ceded territory before the land could be made ready for them. Accordingly, in 1804 the legislature adopted an act "to compel trespassers on the lands south of the Oconee, lately ceded by the Creek Indians, to return within the settled limits of the state." Against this measure a group of representatives drafted an indignant protest, which is reproduced below, and spread it on the records of the House of Representatives. Though admitting that the settlers "have intruded on the lands of this state contrary to right and to the deuties of good citizens," the protesters denounce the repressive measure as a violation of the promises of the 1803 act and of "the charter of their liberties."

By a close vote the House rejected the protest on the ground that it encouraged "a spirit of insurrection and disobedience to the laws of this state." Similar conflicts over the rights of unauthorized settlers were also to occur in federal land policy; and, as Document 11 will show, the defenders of "trespassers" on the public land would not always be in the minority.

---

[4] *Ibid.*

THE FIRST LOTTERY ACT

AN ACT TO MAKE DISTRIBUTION OF THE LATE CESSION OF LANDS,

OBTAINED FROM THE CREEK NATION BY THE UNITED STATES'

COMMISSIONERS, IN A TREATY ENTERED INTO AT OR NEAR

FORT WILKINSON, ON THE 16TH DAY OF JUNE, 1802.—

PASSED MAY 11, 1803.

103. Sec. I.   The territory south of the Oconee and Alatamaha rivers . . . to which the Indian title has been extinguished by treaty, concluded near Fort Wilkinson, on the 16th day of June, 1802: shall, in conformity to the twenty-third section of the first article of the constitution of this state, be laid off into three counties in the following manner. . . .

104. Sec. II.   The lands contained in the several districts shall be divided by lines running parallel with the dividing lines of districts, and by others crossing them at right angles, so as to form tracts of forty-five chains square, containing 202½ acres each, plainly and distinctly marked, in a manner different from the ordinary mode heretofore pursued, for marking lines in this state, to be pointed out by the surveyor general; except the county of Wayne, which shall be laid off into tracts of seventy chains square, and to contain 490 acres each, unless where the line which is to form a temporary boundary between the said territory and Creek Indians, or the course of navigable rivers, may render it impracticable, and then this rule shall be departed from no further than such particular circumstances may require; and all fractional parts of surveys, which may be created by the courses of navigable rivers, by the temporary

From Oliver H. Prince, *Digest of the Laws of the State of Georgia* (Milledgeville: Grantland & Orme, 1822), pp. 284–287.

boundary line, or other unavoidable circumstances, and all islands within the limits of said territory, and lying southwest of the middle or main source of the Oconee or Alatamaha rivers, shall be reserved and sold, and the funds arising therefrom, be appropriated in such manner as a future legislature may direct.

106. Sec. VIII. . . . Every free male white person, twenty-one years of age and upwards, being a citizen of the United States, and an inhabitant of this state, twelve months immediately preceding the passage of this act, or who has paid a tax towards the support of government, (including such as may be absent on lawful business,) shall be entitled to one draw; every free white male person of like description, having a wife, legitimate child or children, under twenty-one years of age, shall be entitled to two draws; and all widows having a legitimate child or children under the age of twenty-one years, who have resided twelve months in this state immediately preceding the passage of this act, shall be entitled to two draws; and all families of orphans, under twenty-one years of age, having no parents living, shall be entitled to one draw.

107. Sec. IX. Lists of persons entitled to draw, in conformity to the provisions of this act, shall be taken and made out, within three months from the passage thereof, by any three or more of the justices of the inferior courts of the respective counties, or such fit and proper persons as they may appoint, not exceeding one for each county, who shall, previous to their entering on the duties of their appointment, severally enter into bond and security, to be approved by the said justices, in such reasonable sum as they may deem necessary, for the faithful discharge of the trust reposed in them, and also take and subscribe an oath in writing, faithfully to perform the duties required of them by this act. And it shall be the duty of the said justices, or any three or more of them, or such persons as they may appoint, to attend at the court-houses of the respective counties, on as many several days as the said justices

may deem necessary and appoint, for the purpose of taking and making out such lists, giving at least ten days previous notice of such attendance by advertisement, at five or more of the most public places in the respective counties; and the names of all persons entitled to draw, with the number of draws to which they may be entitled, shall be entered into a book, to be provided for that purpose in each county, which said list or book shall, immediately after the same shall have been completed and transcripts thereof deposited in the clerk's office of the superior courts be transmitted by the said justices to his excellency the governor. . . .

109. Sec. XVI.   Immediately after the boundary line shall be run agreeably to this act, five commissioners to be appointed by the legislature, shall, at the most eligible and suitable place at or near the head of navigation on the south side of the Oconee river, lay out a tract of land containing 3240 acres, or sixteen of the aforementioned tracts of 202½ acres each, as laid off by the district surveyors; which is hereby reserved and set apart for a town, to be called and known by the name of Milledgeville; and shall on such part as they may deem most proper, lay off lots containing one acre each; and shall lay a plan of the said tract of land, together with a plan of the town before the next general assembly, and such number of lots shall be disposed of as they may deem expedient.

An Act to alter and amend the foregoing.—Passed December 6, 1803.

110. Sec. I.   The person against whose names any survey or surveys of land shall be drawn in pursuance of the before-recited act, or their legal representatives, shall be entitled to receive grants for the same, vesting in them fee simple titles free of purchase, immediately on paying into the treasury of this state, the sum of four dollars per hundred acres, in lieu of

all fees of office and other charges, for surveying and granting the said land, any thing in the said act contained to the contrary notwithstanding.

PROTEST ON THE REMOVAL OF TRESPASSERS

Mr. Walker then moved in behalf of himself and the persons whose names are thereunto subscribed the following protest, to wit:

PROTEST

Anxious as we are to guard with vigilant circumspection, the constitution of our country, which we have more than once sworn to support; and solicitous as we are for the harmony, prosperity and happiness of the good people of the state of Georgia, whose interest to promote, we have solemnly appealed to the great disposer of events—We should deem it a departure from that duty which we owe those persons who have honored us with their confidence, as well as a departure from that duty we owe ourselves, as members of this legislature, were we to let the act entitled, an act to compel trespassers on the lands south of the Oconee, lately ceded by the Creek Indians, to return within the settled limits of the state pass, without solemnly protesting against it.

Among the reasons which produced our opposition to the passage of this act, we have thought proper to enumerate the following:

1st. For that the said act is a violation of the 10th Sec. of the 1st. Art. of the federal constitution, which declares that "no

From Georgia *Journal of the House of Representatives,* December 3, 1804, pp. 53–54.

state shall pass any bill of attainder, or law impairing the obligation of contracts."

To prove this, we have only to compare the act now on its passage, with the law passed the [11th] day of [May][1] 1803, entitled an act to make distribution of the late cession of land obtained from the Creek nation, by the U. States commissioners, in a treaty entered into at or near Fort Wilkinson, on the 16th day of June, 1802.

The law just mentioned gave each citizen of the state of Georgia, a right to a ticket or draw in said lottery upon his paying a certain sum of money therein stipulated: when the citizen had paid this stipulated price, the contract was no longer executory but executed, both parties were bound, nor could the contract be annulled, but by mutual consent. Notwithstanding this proposition is one founded in reason, and one which cannot be denied, until a knowledge of the law of contracts shall become extinct. Yet has this legislature in violation of the above recited clause of the constitution, passed an act, which in its tendency must necessarily annul the contract, thus entered into and executed between the state and her citizens, in as much as it declares that unless persons who shall have settled on the south side of the Oconee, and shall not return upon the issuing of the governors proclamation, commanding them to return, that they shall forfeit all their right in said lottery. Thereby in effect inflicting in part the pains of an attainder, in farther derogation of the aforementioned clause of the constitution.

2ndly. For that the mode pointed out by said act, for ascertaining refractory persons, is incompatible with the genius and spirit of a free government, in as much as it establishes a set of spies, informers, and inquisitors, who are empowered to report at discretion to the executive, the names of such persons. Thus

---

[1] The date has been added by the present editor. [ED.]

placing it in the power of those inquisitors, to exercise a spirit of favoritism, or malevolence at discretion, in effect leaving it optional with them to say what persons shall continue in the occupancy of the soil, and who shall be forced from their houses, and compelled to seek subsistance from the munificence of those who from motives of charity and humanity, may feel themselves bound to administer to their relief, thereby prostrating that equality of rights which is the boast of free-men, and to guarantee which, our incomparable constitution was formed.

3dly. For that the said act authorises the governor to call forth military force, against persons from other states, in case of disobedience to his proclamation. We conceive but few arguments are necessary to prove the impropriety of this extraordinary measure; by this act an unwarrantable distinction is created between persons who were inhabitants of Georgia at the time of the passage of the first act disposing of this territory, and those who have emigrated to this state since that time, which is contrary to the 2d Sec. of the 4th Art. of the federal constitution—independent of this consideration, we view in the progress of this law all the horrors of a civil war.

4thly. For that all those enormities might have been completely done away, by carrying into immediate effect the lottery under the act making distribution of the aforesaid tract of territory, pursuant to contract, made with the good people of this state, which contract we humbly conceive has been violated to the great injury of our citizens, by the refusal on the part of the majority of this house to comply with the requisitions thereof.

Whilst the undersigned depricate the measures adopted by a majority of this house, because they consider it a violation of the charter of their liberties, yet they do not hesitate unequivocally to declare that in their opinion, those persons who are now settled on the south side of the Oconee river, have intruded on the lands of this state contrary to right and to the deuties of good citizens; therefore merit the censure of this house, and of every friend to his country.

T. FLOURNOY	W. FITZPATRICK
F. WALKER	M. SPEER
W. W. BIBB	WM. CONE
B. HALL	E. HOBSON WOODFORD
TIM. BARNARD, JUN.	MABRY
E. FAINE	

9. Thomas J. D. Fuller: The Public Domain as a Source of Revenue

The case of Georgia illustrates the issues of land disposal and to some degree foreshadowed the direction of later policy, but the major decisions regarding the public domain were those of the federal government. This is so for the obvious reason that by far the greater share of the unoccupied lands was the property of the nation rather than of the states. East of the Mississippi, the entire Old Northwest, as well as Alabama, Mississippi, and Florida constituted "public land states." West of the Mississippi, only Texas—by inheritance from its days as a Republic—retained possession of its own broad expanses of open land. The total area of unoccupied land at the disposal of the federal government during the period was almost 1,300,000,000 acres or about 2,000,000 square miles. No authority ever had so lordly a domain to divide, and it is not surprising that the land question took a major place in congressional debate.

In these debates there were two principal points of view. The one was that the public domain should be used primarily as a source of revenue for the nation as a whole. The other was that the primary purpose of land disposal was to promote settlement and western expansion.

The revenue policy had obvious and strong attractions; the return from land sales could reduce the amount of taxation or, alternatively, increase the government expenditures. Different uses of the resource were prominent at different stages in the debate. The first Congress pledged the revenues from public domain as security for the public debt. "If timely and judiciously applied," said Washington, "they may save the necessity of burthening our citizens with new taxes for the extinguishment of the principal."[1] Many years later, a House committee proposed that the federal government issue bonds on the security of the public domain, in order to pay off the debts of the states that had defaulted on the obligations they had incurred for internal improvements and other purposes.[2] A revenue policy was also appealing when surpluses were expected or at hand. John Quincy Adams looked to the land revenues as the source of a national revolving fund that would provide "unfailing streams of improvement from the Atlantic to the Pacific Ocean."[3] In 1833 Henry Clay secured passage of a bill, which Andrew Jackson vetoed, for distributing the land revenue to the states so that they could construct their own internal improvements.

As the frontier advanced, concern over revenue from land sales tended to give way to concern for the promotion of settlement. Yet in the 1852 debate on a homestead bill, Congressman Fuller of Maine declared without qualification that the only proper use of the public domain was as a fiscal resource for the nation as a whole. The bill, he said, is "partial and unjust." The public domain is the property of the whole people. Part of it was given to the nation by certain of the original states on the express condition that it should be used

---

[1] Third Annual Message, October 25, 1791, in James D. Richardson, *A Compilation of the Messages and Papers of the Presidents, 1789–1903* (New York: Bureau of National Literature and Art, 1897–1920), vol. I, p. 108.

[2] *House Report No. 296*, 27th Congress, 3rd Session, March 2, 1843. John Quincy Adams was a member of the Committee.

[3] First Annual Message, December 6, 1825, in Richardson, *Messages and Papers of the Presidents*, vol. II, p. 305.

only for the "common benefit." The rest was obtained through
the efforts of the United States as a whole. Congress has
therefore no right to take away part of the common heritage
and give it to a "select favored few."

Mr. Fuller.—I regard the bill as *unconstitutional, partial,*
and *unjust* in its provisions. . . .

. . . I deny that this Government holds the public domain by
such a *tenure* as that it is susceptible of any such severance and
partition as is prayed for by the bill. I ask by what right—by
what warrant—by what title deeds—a certain class of persons,
aliens and foreigners, or citizens of a limited age—of a particular condition in their domestic relations—of a particular condition in their pecuniary affairs—as they chanced to be, on the
1st day of January, 1852, appear here and claim that all, or any
portion of the public lands—the common property of the whole
people of the United States—shall gratuitously be set off to
them, by metes and bounds, and thereafter be held and owned
in severalty, to the exclusion of a much greater portion of the
people, possessing equal rights and equal privileges.

Sir, if there be any one subject, having a political or legislative bearing, upon which the American people are more sensi-
tive than any other, it is, the partial and unequal bestowment
of Government favors, pensions or bounties. The axiom that
"the blessings of Government, like the dews of heaven, should
fall alike equally upon all," meets with an affirmative response
from every breast. . . .

If you open the door for the distribution of the public lands,
there is no stopping-place; each successive Congress must ex-

---

From *Congressional Globe,* 32nd Congress, 1st Session, March 30, 1852,
Appendix, pp. 386-390.

ceed its predecessor until every man, woman, and child shall receive their quarter section, or else universal dissatisfaction will follow. . . .

I hold that the proceeds of these lands should be paid into the common Treasury and thereby lighten the burdens common to us all. I hold, sir, that the public domain is as much a legitimate source of revenue to this Government as duties on imports, and should be so applied. . . .

Now, sir, I come to the main subject of my argument, and I affirm these three positions as applicable to our public lands:

1. That the public lands shall be *disposed of* for the use and common benefit of all the people of the United States, as a whole.

2. That each State shall participate in that common benefit, according to its respective and proper proportion in the general charge and expenditure.

3. That they shall not be disposed of for any other use or purpose whatsoever.

Now, sir, this bill proposes to divert these lands from the *general charge and expenditure,* and to bestow them, not upon all the people, but upon a *select favored few.* Is this honestly executing the trust? The seven States from whom the United States derived its title, and all its claim, are now represented upon this floor by eighty-seven Representatives. I ask you if you can sit quietly by and witness so gross and palpable a violation of the objects and purposes for which these grants were made—yea, more—be instrumental in thus violating the sacred compact? From the perusal of these deeds of cessions it will be noticed that four of them, New York, Massachusetts, Connecticut, and South Carolina, contain the language that the cessions were made.

First, New York—"for the only use and benefit of such of the United States." &c

Second, Massachusetts—"be disposed of for the common benefit."

Third, Connecticut—"for the common use and benefit of said states."

Fourth, South Carolina—"for the common benefit of the Union."

The deeds of Virginia, North Carolina, and Georgia contain not only the same language, but go further, and prescribe how the common benefit is to be realized, and *in what proportion* each State shall share in this common fund, *viz.*: according "to *the respective and usual proportion in the general charge and expenditure.*" What is this general charge? Has it ceased to exist? Your common treasury has a continual drain and charge upon it—increasing most fearfully within the past few years. And yet you propose to divert from it a portion of its accustomed supply.

These conveyances are in terms perpetual; no change in the destination of the funds, arising from their *disposal,* is contemplated. It is for the payment of no particular debt, to which they stand pledged, but for the *"common benefit"*—*"common use"* of the United States, so long as a charge remains upon the treasury. These donors or grantors, for the purpose of preventing themselves at any future day from being deprived of their *"share,"* or *proportion,* and to clinch the nail, so far as confidence could be reposed in the integrity of man, added the words, *"to be faithfully and bona fide applied for that purpose, and for no other use or purpose whatsoever."* Such, sir, is the language of the deeds under which you hold your title in trust, which trust appears on their face; and I submit whether, from these deeds, I have not made good my three propositions. . . .

But, it may be said, the deeds from the seven old States cover but a small portion of the territory of the United States. Now, the fact is that a consideration in money was actually paid by the United States in each of the three treaties made with France, Spain, and Mexico—thirty-five millions in the aggregate—besides the accumulating interest, and the yielding up of Texas to Spain, and the expense of two wars, which formed only a part of the consideration for the acquisition of the remaining territory. Can the Government do that *indirectly* which it cannot constitutionally do *directly?* This territory represents money to the extent it has been paid for it—the land cannot be appropriated to any other object than the money could have been before it was turned into land. If this reasoning be incorrect, the Government is without limitation as to the purposes for which it may appropriate money. All it has to do is to turn money into *"stocks"* or *"lands,"* and then it may make appropriations for any conceivable object, and thus accomplish by indirect means what it cannot and ought not to accomplish by direct means. If the land States, by reason of the public domain being within their exterior limits, have superior rights to, or claims over, this *"common property,"* so have the old States to the custom houses, forts, arsenals, and other public property situated within *their* limits. Where is the distinction? In the latter case the old States *ceded* their jurisdiction—in the former case the new States, in quite as solemn and formal a manner, pledged their faith not to assert property or jurisdiction over the public domain. . . .

Our present system is, in my opinion, just and equal toward all sections and interests of the country. I seek no change—I desire none. I ask nothing for my own section of country that I am unwilling to extend to every other section. I disclaim all sectional feeling. I believe our past growth has been greatly promoted by the existing policy. If it shall be materially changed, it cannot fail to produce gloomy apprehensions for the future growth and prosperity of the people. Our present land system operates like a great balance wheel upon our political institutions. It regulates the value of real property; it controls the wages of labor; and so long as one day's work will purchase an acre of productive land, and secure a certain and sure title, directly from the Government—Eastern manufacturers can never control the wages of labor. The value of real property in the agricultural regions of the older States is ad-

justed, in a great measure, by this system. As our population
increases and becomes more dense, they will emigrate to this
broad domain, occupy and cultivate the soil, establish schools
and churches, and form settlements, and thereby avoid those
evils incident to a more dense and thickly settled country. But
offering extraordinary and unusual inducements for settlement
will not increase the number of good and reliable settlers. Such
settlers multiply only by time and the natural course of events.
I trust, sir, that our public domain may be long so held, and
that our children, and our children's children, may always have
the privilege of resorting to it for settlement and support, and
at an unvarying price, with a certainty of title, until the almost
countless acres of our unoccupied domain shall be covered with
a virtuous, industrious, and happy people.

10. Thomas Hart Benton: A Land Policy to Encourage Settlement

After thirty years as United States Senator from Missouri,
Thomas Hart Benton published a voluminous memoir recount-
ing the political battles in which he and his country had been
engaged. In this a chapter is devoted to what he considered
"a great amelioration" in federal land policy and to his own
part in helping to bring it about. The improvement was steady
progress away from the policy of using the public land as a
source of revenue toward that of using it as an instrument for
the promotion of settlement.

Benton's chapter begins with a quotation from Edmund
Burke and finds supporting examples in American colonial
history and in the contemporary policies of South American
republics and the Shah of Persia. Like the rest of the book, it
consists largely of passages from the author's speeches in the
Senate. Its particular value lies in its résumé of the series of

issues over which successive stages of the campaign were
fought and in its statement of the philosophy of those who
favored greater liberality in land alienations. An early victory,
to which Document 11 will be devoted, was to give rights of
preemption at the minimum price to those who had settled on
the land before it was put up for sale. The uniform minimum
price was itself an evil, in Benton's eyes, and a second achievement would be to secure adoption of the principle of "graduation," that is, a progressive reduction in the prices of land
remaining "in market unsold." The third and final stage should
be to give up the "merchandizing" of the public domain and
to make donations of land "in parcels suitable to their wants,
to meritorious cultivators."

For such a direction of policy Benton's basic argument is
two-fold. In the first place, settlement and cultivation are more
important objectives than maximization of the immediate
revenue to be obtained from selling the land. This is true in
the long run, even from the narrow point of view of the public
treasury, and it is clearly true from the broader viewpoint of
national development. In the second place, the settlement to
be encouraged should have a particular social structure.
"Tenantry is unfavorable to freedom. . . . The freeholder, on
the contrary, is the natural supporter of a free government;
and it should be the policy of republics to multiply their freeholders, as it is the policy of monarchies to multiply tenants.
We are a republic, and we wish to continue so: then multiply
the class of freeholders; pass the public lands cheaply and
easily into the hands of the people."

About the year 1785 the celebrated Edmund Burke brought
a bill into the British House of Commons for the sale of the
crown lands, in which he laid down principles in political
economy, in relation to such property, profoundly sagacious in

---

From "A Senator for Thirty Years" (Thomas Hart Benton), *Thirty Years'
View* (New York: D. Appleton & Co., 1854), vol. I, pp. 102–107.

themselves, applicable to all sovereign landed possessions, whether of kings or republics—applicable in all countries— and nowhere more applicable and less known or observed, than in the United States. In the course of the speech in support of his bill he said:

> Lands sell at the current rate, and nothing can sell for more. But be the price what it may, a great object is always answered, whenever any property is transferred from hands which are not fit for that property, to those that are. The buyer and the seller must mutually profit by such a bargain; and, what rarely happens in matters of revenue, the relief of the subject will go hand in hand with the profit of the Exchequer. . . . The revenue to be derived from the sale of the forest lands will not be so considerable as many have imagined; and I conceive it would be unwise to screw it up to the utmost, or even to suffer bidders to enhance, according to their eagerness, the purchase of objects, wherein the expense of that purchase may weaken the capital to be employed in their cultivation. . . . The principal revenue which I propose to draw from these uncultivated wastes, is to spring from the improvement and population of the kingdom; events infinitely more advantageous to the revenues of the crown than the rents of the best landed estate which it can hold. . . . It is thus I would dispose of the unprofitable landed estates of the crown: *throw them into the mass of private property:* by which they will come, through the course of circulation and through the political secretions of the State, into well-regulated revenue. . . . Thus would fall an expensive agency, with all the influence which attends it.

I do not know how old, or rather, how young I was, when I first took up the notion that sales of land by a government to its own citizens, and to the highest bidder, was false policy; and that gratuitous grants to actual settlers was the true policy, and their labor the true way of extracting national wealth and strength from the soil. It might have been in childhood, when reading the Bible, and seeing the division of the promised land among the children of Israel: it might have been later, and in learning the operation of the feudal system in giving lands to those who would defend them: it might have been in early life in Tennessee, in seeing the fortunes and respectability of many families derived from the 640 acre head-rights which the State of North Carolina had bestowed upon the first settlers. It was certainly before I had read the speech of Burke from which the extract above is taken; for I did not see that speech until 1826; and seventeen years before that time, when a very young member of the General Assembly of Tennessee, I was fully imbued with the doctrine of donations to settlers, and acted upon the principle that was in me, as far as the case admitted, in advocating the pre-emption claims of the settlers on Big and Little Pigeon, French Broad, and Nolichucky. And when I came to the then Territory of Missouri in 1815, and saw land exposed to sale to the highest bidder, and lead mines and salt springs reserved from sale, and rented out for the profit of the federal treasury, I felt repugnance to the whole system, and determined to make war upon it whenever I should have the power. The time came round with my election to the Senate of the United States in 1820: and the years 1824, '26, and '28, found me doing battle for an ameliorated system of disposing of our public lands; and with some success. The pre-emption system was established, though at first the pre-emption claimant was stigmatized as a trespasser, and repulsed as a criminal; the reserved lead mines and salt springs, in the State of Missouri, were brought into market, like other lands; iron ore lands, intended to have been withheld from sale, were rescued from that fate, and brought into market. Still the two repulsive features of the federal land system—sales to the highest bidder, and donations to no one—with an arbitrary minimum price which placed the cost of all lands, good and bad, at the same uniform rate (after the auctions were over), at one dollar twenty-five cents per acre. I resolved to move against the whole system, and especially in favor of graduated prices, and donations to actual and destitute settlers. I did so in a bill, renewed annually for a long time; and in speeches which had

more effect upon the public mind than upon the federal legislation—counteracted as my plan was by schemes of dividing
the public lands, or the money arising from their sale, among
the States. It was in support of one of these bills that I produced the authority of Burke in the extract quoted; and no one
took its spirit and letter more promptly and entirely than President Jackson. He adopted the principle fully, and in one of his
annual messages to Congress recommended that, as soon as the
public (revolutionary) debt should be discharged (to the payment of which the lands ceded by the States were pledged),
that they should *cease to be a subject of revenue, and be disposed of chiefly with a view to settlement and cultivation.* His
terms of service expired soon after the extinction of the debt,
so that he had not an opportunity to carry out his wise and
beneficent design.

Mr. Burke considered the revenue derived from the sale of
crown lands as a trifle, and of no account, compared to the
amount of revenue derivable from the same lands through their
settlement and cultivation. He was profoundly right! and
provably so, both upon reason and experience. The sale of the
land is a single operation. Some money is received, and the
cultivator is disabled to that extent from its improvement and
cultivation. The cultivation is perennial, and the improved condition of the farmer enables him to pay taxes, and consume
dutiable goods, and to sell the products which command the
imports which pay duties to the government, and this is the
"well-regulated revenue" which comes through the course of
circulation, and through the "political secretions" of the State,
and which Mr. Burke commends above all revenue derived
from the sale of lands. Does any one know the comparative
amount of revenue derived respectively from the sales and
from the cultivation of lands in any one of our new States
where the federal government was the proprietor, and the
auctioneer, of the lands? and can he tell which mode of
raising money has been most productive? Take Alabama, for

example. How much has the treasury received for lands sold within her limits? and how much in duties paid on imports purchased with the exports derived from her soil? Perfect exactitude cannot be attained in the answer, but exact enough to know that the latter already exceeds the former several times, ten times over; and is perennial and increasing for ever! while the sale of the land has been a single operation, performed once, and not to be repeated; and disabling the cultivator by the loss of the money it took from him. Taken on a large scale, and applied to the whole United States, and the answer becomes more definite—but still not entirely exact. The whole annual receipts from land sales at this time (1850) are about two millions of dollars: the annual receipts from customs, founded almost entirely upon the direct or indirect productions of the earth, exceed fifty millions of dollars! giving a comparative difference of twenty-five to one for cultivation over sales; and triumphantly sustaining Mr. Burke's theory. I have looked into the respective amounts of federal revenue, received into the treasury from these two sources, since the establishment of the federal government; and find the customs to have yielded, in that time, a fraction over one thousand millions of dollars net—the lands to have yielded a little less than one hundred and thirty millions gross, not forty millions clear after paying all expenses of surveys, sales and management. This is a difference of twenty-five to one—with the further difference of endless future production from one, and no future production from the land once sold; that is to say, the same acre of land is paying for ever through cultivation, and pays but once for itself in purchase.

Thus far I have considered Mr. Burke's theory only under one of its aspects—the revenue aspect: he presents another—that of population—and here all measure of comparison ceases. The sale of land brings no people: cultivation produces population: and people are the true wealth and strength of nations. These various views were presented, and often enforced, in the course of the several speeches which I made in support of my graduation and donation bills: and, on the point of population, and of freeholders, against tenants, I gave utterance to these sentiments:

> Tenantry is unfavorable to freedom. It lays the foundation for separate orders in society, annihilates the love of country, and weakens the spirit of independence. The farming tenant has, in fact, no country, no hearth, no domestic altar, no household god. The freeholder, on the contrary, is the natural supporter of a free government; and it should be the policy of republics to multiply their freeholders, as it is the policy of monarchies to multiply tenants. We are a republic, and we wish to continue so: then multiply the class of freeholders; pass the public lands cheaply and easily into the hands of the people; sell, for a reasonable price, to those who are able to pay; and give, without price, to those who are not. I say give, without price, to those who are not able to pay; and that which is so given, I consider as sold for the best of prices; for a price above gold and silver; a price which cannot be carried away by delinquent officers, nor lost in failing banks, nor stolen by thieves, nor squandered by an improvident and extravagant administration. It brings a price above rubies—a race of virtuous and independent laborers, the true supporters of their country, and the stock from which its best defenders must be drawn. . . .

In favor of low prices, and donations, I quoted the example and condition of the Atlantic States of this Union—all settled under liberal systems of land distribution which dispensed almost (or altogether in many instances) with sales for money. I said:

> These Atlantic States were donations from the British crown; and the great proprietors distributed out their possessions with a free and generous hand. A few shillings for a hundred acres, a nominal quitrent, and gifts of a hundred, five hundred, and a thousand acres, to actual settlers: such were the terms on which they dealt out the soil which is now covered by a nation of free-men. Provinces, which now form sovereign States, were sold from hand to hand, for a less sum than the federal government now

demands for an area of two miles square. . . . Well it was for every State in this Union, that their soil was sold for a song, or given as a gift to whomsoever would take it. Happy for them, and for the liberty of the human race, that the kings of England and the "Lords Proprietors," did not conceive the luminous idea of waiting for the rise, and sticking to a *minimum* of $1 25 per acre. Happy for Kentucky, Tennessee, and Ohio, that they were settled under *States,* and not under the federal government. To this happy exemption they owe their present greatness and prosperity. When they were settled, the State laws prevailed in the acquisition of lands; and donations, pre-emptions, and settlement rights, and sales at two cents the acre, were the order of the day. I include Ohio, and I do it with a knowledge of what I say: for ten millions of her soil,—that which now constitutes her chief wealth and strength,—were settled upon the liberal principles which I mention. The federal system only fell upon fifteen millions of her soil; and, of that quantity, the one half now lies waste and useless, paying no tax to the State, yielding nothing to agriculture, desert spots in the midst of a smiling garden, "waiting for the rise," and exhibiting, in high and bold relief, the miserable folly of prescribing an arbitrary *minimum* upon that article which is the gift of God to man, and which no parental government has ever attempted to convert into a source of revenue and an article of merchandise.

Against the policy of holding up refuse lands until they should rise to the price of good land and against the reservation of saline and mineral lands, and making money by boiling salt water, and digging lead ore, or holding a body of tenantry to boil and dig, I delivered these sentiments:

I do trust and believe, Mr. President, that the Executive of this free government will not be second to George the Third in patriotism, nor an American Congress prove itself inferior to a British Parliament in political wisdom. I do trust and believe that this whole system of holding up land for the rise, endeavoring to make revenue out of the soil of the country, leasing and renting lead mines, salt springs, and iron banks, with all its train of penal laws and civil and military agents, will be condemned and abolished. . . .

Argument and sarcasm had their effect, in relation to the mineral and saline reserves in the State in which I lived—the State of Missouri. An act was passed in 1828 to throw them into the mass of private property—to sell them like other public lands. And thus the federal government, in that State, got rid of a degrading and unprofitable pursuit; and the State got citizen freeholders instead of federal tenants; and profitably were developed in the hands of individuals the pursuits of private industry which languished and stagnated in the hands of federal agents and tenants. . . .

I quoted the example of all nations, ancient and modern, republican and monarchical, in favor of giving lands, in parcels suitable to their wants, to meritorious cultivators; and denied that there was an instance upon earth, except that of our own federal government, which made merchandise of land to its citizens—exacted the highest price it could obtain—and refused to suffer the country to be settled until it was paid for. The "promised land" was divided among the children of Israel—the women getting a share when there was no man at the head of the family—as with the daughters of Manasseh. All the Atlantic States, when British colonies, were settled upon gratuitous donations, or nominal sales. Kentucky and Tennessee were chiefly settled in the same way. The two Floridas, and Upper and Lower Louisiana, were gratuitously distributed by the kings of Spain to settlers, in quantities adapted to their means of cultivation—and with the whole vacant domain to select from according to their pleasure. Land is now given to settlers in Canada; and £30,000 sterling, has been voted at a single session of Parliament, to aid emigrants in their removal to these homes, and commencing life upon them. The republic of Colombia now gives 400 acres to a settler: other South American republics give more or less. Quoting these examples, I added:

Such, Mr. President, is the conduct of the free republics of the South. I say republics: for it is the same in all of them, and it would be tedious and monotonous to repeat their numerous decrees. In fact, throughout the New World, from Hudson's Bay to Cape Horn (with the single exception of these United States), land, the gift of God to man, is also the gift of the government to its citizens. Nor is this wise policy confined to the New World. It prevails even in Asia; and the present age has seen—we ourselves have seen—published in the capital of the European world, the proclamation of the King of Persia, inviting Christians to go to the ancient kingdom of Cyrus, Cambyses and Darius, and there receive gifts of land—first rate, not refuse—with a total exemption from taxes, and the free enjoyment of their religion. Here is the proclamation: listen to it.

The Proclamation

"Mirza Mahomed Saul, Ambassador to England, in the name, and by the authority of Abbas Mirza, King of Persia, offers to those who shall emigrate to Persia, gratuitous grants of land, good for the production of wheat, barley, rice, cotton, and fruits,—free from taxes or contributions of any kind, and with the free enjoyment of their religion; *the king's object being to improve his country.*

"London, July 8th, 1823."

The injustice of holding all lands at one uniform price, waiting for the cultivation of the good land to give value to the poor, and for the poorest to rise to the value of the richest, was shown in a reference to private sales, of all articles; in the whole of which sales the price was graduated to suit different qualities of the same article. The heartless and miserly policy of waiting for government land to be enhanced in value by the neighboring cultivation of private land, was denounced as unjust as well as unwise. The new States of the West were the sufferers by this federal land policy. They were in a different condition from other States. In these others, the local legislatures held the primary disposal of the soil,—so much as remained vacant within their limits,—and being of the same community, made equitable alienations among their constituents. In the new States it was different. The federal government held the primary disposition of the soil; and the majority of Congress (being independent of the people of these States), was less heedful of their wants and wishes. They were as a stepmother, instead of a natural mother: and the federal government being sole purchaser from foreign nations, and sole recipient of Indian cessions, it became the monopolizer of vacant lands in the West: and this monopoly, like all monopolies, resulted in hardships to those upon whom it acted. Few, or none of our public men, had raised their voice against this hard policy before I came into the national councils. My own was soon raised there against it: and it is certain that a great amelioration has taken place in our federal land policy during my time: and that the sentiment of Congress, and that of the public generally, has become much more liberal in land alienations; and is approximating towards the beneficent systems of the rest of the world. But the members in Congress from the new States should not intermit their exertions, nor vary their policy; and should fix their eyes steadily upon the period of the speedy extinction of the federal title to all the lands within the limits of their respective States;—to be effected by pre-emption rights, by donations, and by the sale (of so much as shall be sold), at graduated prices,—adapted to the different qualities of the tracts, to be estimated according to the time it has remained in market unsold—and by liberal grants to objects of general improvement, both national and territorial.

11. The Debate over Preemption for Squatters

The issue of preemption, on which Senator Benton's position has already been recorded, provided a significant clash between federal law and frontier custom. What the law contemplated was an orderly system under which the government first surveyed the land of a particular area, dividing it into sections and quarter sections, and then offered it at public auction, setting a minimum price per acre, which after 1820 was $1.25, but collecting as much more for each parcel as competitive bidding might produce. What took place in many parts of the frontier was a much more disorderly and spontaneous process, under which settlement preceded survey and the pioneers chose plots of land and began to cultivate and improve them before legal title could be secured. Then, when the land was finally put up for auction, these squatters considered that they were entitled to buy the land they had occupied at the minimum price, and in many cases banded together in "claims associations" to make sure, by moral or physical force, that no outsider or speculator should be permitted to outbid them.[1]

Congress recognized the preemptive rights of the squatters in several special cases and in a more general law that was in effect during part of the decade of the 1830's. In 1838, the Senate engaged in an unusually vigorous debate over the permanent adoption of the principle. In one of the passages quoted, Daniel Webster argues that it would be futile to oppose such deeply rooted local customs and wrong to deprive the squatters of the benefit of the improvements they had made. Henry Clay, on the other hand, insists that no concessions should be made to these "club law men." They are "a lawless rabble" and deserve no more consideration than as if they had stolen goods from a warehouse rather than lands from the public domain. Senator Tipton of Indiana rises to defend the squatters of his own state against Clay's description of them. They are, he says, "industrious and enterprising," most of them poor, but "honorable, peaceable, law-abiding citizens."

The preemptive right of the actual settler to buy 160 acres at the minimum price was finally established in 1841. As Stephen A. Douglas remarked long afterward, "the settlers

---

[1] Benjamin Horace Hibbard, *A History of the Public Land Policies* (New York: Macmillan, 1934), ch. 11.

made a preemption law of their own ... each with his pistol and Bowie knife ... whenever Congress failed to give them one."[2] In the end it was the settlers' law that Congress enacted.

SPEECH OF SENATOR DANIEL WEBSTER

...The result of these causes is, that settlements have become quite extensive, and the number of people very large. In that part of Wisconsin which lies west of the Mississippi there are supposed to be from thirty to fifty thousand inhabitants. Over this region Congress has extended civil government, established courts of law, and encouraged the building of villages and towns, and yet the country has not been brought into the market for sale, except it may be small quantities for the sites of villages and towns. In other parts of Wisconsin a similar state of things exists, especially on and near the border of Lake Michigan, where numerous settlements have been made and commercial towns erected, some of them already of considerable importance, but where the title to the land still remains in the Government. Similar cases exist in Indiana, Illinois, and Michigan, and probably, also, in the Southwestern States.

Now, said Mr. W. the practical question is, what is to be done in these cases? What are we to do with those settlers, their improvements, and the lands on which they live? Is there any one who would propose or desire that these lands should be put up at open auction, improvements and all, and sold to the highest bidder, without any regard whatever to the interest

---

[2] *Congressional Globe,* 36th Congress, 1st Session, p. 2040.

From *Congressional Globe,* 35th Congress, 2nd Session, January 27, 1838, Appendix, p. 136.

or protection of the settlers? For my part, I could propose no such thing, nor by any means consent to any such thing.

Nor do I suppose that there could be such an auction, and that other persons could attend and bid at it freely, and over-bid the actual settlers for their own settlements and improvements, without disturbance and violation of the public peace. Nor would a dollar of money, in my judgment, be realized by the Treasury by such a course of proceeding, beyond what would be received for the same lands under this law. As to the general justice of the bill, its policy, or the degree of indulgence which it holds out to those who have become settlers, it ought to be remembered—

1. That it applies only to those who have now already settled on the public lands. And I am quite willing to concur with others in carrying out the recommendations of the President's message, by adopting such measures as may be thought wise and reasonable for the future, as shall prevent the recurrence hereafter of any necessity for laws like this.

2. The bill makes no donation, or gratuity. It grants only a pre-emption right—a right of previous purchase, at the price for which the greater part of the public lands has been, and now is, actually sold.

3. It gives this right only to the extent of one quarter section—not more than a reasonable quantity for a farm, in the estimation of the inhabitants of these new and vast regions.

4. It gives the right only to heads of families, or house-holders, actually settled and residing on the tract.

And, in my opinion, it is much in favor of this bill, that what it does grant, it grants (where the requisite proof is made) at once and for ever, without mischievous qualifications, and conditions subsequent, such as formed part of the bill of last year.

It has been proposed to amend this bill, so as to limit its benefits to native or naturalized citizens of the United States. Although I have heretofore been disposed to favor such a proposition, yet, on the whole, I think it ought not to pass; because such a limitation has been altogether unknown, in our general system of land sales, and to introduce it here, where we are acting on rights already acquired, would be both invidious and unjust.

It has been proposed, also, so to amend the bill as to require that the settler, in addition to the dollar and a quarter per acre, should pay one-half the actual value of the land above that sum; this value to be ascertained by appraisers, appointed by the Register of the Land Office. I could not agree to this amendment; because, in the first place, we have never adopted the principle of selling lands on appraisement; but, secondly and mainly, because, if these settlers have had any ground or reason to expect a pre-emption right from Congress, (which is the substantial foundation of the bill,) they had had, and now have, reason to expect it, on the same terms on which it has been granted to others.

Mr. President, that there may be some undeserving persons among these settlers, I do not doubt. That the advantages of this bill may be enjoyed, in some cases, by those who are not actual settlers, with honest, *bona fide* purpose of permanent residence, is very probable. But I believe the great majority of the cases to which the bill will apply will be such as ought to be relieved. I believe the bill is the readiest way of quieting these titles and possessions, which the public interest requires should, in some way, be quieted without further delay. Indeed, no course is proposed, but either to pass this bill, or to bring the lands at once to public auction, open to the biddings of all. This last course, I am persuaded, would result in no gain whatever to the Treasury, whilst it might be attended with serious inconveniences to the public, and would be sure to throw whole neighborhoods, villages, and counties, into a state of much excitement, much perplexity, and much distress. Both for the general interests of the country, and for the interest and protection of the settler, I am of opinion that the bill ought to pass.

SPEECH OF SENATOR HENRY CLAY

I dare say there are members in this, and the other House, ready to pronounce that a more honest, deserving set of men, than these "club law men" does not exist: men who openly violate the laws—men whose moral sense would be violated by an enforcement of the existing laws, as they had been told by a Senator on that floor. Whose moral sense? Why the moral sense of these club law men, who band themselves together, and overawe and set at defiance the officers of the Government. What pretence had these lawless men for roving about the country and seizing by violence on the choicest spots of land?

He read a statement, by which it appeared that there were in the State of Illinois millions of acres of as fine farming lands as the sun ever shone upon, that could be entered by any man who was willing to pay his dollar and a quarter per acre for it. And all the new States contained an abundance of the best land which could be obtained by the settlers on the same easy terms. The honorable Senator from Michigan (Mr. Lyon) had made the notable discovery that it was the settlement of land which constituted its value. No, sir, said Mr. C. it is the fertility of the soil, the natural advantages of the tract, and its capacity to yield a profitable return for the capital and labor expended on it, which gave value to the land; and there were millions upon millions of acres of such land that would readily find purchasers were it not for the practices introduced by this pre-emption system. He had had occasion to say that prior to 1830 there was no general pre-emption law. The laws of that description, passed before that time, were all founded on particular circumstances, limited as to the territory and limited as to their duration. The first pre-emption law originated in 1830, and was one of the fatal series of experiments which grew up

From *Congressional Globe*, 35th Congress, 2nd Session, January 29, 1838, Appendix, p. 139.

under the late Administration, and been followed by the present, and the effects of which he feared would be felt for years. But this system expired two years ago, and owing to the abuses and corruptions which sprung from it, it came into general disrepute. Why, said Mr. C. do you not recollect the scenes enacted at the Chicago sales? The moment the sale commenced, there were persons present ready to oppose the sale of every tract offered crying out "settler's claim, settler's claim," and the sale was interrupted in the most disgraceful and outrageous manner.

In consequence of the abuses that had been practised under this system, it became so odious that it could not have found a vote in either House to support it. No one ever thought of reviving it until the last session, and all the unauthorized settlements that have been since made on the public lands, have been made in violation, not only of the known laws, but in violation of the well ascertained sense of Congress. He had shown that there were one hundred and fourteen millions of acres of land already surveyed, and in the market—that there was no want of elbow room—no want of good land for the settler to choose from, on paying for it; and there was therefore no reason why the settlers should move off, and seize upon lands not yet surveyed.

That gentleman [Senator Daniel Webster] stated as one of the strongest reasons why he should vote for this bill, that a state of things with regard to these settlers existed, which could not be met—that encouraged by former pre-emption laws, they had gone and settled upon these lands, and could not now be removed. Sir, said Mr. C. I will meet them with the laws of the country. Let the lands be exposed to public sale, and afterwards at private sale, and then put in force, if necessary, the existing laws, and remove these lawless intruders from the property they have forcibly appropriated to their own use. What right had they to the public domain more than any other description of plunderers to the goods they may seize upon? An auctioner has his warehouse broken open by a lawless body of armed men: one man seizes upon a bale, another upon a hamper, and another upon something else, and says he has a right to take it at his own price. When other purchasers come to auction, and say Mr. Auctioneer, why not give me these goods on as cheap terms as these gentlemen who have broken open your warehouse obtained theirs. Why, what sort of answer would it be to say that the gentlemen are preemptioners, their moral sense has been outraged by locking up these goods, and keeping them from their use, and as they particularly wished for this bale or hamper at their own price, and are honest, industrious men, who are unable to give the real value for the goods, they have taken this natural and harmless method of getting possession of them. In a country like this, where there are one hundred and fourteen millions of good land open to sale at the lowest price, you find (said Mr. C.) these men, in opposition to the laws, and in opposition to the known sense of the Legislature, going further to the West, seizing from latitude to latitude upon the choicest spots of the public lands, and their moral sense is so wounded by the nation wishing to retain the lands in their own hands, that they must have them at their own price.

SPEECH OF SENATOR JOHN TIPTON

I had hoped, (said Mr. T.) when my colleague rose to address the Senate, that he would have defended our constituents, who are settlers upon the public lands, from the unjustifiable assaults made upon them on this floor; but as he did not see proper to do so, I feel it to be my duty to defend their reputation. I could wish that the task had fallen into abler

From *Congressional Globe*, 35th Congress, 2nd Session, January 27, 1838, Appendix, p. 134.

hands. There are those more able, but none more willing, than myself, to do justice to the people of that noble young State, whose servant I am. I have an account to settle with the honorable Senator from Kentucky, (Mr. Clay,) in doing which I shall in part reply to the remarks of my colleague. I will not attempt to prolong the debate by entering into a discussion of the merits of the bill now before the Senate. I only desire to correct the errors into which that honorable Senator has fallen in relation to a very respectable portion of the State which I have the honor, in part, to represent here. I was called out of the Senate chamber yesterday for a few moments, on business, whilst the pre-emption bill was under discussion. When I returned to the chamber, the honorable Senator to whom I have alluded was closing his remarks, in opposition to the bill, by reading extracts from a newspaper, published in Indiana. I had not, consequently, an opportunity of hearing all his remarks, nor do I find them reported in the morning papers, but I am informed that he indulged in harsh expressions against the citizens of my State, whom he was pleased to denominate as "squatters on the public lands." I hope he was misunderstood. If that honorable Senator had only alluded to settlers on the public lands in Indiana, in speaking of them in connection with the people of other States, I would not have felt constrained to reply; but he has more than once or twice, on different days, during this debate dwelt it would seem with peculiar emphasis on the squatters on those valuable public lands in Indiana, applying to those who occupied them remarks that shall not go unanswered or uncontradicted. I will repeat as nearly as I can what was told yesterday, and if I go wrong he can correct me. I understood that he denounced the settlers on the lands as a lawless banditti of land robbers, unjustly grasping at the public treasure.

[Here Mr. Clay rose, and said that he would repeat what he did say on the occasion referred to by the honorable Senator from Indiana. He did say that the squatters on the public lands were a lawless rabble; that they might as well seize upon our forts, our arsenals, or on the public treasure, as to rush out and seize on the public lands.]

Mr. Tipton resumed. The Senator admits that the expressions used by him amounted to what I have repeated. Does he not know that the laws to prevent trespass on the public lands have never, in a single instance, been put in force for many years, but have stood as a dead letter on our statute books for a quarter of a century? That the emigrants from the old to the new States are in the constant habit of entering upon the best public land they could find, building cabins to shield their families from the pelting of the storm, and cultivating the soil, regardless whether the land had been surveyed or not, with the expectation and intention of paying the Government for the lands whenever they should be brought into market. Has it not been the constant practice of Congress to pass laws to protect the actual settler from the iron grasp of the speculator? And is it just to call those industrious and enterprising citizens, who settle on the public lands with intention to purchase as soon as they come into market, a lawless rabble? I think not. Does the honorable Senator know that the people of four entire counties in Indiana—Porter, Lake, Newton, and Pulaski, with a portion of Miami and other counties—are settlers on the public lands? They are emigrants from the older States, seeking a home in the West.

It is true, sir, most of them are poor, but I trust and believe they are honest. I know them to be honorable, peaceable, law-abiding citizens, who would scorn a dishonorable action as much as the Senator himself. I am personally acquainted with many of them: they are educated, moral, and highly respectable. Many of them would lose nothing by a comparison with members on this floor; and if the honorable Senator holds a different opinion, it is because he has been misinformed. . . .

12. Andrew Johnson:
The Case for the Homestead Bill

In the final decade of our period, the effort to encourage settlement by small farmers was concentrated on the proposal of free homesteads. The extreme land reformers, who had coined the effective slogans of "Lands for the Landless" and "Vote Yourself a Farm,"[1] wished indeed to make this the only method of land disposal, and to see to it that the effects would be made permanent by providing that the land thus granted should never afterwards be combined into parcels of more than 160 acres. These restrictions, however, stood little chance of congressional acceptance, and most of the proponents of the homestead were prepared to give full title to a quarter section of land to any actual settler who had completed five years of bona fide residence and occupation.

Andrew Johnson introduced bills of this type in several sessions of Congress, first as a Representative and later as a Senator from Tennessee. His argument in 1850, like those he advanced in other years, ran in broad and general terms. The government has more lands than it can now use and many individuals need lands which they do not have. What right, then, has the government to keep the people from cultivating these lands and thus contributing to the national prosperity? The increased income which the settlers will earn will make them more substantial taxpayers and therefore enhance rather than diminish the security behind the public debt. This, however, was not Johnson's principal concern. "He would now show that [the plan] would not only make money for the Govern-

---

[1] Helene S. Zahler, *Eastern Workingmen and National Land Policy, 1829–1862* (New York: Columbia University Press, 1941). Appendices reprint the "Vote Yourself a Farm" pamphlet and a Land Reform poem with the following refrain:

Oh! Millions of hands want acres
And millions of acres want hands!

ment but that it would make better men." Ireland, with its landed aristocracy and starving people, offers the example to be avoided. By contrast, the Homestead bill would make the common man an independent citizen and home owner; and Johnson's peroration pictures him living with his family under a more thoroughly American, if less literary, version of the Jeffersonian vine and fig tree.

The passage reprinted below comes from the brief form of the speech as it was taken down by the reporter for the *Congressional Globe*. When Johnson elaborated it for the record, he added two comments of a more personal nature. One was "that he was no agrarian, no leveller, as they were termed in modern times." The other is of particular interest as coming from a man who was to attain the presidency under tragic circumstances. "He would rather have the honor and the credit of being instrumental in the accomplishment of this great scheme, than to be President of the United States *forty times*."[2]

Mr. Johnson, of Tennessee, then addressed the House at length, in explanation of the objects contemplated by this bill. He looked upon it as a measure of great importance. Five years ago he had introduced a similar proposition, to give to every citizen, the head of a family, a portion of the public lands, for the purpose of settlement, and on which he might establish for himself a home. There were many gentlemen who at that time regarded the plan as impracticable, and as unlikely to lead to any useful results. But since that time the public mind had taken up the subject. It had been widely discussed out of doors, and Congress had at various periods made liberal donations of the public domain, in aid of public institutions, and in

---

From *Congressional Globe*, 31st Congress, 1st Session, July 25, 1850, Part II, pp. 1449–1450.

---

[2] *Congressional Globe*, 31st Congress, 1st Session, Appendix, p. 952.

recompense for public services. He now came forward to ask for a participation in this bounty, in the name of the common man, who, by his toil and sweat, had quietly and effectually contributed to the support of the Government. For that class of our citizens he desired to ask that they also may be permitted to come in for a share of these public lands.

. . . By whom are these public lands owned? They are held by the Government of the United States as agent for the people of the United States. By whom were these public lands acquired? They were acquired by the Federal Government for the people. We have now a greater aggregate of public lands than we have any use for. But numerous individuals among us have no portion of these lands. As a whole, therefore, we have too much, while, as individuals, we have too little. He desired to know on what ground the Government was justified in withholding these lands from those citizens who may be desirous to go on them for the purpose of cultivation. By what authority did the Government withhold these lands? Did the Constitution of the United States provide any such authority? No. Was it to be found in any of these great principles which lie at the foundation of all natural rights? Not so. The proper object of our Government, and of all Governments, is to effect the greatest possible good to the greatest possible number.

He denied the right of the Government to take $160 or $200 from any citizen of the United States as the purchase of one hundred and sixty acres of the public domain, thus denying the right of any other citizen who did not pay the same amount, to a settlement on any part of the public domain. This exclusion of the citizens from the cultivation of the public lands, destroyed one of the elements of national prosperity. The necessity for the cultivation of the earth was imposed on man by the law of his nature. Unless he obeys that law, he cannot continue to exist. What right, then, has any Government, instituted for the benefit of a community, to withhold from those over whom it is extended, the right to do that which is necessary to sustain life? No man ought to be prevented from enjoying this right, because he cannot pay for it an equivalent in money. Like the air, or like heat, it is the property of all, intended to be used and enjoyed by all. Hence, therefore, the Government which acts in contravention of this principle, makes war on the interests of those it is bound to protect. . . .

. . . He went on to argue that the general principles which lay at the bottom of the policy illustrated by this bill, if worked out, would produce the most beneficial melioration in the condition of man; putting an end to war and famine, and many other evils which arise from defective systems of government. He asked gentlemen to take a glance at the condition of Ireland, where, in violation of all these great principles for which he contended, a landed aristocracy held the possession of the soil, while the thousands who were excluded from this class were cut down by starvation. This was the consequence of the violation of that great law which lies at the foundation of all human rights, and which provides that every man shall enjoy the produce of the labor of his own hands, without molestation, and without the interference of Government.

It might be urged as an objection to this bill, that the public lands had been pledged for the payment of the public debt. He then reminded the House that the law authorizing a loan, and pledging the public domain, was passed in the month of January; while another law granting large portions of these public lands as bounties to the soldiers who had served in the war with Mexico, did not become a law until the following February. This fact he adverted to as evidence that, even at the time when these lands were thus pledged, Congress did not regard this pledge as tying up its hands in the disposal of these lands. But, admitting it to be true that these lands were thus pledged, he undertook to show that it would be no violation of this pledge to dispose of the public lands, in conformity with the provisions of the bill, because, instead of destroying or depreciating this property, the effect of a general settlement and cultivation of these lands would be an enhancement of their value, and consequently imparted the security to the public creditor. He thought that he could demonstrate this. In the first place, he went on to prove that a settlement of the public lands, as proposed by this bill, would create a new source of public revenue, while it increased the value of the lands.

Were we to take a quarter section of land, which is now totally unproductive, lying in a wild state, and sell it for what it is now worth, how much of the public debt will it pay? It will pay very little. What would be the effect of the adoption of the system now proposed? You take a number of your citizens who now give no aid to the support of the Government, and place them in a condition to become contributors to the public Treasury. You give the poor man one hundred and sixty acres of land. He goes upon it, improves his little farm, and gradually acquires means which enable him to purchase something beyond the mere necessaries of life. He looks around him for luxuries; and as these are imported articles, and are subject to a duty at the customhouse, by their purchase, he becomes a contributor to the revenue. Suppose that he expends on articles of this class one hundred dollars in the course of a year, and there is a duty of thirty per cent. on these articles, the purchaser becomes a contributor to the Treasury to that amount, paying thirty dollars towards the public revenue. Thus, by giving the poor man a portion of the public lands, you enable him to contribute to the expenses of the Government. In seven years you thus enable him to pay more than the original value of the land. . . .

. . . But it does not stop here. Every seven years thereafter, he will continue to pay this $30 annually. . . .

But this was not all the benefits which would result from the adoption of the system contained in this bill. He would now show that it would not only make money for the Government, but that it would make better men. By placing in the hands of man the means of providing for the wants and comforts of life, you elevate him to a higher rank as a citizen. He has a home, where his wife and children reside; he has a property to improve and defend. When the election day rolls around, he comes to the ballot-box, and exercises his franchise with that independence which becomes a free citizen. He there maintains his rights, looks his neighbor in the face, and then returns to the home where his dearest affections are centered. If he could do as he wished, this bill should never go to the Committee of the Whole on the state of the Union, or to the Speaker's table, where it would not again be heard of. It should become a law at once, and we should then see every citizen in the enjoyment of his home, his horse, his stable, and his barn, and his wife milking her own cow and churning her own butter.

13. James Buchanan:
The Case Against the Homestead Bill

In February, 1859, advocates of two proposals were competing to get their respective measures to a vote on the floor of the Senate. One was the Homestead Bill. The other was a bill for the annexation of Cuba, which would have provided an extension of the slave area of the United States. Robert Toombs of Georgia declared that it would be ridiculous to put aside a great question of national policy to take up a demagogic proposal to make donations to "lacklanders." Benjamin F. Wade of Ohio was recorded as winning "Applause from the galleries" with the retort that: "The question will be, shall we give niggers to the niggerless, or land to the landless?"[1] By the end of our period, the question of the public lands, like so many others, had become entangled with the great issue of slavery.

---

[1] *Congressional Globe*, 31st Congress, 2nd Session, February 25, 1859, Part II, pp. 1353–1354.

By this time Andrew Johnson was one of the few southerners supporting the Homestead bill. Some of the attacks of his colleagues were aimed at the inclusion of immigrants among its beneficiaries. Jefferson Davis was opposed to using the public lands "as a fund with which to empty the pauper houses of Europe." Senator Johnson of Arkansas added to a warning against this "unnatural" stimulus to immigration an argument not very often heard in the American debates, that more liberal land policy would lead to excessive diffusion of settlement, "a rush and scattering of population over an immense surface, followed by a recoil, and all its disastrous consequences." Johnson of Tennessee made a vigorous defence of homesteads for immigrants. It was, he argued, good economic policy to let foreign nations "grow men . . . and incur the expense of raising them, and send able-bodied men here, men that are grown with muscles and sinews, ready to be brought in contact with the soil, which is to result in production and adding to the national wealth."[2]

The Homestead Bill passed the Congress, modified to require a payment of twenty-five cents per acre in an attempt to quiet constitutional objections, but President Buchanan returned it with his veto. Brushing aside the token payment, the message declares that the bill provides for unconstitutional donations, reducing the revenues and wasting the national inheritance, and that it "lays the ax to the root of our present admirable land system." It is unfair to earlier settlers, who have paid a price for lands similar to those which their competitors will obtain without price, and it is unfair to classes other than farmers. In reply to the arguments often advanced that the homesteads would provide an outlet for oppressed eastern wage earners, Buchanan comments realistically on the difficulties they would find in "entering upon a new occupation for which their habits of life have rendered them unfit."[3] Most of

---

[2] *Congressional Globe*, 36th Congress, 1st Session, pp. 1799, 2035. For the argument against undue diffusion, see Document 17 below.

[3] It is now recognized that few eastern wage earners ever took up farms on the frontier. Carter Goodrich and Sol Davison, "The Wage Earner and the Westward Movement," *Political Science Quarterly* L (1935), 161–185; LI (1936), 61–116.

the message is soberly argued, but its final paragraph applies to the measure the epithet "agrarian," which Johnson had been so anxious to avoid. The veto was sustained, and for our period Buchanan had the final word on land policy. But the Republican platform of 1860 contained a homestead plank, and the bill would be enacted in 1862 when its southern opponents were no longer in the halls of Congress.

VETO MESSAGE

Washington, June 22, 1860
To the Senate of the United States:

I return with my objections to the Senate, in which it originated, the bill entitled "An act to secure homesteads to actual settlers on the public domain, and for other purposes," presented to me on the 20th instant.

This bill gives to every citizen of the United States "who is the head of a family," and to every person of foreign birth residing in the country who has declared his intention to become a citizen, though he may not be the head of a family, the privilege of appropriating to himself 160 acres of Government land, of settling and residing upon it for five years; and should his residence continue until the end of this period, he shall then receive a patent on the payment of 25 cents per acre, or one-fifth of the present Government price. During this period the land is protected from all the debts of the settler.

This bill also contains a cession to the States of all the public lands within their respective limits "which have been subject to sale at private entry, and which remain unsold

From James D. Richardson, *A Compilation of the Messages and Papers of the Presidents, 1789–1903* (New York: Bureau of National Literature and Art, 1897–1920), vol. V, pp. 608–614.

after the lapse of thirty years." This provision embraces a present donation to the States of 12,229,731 acres, and will from time to time transfer to them large bodies of such lands which from peculiar circumstances may not be absorbed by private purchase and settlement.

To the actual settler this bill does not make an absolute donation, but the price is so small that it can scarcely be called a sale. It is nominally 25 cents per acre, but considering this is not to be paid until the end of five years, it is in fact reduced to about 18 cents per acre, or one-seventh of the present minimum price of the public lands. In regard to the States, it is an absolute and unqualified gift.

1. This state of the facts raises the question whether Congress, under the Constitution, has the power to give away the public lands either to States or individuals. On this question I expressed decided opinion in my message to the House of Representatives of the 24th February, 1859, returning the agricultural-college bill.[4] This opinion remains unchanged. The argument then used applies as a constitutional objection with greater force to the present bill. *There* it had the plea of consideration, growing out of a specific beneficial purpose; *here* it is an absolute gratuity to the States, without the pretext of consideration. I am compelled for want of time in these the last hours of the session to quote largely from this message.

I presume the general proposition will be admitted that Congress does not possess the power to make donations of money already in the Treasury, raised by taxes on the people, either to States or individuals.

But it is contended that the public lands are placed upon a different footing from money raised by taxation and that the proceeds arising from their sale are not subject to the limitations of the Constitution, but may be appropriated or given away by Con-

---

[4] Document 38 is taken from this earlier message but does not contain the passage which President Buchanan quotes here. [ED.]

gress, at its own discretion, to States, corporations, or individuals for any purpose they may deem expedient.

The advocates of this bill attempt to sustain their position upon the language of the second clause of the third section of the fourth article of the Constitution, which declares that "the Congress shall have power to dispose of and make all needful rules and regulations respecting the territory or other property belonging to the United States." They contend that by a fair interpretation of the words "dispose of" in this clause Congress possesses the power to make this gift of public lands to the States for purposes of education.

It would require clear and strong evidence to induce the belief that the framers of the Constitution, after having limited the powers of Congress to certain precise and specific objects, intended by employing the words "dispose of" to give that body unlimited power over the vast public domain. It would be a strange anomaly indeed to have created two funds—the one by taxation, confined to the execution of the enumerated powers delegated to Congress, and the other from the public lands, applicable to all subjects, foreign and domestic, which Congress might designate; that this fund should be "disposed of," not to pay the debts of the United States, nor "to raise and support armies," nor "to provide and maintain a navy," nor to accomplish any one of the other great objects enumerated in the Constitution, but be diverted from them to pay the debts of the States, to educate their people, and to carry into effect any other measure of their domestic policy. This would be to confer upon Congress a vast and irresponsible authority utterly at war with the well-known jealousy of Federal power which prevailed at the formation of the Constitution. The natural intendment would be that as the Constitution confined Congress to well-defined specific powers, the funds placed at their command, whether in land or money, should be appropriated to the performance of the duties corresponding with these powers. If not, a Government has been created with all its other powers carefully limited, but without any limitation in respect to the public lands. . . .

2. It will prove unequal and unjust in its operation among the actual settlers themselves.

The first settlers of a new country are a most meritorious class. They brave the dangers of savage warfare, suffer the privations of a frontier life, and with the hand of toil bring the wilderness into cultivation. The "old settlers," as they are everywhere called, are public benefactors. This class have all paid for their lands the Government price, or $1.25 per acre. They have constructed roads, established schools, and laid the foundation of prosperous commonwealths. Is it just, is it equal, that after they have accomplished all this by their labor new settlers should come in among them and receive their farms at the price of 25 or 18 cents per acre? Surely the old settlers, as a class, are entitled to at least equal benefits with the new. If you give the new settlers their land for a comparatively nominal price, upon every principle of equality and justice you will be obliged to refund out of the common Treasury the difference which the old have paid above the new settlers for their land.

3. This bill will do great injustice to the old soldiers who have received land warrants for their services in fighting the battles of their country. It will greatly reduce the market value of these warrants. Already their value has sunk for 160-acre warrants to 67 cents per acre under an apprehension that such a measure as this might become a law. What price would they command when any head of a family may take possession of a quarter section of land and not pay for it until the end of five years, and then at the rate of only 25 cents per acre? The magnitude of the interest to be affected will appear in the fact that there are outstanding unsatisfied land warrants reaching back to the last war with Great Britain, and even Revolutionary times, amounting in round numbers to seven and a half millions of acres.

4. This bill will prove unequal and unjust in its operation, because from its nature it is confined to one class of our people. It is a boon exclusively conferred upon the cultivators of the soil. Whilst it is cheerfully admitted that these are the most

numerous and useful class of our fellow-citizens and eminently deserve all the advantages which our laws have already extended to them, yet there should be no new legislation which would operate to the injury or embarrassment of the large body of respectable artisans and laborers. The mechanic who emigrates to the West and pursues his calling must labor long before he can purchase a quarter section of land, whilst the tiller of the soil who accompanies him obtains a farm at once by the bounty of the Government. The numerous body of mechanics in our large cities can not, even by emigrating to the West, take advantage of the provisions of this bill without entering upon a new occupation for which their habits of life have rendered them unfit.

5. This bill is unjust to the old States of the Union in many respects; and amongst these States, so far as the public lands are concerned, we may enumerate every State east of the Mississippi with the exception of Wisconsin and a portion of Minnesota.

It is a common belief within their limits that the older States of the Confederacy do not derive their proportionate benefit from the public lands. This is not a just opinion. It is doubtful whether they could be rendered more beneficial to these States under any other system than that which at present exists. Their proceeds go into the common Treasury to accomplish the objects of the Government, and in this manner all the States are benefited in just proportion. But to give this common inheritance away would deprive the old States of their just proportion of this revenue without holding out any the least corresponding advantage. Whilst it is our common glory that the new States have become so prosperous and populous, there is no good reason why the old States should offer premiums to their own citizens to emigrate from them to the West. That land of promise presents in itself sufficient allurements to our young and enterprising citizens without any adventitious aid. The offer of free farms would probably have a powerful effect in encouraging emigration, especially from States like Illinois, Tennessee, and Kentucky, to the west of the Mississippi, and could not fail to reduce the price of property within their limits. An individual in States thus situated would not pay its fair value for land when by crossing the Mississippi he could go upon the public lands and obtain a farm almost without money and without price.

6. This bill will open one vast field for speculation. Men will not pay $1.25 for lands when they can purchase them for one-fifth of that price. Large numbers of actual settlers will be carried out by capitalists upon agreements to give them half of the land for the improvement of the other half. This can not be avoided. Secret agreements of this kind will be numerous. In the entry of graduated lands the experience of the Land Office justifies this objection.

7. We ought to maintain the most perfect equality between native and naturalized citizens. They are equal, and ought always to remain equal, before the laws. Our laws welcome foreigners to our shores, and their rights will ever be respected. Whilst these are the sentiments on which I have acted through life, it is not, in my opinion, expedient to proclaim to all the nations of the earth that whoever shall arrive in this country from a foreign shore and declare his intention to become a citizen shall receive a farm of 160 acres at a cost of 25 or 20 cents per acre if he will only reside on it and cultivate it. The invitation extends to all, and if this bill becomes a law we may have numerous actual settlers from China and other Eastern nations enjoying its benefits on the great Pacific Slope. The bill makes a distinction in favor of such persons over native and naturalized citizens. When applied to such citizens, it is confined to such as are the heads of families, but when applicable to persons of foreign birth recently arrived on our shores there is no such restriction. Such persons need not be the heads of families provided they have filed a declaration of intention to become citizens. Perhaps this distinction was an inadvertence, but it is, nevertheless, a part of the bill.

8. The bill creates an unjust distinction between persons claiming the benefit of the preemption laws. Whilst it reduces the price of the land to existing preemptors to 62½ cents per acre and gives them a credit on this sum for two years from the present date, no matter how long they may have hitherto enjoyed the land, future preemptors will be compelled to pay double this price per acre. There is no reason or justice in this discrimination.

9. The effect of this bill on the public revenue must be apparent to all. Should it become a law, the reduction of the price of land to actual settlers to 25 cents per acre, with a credit of five years, and the reduction of its price to existing preemptors to 62½ cents per acre, with a credit of two years, will so diminish the sale of other public lands as to render the expectation of future revenue from that source, beyond the expenses of survey and management, illusory. The Secretary of the Interior estimated the revenue from the public lands for the next fiscal year at $4,000,000, on the presumption that the present land system would remain unchanged. Should this bill become a law, he does not believe that $1,000,000 will be derived from this source.

10. This bill lays the ax at the root of our present admirable land system. The public land is an inheritance of vast value to us and to our descendants. It is a resource to which we can resort in the hour of difficulty and danger. It has been managed heretofore with the greatest wisdom under existing laws. In this management the rights of actual settlers have been conciliated with the interests of the Government. The price to all has been reduced from $2 per acre to $1.25 for fresh lands, and the claims of actual settlers have been secured by our preemption laws. Any man can now acquire a title in fee simple to a homestead of 80 acres, at the minimum price of $1.25 per acre, for $100. Should the present system remain, we shall derive a revenue from the public lands of $10,000,000 per annum, when the bounty-land warrants are satisfied, without oppression to any human being. In time of war, when all other

sources of revenue are seriously impaired, this will remain intact. It may become the best security for public loans hereafter, in times of difficulty and danger, as it has been heretofore. Why should we impair or destroy the system at the present moment? What necessity exists for it?

The people of the United States have advanced with steady but rapid strides to their present condition of power and prosperity. They have been guided in their progress by the fixed principle of protecting the equal rights of all, whether they be rich or poor. No agrarian sentiment has ever prevailed among them. The honest poor man, by frugality and industry, can in any part of our country acquire a competence for himself and his family, and in doing this he feels that he eats the bread of independence. He desires no charity, either from the Government or from his neighbors. This bill, which proposes to give him land at an almost nominal price out of the property of the Government, will go far to demoralize the people and repress this noble spirit of independence. It may introduce among us those pernicious social theories which have proved so disastrous in other countries.

JAMES BUCHANAN

PART THREE

THE ENCOURAGEMENT
OF MANUFACTURES

14. Thomas Jefferson:
"The Husbandman" and "The Manufacturer"

In the mainly rural America of the early days of the Republic, proposals for the encouragement of manufactures had to encounter the opposition of a deep-rooted preference for agrarian rather than industrial ways of life. The classic expression of this feeling comes from Thomas Jefferson's *Notes on Virginia.* The passage, which is cited below, is a brief one, but it is based on an analysis of the special economic position of the country as well as on emphatic judgment of relative values. Husbandry breeds virtue and manufacture breeds corruption. In the older countries manufacture is nevertheless a necessary evil, but in America the evil may be almost entirely avoided. "The immensity of land courting the industry of the husbandman" makes it possible to concentrate on agriculture, and manufactured goods may readily be obtained from Europe.

This passage was written before independence had been won, and the experiences of the new nation and Jefferson's own responsibilities forced him to some modifications of this extreme position. His second annual message, on December 15, 1802, acknowledged somewhat guardedly the duty to "protect the manufactures adapted to our circumstances."[1] The circumstances changed abruptly when the Embargo and the War of

---

[1] Richardson, *Messages and Papers of the Presidents,* vol. I, p. 346.

1812 interrupted the easy commercial intercourse with Europe on which Jefferson's position had rested. American manufactures grew rapidly to meet the emergency and Jefferson recognized their value and was prepared to afford them some continuing protection. His changed viewpoint was expressed in a letter to Benjamin Austin of Boston (reprinted below) citing the experiences of the intervening thirty years as reason for modifying the position taken in the *Notes on Virginia.* "We must now," he said, "place the manufacturer by the side of the husbandman."

Jefferson, however, had not become a convert to the policy of a high tariff. A still later letter, to which Professor Dorfman calls attention, attacked the extreme protectionists for trying to take the earnings of agriculture, the more depressed branch of industry, and "put them into the pockets of the other," manufacturing, "the most flourishing of all." In this way the more "favored branches of manufactures, commerce and navigation" were "riding and ruling over the plundered ploughman and beggared yeomanry."[2] Jefferson retained his partisanship for the yeoman; and the speeches of Thomas Benton and Andrew Johnson, cited in Part Two, are evidence of the long-continued influence in American politics of this Jeffersonian attachment to agrarian values.

NOTES ON VIRGINIA

QUERY XIX—THE PRESENT STATE OF MANUFACTURES, COMMERCE, INTERIOR AND EXTERIOR TRADE

We never had an interior trade of any importance. Our exterior commerce has suffered very much from the beginning

---

From Albert Ellery Bergh, ed., *The Writings of Thomas Jefferson* (Washington: Thomas Jefferson Memorial Association, 1903), vol. II, pp. 228–230. The "Notes" were written in 1781 and 1782 and first published in 1785.

---

[2] Joseph Dorfman, *The Economic Mind in American Civilization, 1606–1865* (New York: The Viking Press, 1946), vol. I, pp. 443–444. The letter was written to William B. Giles of Virginia on December 26, 1825. Bergh, ed., *The Writings of Thomas Jefferson,* vol. XVI, pp. 147, 149–150.

of the present contest. During this time we have manufactured within our families the most necessary articles of clothing. Those of cotton will bear some comparison with the same kinds of manufacture in Europe; but those of wool, flax and hemp are very coarse, unsightly, and unpleasant; and such is our attachment to agriculture, and such our preference for foreign manufactures, that be it wise or unwise, our people will certainly return as soon as they can, to the raising raw materials, and exchanging them for finer manufactures than they are able to execute themselves.

The political economists of Europe have established it as a principle, that every State should endeavor to manufacture for itself; and this principle, like many others, we transfer to America, without calculating the difference of circumstance which should often produce a difference of result. In Europe the lands are either cultivated, or locked up against the cultivator. Manufacture must therefore be resorted to of necessity not of choice, to support the surplus of their people. But we have an immensity of land courting the industry of the husbandman. Is it best then that all our citizens should be employed in its improvement, or that one half should be called off from that to exercise manufactures and handicraft arts for the other? Those who labor in the earth are the chosen people of God, if ever He had a chosen people, whose breasts He has made His peculiar deposit for substantial and genuine virtue. It is the focus in which he keeps alive that sacred fire, which otherwise might escape from the face of the earth. Corruption of morals in the mass of cultivators is a phenomenon of which no age nor nation has furnished an example. It is the mark set on those, who, not looking up to heaven, to their own soil and industry, as does the husbandman, for their subsistence, depend for it on casualties and caprice of customers. Dependence begets subservience and venality, suffocates the germ of virtue, and prepares fit tools for the designs of ambition. This, the natural progress and consequence of the arts, has sometimes perhaps been retarded by accidental circumstances; but, generally speaking, the proportion which the aggregate of the other classes of citizens bears in any State to that of its husbandmen, is the proportion of its unsound to its healthy parts, and is a good enough barometer whereby to measure its degree of corruption. While we have land to labor then, let us never wish to see our citizens occupied at a work-bench, or twirling a distaff. Carpenters, masons, smiths, are wanting in husbandry; but, for the general operations of manufacture, let our workshops remain in Europe. It is better to carry provisions and materials to workmen there, than bring them to the provisions and materials, and with them their manners and principles. The loss by the transportation of commodities across the Atlantic will be made up in happiness and permanence of government. The mobs of great cities add just so much to the support of pure government, as sores do to the strength of the human body. It is the manners and spirit of a people which preserve a republic in vigor. A degeneracy in these is a canker which soon eats to the heart of its laws and constitution.

LETTER TO BENJAMIN AUSTIN

Monticello, January 9, 1816

DEAR SIR,

You tell me I am quoted by those who wish to continue our dependence on England for manufactures. There was a time when I might have been so quoted with more candor, but within the thirty years which have since elapsed, how are circumstances changed! We were then in peace. Our independent place among nations was acknowledged. A commerce which offered the raw material in exchange for the same

---

From Bergh, ed., *The Writings of Thomas Jefferson*, vol. XIV, pp. 389–392.

material after receiving the last touch of industry, was worthy of welcome to all nations. It was expected that those especially to whom manufacturing industry was important, would cherish the friendship of such customers by every favor, by every inducement, and particularly cultivate their peace by every act of justice and friendship. Under this prospect the question seemed legitimate, whether, with such an immensity of unimproved land, courting the hand of husbandry, the industry of agriculture, or that of manufactures, would add most to the national wealth? And the doubt was entertained on this consideration chiefly, that to the labor of the husbandman a vast addition is made by the spontaneous energies of the earth on which it is employed: for one grain of wheat committed to the earth, she renders twenty, thirty, and even fifty fold, whereas to the labor of the manufacturer nothing is added. Pounds of flax, in his hands, yield, on the contrary, but pennyweights of lace. This exchange, too, laborious as it might seem, what a field did it promote for the occupations of the ocean; what a nursery for that class of citizens who were to exercise and maintain our equal rights on the element? This was the state of things in 1785, when the *Notes on Virginia* were first printed; when, the ocean being open to all nations, and their common right in it acknowledged and exercised under regulations sanctioned by the assent and usage of all, it was thought that the doubt might claim some consideration. But who in 1785 could foresee the rapid depravity which was to render the close of that century the disgrace of the history of man? Who could have imagined that the two most distinguished in the rank of nations, for science and civilization, would have suddenly descended from that honorable eminence, and setting at defiance all those moral laws established by the Author of nature between nation and nation, as between man and man, would cover earth and sea with robberies and piracies, merely because strong enough to do it with temporal impunity; and that under this disbandment of nations from social order, we should have been despoiled of a thousand ships, and have thousands of our citizens reduced to Algerine slavery. Yet all this has taken place. One of these nations interdicted to our vessels all harbors of the globe without having first proceeded to some one of hers, there paid a tribute proportioned to the cargo, and obtained her license to proceed to the port of destination. The other declared them to be the lawful prize if they had touched at the port, or been visited by a ship of the enemy nation. Thus were we completely excluded from the ocean. Compare this state of things with that of '85, and say whether an opinion founded in the circumstances of that day can be fairly applied to those of the present. We have experienced what we did not then believe, that there exist both profligacy and power enough to exclude us from the field of interchange with other nations; that to be independent for the comforts of life we must fabricate them ourselves. We must now place the manufacturer by the side of the agriculturist. The former question is suppressed, or rather assumes a new form. Shall we make our own comforts, or go without them, at the will of a foreign nation? He, therefore, who is now against domestic manufacture, must be for reducing us either to dependence on that foreign nation, or to be clothed in skins, and to live like wild beasts in dens and caverns. I am not one of these; experience has taught me that manufactures are now as necessary to our independence as to our comfort; and if those who quote me as of a different opinion, will keep pace with me in purchasing nothing foreign where an equivalent of domestic fabric can be obtained without regard to difference of price, it will not be our fault if we do not soon have a supply at home equal to our demand, and wrest that weapon of distress from the hand which has wielded it. If it shall be proposed to go beyond our own supply, the question of '85 will then recur, will our *surplus* labor be then most beneficially employed in the culture of the earth, or in the fabrications of art? We have time yet for consideration, before that question will press upon us; and the maxim to be applied will depend on the circumstances which shall then exist; for in so complicated a science as political economy, no one axiom can be laid down as wise and expedient for all times and circumstances, and for their contraries. Inattention to this is what has called for this explanation, which reflection would have rendered unnecessary with the candid, while nothing will do it with those who use the former opinion only as a stalking horse, to cover their disloyal propensities to keep us in eternal vassalage to a foreign and unfriendly people.

15. Alexander Hamilton: "The Incitement and Patronage of Government"

Hamilton's *Report on Manufactures,* presented in 1791, is still regarded as the classic statement of the case for the encouragement of manufactures in the national interest. The Report begins with a reasoned argument against the prevalent viewpoint, illustrated in the previous selection, that agriculture was superior to industry. It proceeds to an enumeration of the positive advantages to be gained by manufacturing, and it attempts to refute the economic arguments that shortages of labor and capital would make it unprofitable in the American case. On the basis of an extensive correspondence similar to that on which Gallatin would later base his *Report on Roads and Canals,*[1] Hamilton reviews the progress already made in the various branches of manufacturing. A final section discusses the means by which encouragement might best be given.

---

[1] See Document 1 above. Arthur H. Cole, ed., *Industrial and Commercial Correspondence of Alexander Hamilton Anticipating His Report on Manufactures* (Chicago: A. W. Shaw Co., 1928).

The Report on Manufactures has perhaps been quoted more often than any other document in American economic history, and its full text is readily available.[2] The present selection is therefore confined to three brief passages which have sometimes been overlooked or on which later writers have differed in their interpretations.

The first of these relates to the advantages claimed for manufactures in the use and development of human capacities. Together with the often quoted claim that industry would put idle women and children to productive work, it advances the more developmental argument that the new employment would draw forth and utilize a greater "diversity of talents."

The second passage develops what in later discussion became known as the "infant industry" argument. Why, it asks, cannot the matter be left to what Hamilton, earlier in *The Report,* had called "the quick-sighted guidance of private interest?" Why will not manufactures "grow up as soon and as fast as the natural state of things . . . may require?" Hamilton's answer emphasizes the barriers placed in the way of such a natural development by the "artificial" means employed by the older nations to protect their own manufactures against competition. But he notes also the obstacles of human inertia and habit, which should be counteracted by the "incitement" of an active government, and the economic "obstacles inseparable from first experiments." A new industry will necessarily operate at high costs, and it will require the aid of government to overcome its initial difficulties.

A third and little-remembered passage, which concludes *The Report,* is part of Hamilton's discussion of the methods by which the necessary encouragement should be given. Protective duties on imports are of course in the list and are cited first, although outright subsidy would be in some ways preferable. But the Report also recommends a variety of other

---

[2] E.g., Alexander Hamilton, *Papers on Public Credit, Commerce, and Finance,* Samuel McKee, Jr., ed., in "American Heritage Series," No. 18 (New York: Bobbs-Merrill, 1957).

methods and the establishment of what now might be called a National Planning Board to administer them. The duties of the "commissioners" should be to stimulate invention and technical progress by offering premiums "both honorable and lucrative" and to arrange for the importation of machinery and experts and workmen with the necessary skills.

This last recommendation went unheeded. No such commission was established or seriously considered, and none of its functions was ever undertaken by the national government, except indirectly through the patent system. Future debate and decision on the encouragement of manufactures were to turn almost entirely on the single issue of the protective tariff.

As to the additional employment of classes of the community not originally engaged in the particular business.

This is not among the least valuable of the means, by which manufacturing industries contribute to augment the general stock of industry and production. In places where those institutions prevail, besides the persons regularly engaged in them, they afford occasional and extra employment to industrious individuals and families, who are willing to devote the leisure resulting from the intermissions of their ordinary pursuits to collateral labors, as a resource for multiplying their acquisitions or their enjoyments. The husbandman himself experiences a new source of profit and support, from the increased industry of his wife and daughters, invited and stimulated by the demand of the neighboring manufactories.

Besides this advantage of occasional employment to classes having different occupations, there is another, of a nature allied

From "Report on Manufactures," 2nd Congress, 1st Session, House Report No. 31, December 5, 1791, *American State Papers, Finance*, vol. I, pp. 126–129, 144.

to it, and of a similar tendency. This is the employment of persons who would otherwise be idle, and in many cases, a burthen on the community, either from the bias of temper, habit, infirmity of body, or some other cause, indisposing or disqualifying them for the toils of the country. It is worthy of particular remark, that in general, women and children are rendered more useful, and the latter more early useful, by manufacturing establishments, than they would otherwise be. Of the number of persons employed in the cotton manufactories of Great Britain, it is computed that four-sevenths, nearly, are women and children; of whom the greatest proportion are children, and many of them of a tender age.

And thus it appears to be one of the attributes of manufactures, and one of no small consequence, to give occasion to the exertion of a greater quantity of industry, even by the same number of persons, where they happen to prevail, than would exist if there were no such establishments. . . .

As to the furnishing greater scope for the diversity of talents and dispositions, which discriminate men from each other.

This is a much more powerful mean of augmenting the fund of national industry, than may at first sight appear. It is a just observation, that minds of the strongest and most active powers for their proper objects, fall below mediocrity, and labor without effect, if confined to uncongenial pursuits. And it is thence to be inferred, that the results of human exertion may be immensely increased by diversifying its objects. When all the different kinds of industry obtain in a community, each individual can find his proper element, and can call into activity, the whole vigor of his nature. And the community is benefitted by the services of its respective members, in the manner in which each can serve it with most effect.

If there be any thing in a remark often to be met with, namely, that there is, in the genius of the people of this country, a peculiar aptitude for mechanic improvements, it would operate as a forcible reason for giving opportunities to the exercise of that species of talent, by the propagation of manufactures.

As to the affording a more ample and various field for enterprise.

This also is of greater consequence in the general scale of national exertion, than might, perhaps, on a superficial view be supposed, and has effects not altogether dissimilar from those of the circumstance last noticed. To cherish and stimulate the activity of the human mind, by multiplying the objects of enterprise, is not among the least considerable of the expedients by which the wealth of a nation may be promoted. Even things in themselves not positively advantageous, sometimes becomes so, by their tendency to provoke exertion. Every new scene which is opened to the busy nature of man to rouse and exert itself, is the addition of a new energy to the general stock of effort.

The spirit of enterprise, useful and prolific as it is, must necessarily be contracted or expanded, in proportion to the simplicity or variety of the occupations and productions which are to be found in a society. It must be less in a nation of mere cultivators, than in a nation of cultivators and merchants; less in a nation of cultivators and merchants, than in a nation of cultivators, artificers, and merchants. . . .

The remaining objections to a particular encouragement of manufactures in the United States, now require to be examined.

One of these turns on the proposition, that industry, if left to itself, will naturally find its way to the most useful and profitable employment. Whence it is inferred, that manufactures, without the aid of government, will grow up as soon and as fast as the natural state of things and the interest of the community may require.

Against the solidity of this hypothesis, in the full latitude of the terms, very cogent reasons may be offered. These have relation to the strong influence of habit and the spirit of imitation; the fear of want of success in untried enterprises; the intrinsic difficulties incident to first essays towards a competition with those who have previously attained to perfection in the business to be attended; the bounties, premiums, and other artificial encouragements, with which foreign nations second the exertions of their own citizens, in the branches in which they are to be rivalled.

Experience teaches, that men are often so much governed by what they are accustomed to see and practise, that the simplest and most obvious improvements, in the most ordinary occupations, are adopted with hesitation, reluctance, and by slow gradations. The spontaneous transition to new pursuits, in a community long habituated to different ones, may be expected to be attended with proportionably greater difficulty. When former occupations ceased to yield a profit adequate to the subsistence of their followers; or when there was an absolute deficiency of employment in them, owing to the superabundance of hands, changes would ensue; but these changes would be likely to be more tardy than might consist with the interest either of individuals or of the society. In many cases they would not happen, while a bare support could be ensured by an adherence to ancient courses, though a resort to a more profitable employment might be practicable. To produce the desirable changes as early as may be expedient, may therefore require the incitement and patronage of government.

The apprehension of failing in new attempts, is, perhaps, a more serious impediment. There are dispositions apt to be attracted by the mere novelty of an undertaking; but these are not always those best calculated to give it success. To this, it is of importance that the confidence of cautious, sagacious, capitalists, both citizens and foreigners, should be excited. And to inspire this description of persons with confidence, it is essential that they should be made to see in any project which is new—and for that reason alone, if for no other—precarious, the prospect of such a degree of countenance and support from government, as may be capable of overcoming the obstacles inseparable from first experiments.

The superiority antecedently enjoyed by nations who have pre-occupied and perfected a branch of industry, constitutes a more formidable obstacle than either of those which have been mentioned, to the introduction of the same branch into a country in which it did not before exist. To maintain, between the recent establishments of one country, and the long matured establishments of another country, a competition upon equal terms, both as to quality and price, is, in most cases, impracticable. The disparity, in the one, or in the other, or in both, must necessarily be so considerable, as to forbid a successful rivalship, without the extraordinary aid and protection of government.

But the greatest obstacle of all to the successful prosecution of a new branch of industry in a country in which it was before unknown, consists, as far as the instances apply, in the bounties, premiums, and other aids, which are granted in a variety of cases, by the nations in which the establishments to be imitated are previously introduced. It is well known (and particular examples, in the course of this report, will be cited) that certain nations grant bounties on the exportation of particular commodities, to enable their own workmen to undersell and supplant all competitors, in the countries to which those commodities are sent. Hence the undertakers of a new manufacture have to contend, not only with the natural disadvantages of a new undertaking, but with the gratuities and remunerations which other governments bestow. To be enabled to contend with success, it is evident that the interference and aid of their own governments are indispensable. . . .

Let a certain annual sum be set apart, and placed under the management of commissioners, not less than three, to consist of certain officers of the Government and their successors in office.

Let these commissioners be empowered to apply the fund

confided to them, to defray the expenses of the emigration of artists, and manufacturers in particular branches of extraordinary importance; to induce the prosecution and introduction of useful discoveries, inventions, and improvements, by proportionate rewards, judiciously held out and applied; to encourage by premiums, both honorable and lucrative, the exertions of individuals and of classes, in relation to the several objects they are charged with promoting; and to afford such other aids to those objects as may be generally designated by law.

The commissioners to render to the Legislature an annual account of their transactions and disbursements; and all such sums as shall not have not been applied to the purposes of their trust, at the end of every three years, to revert to the treasury. It may, also, be enjoined upon them not to draw out the money, but for the purpose of some specific disbursement.

It may, moreover, be of use to authorize them to receive voluntary contributions, making it their duty to apply them to the particular objects for which they may have been made, if any shall have been designated by the donors.

There is reason to believe that the progress of particular manufactures has been much retarded by the want of skilful workmen. And it often happens, that the capitals employed are not equal to the purposes of bringing from abroad workmen of a superior kind. Here, in cases worthy of it, the auxiliary agency of Government would, in all probability, be useful. There are also valuable workmen in every branch, who are prevented from emigrating, solely, by the want of means. Occasional aids to such persons, properly administered, might be a source of valuable acquisitions to the country.

The propriety of stimulating by rewards the invention and introduction of useful improvements, is admitted without difficulty. But the success of attempts in this way, must evidently depend much on the manner of conducting them. It is probable that the placing of the dispensation of those rewards under some proper discretionary direction, where they may be accompanied by collateral expedients, will serve to give them the surest efficacy. It seems impracticable to apportion, by general rules, specific compensations for discoveries of unknown and disproportionate utility.

The great use which may be made of a fund of this nature, to procure and import foreign improvements, is particularly obvious. Among these, the article of machines would form a most important item.

The operation and utility of premiums have been adverted to, together with the advantages which have resulted from their dispensation, under the direction of certain public and private societies. Of this, some experience has been had, in the instance of the Pennsylvania Society for the promotion of manufactures and useful arts; but the funds of that association have been too contracted to produce more than a very small portion of the good to which the principles of it would have led. It may confidently be affirmed, that there is scarcely any thing which has been devised, better calculated to excite a general spirit of improvement, than the institutions of this nature. They are truly invaluable.

In countries where there is great private wealth, much may be effected by the voluntary contributions of patriotic individuals; but in a community situated like that of the United States, the public purse must supply the deficiency of private resource. In what can it be so useful, as in prompting and improving the efforts of industry?

All which is humbly submitted.

ALEXANDER HAMILTON
Secretary of the Treasury

16. New York State Aid to Manufactures

Several of the states undertook measures to encourage manufactures, acting in the spirit of Hamilton's *Report* and using some of the methods which he recommended. One of the larger of these early programs, that of New York, has recently been analyzed by Dr. Reubens.[1] The principal method of aid was the loan, and between 1790 and 1820 special acts were passed lending a total of $273,000 to forty-eight new or prospective manufacturing enterprises.

Two of these measures, reproduced below, illustrate the small scale of the proposed operations, and their preambles set out the reasons for public encouragement. Capital is scarce, and the companies will bring "valuable artisans" into the state and introduce machinery which will be "of great public utility." A similar justification was given for a measure chartering the New York Manufacturing Company. The statute cited "the difficulty of inducing persons to invest their money in untried enterprises, however important to the general welfare"; and the state's approval was given on condition that the company obtain the patents to certain machinery and that it should *not* carry on manufactures in other states.[2]

In his Governor's Message of 1818, De Witt Clinton advocates further encouragement to manufactures on the basis of the "home market" argument that was later to become better known as part of the American System of Henry Clay. Agriculture needs the incentive of good markets, and these can best be created by building up a domestic manufacturing interest. Primary responsibility rests with the federal government and its tariff-making power, but the actions of the state government and the public spirit of its citizens can also assist in the promotion of American manufactures.

In another message, Clinton, like Hamilton, proposes rewards or bounties for improvements in manufacturing as well as in agriculture; and he reports the "propitious" results of such encouragement already given in the special case of manufactures produced in the home. In his 1820 message, Clinton recommends further loans to manufacturing companies. In 1831, however, a committee of the legislature, commenting on a report of the Comptroller showing many of the loans unpaid,

---

[1] Beatrice G. Reubens, "State Financing of Private Enterprise in Early New York," unpublished Ph.D. dissertation, Columbia University, 1960.

[2] *Laws of the State of New York*, 35th Session, 1812, pp. 509–512.

made a declaration that completely repudiated the developmental premises on which they had been based:

> A large part, in amount, of these loans were made under special acts of the Legislature, passed on the applications of individuals who had undertaken some new business or enterprise which it was considered matter of public policy to patronize; or who, under particular circumstances, were considered as entitled to aid and facilities from the government: and it need scarcely be suggested, that the fact of these borrowers applying to the Legislature affords pretty convincing proof, that the property which they offered as security was not sufficient to enable them to obtain loans from private individuals or companies.[3]

LOANS TO MANUFACTURERS

AN ACT TO LOAN MONEY FOR THE ENCOURAGEMENT OF

CERTAIN USEFUL MANUFACTORIES.—

PASSED APRIL 6, 1808

WHEREAS Benjamin Peck and Job Wilkinson, have, by their memorial, represented to the legislature, that they have it in contemplation to erect a manufactory for spinning cotton yarn and manufacturing cotton cloth, in the village of Waterford, and that the expense will be greater than they can meet, and have prayed legislative aid in the premises; Therefore,

I. *Be it enacted by the People of the State of New-York, represented in Senate and Assembly,* That the treasurer of this state pay, on the warrant of the comptroller, to the said Benjamin Peck and Job Wilkinson, the sum of two thousand dollars,

---

From *Laws of the State of New York*, 31st Session, 1808, pp. 324–325; 35th Session, 1812, pp. 487–488.

[3] "Report of the Committee of Ways and Means, on the finances of the state," February 26, 1831, New York *Assembly Documents*, 54th Session, 1831, No. 224, p. 38.

out of any monies in the treasury not otherwise appropriated; *Provided,* That the said Benjamin Peck and Job Wilkinson, shall previous to receiving the money above directed to be paid by virtue of this act, enter into a bond, jointly and severally, to the people of the State of New-York, conditioned for the faithful payment of two thousand dollars, in four years from the date of the said obligation, together with interest annually for the same, at the rate of six per cent per annum; and shall also execute to the said people a good and sufficient mortgage, upon such unincumbered real estate as the comptroller shall think sufficient (exclusive of any buildings erected on the same) for securing double the said sum of money, with the interest on the same as aforesaid, which said mortgage shall previously be duly recorded at full length, at the expense of the said Benjamin Peck and Job Wilkinson, in the proper county: *And provided also,* That before any money shall be advanced or loaned as hereby directed, the said Benjamin Peck and Job Wilkinson shall give such surety to the comptroller as he shall judge sufficient, that the money received by them, in virtue of the act, shall bona fide be applied to the purpose of prosecuting the said manufactories within this state.

II. *And be it further enacted,* That it shall and may be lawful for the comptroller to loan of the monies now in the treasury, or of the first monies that may be paid in, of the fund appropriated to the use of common schools, to George Booth, a sum not exceeding five thousand dollars, for a term of five years, on such terms and conditions as are contained in the second section of the act entitled "an act for the encouragement of common schools;" *Provided,* That the said George Booth, shall execute a bond, with sufficient sureties, to be approved of by the comptroller, conditioned that the said George Booth shall apply the aforesaid sum so loaned in extending and promoting a woollen manufactory, in the town of Poughkeepsie, in this state.

III. And whereas Charles Joy, has established a manufactory for spinning linen and hemp twine and yarn, at Schaghticoke, in the county of Rensselaer, by machinery, which is a saving of much labor, and promises to be of great public utility, and has prayed for a loan of money for the purpose of making his establishment more extensive; Therefore, *Be it further enacted,* That the comptroller be and he is hereby directed to loan to the said Charles Joy, one thousand five hundred dollars, to be appropriated for the sole purpose of manufacturing yarn and twine, for the term of five years, at six per cent; *Provided,* the said Charles Joy, previous to receiving the said money, so to be loaned as aforesaid, shall enter into bonds and give good and ample security, by a mortgage on lands to be approved of by the comptroller, in double the sum so to be loaned, conditioned to be paid at the expiration of the said term, with annual interest, as specified in the first section of this act: *And provided also,* That before any monies shall be loaned as hereby directed, the said Charles Joy shall also give such surety to the comptroller, as he shall deem sufficient, that the money received by him, in virtue of this act, shall be bona fide applied to the purpose contemplated.

AN ACT AUTHORISING THE COMPTROLLER TO LOAN MONEY TO

SETH CAPRON AND THE MILTON MANUFACTURING COMPANY.—

PASSED JUNE 12, 1812

WHEREAS Seth Capron hath, by his petition to the legislature, represented, that by his great exertions he has succeeded in introducing a number of valuable artizans into this state, and in organizing several extensive associations for carrying on the manufacture of cotton and wool: And whereas it appears by his representation, that in the course of his said undertaking he has expended large sums of money, and incurred extensive pecuniary responsibility, and prays that a loan may be made to him to enable him to complete the valuable works already commenced; Therefore,

I. *Be it enacted by the People of the State of New-York, represented in Senate and Assembly,* That the comptroller be and he is hereby authorised to loan to the said Seth Capron, six thousand dollars out of the first monies which shall be in the treasury, arising from the school fund, at the rate of six per centum per annum: *Provided,* That the said Seth Capron shall execute a bond to the people of this state, conditioned for the annual payment of the interest, and for the repayment of the principal in seven years, and secure the same, by mortgage, on sufficient real estate within this state, to be approved by the comptroller.

II. *And be it further enacted,* That it shall be lawful for the comptroller to loan to the Milton manufacturing society, in the county of Saratoga, six thousand dollars out of the first monies which shall be in the treasury, arising from the school fund, at the rate of six per centum per annum: *Provided,* That the said Milton manufacturing society shall execute a bond to the people of this state, conditioned for the annual payment of the interest, and for the repayment of the principal in seven years, and secure, or procure the same to be secured, by mortgage, on sufficient real estate within this state, to be approved by the comptroller.

DE WITT CLINTON:

"THE HONORABLE PREFERENCE"

GOVERNOR'S MESSAGE, 1818

As Agriculture is the source of our subsistence, the basis of our strength, and the foundation of our prosperity, it is pleasing to observe the public attention awakened to its importance, and associations springing up, in several counties, to cherish

From New York *Assembly Journal,* January 27, 1818, pp. 7–8.

its interests. Having received but a small portion of direct encouragement from government, it has been left to its own energies; and, supported by a fertile soil, cherished by a benign climate, cultivated by industry, and protected by liberty, it has diffused its bounties over the country, and has relieved the wants of the old world. Relying hitherto almost exclusively on the fertility of our soil, and the extent of our possessions, we have not adopted those improvements which the experience of modern times has indicated. And it has not been sufficiently understood that Agriculture is a science as well as an art; that it demands the labor of the mind as well as of the hands; and that its successful cultivation is intimately allied with the most profound investigations of philosophy, and the most elaborate exertions of the human mind.

If not the exclusive duty, it is certainly the peculiar province of the state governments, to superintend and advance the interests of Agriculture. . . .

Good markets for agricultural productions are the vital incentive to agricultural industry; and nothing tends more directly to the promotion of these, than the establishment of cheap and easy modes of transportation; and the erection of flourishing villages, towns and cities, under the auspices of commerce, trade and manufactures. As foreign markets are always fluctuating in their prices, and uncertain as to their exigencies, we must rely principally on our own internal consumption, for the staple and permanent support of Agriculture. But this can only be effected by the excitement of other kinds of industry, and the creation of a great manufacturing interest. The excessive importation of foreign fabrics was the signal of ruin to institutions founded by enterprising industry, reared by beneficial skill, and identified with the general welfare. The raw materials of iron, woollen and cotton manufactures are abundant, and those for the minor and auxiliary ones, can, in most cases, be procured at home with equal facility. Nothing is wanting to destroy foreign competition but the steady protection of the government, and the public spirit of the country.

High duties, and prohibiting provisions applied to foreign productions, afford the most efficient encouragement to our manufactures; and these measures appertain to the legitimate functions of the national government. But much may be done by the state government, by liberal accommodations, by judicious exemptions, and by the whole weight of its influence; and much more may be accomplished by the public spirit of the community. For I am persuaded, that if every citizen who adopts the fabrics of other nations, would seriously consider that he is not only paying taxes for the support of foreign governments, but that he participates in undermining one of the main pillars of our productive industry, he would imitate the honorable preference which you have evinced . . . in favor of American Manufactures.

GOVERNOR'S MESSAGE, 1825

. . .

The useful arts, connected as they are with the comforts and conveniences of life, deserve at all times the fostering care of government. In a community where labour is high and in constant demand—where the genius of the people is prolific in inventions of vast value, and where every new discovery that diminishes manual labor becomes of immediate consequence, it seems wise to hold forth such rewards as may stimulate ingenuity and indemnify expense. The national government, under existing laws, can do but little; and even when letters patent are granted, their validity is frequently drawn into question, with all the expense and vexation of incidental litigation. Would it not be sound policy to reward with liberality the authors of such inventions as produce a saving of labour in agriculture and mechanical pursuits, and improve the quality and augment the quantity of our products and fabrics? It is perceived with much satisfaction, that the encouragement

From New York *Assembly Journal*, January 4, 1825.

already dispensed has had the most propitious influence, in every direction, on the advancement of household and domestic manufactures. Many articles of exquisite workmanship have been presented at our fairs and exhibitions, greatly creditable to those who furnished, and to those who encouraged them. . . .

17. Friedrich List:
Protection as a National Policy

Hamilton's *Report on Manufactures* had no such immediate impact on public policy as did its companion state papers on the Bank (Document 25) and on the Public Credit. No attention was paid to his idea of a sort of planning board distributing premiums and organizing the importation of technology, and the *Report* seems to have had no decisive influence on the mild degree of protection embodied in the tariffs of his time. It did not receive very wide circulation, and indeed it seems safe to say that it has been read by more twentieth-century students of history than by legislators or voters in its own day.

When Hamilton wrote, American manufacturers were too few and too weak to form an important pressure group. But after the War of 1812, a manufacturing interest—ironmasters, textile men, and others—was strong enough to exert its influence in favor of effective protection; and as a result a later generation of protectionist theorists was able to write with more definite relationship to the actual political struggle. In this group the two principal names were the American, Henry C. Carey, and the German economist living in the United States, Friedrich List.[1] The latter's *Outlines of American Political Economy*, from which selections are given below, was written expressly for use in current agitation. It took the form

---

[1] Joseph Dorfman, *The Economic Mind in American Civilization, 1606–1865* (New York: The Viking Press, 1946), vol. II, pp. 789–805, 575–584.

of a series of letters to Charles J. Ingersoll, who was one of the principal organizers of the national convention of protectionists that met at Harrisburg in 1827. The *American* political economy of List's title is a protectionist one. Like the spokesmen for the "developing" nations of today, List declares that no nation ever became wealthy by agriculture alone. Like Hamilton, he argues that manufactures bring out more of a nation's human capacities or, in List's own term, greater "capital of mind." Like Hamilton also, but rather less skillfully, he develops the argument for the protection of infant industry. What is most characteristic in List's writing is his insistence that political economy should be national and not international, or "cosmopolitical," like the doctrines of Adam Smith and Jean Baptiste Say and their American followers. Nations differ in resources and capabilities and should therefore adopt different policies. List bases his argument on an extended analysis of the economic potential of the United States. From this, unlike the land reformers, he draws the conclusion that rapid agricultural settlement of the West represents an uneconomic "diffusion." In contrast to the Jefferson of the *Notes on Virginia,* who argued that the abundance of land would permit the United States to avoid manufacture and its attendant vice, List argues that that same abundance would permit the nation to develop manufactures without vice.

LETTER I

Reading, 10th July, 1827

. . . I believe it to be a duty of the General Convention at Harrisburg, not only to support the interests of the wool grow-

---

From *Outlines of American Political Economy in a Series of Letters to Charles J. Ingersoll* (Philadelphia: Samuel Barker, 1827). The quotations are from pp. 6–12, 20–26, 31–32. (A copy is in the Seligman Library of Columbia University, which contains a notation in the hand of the late Professor E. R. A. Seligman, founder of the collection, "exceedingly rare original work of List—the father of protection. . . .")

ers and wool manufacturers, but to lay the axe to the root of the tree, by declaring the system of Adam Smith and Co. to be erroneous—by declaring war against it on the part of the American System—by inviting literary men to uncover its errors, and to write popular lectures on the American System —and, lastly, by requesting the governments of the different states, as well as the general government, to support the study of the American System in the different Colleges, Universities, and literary institutions under their auspices. . . .

In consequence of my researches, I found the component parts of political economy to be—1, Individual economy; 2, National economy; 3, Economy of mankind. A. Smith treats of individual economy and economy of mankind. He teaches how an individual creates, increases and consumes wealth in society with other individuals, and how the industry and wealth of mankind influence the industry and wealth of the individual. He has entirely forgotten what the title of his book, "Wealth of Nations," promised to treat. Not taking into consideration the different state of power, constitution, wants and culture of the different nations, his book is a mere treatise on the question, how the economy of the individuals and of mankind would stand, if the human race were not separated into nations, but united by a general law and by an equal culture of mind. This question he treats quite logically; and in this supposition his book contains great truths. If the whole globe were united by a union like the 24 States of North America, free trade would indeed be quite as natural and beneficial as it is now in the union. There would be no reason for separating the interest of a certain space of land, and of a certain number of human beings, from the interests of the whole globe and of the whole race. There would be no national interest, no national law contrary to the freedom of the whole race, no restriction, no war. All would flow in its natural current. English capital and skill, if in superabundance in that island, would overflow to the borders of the Seine and Elbe, of the Rhine and Tagus; they would have fertilized the woods of Bohemia and Poland long before they would flow to the borders of the Ganges and of the St. Lawrence, and every where carry along with them freedom and law. An Englishman would as readily emigrate to Gallicia and Hungary as now a New-Jerseyman emigrates to Missouri and Arkansas. No nation would have to fear for their independence, power and wealth, from the measures of other nations.

This state of things may be very desirable—it may do honour to the heart of a philosopher to wish for it—it may even lie in the great plan of Providence to accomplish it in after ages. But sir, it is not the state of the actual world.

Economy of individuals and economy of mankind, as treated by Adam Smith, teach by what means an individual creates, increases and consumes wealth in society with other individuals, and how the industry and wealth of mankind influence the industry and wealth of individuals. *National Economy* teaches by what means a certain nation, in her particular situation, may direct and regulate the economy of individuals, and restrict the economy of mankind, either to prevent foreign restrictions and foreign power, or to increase the productive powers within herself—or in other words: How to create, in absence of a lawful state, within the whole globe of the earth, a world in itself, in order to grow in power and wealth to be one of the most powerful, wealthy and perfect nations of the earth, without restricting the economy of individuals and the economy of mankind more than the welfare of the people permits.

In my next letter, I shall dwell more upon this subject. For the present remains but space enough to request your indulgence on account of my inability to express myself correctly and elegantly in the language of this country.

Very respectfully your most humble servant,

Fr. List

LETTER II

12th July, 1827

The object of individual economy is merely to obtain the necessities and comforts of life. The object of economy of mankind, or to express it more properly, of *cosmopolitical economy*, is to secure to the whole human race the greatest quantity of the necessities and comforts of life. An individual living in Pennsylvania, considered solely as a part of mankind, has no particular interest that wealth and productive powers should be encreased rather in Vermont or Maine, than in England. If this individual happens to be the agent of a foreign manufactory, he may even be injured in his livelihood by the growing industry of his next neighbours. Nor is mankind interested which spot of the earth, or which people excels in industry; it is benefitted by every increase of industry, and restrictions are as obnoxious to mankind at large, as restrictions of the free intercourse between the twenty four United States would be injurious to the wealth and productive powers of this nation. The idea of *power* is neither applicable to an individual, nor to the whole human race. If the whole globe were to be united by a general law, it would not be of any consequence to a particular people, as regards its freedom and its independence, whether it is strong or weak in population, power, and wealth; as it is now of no consequence for the State of Delaware, as regards her freedom and independence, that her wealth, population, and territory are ten times surpassed by her next neighbour, the State of Pennsylvania. . . .

Indeed so wrong are these adherents of the Scots theory, that in spite of the very name they chose to give their science, they will make us believe that there is nothing of politics in political economy. If their science is properly called *political economy* there must be just as much *politics* in it as *economy*, and if there is no *politics* in it, the science has not got the proper name; it is then nothing else but *economy*. The truth is that the name is right, expressing the very thing these gentlemen mean to treat, but the thing they treat is not consonant to the name. They do not treat *political* economy, but *cosmopolitical* economy.

To complete the science we must add the principles of national economy. The idea of national economy arises with the idea of nations. A nation is the medium between individuals and mankind; a separate society of individuals, who, possessing common government, common laws, rights, institutions, interests, common history, and glory, common defence and security of their rights, riches, and lives, constitute one body, free and independent, following only the dictates of its interest, as regards other independent bodies, and possessing power to regulate the interests of the individuals, constituting that body, in order to create the greatest quantity of common welfare in the interior and the greatest quantity of security as regards other nations. The object of the economy of this body is not only wealth as in individual and cosmopolitical economy, but power and wealth, because national wealth is increased and secured by national power, as national power is increased and secured by national wealth. Its leading principles are therefore not only economical, but political too. The individuals may be very wealthy; but if the nation possesses no power to protect them, it and they may lose in one day the wealth they gathered during ages, and their rights, freedom, and independence too. In a mere economical view, it may be quite indifferent to a Pennsylvanian whether the manufacturer who gives him cloth in exchange for his wheat, lives in Old England or in New England; but in time of war and of restriction, he can neither send wheat to England nor import cloth from there, whilst the exchange with New England would forever be undisturbed. If the manufacturer grows wealthy by this exchange, the inhabitant of Old England increases the power of his enemy in time of war, whilst the manufacturer of New England increases the defence of his nation. In time of peace the farmer of Pennsylvania may do well in buying English guns and gun-powder to shoot game; but in time of war the Englishmen will not furnish him with the means to be shot.

As power secures wealth, and wealth increases power, so are power and wealth, in equal parts, benefitted by a harmonious state of agriculture, commerce and manufactures within the limits of the country.—In the absence of this harmony, a nation is never powerful, and wealthy. A merely agricultural state is dependent for its market as well as for its supply on foreign laws, on foreign good will or enmity. Manufactures, moreover, are the nurses of arts, sciences, and skill, the sources of power and wealth. A merely agricultural people remain always poor. . . .

Nobody can deny these truths. But it is questioned, sir, whether government has a right to restrict individual industry, in order to bring to harmony the three component parts of national industry: and, secondly, it is questioned, whether government does well or has it in its power to produce this harmony by laws and restrictions.

Government, sir, has not only the right, but it is its duty, to promote every thing which may increase the wealth and power of the nation, if this object cannot be effected by individuals. So it is its duty to guard commerce by a navy, because the merchants cannot protect themselves; so it is its duty to protect the carrying trade by navigation laws, because carrying trade supports naval power, as naval power protects carrying trade; so the shipping interest and commerce must be supported by breakwaters—agriculture and every other industry by turnpikes, bridges, canals and rail roads—new inventions by patent laws—so manufactures must be raised by protecting duties, if foreign capital and skill prevents individuals from undertaking them.

In regard to the expediency of protecting measures, I observe that it depends entirely on the condition of a nation whether they are efficacious or not. Nations are as different, in their conditions, as individuals are. There are giants and dwarfs, youths and old men, cripples and well made persons; some are superstitious, dull, indolent, uninstructed, barbarous; others are enlightened, active, enterprising, and civilized; some are slaves, others are half slaves, others free and self-governed; some are predominant over other nations, some independent, and some live more or less in a state of dependency. How wise men can apply general rules to these different bodies, I cannot conceive. I consider so doing no wiser than for physicians to prescribe alike to a child and a giant; to the old and young in all cases the same diet and the same medicine.

Protecting duties in Spain would deprive the Spanish nation of the trifling industry she yet retains.—Having no navy, how could she support such measures? A dull, indolent and superstitious people can never derive any advantage from them, and no foreigner of a sound mind, would submit his capital and his life to a brutal absolute power. . . . Even these United States, after having just converted themselves from a colony to an independent nation, did well to remain for a while in economical vassalage. But after having acquired the strength of a man, it would be absurd to act as a child, as the scripture says: 'when I was a child, I acted as a child, but when I became a man I acted as a man.'

The condition of this nation cannot be compared with the condition of any other nation. The same kind of government and same structure of society were never seen before; nor such general and equal distribution of property, of instruction, of industry, of power and wealth; nor similar accomplishments in the gifts of nature, bestowing upon this people natural riches and advantages of the north, of the south, and of the temperate climates, all the advantages of vast sea shores and of an immense unsettled continent, and all the activity and vigour of youth and of freedom. There is no people, nor was there ever a people, doubling their number every twenty-five years, doubling the number of their states in fifty years, excelling in such a degree of industry, skill and power, creating a navy in a few years, and completing, in a short time, public improvements, which, in former times, would alone have distinguished a nation forever.

As the condition of this nation is unexampled, the effects of her efforts to raise manufactures will be without example; while minor states must submit to the English naval ascendancy, the Americans can raise their heads and look it full in the face. If poor, uninstructed, indolent, and depressed people cannot rise by their own efforts, this free, enterprising, instructed, industrious and wealthy people may. If other people must restrict their ambition, to live in a tolerable dependence and economical vassalage, this nation would do injustice to the call of nature, if it should not look up to full independence, if it should not aspire to an unexampled degree of power to preserve its unexampled degree of freedom and of happiness. But a high degree of power and wealth, a full independence, is never to be acquired, if the manufacturing industry is not brought into harmony with agricultural and commercial industry. Government would therefore not only do well in supporting this industry, but wrong in not doing it.

American national economy, according to the different conditions of the nations, is quite different from English national economy. English national economy, has for its object to manufacture for the whole world, to monopolize all manufacturing power, even at the expense of the lives of her citizens, to keep the world, and especially her own colonies, in a state of infancy and vassalage by political management as well as by the superiority of her capital, her skill and her navy. American economy has for its object to bring into harmony the three branches of industry, without which no national industry can attain perfection. It has for its object to supply its own wants, by its own materials and its own industry—to people an unsettled country—to attract foreign population, foreign capital and skill—to increase its power and its means of defence, in order to secure the independence and the future growth of the nation. It has for its object, lastly, to be free and independent, and powerful, and to let every one else enjoy freedom, power and wealth as he pleases. English national economy is *predominant;* American national economy aspires only to become *independent.*—As there is no similarity in the two systems, there is no similarity in the consequences of it. The country will not be overstocked with woollen goods any more than it is now overstocked with cabinet ware; the manufactories will not produce vice, because every labourer can earn enough to support his family honestly; nobody will suffer or starve from want of labour, because if the labourer cannot earn enough to support his family otherwise, he can cultivate the earth—there is yet room enough for hundreds of millions to become independent farmers.

LETTER IV

18th July, 1827

. . . The question is only whether this nation is enabled—

1. By its natural means to increase its productive power by fostering cotton and woollen manufactories? (capital of nature:)

2. Whether by its present industry, instruction, enterprising spirit, perseverance, armies, naval power, government, (capital of mind) it is reasonably to be expected that it can acquire the necessary skill to complete in a short time its productive power by these manufactories, and whether it can protect them by its political power if acquired? And lastly,

3. Whether there exists so much superabundance of food, utensils, materials, raw stuff, &c. (capital of matter,) as to go on fairly by using the capital of nature and employing the capital of mind.

I. There is pasture enough to raise a hundred millions of sheep, and land enough to raise cotton for the whole world, besides all other materials and provisions. If it would be sheer folly for the Swedish government to establish those manufactories, because it possesses neither opportunity to raise a sufficient quantity of wool and cotton, nor the necessary naval power to secure its supply from abroad, or a foreign market for its manufactures, would it not be equal folly for these United States not to establish and foster them?

II. There exists in the United States a degree of industry, of instruction, of emulation, of enterprising spirit, of perseverance, of unrestricted intercourse in the interior, an absence of all hindrances of industry, a security of property, a market and consumption of necessaries and comforts of life, and a freedom, such as are not to be found in any other country. If the government of Spain could not by any arrangements whatever raise in a hundred years ten prosperous manufacturing establishments, and if raised could never protect them, this country can raise in a few years a hundred, and give them every kind of protection.

III. There exists in these United States an immense quantity, a superabundance of all kinds of necessaries of life, and of labour, to nourish double the present number of inhabitants, to build them houses and shops and mills, to procure them materials and tools. What else is necessary to establish manufactories, and what branch of industry may not be carried on by such means upon the largest scale? . . .

V. Even if there were not capital and skill enough in the country they could be drawn from abroad by political measures. Under number I, I mentioned that capital and knowledge have the tendency to extend themselves over the whole globe, and that they go from those parts where they are in superabundance to those where they are scarce. (To my knowledge the theorists neither observed this tendency, nor did they justice to it.) As this tendency is checked by the policy, &c. of other nations, so it can be restored by counteracting that policy. In securing to foreign capital and skill a premium in this country you will attract them from abroad. The United States have this more in their power than any other nation, because they possess more capital of nature (not yet taken into possession) and more capital of mind than any other nation. Here an immense mass of natural riches have not yet got a proprietor. Here an Englishman finds his language, his laws, his manner of living; the only thing he does not find are the immense taxes and the other evils of his own country. In coming here, any man, from whatever country he comes, if possessing capital, industry and useful knowledge, improves his condition. I know of no other country which enjoys such opportunities and means of attracting foreign capital and skill.

Whilst the United States by protecting duties would attract foreign capital and skill, they would prevent in the interior a very disadvantageous extension of population and capital over an immense continent. I am not, sir, one of those, who estimate the power and wealth of this union by the number of states. As the Roman military power was weakened by the extension of their territory, so, I fear, the power, the progress of civilization, the national strength of this union would be checked by an additional accession of states. Fifty millions of Americans in one hundred states scattered over the whole continent, what would they do?—clear land—raise wheat—and eat it. The whole American history of the next hundred years shall be contained in these three words, if you do not what Jefferson said—place the manufacturer by the side of the farmer. This is the only means of preventing population and capital from withdrawing to the west. Ohio will soon be as populous as Pennsylvania—Indiana as Ohio—Illinois as Indiana; then they will pass over the Mississippi—next the rocky mountains—and at last turn their faces to China instead of England. Pennsylvania and all the eastern and middle states can increase in population, in arts and sciences, civilization and wealth, and the

Union can grow powerful only by fostering the manufacturing interest. This, sir, I think the true *American political economy.*

LETTER V

10th July, 1827

Would the United States act reasonably if they should foster all kinds of manufactories with equal care? By no means. Every improvement must be advanced by steps. A new country like this, increases its productive powers by only fostering those manufactories which employ a number of labourers, and consume great quantities of agricultural produce and raw materials; which can be supported by machinery and by a great internal consumption, (like chemical produce, woollen, cotton, hardware, iron, earthenware, &c. manufactories) and which are not easy to be smuggled. In fostering finer articles with equal care, they would injure the development of the productive powers. Those articles of comfort and luxury, if imported cheaper than we can manufacture them, get in use among all labouring classes, and act as a stimulus in exciting the productive powers of the nation. Its consumption becomes by and by more important, and by and by the time will arrive when these articles, with a moderate encouragement, will be manufactured too within our limits.

Are canals and rail-roads beneficial to a country? Under conditions. In bringing people and produce nearer each other, they support the exchange, and promote labour if labour is properly divided. If not, they may injure certain parts of the country to the advantage of other parts, by increasing competition in the surplus of agricultural produce. So I firmly believe that the eastern parts of Pennsylvania only can derive advantage from those improvements by raising a manufacturing industry, and exchanging the surplus of their manufactures for the agricultural produce of the West.

Machinery and new inventions? For thickly settled countries possessing no commerce, little industry, and a superabundance of labourers, they may be a public calamity; whilst every such improvement in the United States is to be considered as a public blessing. In time I hope the slaves of this country will be made of iron and brass, and set in movement by stone coal instead of whips.

Parsimony? If exercised in the old countries by men who are in possession of immense estates by birth-right, would certainly not be a public blessing; it only would increase the inequality of property at the expense of the lower classes. The parsimony of a farmer living in a new settlement, sparing all his income and bestowing all his time and labour to improve his land, to increase his stock, walking barefoot and wearing self-prepared skins, increases productive powers; because the land would not be improved without it. . . .

LETTER VI

20th July, 1827

As the commerce of a nation wants protection against foreign aggressions, even at the great expense of the country, and even at the risk of a war, so the manufacturing and agricultural interest must be promoted and protected even by sacrifices of the majority of the individuals, if it can be proved that the nation would never acquire the necessary perfection, or could never secure to itself an acquired perfection without such protective measures. This can be proved, and I will prove it. And if the masters and disciples of the cosmopolitical theory are not convinced of this necessity, that is no argument that it does not exist, but proves only that they do not understand the true nature of political economy.

A manufacturing power, like a maritime power, (under which name I comprehend not only the navy but the whole shipping of a country,) is only to be acquired by long exertions. It takes a long time until the labourers are experienced in the different workmanship and accustomed to it; and until the necessary number for every business is at all times to be had. The more, knowledge, experience and skill are wanted, for a particular business, the less, individuals will be willing to devote themselves to it, if they have not a full assurance of their being able to make a living by it for their whole life-time. Every new business is connected with great losses by want of experience and skill for a considerable time. The advancement of every kind of manufactorics, depends upon the advancement of many other kinds, upon the proper construction of houses and works, of instruments and machinery. All this makes the commencement of a new undertaking extremely difficult, whilst the undertakers have to contend with a want of labourers of skill and experience; the first cost of starting a business is the heaviest of all, and the wages of the unskilled labourers in countries which commence manufactories, are higher than the wages of the skilled ones in old manufacturing countries. All cost double prices, and every fault in starting the business causes heavy losses, and sometimes the failure of the whole undertaking. The undertakers possess moreover, in most cases, not a sufficient knowledge of the ways and means to get the first materials profitably, and whilst they are struggling against all these difficulties, they have great exertions to make to get customers, and often to contend with the prejudices of their countrymen, who, not willing to leave their old way in doing business, are in most cases in favour of the foreign manufactories. Often they may be right. New establishments are seldom able to procure such finished articles in the first and second year, as they would in the third and fourth, if supported, and nevertheless their articles must be sold higher. It cannot be expected that the consumers, as individuals by their own accord, should support a manufactory, by purchasing less accomplished articles at higher prices, even if convinced that, in purchasing them, they would encourage the manufactories to improve their products, and to procure them after a while cheaper than foreign manufactures.

All these circumstances are the cause why so many new establishments fail if let alone. Every failure breaks a man, because the greater part of their expenditure in building machinery, in procuring labourers from abroad, &c. is lost. One example of such a failure effects a discouragement of all other new undertakings, and the most advantageous business cannot find afterwards a support from capitalists.

In old manufacturing countries we observe quite the contrary. There are plenty of skilled labourers for every kind of business, at moderate terms, to be had. All buildings, machinery, implements, are in the best condition; the expenditure for them is for the greater part reimbursed by gains already made. On the basis of the already acquired experience and skill, the manufacturer can improve daily his buildings and instruments at moderate expenses; he can save expenditures and perfect his manufactures. The manufacturer himself is possessor of skill, undertaking and capital, and he cannot be exposed to embarrassments by the withdrawal of one of these essential parts, as is the case with new undertakings, where often the undertaker, and the performer, and the possessor of capital are different men, and the whole business can be stopped by the withdrawal of one of them. Credit and confidence of the old manufactures are established; it is therefore as easy for the possessor to get new support from capitalists, as it is difficult for a new undertaker. The credit of his manufactures and his market is established; he can produce finished articles at moderate prices, and yet afford his customers a liberal credit.

Such are the natural differences between an old manufacturing country and a new country just entering into business. The old country, as long as it preserves its freedom, its vigour, its political power, will, in a free intercourse, ever keep down a rising manufacturing power. The Netherlands would never have been deprived of their superior manufacturing power by the English, without the regulations of Edward, Elizabeth, and the following governments, and without the follies of the kings of France and Spain. A new country is, moreover, the less able to contend against the manufacturing power of the old country, the more the interior market of this old country is protected by duties, and the more its competition in the new country is supported by drawbacks, and by an absence of duties in the foreign markets.

18. Protection as an Object of Local Interest

If manufactures are to be encouraged, there remains the problem, as President Madison reminded the Congress, of "selecting the branches more especially entitled to the public patronage."[1] The question would today be recognized as an important one for the planning of economic development, but it received little treatment in the American literature. Madison himself and a number of others suggested priority for the production of the materials of war, and Friedrich List (Document 17) recommended discrimination on more general economic grounds. But when it came to translating the nationalistic principles of Hamilton and List into the detailed schedules of an actual tariff, the most immediate pressures for the inclusion of particular items usually came from those who wished to manufacture them or, more often, had already committed resources to their production.

"Manufactures in the United States," declared the North Carolina Legislature, "are not an object of *general* but of *local* interest."[2] On the other hand, science and agriculture were, in its view, of general interest. The distinction seems a strange

---

[1] Seventh Annual Message, December 5, 1815, in Richardson, *Messages and Papers of the Presidents*, vol. I, p. 563.

[2] *American State Papers, Finance*, 20th Congress, 1st Session, No. 816, vol. V, p. 722.

one, but the sentence will serve to describe an important part of the tariff-making process. It was precisely as objects of local interest that proposals for protection were likely to reach the Congress.

Three illustrations are taken from the flood of resolutions and memorials that were sent to Washington during the discussions that preceded the adoption of the tariff of 1828. One comes from the House of Representatives of Massachusetts together with the plea of a factory that is having to reduce wages, shut down a plant, and discharge employers. The second is the memorial of a "respectable" meeting of wool-growers and wool-manufacturers in upstate New York, joined together because the proposal is to increase duties on raw wool as well as on woolens. The third deals with the much smaller question of umbrella ginghams and silks. On this the Hingham Manufactory presents its petition "humbly" but with an argument that ranges as far as the Brazil Banks.

MEMORIAL OF THE
MASSACHUSETTS LEGISLATURE

In House of Representatives, January 26, 1827

THE SPECIAL COMMITTEE OF THE HOUSE OF REPRESENTATIVES,

TO WHICH WAS REFERRED SO MUCH OF THE GOVERNOR'S

MESSAGE AS RELATES TO THE DEPRESSED STATE OF

OUR WOOLEN MANUFACTURES, HAVE TAKEN THE

SAME SUBJECT INTO CONSIDERATION, AND

RESPECTFULLY REPORT:

That your committee are deeply impressed with the importance of our woolen manufactures as a source of wealth to

---

From *American State Papers, Finance,* 19th Congress, 2nd Session, No. 771, V, 599–600.

this Commonwealth, and as essential to that real independence of foreign nations by which our national resources are to be made adequate to supplying us with every indispensable commodity. Your committee have reason to believe that a large amount of capital is already invested in woolen manufactures, which now give employment and support to thousands of our citizens, and that an additional amount of capital will seek similar investments if our manufactures obtain relief from their present embarrassments.

This relief must proceed from measures devised and adopted by the wisdom of Congress, and calculated to protect our own manufactures from the ruinous competition of an overgrown foreign manufacturing interest. To Congress is given, by the Constitution, the power to "regulate commerce;" and your committee cannot doubt that, in the existing emergency, Congress will exercise this power in the manner most conducive to the mutual benefit of our manufacturing, agricultural, and commercial interests. The period has gone by when it can be successfully urged that the protection of the first of these great interests must be injurious to the others. Commerce and agriculture find their best resources and support in manufacturing industry and its results, and, reciprocally, manufactures create new markets for the products of agriculture and commerce, and breathe new life into the labors of the husbandman and the enterprise of the merchant. To the wisdom of Congress, therefore, your committee look for such measures as are calculated to relieve our woolen manufactures in their present depressed condition, and they accordingly recommend the adoption of a resolve herewith submitted.

Per order of the committee.

JOHN BRAZER DAVIS
Chairman

"*Resolved,* That the House of Representatives of the Commonwealth of Massachusetts is deeply impressed with the importance of our woolen manufactures as a source of national wealth and power, and have full confidence in the wisdom of Congress to devise and adopt such measures as shall relieve them in their present depression."

Boston, January 26, 1827

DEAR SIR:

As it is possible that the fate of the new tariff on woolens may not have been decided on the receipt of this letter, and conceiving that a few statements of facts may be of some service to us, I take the liberty of forwarding to you two votes passed yesterday by the Wolcott Woolen Manufacturing Company, in consequence of the great losses they have met with during the past year, their accounts having been made up to the 31st December, 1826, and show a loss of more than ten per cent. upon their capital stock, not by bad debts, as they do not exceed one hundred dollars, but in consequence of the large quantity of woolens sent to this country from England and Germany, and sold at auction at a very great loss, if the fair duties had been paid upon them.

The Wolcott Woolen Manufacturing Company have been incorporated several years; they have the most approved machinery, and the cloths made at the factory have been sold from $1 75 to $10 37½ per yard; they obtained the medal of the New England Society for the best cloth exhibited in October last; there has been manufactured at the factory during the past year forty-four thousand five hundred and seventy-five yards broadcloth, valued at from $1 50 to $8 per yard. The losses by other woolen manufactories must be about equal to ours; and we must suspend the business entirely, unless the Government grant us some protection by an increase of duties.

In the factory at Woodstock, to which the second vote refers, we have had in full operation the last year fifteen broad hand-looms and other necessary machinery for making superfine cloths; you will observe that mill is to be closed as soon as possible; and at Southbridge we have had sixteen power-looms and five hand-looms in operation, together with the necessary machinery for finishing, &c. One-fourth part of the hands employed there are to be dismissed immediately, and the wages of those retained are to be reduced; and it is our intention to continue to lessen the number employed until the work is entirely suspended, unless we get some relief from Congress during the present session.

With the hope that you will afford us all the assistance in your power, I remain, with great respect, your obedient servant,

SAMUEL TORREY

HON. DANIEL WEBSTER

At a meeting of the directors of the Wolcott Woolen Manufacturing Company, holden on Thursday, January 25, 1827.

Present: Wm. Payne, president, Ebenezer T. Andrews, John Williams, and S. Torrey.

Voted, That the agent be required to dismiss, as soon as possible, one-fourth part of the hands now employed in the factory at Southbridge; and that the wages of those retained in the employ of the company be reduced, so as to average about twenty per cent. from the prices now paid.

Voted, That the agent be required to have finished all the cloth now in preparation at Woodstock, and to suspend all business there by the 1st of April next, if possible.

A true copy of the record.

Attest: SAMUEL TORREY
Clerk

MEMORIAL OF THE WOOL-GROWERS AND MANUFACTURERS OF MADISON COUNTY, NEW YORK

IN FAVOR OF INCREASE OF DUTIES ON IMPORTS

Communicated to the House of Representatives February 4, 1828

At a numerous and respectable meeting, composed of manufacturers, agriculturists, wool-growers, and others friendly to the promotion of American industry, held, pursuant to public notice, at the house of P. Munger, in Morrisville, in the county of Madison and State of New York, on the 21st December, 1827, General Erastus Cleaveland was called to the chair, and Amos Crocker chosen secretary.

Resolved, That a committee be appointed to draught and present for consideration resolutions and a memorial expressing the sense of the meeting on the subject for which it was called.

Resolved, That the said committee consist of Curtis Hoppin, Willard Welton, William Berry, and Bennet Bicknell.

Whereupon the committee, after a recess, reported the following resolutions and memorial; which were unanimously adopted, to wit:

Resolved, That we approve of the proceedings of the Harrisburg convention, held on the 31st day of July last, in recommending and urging upon Congress to extend an adequate protection and encouragement to the growing of wool, hemp, flax, and the manufacture of woolens, iron, steel, and other articles of domestic productions.

Resolved, That we fully approve of the proceedings of the meeting of agriculturists, manufacturers, and others friendly to

From *American State Papers, Finance,* 20th Congress, 1st Session, No. 846, V, 847.

the encouragement of American industry, held at the Capitol, in the city of Albany, on the 26th day of November last, and of the resolutions passed at said meeting.

Resolved, as the sense of this meeting, That the agricultural interest of this county would be greatly promoted by an increased duty on imported liquors.

The memorial of the wool-growers and manufacturers of wool, in the county of Madison, State of New York, convened, pursuant to public notice, at Morrisville, December 21, 1827, respectfully represents: That they inhabit a section of country nearly equidistant from the extremes of the said State, which, for growing of wool, is equal, in salubrity of climate and fertility of soil, to any other in the same latitude of our hemisphere.

Our yeomanry, aware of the advantage coincident with the principles of domestic political economy, have availed themselves of the opportunities collateral to their situation.

Stimulated by the revising the tariff of 1824, a large proportion of our citizens have entered extensively and at great expense into the growing of wool, inasmuch that the wool has become an important staple of the country. Our manufacturers, possessing the advantages of hydraulic and scientific power, animated by the same principles, encouraged by the same law, unwearied in their industry, and liberal in their enterprises, have invested a great amount of capital; have created a business where little before existed; affording the means of subsistence and consumption for a numerous population. Such briefly is the location, and such the condition of your memorialists.

We assume as a fact, that Congress designed by the tariff of 1824 to afford to the great agricultural and manufacturing interests of the United States an adequate protection; under the faith of the guarantee implied by that law your memorialists have invested their capital. We have gone industriously to work to build up an interest which Congress and national economy assured us and the world they would protect—but our business languishes.

Not a woolen factory within the circle of our acquaintance, however industrious and prudent in its management, but assures us of a losing business; our flocks of sheep are reduced to less than half their former value; and lands, though not so much affected, are essentially reduced in price. In searching for causes, the effects of which are so alarming, we are led to discover some defect in the tariff system of 1824, which the ingenuity of foreign manufacturers and growers of wool have turned much to their advantage. That law imposes an ad valorem duty; allows the foreigner to set a value to his own invoices; while the state of trade and manufactures in England and other European countries permits this value to be placed so low that the American manufacturers and wool-growers are overborne by undervalued cloths and wool; and the revenue, too, is defrauded by that which ruins the citizens. Large quantities of broad flannels and pelts have been introduced to evade the duty and embarrass our citizens. Every expedient which the ingenuity of foreign manufacturers and merchants could devise have been resorted to to prostrate the American system; and, we may add, they have been eminently successful. But far more than this, the statesmen of Great Britain, with an eye ever watchful of her agricultural and manufacturing interest and scientific power, the secret of her wealth, have interposed their guardian care, and, by a reduction of her duties from six pence to a halfpenny per pound on imported wool, have virtually countervailed the effect of the American system. . . .

. . . In order, then, to counteract this British legislation, and give the protection intended by the American law, it is incumbent on Congress to increase the duty to 48 per cent. Should this be done, the foreign article will not be enhanced to the American consumer beyond its old prices, because what is added to the duty will be taken from the cost. Will you allow the British Parliament thus virtually to repeal the law passed for the protection of American manufacturers and wool-growers? We think the genius, the interest, and independence of Americans forbid the idea. We derive the confidence of this from various considerations. As manufacturers, we desire that the materials of our fabrics should be grown in our country, relieving us from a dependence upon precarious, uncertain, and foreign supply; while, as wool-growers, demonstration is clear, that, with the fall of American manufactures, our enterprises as wool-growers must be abandoned.

MEMORIAL OF THE
HINGHAM UMBRELLA MANUFACTORY

FOR SPECIFIC DUTY ON IMPORTED UMBRELLAS

Communicated to the House of Representatives
March 3, 1828

To the Senate and House of Representatives of the United States in Congress assembled:
    This memorial of the proprietors of the Hingham Umbrella Manufactory humbly showeth: That the duty of 7½ cents per square yard on imported cotton cloths of inferior qualities induces the manufacture of almost every description of low price cotton goods excepting umbrella ginghams. This article, although legally subject to the square yard duty when imported in the piece, is nevertheless admitted to entry as a component part of umbrellas, at an ad valorem duty of 30 per centum. The protecting duty of 7½ cents the square yard being thus virtually evaded, as respects umbrella ginghams, there exists no

From *American State Papers, Finance*, 20th Congress, 1st Session, No. 874, V, 897–898.

inducement to manufacture them in this country, and, therefore, the American umbrella makers are dependent on England for their supply of this article, on which they are compelled to pay a square yard duty amounting to about 60 per centum.

Owing to the unequal operation of the tariff in this particular, it is impossible for the American manufacturers of umbrellas to hold a competition with those of England; and, consequently, the profit on the labor of making umbrellas, *even for the consumption of the United States,* is thrown into the hands of foreigners. The *square yard* duty on a sufficient quantity of gingham to cover an umbrella amounts to more than the *ad valorem duty* on an *entire umbrella* when imported in a manufactured state. This your memorialists conceive to be neither equitable nor politic; and they believe it was never the intention of Congress that the law should operate in this way, to the prejudice of American industry. Therefore, your memorialists humbly pray that the evil of which they complain may be remedied by laying a *specific duty* on imported cotton umbrellas of such an amount as will place the American umbrella manufacturer on an *equal* footing (at least) with the English; and, at the same time, prevent those impositions on the revenue which your memorialists believe have been too frequently practiced by invoicing umbrellas below their actual cost. Your memorialists further pray that silk umbrellas, made in the United States, may be entitled to a drawback, when exported, equal to the amount of duty which may have been paid on the silk cloth, which would enable this country to supply the West India and South American markets with umbrellas. By granting these petitions your memorialists believe that the important fisheries to the Brazil Banks (whence the whalebone is derived) would be fostered and extended. And your memorialists will ever pray.

The proprietors of the Hingham Umbrella Manufactory, by their agent,

LEWIS GROSVENOR

Hingham, February 21, 1828

19. A Southern Remonstrance
Against Protection

In the appeals sent to the Congress during the discussions of 1827 and 1828, opposition to the proposed increases in duties was expressed by the chambers of commerce of New York and Baltimore representing the interest in foreign trade, by hardware manufacturers concerned over the duty on iron, and by groups of citizens in northern rural areas, as well as by legislatures and groups of citizens in the southern states. Yet from this time on the most unified and implacable opposition to the protective policy was to come from the South. Manufacturing was a northern interest. Farmers of the North and West were brought within the protective system by duties on some of their products such as wool, hemp, and flax; and advocates of the "American System" appealed to them on the ground that the growth of manufacturing would give them a dependable "home market" for their produce. Southerners, on the other hand, except for the sugar planters of Louisiana, raised no products that could gain any advantage from tariff protection. As a region depending primarily on the export of cotton, the South came to see the tariff as an instrument to favor other sections of the country at its expense.

An early expression of this viewpoint is contained in the Remonstrance of the Alabama Legislature, which is reproduced below. It begins, like so many other documents of the period, with an argument on constitutional grounds. It denounces as improper the campaign of protectionist propaganda launched by the Harrisburg Convention.[1] The so-called "American system," it argues, is really the "British system" of monopoly and protection. It will make "nabobs" of some and "paupers" of others and proposes to favor what is already the most prosperous part of the economy at a time when agricul-

---

[1] See Document 17 above. [ED.]

ture is languishing and the mercantile and shipping interests partake of the languor. The effect will be to make the southern and southwestern states "dependent tributaries to the greedy monopolists of the north and east."

In spite of this and other protests, the so-called "Tariff of Abominations," embodying most of the disputed increases, was adopted in 1828. In a notable speech before the Senate in 1830, Senator George McDuffie of South Carolina developed the economic argument that duties on imports were in effect duties on the export of the South. He twitted the northern states for encouraging manufactures at the expense of others rather than with their own means:

> How, then, has it come to pass, that, while the manufacturers have been, for more than ten years past, clamoring at our doors for protection, the Legislature of no single State of the Union, so far as I am informed, has ever appropriated a cent, or raised a finger, to sustain these languishing and suffering interests, which certainly have a claim upon the States for protection, if indeed they have any claim at all? . . . The moral sense of this nation would not tolerate the avowal, that the State of Massachusetts, for example, will not tax her own citizens to afford protection to her own manufactures, because the Federal Government can be made the unrighteous instrument of taxing the people of the southern States for the purpose of affording that protection.[2]

Protests against the tariff acts of 1828 and 1832 culminated in the great Nullification controversy of 1833 in which McDuffie's state of South Carolina claimed the right to hold the measures invalid. A compromise act of 1833 began a process of tariff reduction and, though rates were again raised for the years 1842–1846, the remainder of the ante bellum era was one of

---

[2] The major portions of this speech are reprinted in Guy Stevens Callender, *Selections from the Economic History of the United States, 1765–1860* (Boston: Ginn & Co., 1909), pp. 514–536. See especially pp. 516, 526–527.

Senator McDuffie would not have had to alter his argument greatly if he had been informed of the modest New York program described in Document 16, which had already been abandoned.

only moderate protection. The notable growth of manufacturing in the decade of the 1850's, which did so much to strengthen the relative position of the North, took place under the shelter of much lower duties than those that were to prevail after the Civil War.

AGAINST INCREASE OF DUTIES ON IMPORTS

Communicated to the House of Representatives February 4, 1828

A JOINT REMONSTRANCE TO THE CONGRESS OF THE UNITED STATES

AGAINST THE POWER ASSUMED TO PROTECT CERTAIN BRANCHES

OF DOMESTIC INDUSTRY AT THE EXPENSE OF OTHERS,

AND THE POLICY OF THE MEASURE

To the honorable the Senate and House of Representatives of the United States of America in Congress assembled:

The General Assembly of Alabama, alive to the rights of the people they serve and the interest of the country in which they live, (however painful the duty,) feel themselves called on by the crisis to protest most solemnly against the principle asserted by the General Government to control the labor of the nation by protecting certain branches of domestic industry at the expense of others. We do not complain of the power to raise revenue or regulate commerce. These powers are expressly granted to preserve the existence and promote the harmony and prosperity of the Government. Nor do we complain of the

---

From *American State Papers, Finance,* 20th Congress, 1st Session, No. 847, V, 848–849.

incidental protection that may result from a well adjusted "tariff" imposed on the importation of foreign goods with a view to revenue alone, nor yet of the occasional inequalities that must attend the operation of any general system. The power to raise revenue is essential to the existence of Government, and is expressly and distinctly granted in the Constitution. It is a power entirely safe, and every way compatible with limited and free government, because it has a boundary so well defined by the wants of the Government as rarely to be transcended. The power to regulate commerce was obviously given to avoid the conflicting systems that would necessarily arise in the different States if each had retained a separate control of the subject. That power is connected with the other, and was given to equalize the duties in the different States. It is not of these powers that we complain, but it is the assertion of another and a very different one. It is the assertion of the power to impose a duty on any article of foreign commerce, not because we want revenue, or the regulations of commerce as such require improvement, but because we want to exclude the foreign in favor of the domestic fabric. This power is not granted in the Constitution, and must be sustained, if at all, by the pliable doctrine of implication; and as it is not necessary to the power to raise revenue or regulate commerce, it cannot be sustained as an incidental or implied power; on the contrary, it is a substantial, distinct power, resting on assumption, and fraught with frightful danger. It has no limit but the caprice of those who assert its existence, and is necessarily subject to all the varying views of supposed convenience and the fugitive conceits of expediency. The unlimited nature of this power, and the dangerous purposes to which it may be applied, renders it odious and unfit to mingle in human affairs. Its natural offspring is monopoly, and its natural tendency is to divide the community into nabobs and paupers, to accumulate overgrown wealth in the hands of the few, and to extend the poverty, the vices, and the miseries of the many. This alarming principle leads to the union of the worst of human passions. Cupidity and ambition, under its deleterious influence minister to each other at the expense of the community. Cupidity will barter worlds for money, and unchastened ambition will filch from the poor man's toil a portion of its just reward to appease the cupidity of the cold calculating monopolist. In this sordid and selfish exchange of equivalents, each accords to the other what is most highly prized without feeling the loss. As the ambitious man cares not for money, nor the monopolist for rank and power, will not the seductive influence of these passions destroy the equipoise of the General Government, and throw its destructive weight upon any portion of the Union that may be necessary to promote their views? Is fate more certain or destiny more inevitable? Can a power leading, in the dawn of its existence, to a combination so incompatible with freedom exist in a free Government? Shall it be assumed or raised by implication for purposes so oppressive? Shall its oppressive character be obscured by the magic of a name? Can the cabalistic appellation of "American system" change the essential character of the principle? These are portentous questions to all concerned, and the crisis calls for the greatest exertions of the friends of limited Government. Already has the manufacturing interests assumed an organized form, and exhibited a concert and systematic combination against all the other great interests of the nation. Union of councils and immense wealth enable the manufacturing corps to sustain a set of agents to attend the sessions of Congress to importune and press their claims upon the attention of the National Legislature. Not content with the importunity of individual agents, a solemn convention has been convoked at Harrisburg, consisting of delegaes from various States, to execute a writ of inquiry, as it would seem, upon the agricultural and other interests of the country, and indicate to Congress, in a more commanding form, how much further the scheme of oppression can be prudently pressed. The right to assemble and petition Congress for the redress of grievances can give no sanction to such a convention. The other languishing interests of the country might well raise a voice of supplication; but for the most pampered and, beyond question, the most flourishing interest in the country to affect a distress that does not exist, and urge Congress for a license to extort from the poor man's toil a still greater portion of its just reward, is a plain insult to the understanding as well as an overt act of tyranny and oppression. In the conflicts of party strife the timid and the silent are apt to be shoved aside to make room for the bold and aspiring; when further exaction is thus urged, to be silent would be criminal. If our rights must be usurped, and our wealth drained to pamper monopolists, we will yield them only when the last inch of ground has been defended with the spirit of freemen. Is it desirable here to imitate the policy of England, and pursue a system that takes from the laborer more and more the proceeds of his toil, until pauperism pervades the land? The policy that takes from one class of laborers the proceeds of their toil to fill the pockets of another must be intrinsically unjust and inimical to freedom. The inevitable tendency of such a system is to accumulate the wealth of the country into a few hands. The rich become more and more rich, without becoming more virtuous or happy; and the poor are pressed down from one point of depression to another, until the extreme of pauperism and consequent misery, vice, and degradation is attained. This picture is not drawn from fancy, but from the solemn admonitions of history. England has pursued the infatuated system of monopoly and protection, of balances and counterbalances, until the middle class of society, once the pride and strength of the nation, is nearly extinguished and merged in the other two, and the nation is divided into a small number ruinously rich, and the millions of paupers who infest the poor-house and cook-shops of the nation. The sponge of monopoly has absorbed nearly the whole wealth of the nation, and drawn it into a few hands, gradually diminishing in number. The nation, it is true, presents a splendid and magnificent exterior, dazzling and captivating the distant spectator, but an interior of extended wretchedness, vice, and misery. Of 21,000,000 of people, less than 300,000 are said to own the whole of the immense public debt, and nearly the whole of the landed property of the nation.

The balance of the nation are in a state of pauperism varying only in degree, taxed to the bone, and doomed to ceaseless toil for a scanty and wretched subsistence. This appalling mass of wretchedness, vice, and poverty, is the practical result of the *"British system"* of monopoly and protection, of balances and counterbalances, in the scheme of restriction, and regulating labor for a series of years, pursued by the magnificent and splendid Government of a wretched and impoverished people.

Let it not be said that the "American system" of monopoly and protection will have different tendencies or lead to different results; the artifice is two shallow to deceive. We cannot disguise the fact that we are struggling with fearful odds, and contending with an organized body of monopolists, who act in concert, and, like the tiger that has tasted blood, prowls for more with increased voracity. Already pampered into fearful importance by partial legislation, they goad and importune Congress for further exactions from the planting interest.

The *allied powers* of avarice, monopoly, and ambition, through the Harrisburg convention, and every subordinate channel of importunity at their command, call for a further subsidy on the labor of the south and southwest, in the shape of a woolens bill, to pamper the gentlemen wool-growers and wool-carders of the northeast; and this, too, at a time when agriculture is languishing and prostrate, yielding a bare support to those who pursue it, and the mercantile and shipping interests partaking of the languor, and manufacturers alone in a flourishing and prosperous condition. The interest least in need thus urging, by aid of such powerful political machinery, a further tribute from the interest least able to bear it, is surely sufficient to prove to Congress how vain and fruitless is the attempt to satisfy the inordinate cravings of the monopolists. One exaction leads to another, and every concession generates a new and more exorbitant demand.

When combinations thus formidable endeavor to throw the overgrown weight of the General Government upon the southern and southwestern States, dry up their commerce by sapping its foundation, degrade them from the proved equality of the compact into the humiliating condition of dependent tributaries to the greedy monopolists of the north and east, the victims would deserve the oppression were they not promptly to interpose the most determined and unyielding resistance.

Let it not be again said that because the southwest and south send no agents to beset the members of Congress, and have foreborne to petition or remonstrate in every village, or to call a counter-convention, that they are so recreant to duty as to acquiesce in the proposed oppression. On the contrary, let it be distinctly understood that Alabama, in common with the southern and southwestern States, regards the power assumed by the General Government to control her internal concerns by protecting duties beyond the fair demands of the revenue as a palpable usurpation of a power not given by the Constitution, and the proposed woolens bill as a species of oppression little less than legalized pillage on the property of her citizens, to which she can never submit until the constitutional means of resistance shall be exhausted.

SAMUEL W. OLIVER, *Speaker of the House of Representatives*
NICHOLAS DAVIS, *President of the Senate*

JOHN MURPHY

Approved January 15, 1828

PART FOUR

THE PROTECTION OF

COMMERCE

20. Alexander Hamilton: "The Importance of the Union in a Commercial Light"

The interests of commerce were very much in the minds of the men who framed the Constitution. The Philadelphia Convention itself was the outgrowth of an earlier interstate convention on commercial policy held at Annapolis; and the "importance of the Union, in a commercial light," was one of the points that "commanded the most general assent."

During the campaign for ratification of the Constitution by the state of New York, the case in its favor was presented in a remarkable series of newspaper articles written by Alexander Hamilton, James Madison, and John Jay. Number XI of this series of Federalist papers, written by Hamilton, was devoted to commercial policy.

Formation of the Federal Union would, he argued, promote both internal and foreign commerce. Trade within the nation would benefit from the removal of barriers between the states, and foreign trade could only be promoted by a government that spoke with one voice rather than with thirteen. Finding an argument for the tariff power quite different from those emphasized in Part Three, Hamilton developed the point that a government able to establish uniform duties on imports would be in an effective bargaining position from which to negotiate commercial treaties opening foreign markets to American goods. Only an effective central government, moreover, would be able to foster a merchant marine, so that we might have an "ACTIVE COMMERCE in our own bottoms," and to protect it by an adequate Navy.

THE FEDERALIST, NO. XI

To the People of the State of New York:

The importance of the Union, in a commercial light, is one of those points about which there is least room to entertain a difference of opinion, and which has, in fact, commanded the most general assent of men who have any acquaintance with the subject. This applies as well to our intercourse with foreign countries as with each other.

There are appearances to authorize a supposition that the adventurous spirit, which distinguishes the commercial character of America, has already excited uneasy sensations in several of the maritime powers of Europe. They seem to be apprehensive of our too great interference in that carrying trade, which is the support of their navigation and the foundation of their naval strength. Those of them which have colonies

---

From "Publius" (Alexander Hamilton), *Independent Journal,* New York, November 24, 1787; reprinted in Henry Cabot Lodge, ed., *The Federalist* (New York: G. P. Putnam's Sons, 1923), pp. 60–66. This is Number XI of the Federalist papers. It may also be consulted in the modern definitive edition of Hamilton's writings, Harold C. Syrett, ed., *The Papers of Alexander Hamilton,* vol. IV (New York: Columbia University Press, 1962), pp. 339–346.

in America look forward to what this country is capable of becoming, with painful solicitude. They foresee the dangers that may threaten their American dominions from the neighborhood of States, which have all the dispositions, and would possess all the means, requisite to the creation of a powerful marine. Impressions of this kind will naturally indicate the policy of fostering divisions among us, and of depriving us, as far as possible, of an ACTIVE COMMERCE in our own bottoms. This would answer the threefold purpose of preventing our interference in their navigation, of monopolizing the profits of our trade, and of clipping the wings by which we might soar to a dangerous greatness. Did not prudence forbid the detail, it would not be difficult to trace, by facts, the workings of this policy to the cabinets of ministers.

If we continue united, we may counteract a policy so unfriendly to our prosperity in a variety of ways. By prohibitory regulations, extending, at the same time, throughout the States, we may oblige foreign countries to bid against each other, for the privileges of our markets. This assertion will not appear chimerical to those who are able to appreciate the importance of the markets of three millions of people— increasing in rapid progression, for the most part exclusively addicted to agriculture, and likely from local circumstances to remain so—to any manufacturing nation; and the immense difference there would be to the trade and navigation of such a nation, between a direct communication in its own ships, and an indirect conveyance of its products and returns, to and from America, in the ships of another country. Suppose, for instance, we had a government in America, capable of excluding Great Britain (with whom we have at present no treaty of commerce) from all our ports; what would be the probable operation of this step upon her politics? Would it not enable us to negotiate, with the fairest prospect of success, for commercial privileges of the most valuable and extensive kind, in the dominions of that kingdom? When these questions have been asked, upon other occasions, they have received a plausible, but not a solid or satisfactory answer. It has been said that prohibitions on our part would produce no change in the system of Britain, because she could prosecute her trade with us through the medium of the Dutch, who would be her immediate customers and paymasters for those articles which were wanted for the supply of our markets. But would not her navigation be materially injured by the loss of the important advantage of being her own carrier in that trade? Would not the principal part of its profits be intercepted by the Dutch, as a compensation for their agency and risk? Would not the mere circumstance of freight occasion a considerable deduction? Would not so circuitous an intercourse facilitate the competitions of other nations, by enhancing the price of British commodities in our markets, and by transferring to other hands the management of this interesting branch of the British commerce?

A mature consideration of the objects suggested by these questions will justify a belief that the real disadvantages to Britain from such a state of things, conspiring with the prepossessions of a great part of the nation in favor of the American trade, and with the importunities of the West India islands, would produce a relaxation in her present system, and would let us into the enjoyment of privileges in the markets of those islands and elsewhere, from which our trade would derive the most substantial benefits. Such a point gained from the British government, and which could not be expected without an equivalent in exemptions and immunities in our markets, would be likely to have a correspondent effect on the conduct of other nations, who would not be inclined to see themselves altogether supplanted in our trade.

A further resource for influencing the conduct of European nations toward us, in this respect, would arise from the establishment of a federal navy. There can be no doubt that the continuance of the Union under an efficient government, would put it in our power, at a period not very distant, to create a navy which, if it could not vie with those of the great maritime powers, would at least be of respectable weight if thrown into the scale of either of two contending parties. This would be more peculiarly the case in relation to operations in the West Indies. A few ships of the line, sent opportunely to the reinforcement of either side, would often be sufficient to decide the fate of a campaign, on the event of which interests of the greatest magnitude were suspended. Our position is, in this respect, a most commanding one. And if to this consideration we add that of the usefulness of supplies from this country, in the prosecution of military operations in the West Indies, it will readily be perceived that a situation so favorable would enable us to bargain with great advantage for commercial privileges. A price would be set not only upon our friendship, but upon our neutrality. By a steady adherence to the Union, we may hope, erelong, to become the arbiter of Europe in America, and to be able to incline the balance of European competitions in this part of the world as our interest may dictate.

But in the reverse of this eligible situation, we shall discover that the rivalships of the parts would make them checks upon each other, and would frustrate all the tempting advantages which nature has kindly placed within our reach. In a state so insignificant our commerce would be a prey to the wanton intermeddlings of all nations at war with each other; who, having nothing to fear from us, would with little scruple or remorse supply their wants by depredations on our property as often as it fell in their way. The rights of neutrality will only be respected when they are defended by an adequate power. A nation, despicable by its weakness, forfeits even the privilege of being neutral.

Under a vigorous national government, the natural strength and resources of the country, directed to a common interest, would baffle all the combinations of European jealousy to restrain our growth. This situation would even take away the motive to such combinations, by inducing an impracticability of success. An active commerce, an extensive navigation, and a flourishing marine would then be the offspring of moral and physical necessity. We might defy the little arts of the little politicians to control or vary the irresistible and unchangeable course of nature.

But in a state of disunion, these combinations might exist and might operate with success. It would be in the power of the maritime nations, availing themselves of our universal impotence, to prescribe the conditions of our political existence; and as they have a common interest in being our carriers, and still more in preventing our becoming theirs, they would in all probability combine to embarrass our navigation in such a manner as would in effect destroy it, and confine us to a PASSIVE COMMERCE. We should then be compelled to content ourselves with the first price of our commodities, and to see the profits of our trade snatched from us to enrich our enemies and persecutors. That unequalled spirit of enterprise, which signalizes the genius of the American merchants and navigators, and which is in itself an inexhaustible mine of national wealth, would be stifled and lost, and poverty and disgrace would overspread a country which, with wisdom, might make herself the admiration and envy of the world.

There are rights of great moment to the trade of America which are rights of the Union—I allude to the fisheries, to the navigation of the Western lakes, and to that of the Mississippi. The dissolution of the Confederacy would give room for delicate questions concerning the future existence of these rights; which the interest of more powerful partners would hardly fail to solve to our disadvantage. The disposition of Spain with regard to the Mississippi needs no comment. France and Britain are concerned with us in the fisheries, and view them as of the utmost moment to their navigation. They, of course, would hardly remain long indifferent to that decided mastery, of which experience has shown us to be possessed in this valuable branch of traffic, and by which we are able to under-sell those nations in their own markets. What more natural than that they should be disposed to exclude from the lists such dangerous competitors?

This branch of trade ought not to be considered as a partial benefit. All the navigating States may, in different degrees, advantageously participate in it, and under circumstances of a greater extension of mercantile capital, would not be unlikely to do it. As a nursery of seamen, it now is, or, when time shall have more nearly assimilated the principles of navigation in the several States, will become, a universal resource. To the establishment of a navy, it must be indispensable.

To this great national object, a NAVY, union will contribute in various ways. Every institution will grow and flourish in proportion to the quantity and extent of the means concentred towards its formation and support. A navy of the United States, as it would embrace the resources of all, is an object far less remote than a navy of any single State or partial confederacy, which would only embrace the resources of a single part. It happens, indeed, that different portions of confederated America possess each some peculiar advantage for this essential establishment. The more southern States furnish in greater abundance certain kinds of naval stores—tar, pitch, and turpentine. Their wood for the construction of ships is also of a more solid and lasting texture. The difference in the duration of the ships of which the navy might be composed, if chiefly constructed of Southern wood, would be of signal importance, either in the view of naval strength or of national economy. Some of the Southern and of the Middle States yield a greater plenty of iron, and of better quality. Seamen must chiefly be drawn from the Northern hive. The necessity of naval protection to external or maritime commerce does not require a particular elucidation, no more than the conduciveness of that species of commerce to the prosperity of a navy.

An unrestrained intercourse between the States themselves

will advance the trade of each by an interchange of their respective productions, not only for the supply of reciprocal wants at home, but for exportation to foreign markets. The veins of commerce in every part will be replenished, and will acquire additional motion and vigor from a free circulation of the commodities of every part. Commercial enterprise will have much greater scope, from the diversity in the productions of different States. When the staple of one fails from a bad harvest or unproductive crop, it can call to its aid the staple of another. The variety, not less than the value, of products for exportation contributes to the activity of foreign commerce. It can be conducted upon much better terms with a large number of materials of a given value than with a small number of materials of the same value; arising from the competitions of trade and from the fluctuations of markets. Particular articles may be in great demand at certain periods, and unsalable at others; but if there be a variety of articles, it can scarcely happen that they should all be at one time in the latter predicament, and on this account the operations of the merchant would be less liable to any considerable obstruction or stagnation. The speculative trader will at once perceive the force of these observations, and will acknowledge that the aggregate balance of the commerce of the United States would bid fair to be much more favorable than that of the thirteen States without union or with partial unions.

It may perhaps be replied to this, that whether the States are united or disunited, there would still be an intimate intercourse between them which would answer the same ends; but this intercourse would be fettered, interrupted, and narrowed by a multiplicity of causes, which in the course of these papers have been amply detailed. A unity of commercial, as well as political, interests, can only result from a unity of governments. . . .

PUBLIUS

21. A Treaty for
"Reciprocal Liberty of Commerce"

The role of the federal government in fostering foreign commerce took in practice a somewhat different form from that outlined in the *Federalist*. The raising and lowering of import duties, as has been seen, responded much more to internal demands for protection than it did to opportunities for international give-and-take. It was, indeed, only with the Reciprocal Trade Agreements Act of the 1930's that the systematic exchange of reductions in our tariff for reductions in the tariffs of other countries became a major element in American commercial policy.

Bilateral treaties exchanging commercial privileges with other countries on an ad hoc basis also had somewhat less influence on American commerce than had been expected. This was so for two very different reasons. The first was the degree to which its fortunes rose and fell with an extraordinary series of political events abroad and at home. The outlook for American shipping, which faced many restrictions abroad in the 1780's and early 1790's,[1] altered greatly with the outbreak of the Napoleonic Wars. For some years American ships, able to trade with both sets of belligerents, carried the major share of the world's maritime cargoes and reaped the windfall harvest of the neutral trade. Exceptional prosperity, however, gave way to stagnation as restrictions on American commerce were imposed by both Great Britain and France. The United States retaliated with the Embargo Act of 1807. Issues of the protection of the merchant marine played a significant part in

---

[1] Thomas Jefferson, "Report on the Privileges and Restrictions on the Commerce of the United States in Foreign Countries," December 16, 1793, *American State Papers, Foreign Relations*, I, 300–304.

bringing about the War of 1812 with Great Britain, as they had in an earlier period of undeclared warfare with France. Protection of our shipping against piracy led to naval expeditions to the shores of Tripoli and as far as the coast of Sumatra. All this bore out the Hamiltonian argument as to the importance of the navy from a commercial point of view, but it also shows the degree to which the fortunes of commerce depended on foreign policy in general rather than on commercial policy narrowly defined.

In the second place, when the wars were over and more normal commercial negotiations could be resumed, the emphasis tended to shift from special bilateral bargains to the attempt to secure the general privileges of free commerce. As early as 1784, the Continental Congress instructed John Adams, Benjamin Franklin, and Thomas Jefferson to attempt to negotiate treaties with the European nations not on the basis of special bargains, but by the exchange of assurances that each party would give the other all the privileges that it gave to the "most favored" other nation.[2] After the wars American policy returned to this objective.

An intermediate stage in the process is represented by the Commercial Convention with Great Britain, negotiated for the United States by the distinguished team of John Quincy Adams, Henry Clay, and Albert Gallatin and signed in 1815, the year the war ended. The treaty announces the principle of "a reciprocal liberty of commerce," but gives it a somewhat limited application. Duties on American products carried to Great Britain and British possessions in Europe, and port charges on the ships carrying them, are to be the same whether the bottoms are British or American. So also in the carriage of British European goods to the United States. On the other hand, commerce in goods from other areas is not included; American trade to India is subject to special regulations; and

---

2 "Instructions to the Ministers Plenipotentiary appointed to Negotiate Treaties of Commerce with the European Nations," May 7, 1784, in Saul K. Padover, ed., *The Complete Jefferson* (New York: Duell, Sloan & Pearce, 1943), pp. 177–180.

trade with the British West Indies, which had been of such great importance to colonial America, is expressly excluded from the convention. A further and smaller exclusion was required before ratifications were exchanged. When St. Helena was chosen as the site for Napoleon's exile, it was placed out of bounds for American shipping!

GREAT BRITAIN—COMMERCIAL CONVENTION

Washington, December 6, 1815
To the Senate of the United States:
I lay before the Senate, for their consideration and advice, as to a ratification, a convention to regulate the commerce between the United States and Great Britain, signed by their respective plenipotentiaries on the 3d of July last, with letters relating to the same, from the American plenipotentiaries to the Secretary of State; and also the declaration with which it is the intention of the British Government to accompany the exchange of the ratifications of the convention.

JAMES MADISON

A CONVENTION TO REGULATE THE COMMERCE BETWEEN THE
TERRITORIES OF THE UNITED STATES AND HIS BRITANNIC MAJESTY

The United States of America and His Britannic Majesty, being desirous, by a convention, to regulate the commerce and navigation between their respective countries, territories, and people, in such manner as to render the same reciprocally beneficial and satisfactory, have respectively named plenipotentiaries, and given them full powers to treat of and conclude such convention: that is to say, the President of the United States, by and

---

From *American State Papers, Foreign Relations,* 14th Congress, 1st Session, No. 280, IV, 7–8.

with the advice and consent of the Senate thereof, hath appointed for their plenipotentiaries John Quincy Adams, Henry Clay, and Albert Gallatin, citizens of the United States; and His Royal Highness the Prince Regent, acting in the name and on the behalf of His Majesty, has named for his plenipotentiaries the right honorable Frederick John Robinson, vice-president of the committee of privy council for trade and plantations, joint paymaster of His Majesty's forces, and a member of the Imperial Parliament; Henry Goulburn, Esq., a member of the Imperial Parliament, and under Secretary of State; and William Adams, Esq., doctor of civil laws: and the said plenipotentiaries, having mutually produced and shown their said full powers, and exchanged copies of the same, have agreed on and concluded the following articles, viz:

ART. 1. There shall be, between the territories of the United States of America and all the territories of His Britannic Majesty in Europe, a reciprocal liberty of commerce. The inhabitants of the two countries, respectively, shall have liberty freely and securely to come with their ships and cargoes to all such places, ports, and rivers in the territories aforesaid, to which other foreigners are permitted to come, to enter into the same, and to remain and reside in any parts of the said territories, respectively; also to hire and occupy houses and warehouses for the purposes of their commerce; and, generally, the merchants and traders of each nation, respectively, shall enjoy the most complete protection and security for their commerce, but subject always to the laws and statutes of the two countries, respectively.

ART. 2. No higher or other duties shall be imposed on the importation into the United States of any articles the growth, produce, or manufacture of His Britannic Majesty's territories in Europe, and no higher or other duties shall be imposed on the importation into the territories of His Britannic Majesty in Europe of any articles the growth, produce, or manufacture of the United States, than are, or shall be, payable on the like articles being the growth, produce or manufacture of any other foreign country; nor shall any higher or other duties or charges be imposed in either of the two countries, on the exportation of any articles to the United States, or to His Britannic Majesty's territories in Europe, respectively, than such as are payable on the exportation of the like articles to any other foreign country; nor shall any prohibition be imposed on the exportation or importation of any articles the growth, produce, or manufacture of the United States, or of His Britannic Majesty's territories in Europe, to or from the said territories of His Britannic Majesty in Europe, or to or from the said United States, which shall not equally extend to all other nations.

No higher or other duties or charges shall be imposed, in any of the ports of the United States, on British vessels, than those payable in the same ports by vessels of the United States; nor in the ports of any of His Britannic Majesty's territories in Europe on the vessels of the United States, than shall be payable in the same ports on British vessels.

The same duties shall be paid on the importation into the United States of any articles the growth, produce, or manufacture of His Britannic Majesty's territories in Europe, whether such importation shall be in vessels of the United States or in British vessels; and the same duties shall be paid on the importation into the ports of any of His Britannic Majesty's territories in Europe, of any article the growth, produce, or manufacture of the United States, whether such importation shall be in British vessels or in vessels of the United States.

The same duties shall be paid, and the same bounties allowed, on the exportation of any articles the growth, produce, or manufacture of His Britannic Majesty's territories in Europe, to the United States, whether such exportation shall be in vessels of the United States or in British vessels; and the same duties shall be paid, and the same bounties allowed, on the exportation of any articles the growth, produce, or manufacture of the United States, to His Britannic Majesty's territories in Europe, whether such exportation shall be in British vessels or in vessels of the United States.

It is further agreed, that, in all cases where drawbacks are, or may be, allowed upon the re-exportation of any goods the growth, produce, or manufacture of either country, respectively, the amount of the said drawbacks shall be the same, whether the said goods shall have been originally imported in a British or an American vessel. But when such re-exportation shall take place from the United States in a British vessel, or from the territories of His Britannic Majesty in Europe in an American vessel, to any other foreign nation, the two contracting parties reserve to themselves, respectively, the right of regulating or diminishing, in such case, the amount of the said drawbacks.

The intercourse between the United States and His Britannic Majesty's possessions in the West Indies and on the continent of North America shall not be affected by any of the provisions of this article, but each party shall remain in the complete possession of its rights with respect to such an intercourse.

ART. 3. His Britannic Majesty agrees that the vessels of the United States of America shall be admitted, and hospitably received, at the principal settlements of the British dominions in the East Indies, viz: Calcutta, Madras, Bombay, and Prince of Wales's island; and that the citizens of the said United States may freely carry on trade between the said principal settlements and the said United States, in all articles of which the importation and exportation, respectively, to and from the said territories, shall not be entirely prohibited: *Provided, only,* That it shall not be lawful for them, in any time of war between the British Government and any State or Power whatever, to export from the said territories, without the special permission of the British Government, any military stores, or naval stores, or rice. The citizens of the United States shall pay for their vessels, when admitted, no higher or other duty or charge than shall be payable on the vessels of the most favored European nations; and they shall pay no higher or other duties or charges on the importation or exportation of the cargoes of the said vessels than shall be payable on the same articles when imported or exported in the vessels of the most favored European nations. But it is expressly agreed, that the vessels of the United States shall not carry any articles from the said principal settlements to any port or place, except to some port or place in the United States of America, where the same shall be unladen.

It is also understood that the permission granted by this article is not intended to allow the vessels of the United States to carry on any part of the coasting trade of the said British territories; but the vessels of the United States, having in the first instance proceeded to one of the said principal settlements of the British dominions in the East Indies, and then going with their original cargoes, or part thereof, from one of the said principal settlements to another, shall not be considered as carrying on the coasting trade.

The vessels of the United States may also touch for refreshment, but not for commerce, in the course of their voyage to or from the British territories in India, or to or from the dominions of the Emperor of China, at the Cape of Good Hope, the island of St. Helena, or such other places as may be in the possession of Great Britain, in the African or Indian seas; it being well understood that, in all that regards this article, the citizens of the United States shall be subject in all respects to the laws and regulations of the British Government from time to time established.

ART. 4. It shall be free for each of the two contracting parties, respectively, to appoint consuls for the protection of trade to reside in the dominions and territories of the other party; but, before any consul shall act as such, he shall, in the usual form, be approved and admitted by the Government to which he is sent; and it is hereby declared, that in case of illegal or improper conduct towards the laws or Government of the country to which he is sent, such consul may either be punished according to law, if the laws will reach the case, or be sent back; the offended Government assigning to the other the reasons for the same.

It is hereby declared, that either of the contracting parties may except from the residence of consuls such particular places as such party shall judge fit to be excepted.

ART. 5. This convention, when the same shall have been duly ratified by the President of the United States, by and with the advice and consent of their Senate, and by His Britannic Majesty, and the respective ratifications mutually exchanged, shall be binding and obligatory on the United States and His Majesty for four years from the date of its signature; and the ratifications shall be exchanged in six months from this time, or sooner, if possible.

Done at London, this third day of July, in the year of our Lord one thousand eight hundred and fifteen.

> JOHN QUINCY ADAMS
> HENRY CLAY
> ALBERT GALLATIN
> FREDERICK JOHN ROBINSON
> HENRY GOULBURN
> WILLIAM ADAMS

22. The Demand for "A Free and Open Trade"

The preceding selection recorded a part-way stage toward "reciprocal liberty of commerce." The process was virtually completed, as far as American legislation could carry it, by the passage of an 1828 act removing the remaining duties discriminating against the shipping of all foreign countries except those that continued to discriminate against American ships. The principle adopted was that of "free and open trade." This was, of course, not the free trade of the antiprotectionists, since it had no bearing on the right to make tariffs; and it did not affect the coastal trade, which was reserved to American shipping. What it did mean was that the carrying of goods between nations should be open to all on equal terms.

The readings contain arguments presented by Senator Samuel Smith of Maryland both in 1825, when a similar measure failed of adoption, and in 1828, and a contribution to the later debate by Senator Levi Woodbury of New Hampshire, who was to be Attorney General in the administrations of Andrew Jackson and Martin Van Buren. Their arguments move on two planes—the policy of freedom reflects the spirit of an enlightened age, and its adoption will improve the position of Americans in relation to their competitors. "We feel confident that we can excel them in taking advantage of the system, from the superiority of our navigators, and the general enterprise of the country."

American fisheries, "as nurseries of navigation and for the nurture of man,"[1] were subsidized from the early days of the Republic. A subsidy for carrying mail, foreshadowing much later legislation, was applied between 1845 and 1859 on certain steamship lines in the attempt to offset British superiority in the iron ship. But throughout the period of the dominance of sail, through the days of the great clipper ships, the American merchant marine continued to face foreign competition with the confidence expressed by Senator Smith and Senator Woodbury.

SPEECH OF SENATOR SAMUEL SMITH, 1825

DISCRIMINATING DUTIES

The Senate resumed as in Committee of the Whole, the consideration of the bill to repeal so much of the several acts im-

---

[1] Thomas Jefferson, Second Annual Message, December 15, 1802; in Richardson, *Messages and Papers of the Presidents*, vol. I, p. 346.

From *Annals of Congress*, 13th Congress, 3rd Session, February 22, 1825, pp. 263–265.

posing duties on the tonnage of ships and vessels, and on goods, wares, and merchandise, imported into the United States, as imposes a discriminating duty on tonnage between foreign vessels and vessels of the United States, and between goods imported into the United States in foreign vessels and vessels of the United States.

MR. S. SMITH.—Mr. President: It may not be improper for me, as chairman of the committee who presented the bill now under consideration, to give a short history of the subject, and to present a few details taken from official authority. Soon after the adoption of the present Constitution, Congress passed acts laying duties on tonnage and on goods imported into the United States. The law provided that six cents per ton should be paid on ships or vessels of the United States entering any of the ports of the United States, and fifty cents per ton on all foreign ships, and that an additional duty of ten per cent. on the duties payable on all goods imported in vessels of the United States, should be paid on such goods when imported into foreign vessels. These, Mr. President, are what are called "the discriminating duties."

The advantages derived therefrom to the navigation of the United States was such, that in a very few years there was American tonnage sufficient for the carrying of all the productions of our own country, and of other nations to a great extent —in fact, our navigation was second to none but Great Britain, when the late war was commenced.

The effect of those discriminating duties was felt by those foreign nations with whom we had the greatest intercourse. Great Britain, in the Treaty of 1794, reserved the right of countervailing those duties, and the United States bound themselves not to impose any new discriminating duties if Great Britain did countervail—but the wars in which she has constantly been engaged since has prevented its effects from being felt to any considerable extent. The short peace she had after the Treaty of Amiens taught the merchants of South Carolina, however, to know, that the extra duty on cotton imported in an American vessel into Great Britain was so high that it was much better to employ British vessels than to have their cotton carried in their own.

We are now at peace with the European nations. It is our interest that there should be no cause of future misunderstanding with them. If we continue our discriminating duties, and they continue their countervailing duties, the result must be, that our ships will be rendered useless. We cannot carry on equal terms, and of course will not be employed. To prevent the destruction of our navigation, Congress would be compelled to add to the discriminating duties, which would be met by foreign nations with new countervailing duties, and thus a commercial warfare would commence. Is it not, therefore, better, Mr. President, for us agree to meet the nations of Europe on equal terms—the ships of each to be admitted into the ports of the other on the same terms with their own ships? Are we afraid of our want of enterprise, industry, or capital? I hope not. For one, I am ready to agree to the bill on the table, and feel confident that the American merchant is equal in a fair competition to the merchant of any other nation.

SPEECH OF SENATOR LEVI WOODBURY, 1828

The present act proposes to do away the whole of these remaining discriminations. It removes, whenever a reciprocal rule may prevail, all extra duties on tonnage, in all cases, and all extra duties on merchandise in all cases, whether the last be the produce and manufacture of the nation owning the vessel, or usually first shipped there, though not her pro-

From *Register of Debates in Congress*, 20th Congress, 1st Session, February 6, 1828, pp. 239–242.

duce and manufacture: or whether it be produce and manufacture, however frequently re-shipped; or coming from nations
however remote. What are the reasons in favor of these important changes? Do they spring from sound authorities, and
are they well supported by principle? More than twenty years
ago, some of our most sagacious and intelligent merchants
urged this policy upon this country, and one of them, most
venerable for his experience and public services, now in my
eye, attempted its adoption in vain.[1]

. . . It remains for the Senate to decide whether the principles in its favor are such as to meet their full approbation.
Those principles embrace the great paramount one of all
liberal Governments, that trade should be free; that all shackles
on commerce should be stricken off; and, in accordance with
the lights and spirit of the present age, that every thing in
navigation should be left to the fair competition of industry,
enterprise, and skill. That, in a country which justly boasts
of the freedom and superiority of its institutions, nothing is
to be feared from a rivalship on this subject, free as air, and
extensive as the widest range of civilization. Perhaps the only
just limits to this general principle in commercial affairs, are
the necessities, which sometimes exist, to favor the multiplication of seamen and vessels for national defence; or, by discrimination, to obtain a revenue for the customary expenses
of Government. These reasons justified the English navigation
laws in 1651, and our own discriminating duties in 1790; but
would ill apply to our present condition and prospects.

As regards revenue, the discrimination yields but little,
since the foreign tonnage is now so small; and that little is
far from being wanted to meet the ordinary demands of the
Treasury. As regards national defence, we have already a
navy second to none of its size; the appropriations for its
increase are liberal, and our navigation, inferior to only one

---

[1] The reference presumably is to Senator Smith. [ED.]

Power in the world, can now furnish seamen to meet any call whatever, in any national emergency. Again: we are the carriers for other nations, rather than the employers of them to transport for us; and instead of foreign vessels engrossing nearly half the tonnage in our foreign trade, as in the year 1789, or having 100,000 out of 234,000 tons, they now constitute only about eight-hundredths of it, or something like 92,000 out of 1,000,000 tons. Again: we are known by experience, the surest test of all theories, to possess a skill and economy in building vessels, a cheapness in fitting them out, an activity in sailing them, which, without discrimination, would give us an advantage in coping with any commercial Power in existence. Persons of more practical knowledge than myself have, during the last ten years, become convinced, that such are the accurate calculations of our merchants, the youth and agility of our seamen, and the intelligence of our ship-masters, that American vessels can, on an average, make three trips to Europe, while a foreign vessel is making two. It must be maninfest to all, that circumstances like these, rather than any discriminating duty, must always give and maintain to us a superiority and protection, which leave nothing to be feared from the fullest competitions. . . .

. . . The removal of every unequal and odious distinction will promote harmony in our foreign intercourse. It will extend to them the same favors we ask in return. It will reciprocate every privilege. It will invite free and full interchange of surplus commodities of every kind, and remove the usual occasions for angry relations and expensive wars. Where nature, or habit, or political foresight, has given any advantages to one nation over another, she will enjoy them while deserving them. But none will dread a monopoly; and exchanges will profitably happen on those liberal principles, which ought always to distinguish an age of free and thorough inquiry from one of limited enterprise and narrow views . . . .

By this bill we now hold out the olive branch to all. If our terms are accepted, we may obtain most of the transportation now enjoyed by foreigners in the eight or ten hundredths of our foreign tonnage; as they now are enabled to compete with us to that extent, chiefly by the discrimination they enjoy at home. We may relieve our own existing foreign tonnage from some onerous duties, now imposed in some foreign ports. We may send our own products and manufactures, as well as our large exports of foreign articles, to every region unincumbered, wherever nature or custom may render them desirable and useful. On the other hand, by this arrangement, we may enable foreigners to make greater sales of their own produce and manufactures, to cheapen their transportation, to procure at a lower price their wonted supplies, and in these, and other particulars, to become amply remunerated for every indulgence granted to strangers. But, whether accepted or not, by nations, other than those who already have adopted the basis of this bill, we shall, at all events, by its passage, act in conformity to the boasted principles of our free Government. We shall second the liberal spirit of the present age; and if our advances are repulsed with an unconciliating temper, we shall still enjoy the satisfaction of having attempted, on our part, to discharge, with all good fidelity, our duty, both to that age so interesting as our own, and to that country of our birth and affections so forward, if not foremost, in the improvements of that age. . . .

SPEECH OF SENATOR SAMUEL SMITH, 1828

Mr. Smith, of Maryland, had considered this subject for a long time, and was a firm advocate of the principle of the bill. But, so clear a view of the question had been taken by the

From *Register of Debates in Congress*, 20th Congress, 1st Session, February 6, 1828, p. 243.

gentleman from New Hampshire, that, when called on, as a commercial man, to express himself on the subject, he hardly knew what to say. When this country came out of the Revolutionary war, discriminating duties were imposed. At that time Baltimore owned ten times the number of three-masted vessels as New York, and was extensively engaged in the coasting trade. The advantages derived from the passage of that act were instantaneous. The trade of this country was benefitted, and that of Great Britain somewhat prejudiced. That nation then contemplated a retaliation upon us. They waited until a good opportunity offered, and that they found at the negotiation of Mr. Jay's treaty. This treaty enabled them to retaliate the discriminating duty upon us—and, had it not been for the war which ensued, they would have carried all the trade from the United States to Great Britain.

I introduced this subject, said Mr. S. in the year 1802. Our Eastern brethren doubted the policy of the measure. At an after period such an act passed, extending, however, to but a portion of our commerce with foreign countries. What was then the language of our merchants? They said let us alone —give us a free and open trade, and we can take care of ourselves. From that time the principle has gradually gone on. The advantages have been great to the country, and, if this bill pass, they will still be enlarged. It relieves us from the apprehension of retaliatory measures on the part of foreign nations. A free and open trade is the only true American System. It is no new-fangled plan for the benefit of a favored class, but is a policy that has been long acknowledged as good, and satisfactorily tested. We ask no more from other nations; and, if they universally reciprocate the measure, we feel confident that we can excel them in taking advantage of the system, from the superiority of our navigators, and the general enterprise of the country. The prospect in such a case is fair that we shall become the carriers of other nations. He would venture to say that, if this principle were extended to the ports of the Mediterranean, this country would have the carrying trade to a great extent. Holland treats us as she has always treated us, with great liberality. She admits us into the ports of Java. We are, to a considerable extent, the carriers for England, and also for France, since the Convention. And he believed that every Power with which we trade will admit us into their ports on equal terms, if we hold out to them inducements to do so. . . .

23. Thomas Jefferson: An Exploring Expedition to "Extend Commerce"

The two remaining selections of this Part deal with a quite different method "of extending the external commerce of the United States." This was the heading under which President Jefferson asked the Congress to put his proposal for what became the famous Lewis and Clark Expedition.

The proposal itself was contained in the confidential message of December 3, 1803, which began with the quite different question of continuing government "trading-houses with the Indian tribes." What Jefferson suggests is that exploration of the Upper Missouri and a route across the Rockies to the Pacific would lead to a great extension of the American fur trade. The proposal is confidential since part of the exploration would be on territory claimed by Great Britain and part of the purpose would be to direct the trade from British markets. Yet Great Britain would not object to the expedition, regarding it as "a literary pursuit"; and its "literary" achievement in advancing geographical knowledge will be an additional gratification.[1]

---

[1] Document 1, Gallatin's Report, provides another illustration of the strong geographical interest of Jefferson and his circle.

Three years later, in his sixth annual message, the President celebrated the success of the mission in the following paragraph:

The expedition of Messrs. Lewis and Clarke for exploring the river Missouri and the best communication from that to the Pacific Ocean has had all the success which could have been expected. They have traced the Missouri nearly to its source, descended the Columbia to the Pacific Ocean, ascertained with accuracy the geography of that interesting communication across our continent, learnt the character of the country, of its commerce and inhabitants, and it is but justice to say that Messrs. Lewis and Clarke and their brave companions have by this arduous service deserved well of their country.[2]

While the extension of the public commerce among the Indian tribes may deprive of that source of profit such of our citizens as are engaged in it, it might be worthy the attention of Congress in their care of individual as well as of the general interest to point in another direction the enterprise of these citizens, as profitably for themselves and more usefully for the public. The river Missouri and the Indians inhabiting it are not as well known as is rendered desirable by their connection with the Mississippi and consequently with us. It is, however, understood that the country on that river is inhabited by numerous tribes, who furnish great supplies of furs and peltry to the trade of another nation, carried on in a high latitude through an infinite number of portages and lakes shut up by ice through a long season. The commerce on that line could bear no competition with that of the Missouri,

Confidential Message to Congress of January 18, 1803, from Richardson, *Messages and Papers of the Presidents*, vol. I, pp. 353–354.

[2] Richardson, *Messages and Papers of the Presidents*, vol. I, p. 408.

traversing a moderate climate, offering, according to the best accounts, a continued navigation from its source, and possibly with a single portage from the Western Ocean, and finding to the Atlantic a choice of channels through the Illinois or Wabash, the Lakes and Hudson, through the Ohio and Susquehanna, or Potomac or James rivers, and through the Tennessee and Savannah rivers. An intelligent officer, with ten or twelve chosen men, fit for the enterprise and willing to undertake it, taken from our posts where they may be spared without inconvenience, might explore the whole line, even to the Western Ocean, have conferences with the natives on the subject of commercial intercourse, get admission among them for our traders as others are admitted, agree on convenient deposits for an interchange of articles, and return with the information acquired in the course of two summers. Their arms and accouterments, some instruments of observation, and light and cheap presents for the Indians would be all the apparatus they could carry, and with an expectation of a soldier's portion of land on their return would constitute the whole expense. Their pay would be going on whether here or there. While other civilized nations have encountered great expense to enlarge the boundaries of knowledge by undertaking voyages of discovery, and for other literary purposes, in various parts and directions, our nation seems to owe to the same object, as well as to its own interests, to explore this the only line of easy communication across the continent, and so directly traversing our own part of it. The interests of commerce place the principal object within the constitutional powers and care of Congress, and that it should incidentally advance the geographical knowledge of our own continent can not but be an additional gratification. The nation claiming the territory, regarding this as a literary pursuit, which it is in the habit of permitting within its dominions, would not be disposed to view it with jealousy, even if the expiring state of its interests there did not render it a matter of indifference. The appropriation of $2,500 "for the purpose of extending the external commerce of the United States," while understood and considered by the Executive as giving the legislative sanction, would cover the undertaking from notice and prevent the obstructions which interested individuals might otherwise previously prepare in its way.

TH. JEFFERSON

24. A Naval Expedition for "Extending Trade"

"It is very desirable to make our navy an efficient branch of the government, both in extending and protecting commerce and trade." So wrote its Secretary in 1853.[1] *Protection* of commerce had been a recognized function of the Navy from its beginning and had been illustrated in the war against the "Barbary Pirates" and on many other occasions. *Extension* of commerce, on the other hand, through the good offices of government officials abroad, was normally the function of the consular service. An assessment of its cumulative, though conventional and unspectacular, influence could be built up from the volumes of consular reports and the memoirs of merchants.

A more dramatic and less typical illustration of governmental action for the extension of foreign trade is provided by the expeditions of Commodore Matthew C. Perry to Japan in 1853 and 1854. This was an instance in which trade *did* follow a show of the flag. Both in motives and manners, Perry's exploit stands in marked contrast with the government's present-day efforts to aid the so-called "developing" nations, yet there can be no doubt that the expedition helped to set Japan on the way

---

[1] The Secretary of the Navy to Commodore Perry, November 18, 1853, in "Correspondence . . . relative to the Naval Expedition to Japan," *Senate Executive Document* No. 34, 33rd Congress, 2nd Session, Washington, 1855, p. 57.

toward what became an extraordinarily rapid process of economic development.

The documents are taken from the Navy's "Correspondence" as reported to the Congress by President Franklin Pierce. The first is a letter from the Acting Secretary of State to the Secretary of the Navy. This contains the basic instructions for the expedition and declares that arguments or persuasion will need to be "seconded by some imposing manifestation of power," an injunction which the Commodore carried out not merely by the display of his squadron of steam-driven ships but also by setting up on land a short functioning railroad and line of telegraph. The second is the text of the treaty entered into with the Emperor of Japan. The third is a letter of congratulations to Commodore Perry from the American merchants of Canton. Even if some discount is made for its fulsomeness of expression, it indicates that the businessmen in the best position to make a practical appraisal believed that the opening of Japan would be important for the trade of the United States.

COMMODORE MATTHEW PERRY'S INSTRUCTIONS

Department of State
Washington, November 5, 1852

Sir:

As the squadron destined for Japan will shortly be prepared to sail, I am directed by the President to explain the objects of the expedition, and to give some general directions as to the mode by which those objects are to be accomplished.

Since the islands of Japan were first visited by European nations, efforts have constantly been made by the various

---

From "Correspondence . . . relative to the Naval Expedition to Japan," pp. 4–9. The letter is quoted in full, except for brief references to an earlier document. The "Correspondence" was submitted to Congress as a presidential message of January 31, 1855.

maritime powers to establish commercial intercourse with a country whose large population and reputed wealth hold out great temptations to mercantile enterprise. Portugal was the first to make the attempt, and her example was followed by Holland, England, Spain, and Russia; and finally by the United States. All these attempts, however, have thus far been unsuccessful; the permission enjoyed for a short period by the Portuguese to trade with the islands, and that granted to Holland to send annually a single vessel to the port of Nangasaki, hardly deserving to be considered exceptions to this remark.

China is the only country which carries on any considerable trade with these islands.

So rigorously is this system of exclusion carried out, that foreign vessels are not permitted to enter their ports in distress, or even to do an act of kindness to their own people. In 1831, a Japanese junk was blown out to sea, and, after drifting about for several months, was cast ashore near the mouth of the Columbia river, in Oregon. An American ship, the Morrison, undertook to carry the survivors of the crew back to their country, but, on reaching the bay of Yedo, she was fired into from the neighboring shore. She repaired to another part of the island and attempted to land, but meeting with the same reception there, she returned to America with the Japanese on board.

When vessels are wrecked or driven ashore on the islands their crews are subjected to the most cruel treatment. Two instances of this have recently occurred. In the year 1846, two American whaling ships, the Lagoda and the Lawrence, having been wrecked on the island of Niphon, their crews were captured and treated with great barbarity, and it is believed that their lives were spared only through the intercession of the Dutch governor of Nangasaki.

* * *

Every nation has undoubtedly the right to determine for itself the extent to which it will hold intercourse with other nations. The same law of nations, however, which protects a nation in the exercise of this right imposes upon her certain duties which she cannot justly disregard. Among these duties none is more imperative than that which requires her to succor and relieve those persons who are cast by the perils of the ocean upon her shores. This duty is, it is true, among those that are denominated by writers on public law imperfect, and which confer no right on other nations to exact their performance; nevertheless, if a nation not only habitually and systematically disregards it, but treats such unfortunate persons as if they were the most atrocious criminals, such nations may justly be considered as the common enemy of mankind.

That the civilized nations of the world should for ages have submitted to such treatment by a weak and semi-barbarous people, can only be accounted for on the supposition that, from the remoteness of the country, instances of such treatment were of rare occurrence, and the difficulty of chastising it very great. It can hardly be doubted that if Japan were situated as near the continent of Europe or of America as it is to that of Asia, its government would long since have been either treated as barbarians, or been compelled to respect those usages of civilized states of which it receives the protection.

This government has made two attempts to establish commercial intercourse with Japan. In the year 1832, a Mr. Roberts was appointed a special agent of the government, with authority to negotiate treaties with sundry nations in the east, and among others with Japan, but he died before he arrived at the island.

In 1845, Commodore Biddle was sent with two vessels of war to visit Japan and ascertain whether its ports were accessible. He was cautioned, however, "not to excite a hostile feeling, or a distrust of the government of the United States."

He proceeded to Yedo, but was told that the Japanese could trade with no foreign nations except the Dutch and Chinese, and was peremptorily ordered to leave the island and never to return to it. A personal indignity was even offered to Commodore Biddle, and it is not improbable that the barbarity which a short time afterwards was practised by these people towards the crew of the Lagoda, may have been in part occasioned by the forbearance which that excellent officer felt himself bound under his instructions to exercise towards them. . . .

Recent events—the navigation of the ocean by steam, the acquisition and rapid settlement by this country of a vast territory on the Pacific, the discovery of gold in that region, the rapid communication established across the isthmus which separates the two oceans—have practically brought the countries of the east in closer proximity to our own; although the consequences of these events have scarcely begun to be felt, the intercourse between them has already greatly increased, and no limits can be assigned to its future extension.

The duty of protecting those American citizens who navigate those seas is one that can no longer be deferred. In the year 1851, instructions were accordingly given to Commodore Aulick, then commanding our naval forces in the East Indies, to open a negotiation with the government of Japan. It is believed that nothing has been done under these instructions, and the powers conferred on Commodore Aulick are considered as superseded by those now given to Commodore Perry.

The objects sought by this government are—

1. To effect some permanent arrangement for the protection of American seamen and property wrecked on these islands, or driven into their ports by stress of weather.

2. The permission to American vessels to enter one or more of their ports in order to obtain supplies of provisions, water, fuel, &c., or, in case of disasters, to refit so as to enable them to prosecute their voyage.

It is very desirable to have permission to establish a depot for coal, if not on one of the principal islands, at least on some small uninhabited one, of which, it is said, there are several in their vicinity.

3. The permission to our vessels to enter one or more of their ports for the purpose of disposing of their cargoes by sale or barter.

As this government has no right to make treaties for, or to redress the grievances of, other nations, whatever concessions may be obtained on either of the above points, need not, of course, apply in terms to the inhabitants or vessels of any other nation. This government, however, does not seek by this expedition to obtain any exclusive commercial advantage for itself, but, on the contrary, desires and expects that whatever benefits may result from it will ultimately be shared by the civilized world. As there can be no doubt that if the ports of the country are once opened to one nation they would soon be opened to all. It is believed, that for reasons hereinafter mentioned, any reference in your negotiations to the wrongs or claims of other nations, so far from promoting this object, would tend to defeat it.

The next question is, how are the above mentioned objects to be attained?

It is manifest, from past experience, that arguments or persuasion addressed to this people, unless they be seconded by some imposing manifestation of power, will be utterly unavailing.

You will therefore, be pleased to direct the commander of the squadron to proceed, with his whole force, to such point on the coast of Japan as he may deem most advisable, and there endeavor to open a communication with the government, and, if possible, to see the emperor in person, and deliver to him the letter in introduction from the President with which he is charged. He will state that he has been sent across the ocean by the President to deliver that letter to the emperor, and to communicate with his government on matters of importance to the two countries. That the President entertains the most friendly feeling towards Japan, but has been surprised and grieved to learn, that when any of the people of the United States go, of their own accord, or are thrown by the perils of the sea within the dominions of the emperor, they are treated as if they were his worst enemies. He will refer particularly to the cases of the ships Morrison, Lagoda, and Lawrence, above mentioned.

He will inform him of the usages of this country, and of all Christian countries, in regard to shipwrecked persons and vessels, and will refer to the case of the Japanese subjects who were recently picked up at sea in distress and carried to California, from whence they have been sent to their own country; and will state that this government desires to obtain from that of Japan some positive assurance, that persons who may hereafter be shipwrecked on the coast of Japan, or driven by stress of weather into her ports, shall be treated with humanity; and to make arrangements for a more extended commercial intercourse between the two countries. The establishment of this intercourse will be found a difficult, but, perhaps, not an impossible task.

The deep-seated aversion of this people to hold intercourse with Christian nations is said to be owing chiefly to the indiscreet zeal with which the early missionaries, particularly those of Portugal, endeavored to propagate their religion. The commodore will therefore say, that the government of this country, unlike those of every other Christian country, does not interfere with the religion of its own people, much less with that of other nations. It seems that the fears or the prejudices of the Japanese are very much excited against the English, of whose conquests in the east, and recent invasion of China, they have probably heard. As the Americans speak the same language as the English, it is natural that they should confound citizens of the United States with British subjects. Indeed, their barbarous treatment of the crews of the vessels above referred to was partly occasioned by the suspicion that they were really English. . . .

Commodore Perry will, therefore, explain to them that the

United States are connected with no government in Europe. That they inhabit a great country which lies directly between them and Europe, and which was discovered by the nations of Europe about the same time that Japan herself was first visited by them; that the portion of this continent lying nearest to Europe was first settled by emigrants from that country, but that its population has rapidly spread through the country until it has reached the Pacific ocean. That we have now large cities from which, with the aid of steam, Japan can be reached in twenty days. That our commerce with all that portion of the globe is, therefore, rapidly increasing, and that part of the ocean will soon be covered with our vessels. That, therefore, as the United States and Japan are becoming every day nearer and nearer to each other, the President desires to live in peace and friendship with the emperor; but that no friendship can long exist between them unless Japan should change her policy and cease to act towards the people of this country as if they were her enemies. That, however wise this policy may originally have been, it is unwise and impracticable now that intercourse between the two countries is so much more easy and rapid than it formerly was.

If, after having exhausted every argument and every means of persuasion, the commodore should fail to obtain from the government any relaxation of their system of exclusion, or even any assurance of humane treatment of our shipwrecked seamen, he will then change his tone, and inform them in the most unequivocal terms that it is the determination of this government to insist, that hereafer all citizens or vessels of the United States that may be wrecked on their coasts, or driven by stress of weather into their harbors shall, so long as they are compelled to remain there, be treated with humanity; and that if any acts of cruelty should hereafter be practised upon citizens of this country, whether by the government or by the inhabitants of Japan, they will be severely chastised. In case he should succeed in obtaining concessions on any of the points above mentioned, it is desirable that they should be reduced into the form of a treaty, for negotiating which he will be furnished with the requisite powers.

He will also be furnished with copies of the treaties made by this government with China, Siam, and Muscat, which may serve him as precedents in drawing up any treaty he may be able to make. It would be well to have one or more of these translated into the Japanese tongue, which, it is presumed, can be done in China.

He will bear in mind that, as the President has no power to declare war, his mission is necessarily of a pacific character, and will not resort to force unless in self defence in the protection of the vessels and crews under his command, or to resent an act of personal violence offered to himself, or to one of his officers.

In his intercourse with this people, who are said to be proud and vindictive in their character, he should be courteous and conciliatory, but at the same time, firm and decided. He will, therefore, submit with patience and forbearance to acts of discourtesy to which he may be subjected, by a people to whose usages it will not do to test by our standard of propriety, but, at the same time, will be careful to do nothing that may compromit, in their eyes, his own dignity, or that of the country. He will, on the contrary, do everything to impress them with a just sense of the power and greatness of this country, and to satisfy them that its past forbearance has been the result, not of timidity, but of a desire to be on friendly terms with them.

It is impossible by any instructions, however minute, to provide for every contingency that may arise in the prosecution of a mission of so peculiar and novel a character. For this reason, as well as on account of the remoteness of the scene of his operation, it is proper that the commodore should be invested with large discretionary powers, and should feel assured that any departure from usage, or any error of judgment he may commit will be viewed with indulgence.

The government of Holland has communicated to this government that instructions had been given to the superintendent of their factory at Dezima to promote, by every means in his power, the success of the expedition; and the kindness that has heretofore been shown by that officer towards our countrymen in captivity leaves no room for doubt that he will cheerfully fulfil these instructions.

The commissioner of the United States to China has been directed to prefer certain claims of citizens of the United States against that government. As the presence of the squadron might give some additional weight to the demand, you will please direct its commander (if he finds he can do so without serious delay or inconvenience) to touch at Hong-Kong or Macao and remain there as long as he may deem it advisable.

If the squadron should be able, without interfering with the main object for which it is sent, to explore the coasts of Japan and of the adjacent continent and islands, such an exploration would not only add to our stock of geographical knowledge, but might be the means of extending our commercial relations and of securing ports of refuge and supply for our whaling vessels in those remote seas. With this view he will be provided with powers authorizing him to negotiate treaties of amity and navigation with any and all established and independent sovereignties in those regions.

In the event of such a voyage, he will inform himself, as far as practicable, of the population, resources, and natural productions of the country, and procure and preserve specimens of the latter, and the seeds of such plants as may be peculiar to the country.

He will be authorized by this department to draw on the Messrs. Baring Brothers & Co., of London, to a limited amount for the payment of guides, interpreters, messengers, &c., and of other expenses incident to his mission; as also for the purchase of such presents as it may be deemed advisable to make to promote the objects of his mission.

I have the honor to be, very respectfully, your obedient servant,

C. M. CONRAD
Acting Secretary

HON. J. P. KENNEDY
Secretary of the Navy

THE TREATY WITH JAPAN, 1854

The United States of America and the empire of Japan, desiring to establish firm, lasting, and sincere friendship between the two nations, have resolved to fix, in a manner clear and positive, by means of a treaty or general convention of peace and amity, the rules which shall in future be mutually observed in the intercourse of their respective countries; for which most desirable object the President of the United States has conferred full powers on his commissioner, Matthew Calbraith Perry, special ambassador of the United States to Japan; and the august sovereign of Japan has given similar full powers to his commissioners, Hayashi-Daigaku-no-kami, Ido, Prince of Tsus-Sima; Izawa, Prince of Mimasaki; and Udono, member of the Board of Revenue.

And the said commissioners, after having exchanged their said full powers, and duly considered the premises, have agreed to the following articles:

ARTICLE I.—There shall be a perfect, permanent, and universal peace, and a sincere and cordial amity, between the

---

From "Correspondence . . . ," pp. 153–155. In a covering note, Commodore Perry explained that seven Japanese miles were the equivalent of about 10 American miles. Note that Article IX is a most-favored nation clause.

United States of America on the one part, and between their people, respectfully, [respectively,] without exception of persons or places.

ARTICLE II.—The port of Simoda, in the principality of Idzu, and the port of Hakodadi, in the principality of Matsmai, are granted by the Japanese as ports for the reception of American ships, where they can be supplied with wood, water, provisions, and coal, and other articles their necessities may require, as far as the Japanese have them. The time for opening the first-named port is immediately on signing this treaty; the last-named port is to be opened immediately after the same day in the ensuing Japanese year.

NOTE.—A tariff of prices shall be given by the Japanese officers of the things which they can furnish, payment for which shall be made in gold and silver coin.

ARTICLE III.—Whenever ships of the United States are thrown or wrecked on the coast of Japan, the Japanese vessels will assist them, and carry their crews to Simoda or Hakodadi, and hand them over to their countrymen appointed to receive them. Whatever articles the shipwrecked men may have preserved shall likewise be restored, and the expenses incurred in the rescue and support of Americans and Japanese who may thus be thrown upon the shores of either nation are not to be refunded.

ARTICLE IV.—Those shipwrecked persons and other citizens of the United States shall be free as in other countries, and not subjected to confinement, but shall be amenable to just laws.

ARTICLE V.—Shipwrecked men, and other citizens of the United States, temporarily living at Simoda and Hakodadi, shall not be subject to such restrictions and confinement as the Dutch and Chinese are at Nangasaki; but shall be free at Simoda to go where they please within the limits of seven Japanese miles (or *ri*) from a small island in the harbor of Simoda, marked on the accompanying chart, hereto appended;

and shall in like manner be free to go where they please at Hakodadi, within limits to be defined after the visit of the United States squadron to that place.

ARTICLE VI.—If there be any other sort of goods wanted, or any business which shall require to be arranged, there shall be careful deliberation between the parties in order to settle such matters.

ARTICLE VII.—It is agreed that ships of the United States resorting to the ports open to them, shall be permitted to exchange gold and silver coin and articles of goods for other articles of goods, under such regulations as shall be temporarily established by the Japanese government for that purpose. It is stipulated, however, that the ships of the United States shall be permitted to carry away whatever articles they are unwilling to exchange.

ARTICLE VIII.—Wood, water, provisions, coal, and goods required, shall only be procured through the agency of Japanese officers appointed for that purpose, and in no other manner.

ARTCLE IX.—It is agreed, that if, at any future day, the government of Japan shall grant to any other nation or nations privileges and advantages which are not herein granted to the United States and the citizens thereof, that these same privileges and advantages shall be granted likewise to the United States and to the citizens thereof without any consultation or delay.

ARTICLE X.—Ships of the United States shall be permitted to resort to no other ports in Japan but Simoda and Hakodadi, unless in distress or forced by stress of weather.

ARTICLE XI.—There shall be appointed by the government of the United States consuls or agents to reside in Simoda at any time after the expiration of eighteen months from the date of the signing of this treaty; provided that either of the two governments deem such arrangement necessary.

ARTICLE XII.—The present convention, having been concluded and duly signed, shall be obligatory, and faithfully observed by the United States of America and Japan, and by the citizens and subjects of each respective power; and it is to be ratified and approved by the President of the United States, by and with the advice and consent of the Senate thereof, and by the august Sovereign of Japan, and the ratification shall be exchanged within eighteen months from the date of the signature thereof, or sooner if practicable.

In faith whereof, we, the respective plenipotentiaries of the United States of America and the empire of Japan, aforesaid, have signed and sealed these presents.

Done at Kanagawa, this thirty-first day of March, in the year of our Lord Jesus Christ one thousand eight hundred and fifty-four, and of Kayei the seventh year, third month, and third day.

LETTER FROM THE AMERICAN MERCHANTS
OF CANTON

Canton, September 4, 1854

Sir:

We, your countrymen, the undersigned, merchants and residents in China, learning that it is your excellency's intention to leave for the United States on the 11th current, desire to declare to you, before your departure, the sense we entertain of your services in fulfilment of the mission with which you were specially charged by our government to that of Japan, and to acknowledge the promptitude with which you have bestowed the protection so much required by the important interests at stake in this country and its neighborhood during your command in these seas.

From "Correspondence . . . ," pp. 186–187.

Enjoying the advantages of proximity, and with our interest heightened thereby, it has been our privilege twice to witness your departure for the shores of Japan; nor will you have doubted that you went with our best wishes freighted. Participating, indeed, in the hopes and anxieties attending your great enterprise, in perhaps a greater degree than those who were more distant, we may, as your countrymen, now claim the right to anticipate the warm approval, the pride, and satisfaction with which the announcement of your achievements will be hailed in our common country.

But your success, which is so well calculated to enkindle the patriotism and awaken the admiration and gratitude of your countrymen, will not in a less degree elicit the applause of other nations.

You cannot have been unconscious that your audience was the whole civilized world, and that your mission was worthy of man's highest ambition. Whilst this added to your anxieties, it has not lessened your zeal or dazzled your mind; but has called into exercise that rare assemblage of qualities—that union of conciliation with firmness—the happy tact and judgment, which have insured your complete success.

That such will be the award of your own countrymen, and of the people of other nations, we hazard nothing in declaring.

Whilst you have thus elevated yourself to a proud position in the eyes of the world, you have firmly re-established the hold which the name you bear has so long had upon the hearts of your countrymen; and the name of PERRY, which has so long adorned the naval profession, will henceforth be enrolled with the highest in diplomacy. Columbus, De Gama, Cook, La Pérouse, Magellan—these inscribed their names in history by striving with the obstacles of nature. You have conquered the obstinate will of man, and, by overturning the cherished policy of an empire, have brought an estranged but cultivated people into the family of nations. You have done this without violence, and the world has looked on with admiration to see the barriers of prejudice fall before the flag of our country without the firing of a shot.

It is thus that your acts, dictated by your wisdom and inspired by your justice and benevolence, have so auspiciously inaugurated the entrance of Japan into the great family of nations—the consequences of which affect the welfare of the universe; and thus, that in adding lustre to the flag of our country, you have durably inscribed your name upon the history of the world.

In conclusion, permit us to say, that as none of your countrymen can more fully appreciate the value of your services, so none will more sincerely desire to hear of your future welfare; and to request your acceptance of a durable memorial of your visits to China as a testimony of the estimation in which we hold your public services and private character.

Wishing you the highest reward that man can bestow—"that of a whole nation's gratitude"—

> We remain, sir, your countrymen,
>
> [Signed by all the American merchants in Canton.]

His Excellency Commodore MATTHEW C. PERRY,
Commander-in-chief of the Naval Forces U. S. in the
  East India, China, and Japan Seas,
  and late Special Envoy to Japan, &c., &c., &c.

PART FIVE

THE PROVISION OF MONEY
AND CREDIT

25. Alexander Hamilton:
The Case for a National Bank

The federal government assumed an important responsibility
for the provision of credit at a very early stage. The Bank of
the United States was founded by act of Congress in 1791 at
a time when the country possessed only three banks, one in
each of the major northern seaports.

The plan for the Bank was put forward by Alexander
Hamilton in one of his notable reports as Secretary of the
Treasury. It begins with a long and painstaking explanation of
the benefits of banks in general and of their services in making
the capital of a country more effective. Members of the House,
Hamilton admits, will find this superfluous but the body of the
people will need this introduction to an unfamiliar enterprise.
The Bank he proposes will serve these general purposes but
will also be "a political machine, of the greatest importance to
the state." For this reason the Government should provide part
of the capital and receive part of the profits. It should be kept
fully informed regarding the Bank's actions and position, but
should not take part in the Bank's management. The Govern-

ment's own interest, says Hamilton, will be better cared for by private directors guided by the magnet of profit.

What needs most explanation in the proposal is, as Hamilton says, the use of "the public debt" to provide a major fraction of the Bank's capital. The purpose is dual—the bonds are to support the Bank but the Bank is also to support the bonds; and the proposal cannot be explained except with reference to the companion Report on the Public Credit,[1] which forms the other half of Hamilton's financial program. "Funding" of the debt of the Continental Congress and "assumption" by the national government of the debts of the states were to place the credit of the young nation on a satisfactory basis and, as would now be said, improve the climate for foreign investment. They would also bring about a sharp advance in the price of what had been greatly depreciated securities. The Bank "operation" should increase the price still further and bring additional "benefit to the public creditors."

NATIONAL BANK

Treasury Department, December 13th, 1790

IN OBEDIENCE TO THE ORDER OF THE HOUSE OF REPRESENTATIVES,
OF THE NINTH DAY OF AUGUST LAST, REQUIRING THE SECRETARY
OF THE TREASURY TO PREPARE AND REPORT, ON THIS DAY,
SUCH FURTHER PROVISION AS MAY, IN HIS OPINION,
BE NECESSARY FOR ESTABLISHING THE PUBLIC CREDIT,
THE SAID SECRETARY FURTHER RESPECTFULLY REPORTS:

That, from a conviction . . . that a National Bank is an institution of primary importance to the prosperous administration

---

From *American State Papers, Finance,* 1st Congress, 3rd Session, No. 18, I, 67–76.

---

[1] *American State Papers, Finance,* 1st Congress, 3rd Session, No. 6, I, 15 ff.

of the finances, and would be of the greatest utility in the operations connected with the support of the public credit, his attention has been drawn to devising the plan of such an institution, upon a scale which will entitle it to the confidence, and be likely to render it equal to the exigencies of the public. Previously to entering upon the detail of this plan, he entreats the indulgence of the House towards some preliminary reflections naturally arising out of the subject, which he hopes will be deemed neither useless nor out of place. Public opinion being the ultimate arbiter of every measure of government, it can scarcely appear improper, in deference to that, to accompany the origination of any new proposition with explanations, which the superior information of those to whom it is immediately addressed, would render superfluous.

It is a fact, well understood, that public banks have found admission and patronage among the principal and most enlightened commercial nations. They have successively obtained in Italy, Germany, Holland, England, and France, as well as in the United States. And it is a circumstance which cannot but have considerable weight, in a candid estimate of their tendency, that, after an experience of centuries, there exists not a question about their utility in the countries in which they have been so long established. Theorists and men of business unite in the acknowledgement of it.

Trade and industry, wherever they have been tried, have been indebted to them for important aid. And government has been repeatedly under the greatest obligations to them in dangerous and distressing emergencies. That of the United States, as well in some of the most critical conjunctures of the late war, as since the peace, has received assistance from those established among us, with which it could not have dispensed.

With this twofold evidence before us, it might be expected that there would be a perfect union of opinions in their favor. Yet doubts have been entertained; jealousies and prejudices have circulated; and, though the experiment is every day dissipating them, within the spheres in which effects are best known, yet there are still persons by whom they have not been entirely renounced. To give a full and accurate view of the subject, would be to make a treatise of a report; but there are certain aspects in which it may be cursorily exhibited, which may perhaps conduce to a just impression of its merits. . . .

The following are among the principal advantages of a Bank:

First. The augmentation of the active or productive capital of a country. Gold and silver, when they are employed merely as the instruments of exchange and alienation, have been not improperly denominated dead stock; but when deposited in banks, to become the basis of a paper circulation, which takes their character and place, as the signs or representatives of value, they then acquire life, or, in other words, an active and productive quality. This idea, which appears rather subtile and abstract, in a general form, may be made obvious and palpable, by entering into a few particulars. It is evident, for instance, that the money which a merchant keeps in his chest, waiting for a favorable opportunity to employ it, produces nothing till that opportunity arrives. But if, instead of locking it up in this manner, he either deposites it in a bank, or invests it in the stock of a bank, it yields a profit during the interval, in which he partakes, or not, according to the choice he may have made of being a depositor or a proprietor; and when any advantageous speculation offers, in order to be able to embrace it, he has only to withdraw his money, if a depositor, or, if a proprietor, to obtain a loan from the bank, or to dispose of his stock—an alternative seldom or never attended with difficulty, when the affairs of the institution are in a prosperous train. His money, thus deposited or invested, is a fund upon which himself and others can borrow to a much larger amount. It is a well established fact, that banks in good credit, can circulate a far greater sum than the actual quantum of their capital in gold and silver. The extent of the possible excess seems indeterminate; though it has been conjecturally stated at the proportions of two and three to one. This faculty is produced in various ways. 1*st*. A great proportion of the notes which are issued, and pass current as cash, are indefinitely suspended in circulation, from the confidence which each holder has, that he can, at any moment, turn them into gold and silver. 2*dly*. Every loan which a bank makes, is, in its first shape, a credit given to the borrower on its books, the amount of which it stands ready to pay, either in its own notes, or in gold or silver, at his option. But, in a great number of cases, no actual payment is made in either. The borrower frequently, by a check or order, transfers his credit to some other person, to whom he has a payment to make; who, in his turn, is as often content with a similar credit, because he is satisfied that he can, whenever he pleases, either convert it into cash, or pass it to some other hand, as an equivalent for it. And in this manner the credit keeps circulating, performing in every stage the office of money, till it is extinguished by a discount with some person who has a payment to make to the bank, to an equal or greater amount. Thus large sums are lent and paid, frequently through a variety of hands, without the intervention of a single piece of coin. 3*dly*. There is always a large quantity of gold and silver in the repositories of the bank, besides its own stock, which is placed there, with a view partly to its safe keeping, and partly to the accommodation of an institution, which is itself a source of general accommodation. These deposites are of immense consequence in the operations of a bank. Though liable to be redrawn at any moment, experience proves, that the money so much oftener changes proprietors than place, and that what is drawn out is generally so speedily replaced, as to authorize the counting upon the sums deposited, as an *effective fund,* which, concurring with the stock of the bank, enables it to extend its loans, and to answer all the demands for coin, whether in consequence of those loans, or arising from the occasional return of its notes.

These different circumstances explain the manner in which

the ability of a bank to circulate a greater sum than its actual capital in coin is acquired. This, however, must be gradual, and must be preceded by a firm establishment of confidence— a confidence which may be bestowed on the most rational grounds, since the excess in question will always be bottomed on good security of one kind or another. This, every well conducted bank carefully requires, before it will consent to advance either its money or its credit, and where there is an auxiliary capital, (as will be the case in the plan hereinafter submitted) which, together with the capital in coin, define the boundary that shall not be exceeded by the engagements of the bank, the security may, consistently with all the maxims of a reasonable circumspection, be regarded as complete.

The same circumstances illustrate the truth of the position, that it is one of the properties of banks to increase the active capital of a country. This, in other words, is the sum of them: the money of one individual, while he is waiting for an opportunity to employ it, by being either deposited in the bank for safe keeping, or invested in its stock, is in a condition to administer to the wants of others, without being put out of his own reach when occasion presents. This yields an extra profit, arising from what is paid for the use of his money by others, when he could not himself make use of it, and keeps the money itself in a state of incessant activity. In the almost infinite vicissitudes and competitions of mercantile enterprise, there never can be danger of an intermission of demand, or that the money will remain for a moment idle in the vaults of the bank. This additional employment given to money, and the faculty of a bank to lend and circulate a greater sum than the amount of its stock in coin, are, to all the purposes of trade and industry, an absolute increase of capital. Purchases and undertakings, in general, can be carried on by any given sum of bank paper or credit, as effectually as by an equal sum of gold and silver. And thus, by contributing to enlarge the mass of industrious and commercial enterprise, banks become nurseries of national wealth—a consequence as satisfactorily verified by experience, as it is clearly deducible in theory.

Secondly, Greater facility to the Government, in obtaining pecuniary aids, especially in sudden emergencies. This is another, and an undisputed advantage of public banks—one which, as already remarked, has been realized in signal instances among ourselves. The reason is obvious; the capitals of a great number of individuals are, by this operation, collected to a point, and placed under one direction. The mass formed by this union, is, in a certain sense, magnified by the credit attached to it; and while this mass is always ready, and can at once be put in motion, in aid of the Government, the interest of the bank to afford that aid, independent of regard to the public safety and welfare, is a sure pledge for its disposition to go as far in its compliances as can in prudence be desired. There is, in the nature of things, as will be more particularly noticed in another place, an intimate connexion of interest between the Government and the bank of a nation.

Thirdly. The facilitating of the payment of taxes. . . .

It ought not to escape without a remark, that, as far as the citizens of other countries become adventurers in the bank, there is a positive increase of the gold and silver of the country. It is true, that, from this, a half yearly rent is drawn back, accruing from the dividends upon the stock. But as this rent arises from the employment of the capital by our own citizens, it is probable that it is more than replaced by the profits of that employment. It is also likely that a part of it is, in the course of trade, converted into the products of our country: and it may even prove an incentive, in some cases, to emigration to a country in which the character of citizen is as easy to be acquired as it is estimable and important. This view of the subject furnishes an answer to an objection which has been deduced from the circumstance here taken notice of, namely, the income resulting to foreigners from the part of the stock owned by them, which has been represented as tending to drain the country of its specie. In this objection, the original investment of the capital, and the constant use of it afterwards, seem both to have been overlooked. . . .

The establishment of banks in this country seems to be recommended by reasons of a peculiar nature. Previously to the Revolution, circulation was in a great measure carried on by paper emitted by the several local governments. In Pennsylvania alone, the quantity of it was near a million and a half of dollars. This auxiliary may be said to be now at an end. And it is generally supposed that there has been, for some time past, a deficiency of circulating medium. How far that deficiency is to be considered as real or imaginary, is not susceptible of demonstration; but there are circumstances and appearances, which, in relation to the country at large, countenance the supposition of its reality.

The circumstances are, besides the fact just mentioned respecting paper emissions, the vast tracts of waste land, and the little advanced state of manufactures. The progressive settlement of the former, while it promises ample retribution, in the generation of future resources, diminishes or obstructs, in the mean time, the *active* wealth of the country. It not only draws off a part of the circulating money, and places it in a more passive state, but it diverts, into its own channels, a portion of that species of labor and industry which would otherwise be employed in furnishing materials for foreign trade, and which, by contributing to a favorable balance, would assist the introduction of specie. In the early periods of new settlements, the settlers not only furnish no surplus for exportation, but they consume a part of that which is produced by the labor of others. The same thing is a cause that manufactures do not advance, or advance slowly. And notwithstanding some hypotheses to the contrary, there are many things to induce a suspicion, that the precious metals will not abound in any country which has not mines, or variety of manufactures. They have been sometimes acquired by the sword; but the modern system of war has expelled this resource, and it is one upon which it is to be hoped the United States will never be inclined to rely. . . .

The emitting of paper money by the authority of Government is wisely prohibited to the individual States, by the national constitution; and the spirit of that prohibition ought not to be disregarded by the Government of the United States. Though paper emissions, under a general authority, might have some advantages not applicable, and be free from some disadvantages which are applicable to the like emissions by the States, separately, yet they are of a nature so liable to abuse— and, it may even be affirmed, so certain of being abused—that the wisdom of the Government will be shown in never trusting itself with the use of so seducing and dangerous an expedient. In times of tranquillity, it might have no ill consequence; it might even perhaps be managed in a way to be productive of good: but, in great and trying emergencies, there is almost a moral certainty of its becoming mischievous. The stamping of paper is an operation so much easier than the laying of taxes, that a government, in the practice of paper emissions, would rarely fail, in any such emergency, to indulge itself too far in the employment of that resource, to avoid, as much as possible, one less auspicious to present popularity. If it should not even be carried so far as to be rendered an absolute bubble, it would at least be likely to be extended to a degree which would occasion an inflated and artificial state of things, incompatible with the regular and prosperous course of the political economy.

Among other material differences between a paper currency, issued by the mere authority of Government, and one issued by a bank, payable in coin, is this: That, in the first case, there is no standard to which an appeal can be made, as to the quantity which will only satisfy, or which will surcharge the circulation: in the last, that standard results from the demand. If more should be issued than is necessary, it will return upon the bank. Its emissions, as elsewhere intimated, must always be in a compound ratio to the fund and the demand: whence it is evident, that there is a limitation in the nature of the thing; while the discretion of the Government is the only measure of the extent of the emissions, by its own authority. . . .[1]

It is to be considered that such a bank is not a mere matter of private property, but a political machine, of the greatest importance to the State. . . .

The order of the subject leads next to an inquiry into the principles upon which a national bank ought to be organized.

The situation of the United States naturally inspires a wish that the form of the institution could admit of a plurality of branches. But various considerations discourage from pursuing this idea. The complexity of such a plan would be apt to inspire doubts, which might deter from adventuring in it. And the practicability of a safe and orderly administration, though not to be abandoned as desperate, cannot be made so manifest in perspective, as to promise the removal of those doubts, or to justify the Government in adopting the idea as an original experiment. The most that would seem advisable, on this point, is to insert a provision which may lead to it hereafter, if experience shall more clearly demonstrate its utility, and satisfy those who may have the direction, that it may be adopted with safety. It is certain that it would have some advantages, both peculiar and important. Besides more general accommodation, it would lessen the danger of a run upon the bank.

The argument against it is, that each branch must be under a distinct, though subordinate direction, to which a considerable latitude of discretion must, of necessity, be intrusted. And, as the property of the whole institution would be liable for the engagements of each part, that and its credit would be at stake,

---

[1] The Report goes on to consider at length, and reject the possibility that the functions of a National Bank could be performed by the private Bank of North America which is already in existence. [ED.]

upon the prudence of the directors of every part. The mis-management of either branch might hazard serious disorder in the whole.

Another wish, dictated by the particular situation of the country, is, that the bank could be so constituted as to be made an immediate instrument of loans to the proprietors of land; but this wish also yields to the difficulty of accomplishing it. Land is, alone, an unfit fund for a bank circulation. If the notes issued upon it were not to be payable in coin, on demand, or at a short date, this would amount to nothing more than a repetition of the paper emissions, which are now exploded by the general voice. If the notes are to be payable in coin, the land must first be converted into it by sale, or mortgage. The difficulty of effecting the latter, is the very thing which begets the desire of finding another resource; and the former would not be practicable on a sudden emergency, but with sacrifices which would make the cure worse than the disease. Neither is the idea of constituting the fund partly of coin and partly of land, free from impediments. These two species of property do not, for the most part, unite in the same hands. Will the moneyed man consent to enter into a partnership with the landholder, by which *the latter* will share in the profits *which will be* made *by the money of the former?* The money, it is evident, will be the agent or efficient cause of the profits—the land can only be regarded as an additional security. It is not difficult to foresee, that an union, on such terms, will not readily be formed. If the landholders are to procure the money by sale or mortgage of a part of their lands, this they can as well do when the stock consists wholly of money, as if it were to be compounded of money and land.

To procure for the landholders the assistance of loans, is the great desideratum. Supposing other difficulties surmounted, and a fund created, composed partly of coin and partly of land, yet the benefit contemplated could only then be obtained by the bank's advancing them its notes for the whole, or part, of the value of the lands they had subscribed to the stock. If this advance was small, the relief aimed at would not be given; if it was large, the quantity of notes issued would be a cause of *distrust;* and, if received at all, they would be likely to return speedily upon the bank for payment; which, after exhausting its coin, might be under a necessity of turning its lands into money, at any price that could be obtained for them, to the irreparable prejudice of the proprietors.

Considerations of public advantage suggest a further wish, which is—that the bank could be established upon principles, that would cause the profits of it to redound to the immediate benefit of the State. This is contemplated by many who speak of a national bank, but the idea seems liable to insuperable objections. To attach full confidence to an institution of this nature, it appears to be an essential ingredient in its structure, that it shall be under a *private* not a *public* direction—under the guidance of *individual interest,* not of *public policy;* which would be supposed to be, and, in certain emergencies, under a feeble or too sanguine administration, would really be, liable to being too much influenced by *public necessity.* The suspicion of this would, most probably, be a canker that would continually corrode the vitals of the credit of the bank, and would be most likely to prove fatal in those situations in which the public good would require that they should be most sound and vigorous. It would, indeed, be little less than a miracle, should the credit of the bank be at the disposal of the Government, if, in a long series of time, there was not experienced a calamitous abuse of it. It is true, that it would be the real interest of the Government not to abuse it; its genuine policy to husband and cherish it with the most guarded circumspection, as an inestimable treasure. But what government ever uniformly consulted its true interests in opposition to the temptations of momentary exigencies? What nation was ever blessed with a constant succession of upright and wise administrators?

The keen, steady, and, as it were, magnetic sense of their

own interest as proprietors, in the directors of a bank, pointing invariably to its true pole—the prosperity of the institution—is the only security that can always be relied upon for a careful and prudent administration. It is, therefore, the only basis on which an enlightened, unqualified, and permanent confidence can be expected to be erected and maintained. . . .

As far as may concern the aid of the bank, within the proper limits, a good government has nothing more to wish for than it will always possess, though the management be in the hands of private individuals. As the institution, if rightly constituted, must depend for its renovation, from time to time, on the pleasure of the Government, it will not be likely to feel a disposition to render itself, by its conduct, unworthy of public patronage. The Government, too, in the administration of its finances, has it in its power to reciprocate benefits to the bank, of not less importance than those which the bank affords to the Government, and which, besides, are never unattended with an immediate and adequate compensation. Independent of these more particular considerations, the natural weight and influence of a good government will always go far towards procuring a compliance with its desires; and, as the directors will usually be composed of some of the most discreet, respectable, and well informed citizens, it can hardly ever be difficult to make them sensible of the force of the inducements which ought to stimulate their exertions.

It will not follow, from what has been said, that the State may not be the holder of a part of the stock of a bank, and consequently a sharer in the profits of it. It will only follow that it ought not to desire any participation in the direction of it, and, therefore, ought not to own the whole or a principal part of the stock: for, if the mass of the property should belong to the public, and if the direction of it should be in private hands, this would be to commit the interests of the State to persons not interested, or not enough interested in their proper management.

There is one thing, however, which the Government owes to itself and to the community—at least, to all that part of it who are not stockholders—which is, to reserve to itself a right of ascertaining, as often as may be necessary, the state of the bank; excluding, however, all pretension to control. This right forms an article in the primitive constitution of the Bank of North America; and its propriety stands upon the clearest reasons. If the paper of a bank is to be permitted to insinuate itself into all the revenues and receipts of a country; if it is even to be tolerated as the substitute for gold and silver in all the transactions of business; it becomes, in either view, a national concern of the first magnitude. As such, the ordinary rules of prudence require that the Government should possess the means of ascertaining, whenever it thinks fit, that so delicate a trust is executed with fidelity and care. A right of this nature is not only desirable, as it respects the Government, but it ought to be equally so to all those concerned in the institution, as an additional title to public and private confidence, and as a thing which can only be formidable to practices that imply misman-agement. The presumption must always be, that the characters who would be intrusted with the exercise of this right, on be-half of the Government, will not be deficient in the discretion which it may require; at least, the admitting of this presump-tion cannot be deemed too great a return of confidence for that very large portion of it which the Government is required to place in the bank.

Abandoning, therefore, ideas which, however agreeable or desirable, are neither practicable nor safe, the following plan, for the constitution of a National Bank, is respectfully sub-mitted to the consideration of the House.

1. The capital stock of the bank shall not exceed ten millions of dollars, divided into twenty-five thousand shares, each share being four hundred dollars; to raise which sum, subscriptions shall be opened on the first Monday of April next, and shall continue open until the whole shall be subscribed. Bodies politic as well as individuals may subscribe.

2. The amount of each share shall be payable, one-fourth in gold and silver coin, and three-fourths in that part of the public debt, which, according to the loan proposed by the act making provision for the debt of the United States, shall bear an accruing interest, at the time of payment, of six per centum per annum. . . .

6. The totality of the debts of the company, whether by bond, bill, note, or other contract, (credits for deposites excepted) shall never exceed the amount of its capital stock. In case of excess, the directors, under whose administration it shall happen, shall be liable for it in their private or separate capacities. Those who may have dissented may excuse themselves from this responsibility, by immediately giving notice of the fact, and their dissent, to the President of the United States, and to the stockholders, at a general meeting, to be called by the President of the bank, at their request.

7. The company may sell or demise its lands and tenements, or may sell the whole, or any part of the public debt, whereof its stock shall consist; but shall *trade* in nothing except bills of exchange, gold and silver bullion, or in the sale of goods pledged for money lent; nor shall take more than at the rate of six per centum per annum, upon its loans or discounts.

8. No loan shall be made by the bank for the use, or on account, of the Government of the United States, or of either of them, to an amount exceeding fifty thousand dollars, or of any foreign prince or State, unless previously authorized by a law of the United States.

9. The stock of the bank shall be transferable, according to such rules as shall be instituted by the company in that behalf.

10. The affairs of the bank shall be under the management of twenty-five directors, one of whom shall be the President; and there shall be, on the first Monday of January, in each year, a choice of directors, by a plurality of suffrages of the stockholders, to serve for a year. The directors, at their first meeting after each election, shall choose one of their number as President.

11. The number of votes to which each stockholder shall be entitled, shall be according to the number of shares he shall hold, in the proportions following, that is to say: For one share, and not more than two shares, one vote; for every two shares above two, and not exceeding ten, one vote; for every four shares above ten, and not exceeding thirty, one vote; for every six shares above thirty, and not exceeding sixty, one vote; for every eight shares above sixty, and not exceeding one hundred, one vote; and for every ten shares above one hundred, one vote; but no person, co-partnership, or body politic, shall be entitled to a greater number than thirty votes. And, after the first election, no share or shares shall confer a right of suffrage, which shall not have been holden three calendar months previous to the day of election. Stockholders actually resident within the United States, and none other, may vote in the elections by proxy.

12. Not more than three-fourths of the directors in office, exclusive of the President, shall be eligible for the next succeeding year. But the director who shall be President at the time of an election, may always be re-elected.

13. None but a stockholder, being a citizen of the United States, shall be eligible as a director. . . .

20. The bills and notes of the bank, originally made payable, or which shall have become payable, on demand, in gold and silver coin, shall be receivable in all payments to the United States.

21. The officer at the head of the Treasury Department of the United States shall be furnished, from time to time, as often as he may require, not exceeding once a week, with statements of the amount of the capital stock of the bank, and of the debts due to the same, of the moneys deposited therein, of the notes in circulation, and of the cash in hand; and shall have a right to inspect such general accounts in the books of the bank as shall relate to the said statements; provided that this shall not be construed to imply a right of inspecting the account of any private individual or individuals, with the bank.

22. No similar institution shall be established by any future act of the United States, during the continuance of the one hereby proposed to be established.

23. It shall be lawful for the directors of the bank to establish offices wheresoever they shall think fit, within the United States, for the purposes of discount and deposite, only, and upon the same terms, and in the same manner, as shall be practised at the bank, and to commit the management of the said offices, and the making of the said discounts, either to agents specially appointed by them, or to such persons as may be chosen by the stockholders residing at the place where any such office shall be, under such agreements, and subject to such regulations, as they shall deem proper, not being contrary to law, or to the constitution of the bank.

24. And lastly, the President of the United States shall be authorized to cause a subscription to be made to the stock of said company, on behalf of the United States, to an amount not exceeding two millions of dollars, to be paid out of the moneys which shall be borrowed by virtue of either of the acts, the one, entitled "An act making provision for the debt of the United States;" and the other, entitled "An act making provision for the reduction of the public debt;" borrowing of the bank an equal sum, to be applied to the purposes for which the said moneys shall have been procured, reimburseable in ten years, by equal annual instalments; or at any time sooner, or in any greater proportions, that the Government may think fit. . . .

The combination of a portion of the public debt, in the formation of the capital, is the principal thing of which an explanation is requisite. The chief object of this is to enable the creation of a capital sufficiently large to be the basis of an extensive circulation, and an adequate security for it. As has been elsewhere remarked, the original plan of the Bank of North America contemplated a capital of ten millions of dollars, which is certainly not too broad a foundation for the extensive operations to which a national bank is destined. But to collect such a sum in this country, in gold and silver, into one depository, may, without hesitation, be pronounced impracticable. Hence the necessity of an auxiliary, which the public debt at once presents. . . .

The debt composing part of the capital, besides its collateral effect in enabling the bank to extend its operations, and consequently to enlarge its profits, will produce a direct annual revenue of six per centum from the Government, which will enter into the half-yearly dividends received by the stockholders.

When the present price of the public debt is considered, and the effect which its conversion into bank stock, incorporated with a specie fund, would, in all probability, have to accelerate its rise to the proper point, it will easily be discovered that the operation presents, in its outset, a very considerable advantage to those who may become subscribers; and from the influence which that rise would have on the general mass of the debt, a proportional benefit to all the public creditors, and, in a sense which has been more than once adverted to, to the community at large.

The last thing which requires any explanatory remark is, the authority proposed to be given to the President, to subscribe the amount of two millions of dollars on account of the public. The main design of this is, to enlarge the specie fund of the bank and to enable it to give a more early extension to its operations. Though it is proposed to borrow with one hand what is lent with the other, yet the disbursement of what is borrowed, will be progressive, and bank notes may be thrown into circulation, instead of the gold and silver. Besides, there is to be an annual reimbursement of a part of the sum borrowed, which will finally operate as an actual investment of so much specie. In addition to the inducements to this measure, which results from the general interest of the Government to enlarge the sphere of the utility of the bank, there is this more particular consideration, to wit: That, as far as the dividend on the stock shall exceed the interest paid on the loan, there is a positive profit. . . .

All which is humbly submitted,

ALEXANDER HAMILTON
Secretary of the Treasury

26. The Responsibilities of a National Bank

The charter of the first Bank of the United States expired in 1812 and was not renewed. In 1816, however, partly because of financial difficulties during the War of 1812, a second Bank of the United States received a charter similar to that of the first Bank but with provisions for a larger capital and for the appointment by the government of five of its twenty-five directors. The president of the Second Bank, from 1823 until its national charter expired in bitter controversy in 1836, was Nicholas Biddle.

Several present-day writers have described the institution as a central bank in the sense of acting, like the Bank of England before it, as the "lender of last resort" to the rest of the banking community, and as assuming an over-all responsibility for the stability of the financial system as a whole. Fritz Redlich has characterized Biddle as "perhaps . . . the world's very first conscious central banker."[1] If his Bank was a central bank, it was one without any prescribed organic connection with other banks. They had no obligation to maintain reserves with it, and it had no obligation to rediscount their loans. And if it assumed a general responsibility for economic stability, it did

[1] Fritz Redlich, *The Molding of American Banking: Men and Ideas,* Part I, 1781–1840 (New York: Hafner Publishing Co., 1947), ch. 6, especially p. 128. A similar view is presented most persuasively in Bray Hammond, *Banks and Politics in America, From the Revolution to the Civil War* (Princeton: Princeton University Press, 1957).

so long before Wesley Mitchell produced a workable analysis of the business cycle or John Maynard Keynes persuaded statesmen of the importance of aggregate demand to full employment. If these distinctions are kept in mind, it may be useful to examine what ideas of the Bank's central role were held by those who planned the Bank and by Biddle himself.

The "Proposition relating to the national circulating medium," included in a report of Alexander James Dallas as Secretary of the Treasury, states the case for establishment of the Bank. The first emphasis, as the title suggests, is on a "uniform national currency," but the Bank is also to exercise leadership over the other banks in restoring credit and promoting economic recovery. If the Secretary chooses "conciliate" and "aid" rather than "coerce" as companion verbs to "lead," this is perhaps because of his sense of the "delicacy of the subject."

Biddle's own view of the Bank's responsibility toward the economy may be suggested by a confidential letter to the Cashier of the Baltimore Branch, which was written before the period of major controversy. Relying on the foreign exchange position of the country as the indicator of financial difficulty, Biddle diagnoses the immediate problem as "an overbanking which occasions an overtrading." Against this the Bank of the United States must exert its pressure and influence. In the end it may need to borrow abroad in order to protect the other banks "against the effects of their own improvidence." The timing of such intervention, however, is a nice question. To do so too early would unfairly reduce the profits accruing to the Bank's own stockholders.

On another occasion, Biddle was quoted as defining his relation to the state-chartered banks in the following terms:

> The great object is to keep the State banks within proper limits, to make them shape their business according to their means. For this purpose they are called upon to settle, never forced to pay specie, if it can be avoided, but payment is taken in their bills of exchange or suffered to lie occasionally until the bank can turn around; no amount of debt is fixed because the principle we wish to establish is that every bank shall always be ready to provide for its notes.[2]

---

[2] Cited in Redlich, *The Molding of American Banking*, Part I, p. 129.

ALEXANDER J. DALLAS:

"CONCILIATE, AID, AND LEAD"

PROPOSITION RELATING TO THE NATIONAL

CIRCULATING MEDIUM

The delicacy of this subject is only equalled by its importance. In presenting it, therefore, to the consideration of Congress, there is occasion for an implicit reliance upon the legislative indulgence.

By the constitution of the United States Congress is expressly vested with the power to coin money, to regulate the value of the domestic and foreign coins in circulation, and, as a necessary implication from positive provisions, to emit bills of credit, while it is declared by the same instrument that "no State shall coin money, or emit bills of credit." Under this constitutional authority the money of the United States has been established, by law, consisting of coins made with gold, silver, or copper. All foreign gold and silver coins, at specified rates, were placed, in the first instance, upon the same footing with the coins of the United States, but they ceased (with the exception of Spanish milled dollars, and parts of such dollars) to be a legal tender for the payment of debts and demands, in the year 1809.

The constitutional authority to emit bills of credit has also been exercised in a qualified and limited manner. During the existence of the Bank of the United States the bills or notes of the corporation were declared, by law, to be receivable in all payments to the United States; and the Treasury notes, which

From Report on the State of the Finances, 14th Congress, 1st Session, No. 454, *American State Papers, Finance*, III, 17–19.

have been since issued for the services of the late war, have been endowed with the same quality. But Congress has never recognised, by law, the notes of any other corporation; nor has it ever authorized an issue of bills of credit to serve as a legal currency. The acceptance of the notes of banks, which are not established by the federal authority, in payments to the United States, has been properly left to the viligance and discretion of the Executive department; while the circulation of the Treasury notes, employed either to borrow money, or to discharge debts, depends entirely (as it ought to depend) upon the option of the lenders and creditors to receive them.

The constitutional and legal foundation of the monetary system of the United States is thus distinctly seen, and the power of the federal Government to institute and regulate it, whether the circulating medium consist of coin or of bills of credit, must, in its general policy, as well as in the terms of its investment, be deemed an exclusive power. It is true that a system depending upon the agency of the precious metals will be affected by the various circumstances which diminish their quantity, or deteriorate their quality. The coin of a State sometimes vanishes under the influence of political alarms; sometimes in consequence of the explosion of mercantile speculations, and sometimes by the drain of an unfavorable course of trade. But whenever the emergency occurs that demands a change of system it seems necessarily to follow that the authority, which was alone competent to establish the national coin, is alone competent to create a national substitute. It has happened, however, that the coin of the United States has ceased to be the circulating medium of exchange, and that no substitute has hitherto been provided by the national authority. During the last year the principal banks, established south and west of New England, resolved that they would no longer issue coin in payment of their notes, or of the drafts of their customers, for money received upon deposit. In this act the Government of the United States had no participation, and yet the immediate effect of the act was to supersede the only legal currency of the nation. By this act, although no State can constitutionally emit bills of credit, corporations, erected by the several States, have been enabled to circulate a paper medium, subject to many of the practical inconveniences of the prohibited bills of credit.

It is not intended, upon this occasion, to condemn, generally, the suspension of specie payments; for appearances indicated an approaching crisis, which would probably have imposed it as a measure of necessity, if it had not been adopted as a measure of precaution. But the danger which originally induced, and perhaps justified, the conduct of the banks, has passed away, and the continuance of the suspension of specie payments must be ascribed to a new series of causes. The public credit and resources are no longer impaired by the doubts and agitations excited during the war by the practises of an enemy, or by the inroads of an illicit commerce: yet the resumption of specie payments is still prevented, either by the reduced state of the national stock of the precious metals, or by the apprehension of a further reduction to meet the balances of foreign trade, or by the redundant issues of bank paper. The probable direction and duration of these latter causes constitute, therefore, the existing subject for deliberation. While they continue to operate, singly or combined, the authority of the States individually, or the agency of the State institutions, cannot afford a remedy commensurate with the evil; and a recurrence to the national authority is indispensable for the restoration of a national currency.

In the selection of the means for the accomplishment of this important object, it may be asked, 1st. Whether it be practicable to renew the circulation of the gold and silver coins? 2d. Whether the State banks can be successfully employed to furnish a uniform currency? 3dly. Whether a national bank can be employed more advantageously than the State banks for the same purpose? and, 4thly. Whether the Government can itself supply, and maintain a paper medium of exchange, of permanent and uniform value, throughout the United States?

1. As the United States do not possess mines of gold or silver the supply of those metals must, in a time of scarcity, be derived from foreign commerce. If the balance of foreign commerce be unfavorable the supply will not be obtained incidentally, as in the case of the returns for a surplus of American exports, but must be the subject of a direct purchase. The purchase of bullion is, however, a common operation of commerce, and depends, like other operations, upon the inducements to import the article.

The inducements to import bullion arise, as in other cases, from its being cheap abroad, or from its being dear at home. Notwithstanding the commotions in South America, as well as in Europe, there is no reason to believe that the quantity of the precious metals is now (more than at any former period) insufficient for the demand throughout the commercial and civilized world. The price may be higher in some countries than in others; and it may be different in the same country, at different times; but, generally, the European stock of gold and silver has been abundant, even during the protracted war, which has afflicted the nations of Europe.

The purchase of bullion in foreign markets, upon reasonable terms, is, then, deemed practicable; nor can its importation into the United States fail eventually to be profitable. The actual price of gold and silver in the American market would in itself afford, for some time, an ample premium, although the fall in the price must, of course, be proportionate to the increase of the quantity. But it is within the scope of a wise policy to create additional demands for coin, and, in that way, to multiply the inducements to import and retain the metals of which it is composed. For instance, the excessive issue of bank paper has usurped the place of the national money; and, under such circumstances, gold and silver will always continue to be treated as an article of merchandise; but it is hoped that the issue of bank paper will be soon reduced to its just share in the circulating medium of the country; and, consequently, that the coin of the United States will resume its legitimate capacity and character. Again, the Treasury, yielding, from necessity, to the general impulse, has hitherto consented to receive bank paper in the payment of duties and taxes; but the period approaches when it will probably become a duty to exact the payment either in Treasury notes, or in gold or silver coin, the lawful money of the United States. Again, the institutions which shall be deemed proper, in order to remove existing inconveniences, and to restore the national currency, may be so organized, as to engage the interest and enterprise of individuals in providing the means to establish them. And, finally, such regulations may be imposed upon the exportation of gold and silver, as will serve in future to fix and retain the quantity required for domestic uses.

But it is further believed that the national stock of the precious metals is not so reduced, as to render the operation of reinstating their agency in the national currency either difficult or protracted. The quantity actually possessed by the country is considerable; and the resuscitation of the public confidence in bank paper, or in other substitutes for coin, seems alone to be wanting to render it equal to the accustomed contribution for a circulating medium. In other countries, as well as in the United States, the effect of an excessive issue of paper money, to banish the precious metals, has been seen; and, under circumstances much more disadvantageous than the present, the effect of public confidence in national institutions, to recall the precious metals to their uses in exchange, has also been experienced.

Even, however, if it were practicable, it has sometimes been questioned whether it would be politic again to employ gold and silver for the purposes of a national currency. It was long and universally supposed that, to maintain a paper medium without depreciation, the certainty of being able to convert it into coin was indispensable; nor can the experiment which has given rise to a contrary doctrine be deemed complete or conclusive. But whatever may be the issue of that experiment elsewhere, a difference in the structure of the Government, in the physical, as well as the political, situation of the country, and in the various departments of industry, seem to deprive it of any important influence, as a precedent for the imitation of the United States.

In offering these general remarks to the consideration of Congress it is not intended to convey an opinion that the circulation of the gold and silver coins can at once be renewed. Upon motives of public convenience the gradual attainment of that object is alone contemplated; but a strong, though respectful, solicitude is felt that the measures adopted by the Legislature should invariably tend to its attainment.

2d. Of the services rendered to the Government by some of the State banks during the late war, and of the liberality by which some of them are actuated in their intercourse with the Treasury, justice requires an explicit acknowledgment. It is a fact, however, incontestably proved, that those institutions cannot, at this time, be successfully employed to furnish a uniform national currency. The failure of one attempt to associate them with that view has already been stated. Another attempt, by their agency in circulating Treasury notes, to overcome the inequalities of the exchange, has only been partially successful. And a plan recently proposed, with the design to curtail the issues of bank notes, to fix the public confidence in the administration of the affairs of the banks, and to give to each bank a legitimate share in the circulation, is not likely to receive the general sanction of the banks. The truth is, that the charter restrictions of some of the banks, the mutual relation and dependence of the banks of the same State, and even of the banks of different States, and the duty which the directors of each bank conceive they owe to their immediate constituents, upon points of security or emolument, interpose an insuperable obstacle to any voluntary arrangement, upon national considerations alone, for the establishment of a national medium through the agency of the State banks. It is, nevertheless, with the State banks that the measures for restoring the national currency of gold and silver must originate; for, until their issues of paper be reduced, their specie capitals be reinstated, and their specie operations be commenced, there will be neither room, nor employment, nor safety, for the introduction of the precious metals. The policy and the interest of the State banks must, therefore, be engaged in the great fiscal work, by all the means which the Treasury can employ, or the legislative wisdom shall provide.

3d. The establishment of a national bank is regarded as the best, and, perhaps, the only adequate resource to relieve the country and the Government from the present embarrassments. Authorized to issue notes, which will be received in all payments to the United States, the circulation of its issues will be co-extensive with the Union, and there will exist a constant demand, bearing a just proportion to the annual amount of the duties and taxes to be collected, independent of the general circulation for commercial and social purposes. A national bank will, therefore, possess the means and the opportunity of supplying a circulating medium of equal use and value in every State, and in every district of every State. Established by the authority of the Government of the United States, accredited by the Government to the whole amount of its notes in circulation, and entrusted as the depository of the Government with all the accumulations of the public treasure, the national bank, independent of its immediate capital, will enjoy every recommendation which can merit and secure the confidence of the public. Organized upon principles of responsibility, but of independence, the national bank will be retained within its legitimate sphere of action, without just apprehension from the misconduct of its directors, or from the encroachments of the Government. Eminent in its resources, and in its example, the national bank will conciliate, aid, and lead, the State banks in all that is necessary for the restoration of credit, public and private. And acting upon a compound capital, partly of stock, and partly of gold and silver, the national bank will be the ready instrument to enhance the value of the public securities, and to restore the currency of the national coin.

4th. The power of the Government to supply and maintain a paper medium of exchange will not be questioned; but, for the introduction of that medium, there must be an adequate motive. The sole motive for issuing Treasury notes has, hitherto, been to raise money in anticipation of the revenue. The revenue, however, will probably become, in the course of the year 1816, and continue afterwards, sufficient to discharge all the debts, and to defray all the expenses of the Government; and, consequently, there will exist no motive to issue the paper of the Government as an instrument of credit.

It will not be deemed an adequate object for an issue of the paper of the Government, merely that it may be exchanged for the paper of the banks, since the Treasury will be abundantly supplied with bank paper by the collection of the revenue; and the Government cannot be expected to render itself a general debtor, in order to become the special creditor of the State banks.

The co-operation of the Government with the national bank, in the introduction of a national currency, may, however, be advantageously employed by issues of Treasury notes, so long as they shall be required for the public service.

Upon the whole, the state of the national currency, and other important considerations connected with the operations of the Treasury, render it a duty respectfully to propose—

That a national bank be established at the city of Philadelphia, having power to erect branches elsewhere, and that the capital of the bank (being of a competent amount) consist of three-fourths of the public stock, and one-fourth of gold and silver.

All which is respectfully submitted.

A. J. DALLAS
Secretary of the Treasury
Treasury Department, December 6, 1815

NICHOLAS BIDDLE:

"OVERBANKING AND OVERTRADING"

Bank of the United States
March 3, 1828

DEAR SIR:

Your favor of the 28th ult°. was duly received, and I avail myself of the opportunity of answering it, to state precisely what is the present situation of the Bank and the views entertained of its proper course in the present posture of the affairs of the country.

For some months past, the importations from France and England have been very extensive, and without great caution, the results may prove highly disastrous. The low price of our exported articles and tardiness with which the crop of Exchange from the South comes into the market this year, have diminished the means of paying for these importations, and resort has been of course had to the exportation of coin. The natural correction of this evil—for, beyond a certain limit, it

---

From a letter to John White, MS, "President's Letter Book, Private No. 2," pp. 353–356, Nicholas Biddle Papers, Library of Congress. The abbreviations following the title of Cashier stand for Office of Discount and Deposit.

is an evil—is the diminution of the business of those institutions which are the depositories of the coin, which by rendering bank credits less easy, makes them more valuable, and by depriving the importers of these artificial facilities to obtain money, diminishes the means & the temptations to continue these importations, and of course lessens the demand for, and the price of, Exchange. This course which all prudent Banking companies should adopt, is the only true & ultimate restraint on excessive importations. It is therefore a matter of equal surprize and regret that the Banks of New York on whom the pressure of specie has now continued for several months have not until now diminished their discounts one dollar but have gone on discounting as freely as hitherto. The obvious consequence is this. The importers ship specie, or they buy bills from those that do—their goods arrive—are sent immediately to auction. The Banks discount the auction notes, the proceeds of which are drawn out in specie & shipped, thus furnishing the means of continuing indefinitely the circle of operations. As long as they do so—they themselves furnish the means of making the very demands of which they complain. The whole evil therefore lies in an overbanking which occasions an overtrading, and the whole remedy lies in preventing this overbanking. One of our most respectable & extensive merchants trading to France assured me a few days ago, that he was alarmed at these excessive importations & had written to France to send no more, as he anticipated a great glut of French goods with all its train of ruinous consequences. Against these it is the business of the Bank of the U. States to guard. It has accordingly placed itself in an attitude of security and strength, so as to interpose whenever it may be necessary to protect the community. The precise point of that interposition is the interesting question. While the State Banks go on in their present career, it is hardly fair to throw on the Stockholders of the Bank of the U.S. the burden of protecting them against the effects of their own improvidence—of releasing them at the first moment of difficulty by incurring a heavy debt in Europe bearing an interest of five per cent. It seems more just that the Bank of the U.S. should reserve its strength—and let the State Banks feel the pressure which their thoughtlessness occasions. Such is the present position of this Bank. It keeps within its limits—discounts cautiously—and when demands for specie come, turns them over to the State Banks. These operations are coming to their natural result. The State Banks of Phil^a. are already uneasy, & are adopting a prudent course of restrictions. Those of New York will shortly follow the example—and the effect will be a reduction in the rate of Exchange and a stoppage of specie shipments. If those should fail in producing their effect—or if the operation threatens great inconveniences to the community the Bank can and will immediately interfere. But it seems premature to do so at the present moment—while the first effect will be to induce the State Banks to continue their present course—and while the remedy is in their own hands if they have only the prudence to adopt it.

In regard to your Office our impression has been that as the demand for money is habitually small with you and you were more out of reach of the operations which press on New York & Phil^a.—it was not necessary to recommend to you any particular course of restriction. Nevertheless the course of things at present may before long reach you and it would be a very judicious and acceptable co-operation on your part in our present course of measures, if for the present you would abstain from increasing your discounts, and particularly if you would avoid giving facilities to those whose operations are most inconvenient to us. This mutual understanding of our objects will perhaps be more advantageous than any precise stipulation of the mutual credits between the Bank & the Office. The occasion for the restriction will we trust pass when the immediate result expected from it, shall be produced—and it was in this point of view that I regarded our present need of coin as temporary in its duration. It is a fortunate circumstance after the great exhaustion which the country has undergone that the demand for the Canton trade promises to be very small this Spring, and will enable us to return to a more settled state after this immediate crisis is over. Of this of course the earliest intimation will be given to you. In the mean time I have thought it best to state precisely our present position and views.

> With great regard
> Yrs
> N BIDDLE
> *Pres^t.*

JOHN WHITE ESQ^r.
Cashier, Off. Dt. Dept.
Baltimore

27. The Bank as an Organ of "Exclusive Privileges"

The Bank War, the struggle over the proposed recharter of the Second Bank, was one of the bitterest controversies over economic policy that ever took place in the United States. In a sense the conflict still continues, since Pulitzer Prizes have recently been won by eloquent partisans of the two principal protagonists.[1] There remain sharp differences of interpretation as to the classes or economic interests which provided the most significant opposition. The traditional view is that the Bank was destroyed by the agrarian South and West, though it was an open question how much of the objection was that of "hard

---

[1] Arthur M. Schlesinger, Jr., *The Age of Jackson* (Boston: Little, Brown & Co., 1945); Bray Hammond, *Banks and Politics in America* (Princeton: Princeton University Press, 1957).

money" men who were against all bank credit and how much was that of "soft money" men who wanted easier credit from state banks unrestrained by a national institution. Arthur M. Schlesinger, Jr., emphasizes objections on the part of eastern workingmen and sees the opposition to the Bank as a farmer-labor coalition somewhat like that which supported the New Deal. On the other hand, Bray Hammond finds the source of the most implacable and effective opposition in the interests of the state banks, of those of New York City because they resented the primacy of a Philadelphia institution and of bankers and rising businessmen throughout the country who were eager to make money as proprietors of state banks, as borrowers from them, and in both capacities.

Andrew Jackson's veto in 1832 of a bill to recharter the Bank was the decisive act in the War, though more overt hostilities took place later—with the Administration withdrawing the government deposits from the Bank and Biddle retaliating with a general reduction of credit; and bitterness continued until the charter expired in 1836 and Biddle's Bank became a private institution under charter from the state of Pennsylvania. The veto itself appears to be written from a southern and western viewpoint, although it refers also to a group of eastern businessmen who would be ready to bid for the privilege of organizing a national bank. Yet it is quite impossible to determine, either from the passages quoted below or from the remainder of the text, whether the President thought that the Bank had made too much or too little credit available to the South and West. The argument moves on a different plane. The Bank makes profits by doing business in these parts of the country and, since little of its stock is owned there, the effect is to drain money away from southerners and westerners and to give it to easterners and, still worse, to foreign stockholders. The fundamental objection to the Bank is that it is an organ of special privilege, making rich men "richer by act of Congress."

Another western opponent of the Bank, Senator Benton of Missouri, put the argument in similar terms:—"I look upon the Bank as an institution too great and powerful to be tolerated in a government of free and equal laws. . . . A great moneyed power is favorable to great capitalists; for it is the principle of money to favor money."[2] One part of the opposition, the ambitious entrepreneurs described in *Banks and Politics,* opposed the Bank because it put restraints in the way of their own capitalistic enterprise; but another part of the opposition regarded the Bank as the most dangerous expression of developing capitalism rather than as an instrument by which that development might to some degree be regulated and controlled.

ANDREW JACKSON: THE VETO MESSAGE

Washington, July 10, 1832

To the Senate:

The bill "to modify and continue" the act entitled "An act to incorporate the subscribers to the Bank of the United States" was presented to me on the 4th July instant. Having considered it with that solemn regard to the principles of the Constitution which the day was calculated to inspire, and come to the conclusion that it ought not to become a law, I herewith return it to the Senate, in which it originated, with my objections.

A bank of the United States is in many respects convenient for the Government and useful to the people. Entertaining this opinion, and deeply impressed with the belief that some of the powers and privileges possessed by the existing bank are unauthorized by the Constitution, subversive of the rights of the States, and dangerous to the liberties of the people, I felt it my duty at an early period of my Administration to call the attention of Congress to the practicability of organizing an institu-

---

From James D. Richardson, *A Compilation of the Messages and Papers of the Presidents* (New York: Bureau of National Literature and Art, 1897–1920), vol. II, pp. 576–581, 587, 590–591.

---

[2] Thomas Hart Benton, *Thirty Years' View* (New York: D. Appleton & Co., 1854), vol. I, pp. 191, 193.

tion combining all its advantages and obviating these objections. I sincerely regret that in the act before me I can perceive none of those modifications of the bank charter which are necessary, in my opinion, to make it compatible with justice, with sound policy, or with the Constitution of our country.

The present corporate body, denominated the president, directors, and company of the Bank of the United States, will have existed at the time this act is intended to take effect twenty years. It enjoys an exclusive privilege of banking under the authority of the General Government, a monopoly of its favor and support, and, as a necessary consequence, almost a monopoly of the foreign and domestic exchange. The powers, privileges, and favors bestowed upon it in the original charter, by increasing the value of the stock far above its par value, operated as a gratuity of many millions to the stockholders.

An apology may be found for the failure to guard against this result in the consideration that the effect of the original act of incorporation could not be certainly foreseen at the time of its passage. The act before me proposes another gratuity to the holders of the same stock, and in many cases to the same men, of at least seven millions more. This donation finds no apology in any uncertainty as to the effect of the act. On all hands it is conceded that its passage will increase at least 20 or 30 per cent more the market price of the stock, subject to the payment of the annuity of $200,000 per year secured by the act, thus adding in a moment one-fourth to its par value. It is not our own citizens only who are to receive the bounty of our Government. More than eight millions of the stock of this bank are held by foreigners. By this act the American Republic proposes virtually to make them a present of some millions of dollars. For these gratuities to foreigners and to some of our own opulent citizens the act secures no equivalent whatever. They are the certain gains of the present stockholders under the operation of this act, after making full allowance for the payment of the bonus.

Every monopoly and all exclusive privileges are granted at the expense of the public, which ought to receive a fair equivalent. The many millions which this act proposes to bestow on the stockholders of the existing bank must come directly or indirectly out of the earnings of the American people. It is due to them, therefore, if their Government sell monopolies and exclusive privileges, that they should at least exact for them as much as they are worth in open market. The value of the monopoly in this case may be correctly ascertained. The twenty-eight millions of stock would probably be at an advance of 50 per cent, and command in market at least $42,000,000, subject to the payment of the present bonus. The present value of the monopoly, therefore, is $17,000,000, and this the act proposes to sell for three millions, payable in fifteen annual installments of $200,000 each.

It is not conceivable how the present stockholders can have any claim to the special favor of the Government. The present corporation has enjoyed its monopoly during the period stipulated in the original contract. If we must have such a corporation, why should not the Government sell out the whole stock and thus secure to the people the full market value of the privileges granted? Why should not Congress create and sell twenty-eight millions of stock, incorporating the purchasers with all the powers and privileges secured in this act and putting the premium upon the sales into the Treasury?

But this act does not permit competition in the purchase of this monopoly. It seems to be predicated on the erroneous idea that the present stockholders have a prescriptive right not only to the favor but to the bounty of Government. It appears that more than a fourth part of the stock is held by foreigners and the residue is held by a few hundred of our own citizens, chiefly of the richest class. For their benefit does this act exclude the whole American people from competition in the purchase of this monopoly and dispose of it for many millions less than it is worth. This seems the less excusable because some of our citizens not now stockholders petitioned that the door of competition might be opened, and offered to take a charter on terms much more favorable to the Government and country. . . .

It has been urged as an argument in favor of rechartering the present bank that the calling in its loans will produce great embarrassment and distress. The time allowed to close its concerns is ample, and if it has been well managed its pressure will be light, and heavy only in case its management has been bad. If, therefore, it shall produce distress, the fault will be its own, and it would furnish a reason against renewing a power which has been so obviously abused. But will there ever be a time when this reason will be less powerful? To acknowledge its force is to admit that the bank ought to be perpetual, and as a consequence the present stockholders and those inheriting their rights as successors be established a privileged order, clothed both with great political power and enjoying immense pecuniary advantages from their connection with the Government. . . .

By documents submitted to Congress at the present session it appears that on the 1st of January, 1832, of the twenty-eight millions of private stock in the corporation, $8,405,500 were held by foreigners, mostly of Great Britain. The amount of stock held in the nine Western and South-western States is $140,200, and in the four Southern States is $5,623,100, and in the Middle and Eastern States is about $13,522,000. The profits of the bank in 1831, as shown in a statement to Congress, were about $3,455,598; of this there accrued in the nine Western States about $1,640,048; in the four Southern States about $352,507, and in the Middle and Eastern States about $1,463,-041. As little stock is held in the West, it is obvious that the debt of the people in that section to the bank is principally a debt to the Eastern and foreign stockholders; that the interest they pay upon it is carried into the Eastern States and into Europe, and that it is a burden upon their industry and a drain of their currency, which no country can bear without inconvenience and occasional distress. To meet this burden and equalize the exchange operations of the bank, the amount of specie drawn from those States through its branches within the last two years, as shown by its official reports, was about $6,000,000. More than half a million of this amount does not stop in the Eastern States, but passes on to Europe to pay the dividends of the foreign stockholders. . . .

. . . Banking, like farming, manufacturing, or any other occupation or profession, is *a business,* the right to follow which is not originally derived from the laws. Every citizen and every company of citizens in all of our States possessed the right until the State legislatures deemed it good policy to prohibit private banking by law. If the prohibitory State laws were now repealed, every citizen would again possess the right. The State banks are a qualified restoration of the right which has been taken away by the laws against banking, guarded by such provisions and limitations as in the opinion of the State legislatures the public interest requires.

It is to be regretted that the rich and powerful too often bend the acts of government to their selfish purposes. Distinctions in society will always exist under every just government. Equality of talents, of education, or of wealth can not be produced by human institutions. In the full enjoyment of the gifts of Heaven and the fruits of superior industry, economy, and virtue, every man is equally entitled to protection by law; but when the laws undertake to add to these natural and just advantages artificial distinctions, to grant titles, gratuities, and exclusive privileges, to make the rich richer and the potent more powerful, the humble members of society—the farmers, mechanics, and laborers—who have neither the time nor the means of securing like favors to themselves, have a right to complain of the injustice of their Government. There are no necessary evils in government. Its evils exist only in its abuses. If it would confine itself to equal protection, and, as Heaven does its rains, shower its favors alike on the high and the low, the rich and the poor, it would be an unqualified blessing. In the act before me there seems to be a wide and unnecessary departure from these just principles.

Nor is our Government to be maintained or our Union preserved by invasions of the rights and powers of the several States. In thus attempting to make our General Government strong we make it weak. Its true strength consists in leaving individuals and States as much as possible to themselves—in making itself felt, not in its power, but in its beneficence; not in its control, but in its protection; not in binding the States more closely to the center, but leaving each to move unobstructed in its proper orbit.

Experience should teach us wisdom. Most of the difficulties our Government now encounters and most of the dangers which impend over our Union have sprung from an abandonment of the legitimate objects of Government by our national legislation, and the adoption of such principles as are embodied in this act. Many of our rich men have not been content with equal protection and equal benefits, but have besought us to make them richer by act of Congress. By attempting to gratify their desires we have in the results of our legislation arrayed section against section, interest against interest, and man against man, in a fearful commotion which threatens to shake the foundations of our Union. It is time to pause in our career to review our principles, and if possible revive that devoted patriotism and spirit of compromise which distinguished the sages of the Revolution and the fathers of our Union. If we can not at once, in justice to interests vested under improvident legislation, make our Government what it ought to be, we can at least take a stand against all new grants of monopolies and exclusive privileges, against any prostitution of our Government to the advancement of the few at the expense of the many, and in favor of compromise and gradual reform in our code of laws and system of political economy.

I have now done my duty to my country. If sustained by my fellow-citizens, I shall be grateful and happy; if not, I shall find in the motives which impel me ample grounds for contentment and peace. In the difficulties which surround us and the dangers which threaten our institutions there is cause for neither dismay nor alarm. For relief and deliverance let us firmly rely on that kind Providence which I am sure watches with peculiar care over the destinies of our Republic, and on the intelligence and wisdom of our countrymen. Through *His* abundant goodness and *their* patriotic devotion our liberty and Union will be preserved.

ANDREW JACKSON

28. The Bank as a Promoter of "Great Public Interests"

Scholars have listed so many groups and interests as opposing the Second Bank that it is something of a surprise to find a study devoted to an examination of its sources of popular and political support.[1] Yet the bill for recharter received decisive majorities in both Senate and House, including strong support from the West though not from the South. State-chartered banks, moreover, were divided on the issue rather than united in their opposition. Certain of them, in New York City, in Martin Van Buren's stronghold of Albany, and in a few other centers, played an exceptionally effective role in the campaign against the Bank. On the other hand, Nicholas Biddle was able to secure memorials supporting recharter from sixty or seventy state banks, and the more persuasive of these came from the less-developed areas in which shortage of capital was an overriding consideration.

---

[1] Jean Wilburn, *Biddle's Bank: The Crucial Years,* to be published by Columbia University Press.

When President Jackson returned the bill to the Senate with his disapproval, the first and most important speech against the veto was made by Daniel Webster. The issue, he declares, is not whether someone may make a profit from the Bank but whether the institution shall be allowed to perform the functions which the nation and the people need to have performed. If the West owes money to the Bank, this is proof not that its resources are being drained away but that a region that needs and can make good use of capital is obtaining it on better terms than would otherwise be available. "Congress passed the bill, not as a bounty or favor to the present stockholders, . . . but to promote great public interests."

In spite of Webster's peroration, the Constitution and the Union survived the Bank Veto. What did not survive was the principle of national responsibility for the provision of money and credit. The Congress returned to Secretary Dallas's problem of a uniform currency in the national banking legislation of the 1860's, but the government did not renew its early attempt to assume responsibility for the stability of the financial system as a whole until it did so, with more sophisticated means, with the passage of the Federal Reserve Act in 1913.

DANIEL WEBSTER:

SPEECH ON THE BANK VETO

The hour of eleven having arrived, the Senate proceeded to the consideration of the bill for renewing and modifying the charter of the Bank of the United States, with the message of the President of the United States, assigning his reasons for refusing to approve and sign the same. And the question being on passing the bill, said objections notwithstanding.

From *Register of Debates in Congress,* 22nd Congress, 1st Session, July 11, 1832, Part I, pp. 1221–1240.

MR. WEBSTER rose, and addressed the Senate as follows:

Mr. President, no one will deny the high importance of the subject now before us. Congress, after full deliberation and discussion, has passed a bill for extending the duration of the Bank of the United States, by decisive majorities in both Houses. It has adopted this measure not until its attention had been called to the subject in three successive annual messages of the President. The bill having been thus passed by both Houses, and having been duly presented to the President, instead of signing and approving it, he has returned it with objections. These objections go against the whole substance of the law originally creating the bank. They deny, in effect, that the bank is constitutional; they deny that it is expedient; they deny that it is necessary for the public service.

It is not to be doubted that the constitution gives the President the power which he has now exercised; but, while the power is admitted, the grounds upon which it has been exerted become fit subjects of examination. The constitution makes it the duty of Congress, in cases like this, to reconsider the measure which they have passed, to weigh the force of the President's objections to that measure, and to take a new vote upon the question.

Before the Senate proceeds to this second vote, I propose to make some remarks upon these objections. And, in the first place, it is to be observed that they are such as to extinguish all hope that the present bank, or any bank at all resembling it, or resembling any known similar institution, can ever receive his approbation. He states no terms, no qualifications, no conditions, no modifications, which can reconcile him to the essential provisions of the existing charter. He is against the bank, and against any bank constituted in a manner known either to this or any other country. . . . Mr. President, I will not conceal my opinion that the affairs of this country are approaching an important and dangerous crisis. At the very moment of almost unparalleled general prosperity, there appears an unaccountable disposition to destroy the most useful and most approved institutions of the Government. Indeed, it seems to be in the midst of all this national happiness, that some are found openly to question the advantages of the constitution itself; and many more ready to embarrass the exercise of its just power, weaken its authority, and undermine its foundations. How far these notions may be carried, it is impossible yet to say. We have before us the practical result of one of them. The bank has fallen, or is to fall.

It is now certain that, without a change in our public councils, this bank will not be continued, nor will any other be established, which, according to the general sense and language of mankind, can be entitled to the name. In three years and nine months from the present moment, the charter of the bank expires; within that period, therefore, it must wind up its concerns. It must call in its debts, withdraw its bills from circulation, and cease from all its ordinary operations. All this is to be done in three years and nine months; because, although there is a provision in the charter rendering it lawful to use the corporate name for two years after the expiration of the charter, yet this is allowed only for the purpose of suits, and for the sale of the estate belonging to the bank, and for no other purpose whatever. The whole active business of the bank, its custody of public deposites, its transfers of public moneys, its dealing in exchange, all its loans and discounts, and all its issues of bills for circulation, must cease and determine on or before the 3d day of March, 1836; and, within the same period, its debts must be collected, as no new contract can be made with it, as a corporation, for the renewal of loans, or discount of notes or bills, after that time.

The President is of opinion that this time is long enough to close the concerns of the institution without inconvenience. His language is: "The time allowed the bank to close its concerns is ample, and, if it has been well managed, its pressure will be light, and heavy only in case its management has been bad.

If, therefore, it shall produce distress, the fault will be its own." Sir, this is all no more than general statement, without fact or argument to support it. We know what the management of the bank has been, and we know the present state of its affairs. We can judge, therefore, whether it be probable that its capital can be all called in, and the circulation of its bills withdrawn, in three years and nine months, by any discretion or prudence in management, without producing distress. The bank has discounted liberally, in compliance with the wants of the community. The amount due to it on loans and discounts, in certain large divisions of the country, is great; so great, that I do not perceive how any man can believe that it can be paid within the time now limited, without distress. Let us look at known facts. Thirty millions of the capital of the bank are now out, on loans and discounts, in the States on the Mississippi and its waters: ten of these millions on the discount of bills of exchange, foreign and domestic, and twenty millions loaned on promissory notes. Now, sir, how is it possible that this vast amount can be collected in so short a period, without suffering, by any management whatever? We are to remember that when the collection of this debt begins, at that same time the existing medium of payment, that is, the circulation of the bills of the bank, will begin also to be restrained and withdrawn, and thus the means of payment must be limited just when the necessity of making payment becomes pressing. The whole debt is to be paid, and within the same time the whole circulation withdrawn.

The local banks, where there are such, will be able to afford little assistance; because they themselves will feel a full share of the pressure. They will not be in a condition to extend their discounts; but, in all probability, obliged to curtail them. Whence, then, are the means to come for paying this debt, and in what medium is payment to be made? If all this may be done, with but slight pressure on the community, what course of conduct is to accomplish it? How is it to be done? What other thirty millions are to supply the place of these thirty millions, now to be called in? What other circulation or medium of payment is to be adopted, in the place of the bills of the bank? The message, following a singular strain of argument which had been used in this House, has a loud lamentation upon the suffering of the Western States, on account of their being obliged to pay even interest on this debt. This payment of interest is, itself, represented as exhausting their means, and ruinous to their prosperity. But if the interest cannot be paid without pressure, can both interest and pricipal be paid in four years without pressure? The truth is, the interest has been paid, is paid, and may continue to be paid, without any pressure at all; because the money borrowed is profitably employed by those who borrow it, and the rate of interest which they pay is at least two per cent. lower than the actual value of money in that part of the country. But to pay the whole principal in less than four years, losing, at the same time, the existing and accustomed means and facilities of payment created by the bank itself, and do this without extreme embarrassment, without absolute distress, is, in my judgment, impossible. I hesitate not to say that, as this veto travels to the West, it will depreciate the value of every man's property, from the Atlantic States to the capital of Missouri. Its effects will be felt in the price of lands, the great and leading article of Western property; in the price of crops; in the products of labor; in the repression of enterprise; and in embarrassment to every kind of business and occupation. I take this opinion strongly, because I have no doubt of its truth, and am willing its correctness should be judged by the event. Without personal acquaintance with the Western States, I know enough of their condition to be satisfied that what I have predicted must happen. The people of the West are rich, but their riches consist in their immense quantities of excellent land, in the products of these lands, and in their spirit of enterprise. The actual value of money, or rate of interest, with them is high, because their pecuniary capital bears little proportion to their landed interest. At an average rate, money is not worth less than eight per cent. per annum throughout the whole Western country, notwithstanding that it has now a loan, or an advance, from the bank of thirty millions, at six per cent. To call in this loan at the rate of eight millions a year, in addition to the interest on the whole, and to take away, at the same time, that circulation which constitutes so great a portion of the medium of payment throughout that whole region, is an operation which, however wisely conducted, cannot but inflict a blow on the community of tremendous force and frightful consequences. The thing cannot be done without distress, bankruptcy, and ruin to many. . . .

Although, sir, I have spoken of the effects of this veto in the Western country, it has not been because I considered that part of the United States exclusively affected by it.

Some of the Atlantic States may feel its consequences, perhaps, as sensibly as those of the West, though not for the same reasons. The concern manifested by Pennsylvania for the renewal of the charter, shows her sense of the importance of the bank to her own interest, and that of the nation. That great and enterprising State has entered into an extensive system of internal improvements, which necessarily makes heavy demands on her credit and her resources; and by the sound and acceptable currency which the bank affords, by the stability which it gives to private credit, and by occasional advances made in anticipation of her revenues, and in aid of her great objects, she has found herself benefited, doubtless in no inconsiderable degree. Her Legislature has instructed her Senators here to advocate the renewal of the charter at this session; they have obeyed her voice, and yet they have the misfortune to find that, in the judgment of the President, the measure is unconstitutional, unnecessary, dangerous to liberty, and is, moreover, ill-timed. But, Mr. President, it is not the local interest of the West, nor the particular interest of Pennsylvania, or any other State, which has influenced Congress in passing this bill.

It has been governed by a wise foresight, and by a desire to avoid embarrassment in the pecuniary concerns of the country, to secure the safe collection and convenient transmission of public moneys, to maintain the circulation of this country, sound and safe as it now happily is, against the possible effects of a wild spirit of speculation. Finding the bank highly useful, Congress has thought fit to provide for its continuance. . . .

Before proceeding to the constitutional question, there are some other topics, treated in the message, which ought to be noticed. It commenced by an inflamed statement of what it calls the "favor" bestowed upon the original bank by the Government, or, indeed, as it is phrased, the "monopoly of its favor and support;" and through the whole message all possible changes are rung on the "gratuity," the "exclusive privileges," and "monopoly," of the bank charter. Now, sir, the truth is, that the powers conferred on the bank are such, and no other, as are usually conferred on similar institutions. They constitute no monopoly, although some of them are, of necessity, and with propriety, exclusive privileges. "The original act," says the message, "operated as a gratuity of many millions to the stockholders." What fair foundation is there for this remark? The stockholders received their charter not gratuitously, but for a valuable consideration in money, prescribed by Congress, and actually paid. Sometimes the stock has been above par, at other times below par, according to prudence in management, or according to commercial occurrences. But if, by a judicious administration of its affairs, it had kept its stock always above par, what pretence would there be, nevertheless, for saying that such augmentation of its value was a "gratuity" from Government? The message proceeds to declare that the present act proposes another donation, another gratuity, to the same men, of at least seven millions more. It seems to me that this is an extraordinary statement, and an extraordinary style of argument, for such a subject and on such an occasion. In the first place, the facts are all assumed; they are taken for true without evidence. There are no proofs that any benefit to that amount will accrue to the stockholders, nor any experience to justify the expectation of it. It rests on random estimates, or mere conjecture. But suppose the continuance of the charter should prove beneficial to the stockholders, do they not pay for it? They give twice as much for a charter of fifteen years, as was given before for one of twenty. And if the proposed bonus or premium be not, in the President's judgment, large enough, would he, nevertheless, on such a mere matter of opinion as that, negative the whole bill? May not Congress be trusted to decide, even on such a subject as the amount of the money premium to be received by Government for a charter of this kind? But, sir, there is a larger and a much more just view of this subject. The bill was not passed for the purpose of benefiting the present stockholders. Their benefit, if any, is incidental and collateral. Nor was it passed on any idea that they had a right to a renewed charter, although the message argues against such right, as if it had been somewhere set up and asserted. No such right has been asserted by any body.

Congress passed the bill, not as a bounty or a favor to the present stockholders, nor to comply with any demand of right on their part, but to promote great public interests, for great public objects. Every bank must have some stockholders, unless it be such a bank as the President has recommended, and in regard to which he seems not likely to find much concurrence of other men's opinions; and if the stockholders, whoever they may be, conduct the affairs of the bank prudently, the expectation is always, of course, that they will make it profitable to themselves, as well as useful to the public. If a bank charter is not to be granted, because it may be profitable, either in a small or great degree, to the stockholders, no charter can be granted. The objection lies against all banks. Sir, the object aimed at by such institutions is to connect the public safety and convenience with private interests. It has been found by experience that banks are safest under private management, and that Government banks are among the most dangerous of all inventions. Now, sir, the whole drift of the message is to reverse the settled judgment of all the civilized world, and to set up Government banks, independent of private interest, of private control. For this purpose the message labors, even beyond the measure of all its other labors, to create jealousies and prejudices, on the ground of the alleged benefit which individuals will derive from the renewal of this charter. Much less effort is made to show that Government, or the public, will be injured by the bill, than that individuals will profit by it. Following up the impulses of the same spirit, the message goes on gravely to allege that the act, as passed by Congress, proposes to make a present of some millions of dollars to foreigners; because a portion of the stock is holden by foreigners. . . .

. . . Allow me now, sir, to take notice of an argument, founded on the practical operation of the bank. That argument is this. Little of the stock of the bank is held in the West, being chiefly owned by citizens of the Southern and Eastern States, and by foreigners. But the Western and Southwestern States owe the bank a heavy debt, so heavy that the interest amounts to a million six hundred thousand a year. This interest is carried to the Eastern States, or to Europe, annually, and its payment is a burden on the people of the West, and a drain of their currency, which no country can bear without inconvenience and distress. The true character and the whole value of this argument are manifest by the mere statement of it. The people of the West are, from their situation, necessarily large borrowers. They need money capital, and they borrow it because they can derive a benefit from its use, much beyond the interest which they pay. They borrow at six per cent. of the bank, although the value of money with them is at least as high as eight. . . .

From the commencement of the Government it has been thought desirable to invite, rather than to repel, the introduction of foreign capital. Our stocks have all been open to foreign subscriptions, and the State banks, in like manner, are free to foreign ownership. Whatever State has created a debt, has been willing that foreigners should become purchasers, and desirous of it. . . . It is easy to say that there is danger to liberty, danger to independence, in a bank open to foreign stockholders—because it is easy to say any thing. But neither reason nor experience proves any such danger. The foreign stockholder cannot be a director. He has no voice even in the choice of directors. His money is placed entirely in the management of the directors appointed by the President and Senate, and by the American stockholders. So far as there is dependence, or influence, either way, it is to the disadvantage of the foreign stockholder. He has parted with the control over his own property, instead of exercising control over the property or over the actions of others. And, sir, let it now be added, in further answer to this whole class of objections, that experience has abundantly confuted them all. This Government has existed forty-three years, and has maintained, in full being and operation, a bank, such as is now proposed to be renewed, for thirty-six years out of the forty-three. . . .

Mr. President, we have arrived at a new epoch. We are entering on experiments with the Government and the constitution of the country, hitherto untried, and of fearful and appalling aspect. This message calls us to the contemplation of a future, which little resembles the past. Its principles are at war with all that public opinion has sustained, and all which the experience of the Government has sanctioned. It denies first principles. It contradicts truths heretofore received as indisputable. It denies to the judiciary the interpretation of law, and demands to divide with Congress the originations of statutes. It extends the grasp of Executive pretension over every power of the Government. But this is not all. It presents the Chief Magistrate of the Union in the attitude of arguing away the powers of that Government over which he has been chosen to preside; and adopting, for this purpose, modes of reasoning which, even under the influence of all proper feeling towards high official station, it is difficult to regard as respectable. It appeals to every prejudice which may betray men into a mistaken view of their own interests; and to every passion which may lead them to disobey the impulses of their understanding. It urges all the specious topics of State rights, and national encroachment, against that which a great majority of the States have affirmed to be rightful, and in which all of them have acquiesced. It sows, in an unsparing manner, the seeds of jealousy and ill-will against that Government of which its author is the official head. It raises a cry that liberty is in danger, at the very moment when it puts forth claims to power heretofore unknown and unheard of. It affects alarm for the public freedom, when nothing so much endangers that freedom as its own unparalleled pretenses. This, even, is not all. It manifestly seeks to influence the poor against the rich. It wantonly attacks whole classes of the people, for the purpose of turning against them the prejudices and resentments of other classes. It is a State paper which finds no topic too exciting for its use; no passion too inflammable for its address and its solicitation. Such is this message. It remains, now, for the people of the United States to choose between the principles here avowed and their Government. These cannot subsist together. The one or the other must be rejected. If the sentiments of the message shall receive general approbation, the constitution will have perished even earlier than the moment which its enemies originally allowed for the termination of its existence. It will not have survived to its fiftieth year.

29. Georgia: A State Central Bank

Several of the southern states established banks that were intended to meet the special needs of the planters and farmers, particularly for medium or long-term credit. In modern terms, they might perhaps be described as agricultural development banks, though the phrase was not then in use; but they lacked sophisticated devices for meeting the problem raised by the lack of liquidity of the clients' principal assets. As a Georgia Governor said in 1839, restating a point made by Alexander Hamilton in Document 25:

> Land and negroes are unfit instruments for . . . being made
> the basis for issues of bank notes, because they cannot be ex-
> changed into money at the will of the holders, or as the neces-
> sities of commerce may require.[1]

When the Central Bank of Georgia was established in 1828, the intention to encourage agriculture was embodied in the provisions quoted below. The Bank is to give credit on more favorable terms than those that have prevailed, and it is instructed to lend as much as it safely can on longer-term "accommodation" loans rather than on short-term business paper. Good "country" borrowers will not need the backing of "town" endorsers, and the Bank is to distribute its total lending as nearly as possible in proportion to the population of the various counties.

On the other hand, the Central Bank differed from the typical "plantation bank" both in constitution and in history. Its original capital consisted not of claims on the planters' lands but of assets of the state government similar to those which

---

[1] George R. Gilmer, Georgia *Senate Journal*, 1839, p. 16. See also Fritz Redlich, *The Molding of American Banking* (New York: Hafner Publishing Co., 1947), Part I, ch. 7.

formed the basis of the Virginia Fund for Internal Improvement (Document 3). In practice it became a lender to the state as well as to individuals and an instrument for financing Georgia's principal internal improvement, the Western and Atlantic Railroad.[2]

Obviously critical of the unorthodox provisions of the Bank's Charter, Governor John Forsyth in 1829 warned it against the "over anxiety to be popular" that had brought disaster to institutions in other states "similar in character, and formed with like patriotic views."[3] But a later Governor, William Schley, writing under the impact of the crisis of 1837, drew a sharp distinction between the Central Bank that had helped "the people at large" and the private banks that had helped only a few traders in the towns and cities.[4] As late as 1840, Governor Charles J. McDonald, in the message quoted below, praises the Bank for its service in carrying through the depression both the state government and the people. The Bank, however, cannot continue indefinitely to cover the deficits of the state, and the Governor therefore recommends a "resumption" of taxation. In the event, the financial difficulties continued and taxation remained inadequate. In 1842 the Bank's doors were closed to new operations; and its assets were liquidated, at a loss, over the next thirteen years.

Professor Heath has analyzed in modern terms the Bank's accounts and its performance during the depression. His chapter on "Banking Policies" in Georgia reaches the provocative conclusion that the state banks, including the Central Bank, "represented a higher degree of maturity, in the regional stage of banking evolution, than did the United States banks at the national level."[5]

---

[2] See headnote to Document 3.

[3] Georgia *House Journal*, 1829, pp. 15–16.

[4] Georgia *Senate Journal*, 1837, pp. 14–15.

[5] Milton S. Heath, *Constructive Liberalism* (Cambridge: Harvard University Press, 1954), ch. 9, especially p. 230.

THE BANKING ACT OF 1828

WHEREAS, it is deemed expedient and beneficial, both to the State and its citizens, to establish a Bank on the funds of the State, for the purpose of discounting paper, and making loans upon terms more advantageous than has been heretofore customary:

Be it therefore enacted by the Senate and House of Representatives of the State of Georgia in General Assembly met, and it is hereby enacted by the authority of the same, That a Bank shall be established in behalf of the State of Georgia, at Milledgeville, in said State, to be known and called by the name and style of the Central Bank of Georgia, in the manner, and on the conditions and limitations hereinafter expressed. . . .

SEC. 2. *And be it further enacted by the authority aforesaid,* That the money in the treasury of this State, not otherwise appropriated, the shares owned by the State in the Bank of Augusta, in the Planters' Bank of the State of Georgia, in the Bank of the State of Georgia, and in the Bank of Darien; and all bonds, notes, specialties, judgments due the state, and all monies arising from the sales of fractions and town lots heretofore made, (and hereafter to be made,) and all other debts and monies at any time due the state, shall constitute and form the capital stock of said Bank; and the same are hereby appropriated for that purpose, and are, and shall be vested in the President and Directors of said Bank, and their successors in office, as hereinafter prescribed; and shall be and remain the capital stock of said Bank, and subject to the payment of all bills and notes issued by said Bank. . . .

SEC. 3. *And be it further enacted by the authority aforesaid,* That all the taxes hereafter to be collected on account of the

From Georgia *Laws,* December 22, 1828, pp. 34–39.

state, and all its dividends arising from stock in other Banks, shall be deposited in said Bank, to aid and facilitate its operations, subject nevertheless to all the drafts on the part of the state, authorised by legal appropriations—Provided nothing in this act shall be so construed as to interfere with the appropriations of the proceeds of the Bank stock heretofore set apart for the purposes of Internal Improvement and Education. . . .

SEC. 19. *And be it further enacted by the authority aforesaid,* That the bills or notes of the said corporation shall be receivable in payment of all taxes and debts due to the State.

SEC. 20. *And be it further enacted by the authority aforesaid,* That the Directors of said Bank shall not require town indorsers upon any note or obligation made payable at said Bank, where the country indorsers are deemed amply responsible to secure the payment of the same; and no notice or protest shall be necessary to charge any indorser, nor shall any charge be made by any notary public, for noting for nonpayment, or protesting any note due at the Bank.

SEC. 21. *And be it further enacted by the authority aforesaid,* That on all accommodation notes running at said Bank, the makers thereof shall renew their notes once in six months, at least, by paying up the interest in advance, at the rate of six per centum per annum, or for shorter periods, as the said makers may think proper: *Provided nevertheless,* That the Directors may call at any time on the maker of any discounted note for additional security, and if he shall refuse or neglect to comply, within twenty days after notice, said note shall be deemed and considered due, and suit shall be [commenced] immediately.

SEC. 22. *And be it further enacted by the authority aforesaid,* That the Directors of said Bank, shall loan as much money upon accommodation paper, as the interest and safety of said Bank will permit: and they shall not require to be paid upon such accommodation loans, more than twenty per centum per annum, of the principal thereof, unless the exigencies of the Bank shall require it. . . .

SEC. 25. *And be it further enacted by the authority aforesaid,* That the Directors of said Bank shall distribute their loans as equally as practicable, among the citizens of this State, having due regard to the population of the different counties. And no loan made by said Bank to any one person, or body corporate, or any society or collection of persons whatsoever, shall exceed twenty-five hundred dollars—Nor shall the Directors of the Central Bank at any time put in circulation, the bills thereof to a greater amount than the aggregate of specie and bills of the other chartered Banks of this State, and the bills of the Bank of the United States, in its vault.

CHARLES J. McDONALD:

"A BENEFACTOR OF THE PEOPLE"

The difficulties which have embarrassed the Commerce of the world, and produced in many places distress and ruin, have been felt by our people, but not so severely as in many States of the Union. The restless spirit of speculation which seemed to have taken possession of the country, exciting the public mind to a state of delirium, abstracting many of the people from their customary pursuits, with the inspiring hope of the sudden accumulation of fortune, has been the chief and prolific source of our embarrassments. Debts were contracted without reflection; or, upon the wild supposition that the staple commodity of the South, the great regulator of the value of property, would maintain an undiminished price, and habits of prodigality as extravagant as this unwarrantable expectation,

From Georgia *Senate Journal,* 1840, pp. 9–13.

were indulged. Men who never before yielded to delusive temptations, caught the contagion, and those alone escaped who trusted themselves not within the sphere of its infection. When the paroxism was over, and the day of retribution came, and brought with it that sober consideration which the debtor, disappointed in his imaginary means, realizes, when thrown upon his actual resources to meet his engagements, the true condition of the country was known, and it was one of extraordinary pressure. Fortunately for the debtor class of the community, the severity of the times has been greatly mitigated by the magnanimous forbearance of many creditors to urge the collection of their debts, and by the timely aid afforded by the Central Bank. This institution, with a liberality becoming it, administered to the general relief with all the means at its command. It could not have done more without exposing its issues to a ruinous depreciation, which would have been far more calamitous, than the evils intended to be remedied by its kind interposition. Though the late distribution has been liberal, it has come far short of relieving the embarrasments of the people. It is impossible, and perhaps inconsistent with the principles of sound policy, for the Government to undertake to protect the citizen from the consequences of imprudence or miscalculation. A reliance of this sort would beget a dependence destructive of individual enterprize, engender and cherish habits of reckless speculation, and foster a spirit of indifference to active and industrious pursuits, hostile to the welfare of society. Habits of industry and a rigid economy that would forbid the expenditures of the year to equal the lowest estimate of the probable income, and a firm resistance of the allurements to speculation, held out by the tempting prospects of unreasonable gain, are sure guarantees of immunity from pecuniary troubles, as well as of individual prosperity. . . .

The Central Bank, under the management of an able and experienced Board of Directors, in addition to the distribution already alluded to, has afforded to the Commissioners of the Western and Atlantic Rail Road, important facilities which have enabled them to discharge many of their heavy obligations which it was expected would have been met by the sale of State Bonds. This measure, warranted by law, was also dictated by a sense of justice to contractors who had labored faithfully in this great work, and had incurred heavy liabilities, relying on the punctuality of the Commissioners. It has also made arrangements for the payment of the New York debt, which, unless prevented by the unexpected default of debtors, will be extinguished early in the next year, by which the State will be relieved from the disgrace inflicted upon it, by permitting its credit to be sacrificed. It has met all the appropriations of the Legislature, including the amount set apart for the support of Common Schools. Though these operations of the Bank have resulted in great advantage to the State and people, they have left in circulation a large amount of its notes which must be so reduced, before further accommodations can be granted, as to save the country from the enormous mischiefs of a depreciated currency. It is to be hoped that this Bank, so long the benefactor of the people, will, with its ample assets, be enabled to counteract the ungenerous efforts of other Banks to discredit its issues, provided its liabilities are not increased by legislative requisitions. If however, the appropriations of the Legislature, which are annually increasing in amount, are to be met by the Central Bank, their payment must be made in the notes of the Bank, for the redemption of which no fund is provided; it must cease its operations as a Bank, collect its debts, speedily recall its circulation, which creates an obligation paramount to all others, and wind up its affairs. As a timely provision against a measure of this sort, I would recommend to the Legislature a resumption of the entire amount of State taxes, which have for some years been given to the counties, with but little benefit to them, but greatly to the injury of the finances of the State.

30. Martin Van Buren and Joshua Forman: The Innovation of the Safety Fund

When Martin Van Buren looked back on his forty-eight days as Governor of New York, he put first on his list of achievements the law creating the Safety Fund "to protect the public and more particularly the laboring classes . . . from losses through bank failures." The idea for the measure came, as Van Buren acknowledged, from Joshua Forman of Onondaga. Described by Van Buren as "a plain but practical and far-seeing man,"[1] Forman had at an earlier time played an effective part in the decision to carry New York's canal all the way to Lake Erie (Document 4).

The Governor's Inaugural Message pointed out that the charters of most of the state's banks were about to expire and urged the Legislature to take the opportunity to make a decisive improvement in the banking system. He rejected the alternatives of doing without banks or of relying solely on the Bank of the United States, and he argued that renewal of the charters of the existing banks would cause less disturbance to the economy than the creation of a new bank owned by the state. New or renewed charters should, however, be granted on a different basis. Instead of demanding a large bonus to the state, the conditions imposed should "refer exclusively to the safety and stability of the institution." "The solvency of the banks, and the consequent stability of their paper, is," he said, "the principal and almost the only point, in which the public has much interest."[2]

The later message containing the actual proposal is more

---

[1] *Autobiography of Martin Van Buren, ca.* 1854, in *Annual Report of the American Historical Association for the Year 1918* (Washington: U.S. Government Printing Office, 1920), pp. 221–222.

[2] New York *Senate Journal,* January 6, 1829, pp. 8–11.

Forman than Van Buren. The Governor provides a brief introduction, but the Plan itself and a covering letter are Forman's.
The letter contains the forthright statement that the "system
interferes with the interests and policy of the existing banks
where they interfere with the public good." The Governor did
not, however, find it politic to use an earlier version of the
letter in which Forman had suggested that only legislators
looking for bribes would be likely to oppose the measure and
had quoted a banker as admitting the merits of the argument
but thinking "that leaving things as they are he would make
more money."[3]

The essential features of the Plan are the Safety Fund itself,
which is to be raised by assessments on all the banks and used to
pay the creditors of banks that fail, and "full but confidential"
inspection, intended to make failures less likely. The inspection
is to be carried out by a board of commissioners of whom, in
the act as adopted, two are to be elected by the banks themselves—one from New York City and the other from the rest
of the state—and the third to be appointed by the governor.

The Safety Fund Plan was adopted in several other states,
and officials of the Federal Deposit Insurance Corporation cite
it as a precedent for the twentieth-century measure that they
administer.[4] It was, however, superseded in New York by the
free banking system initiated in 1838 (Document 36), which
abandoned the principle of insurance and backed the note
issue by a reserve of government bonds. This idea, which is a
variant of one of Forman's suggestions, was in turn to be
adopted in the National Banking Act of 1863. A third notable
development in state regulation was the Louisiana Act of 1842,
which relied on short-term commercial paper as a major part
of the reserve against liabilities, an idea that is embodied in the
present Federal Reserve System. Joshua Forman's Safety Fund

---

[3] Letter from James Forman to Martin Van Buren, January 24, 1829,
Van Buren Papers, Manuscript Division, Library of Congress.

[4] Carter H. Golembe, "The Deposit Insurance Legislation of 1933:
An Examination of Its Antecedents and Its Purposes," *Political Science
Quarterly*, LXXV (1960), 181–200.

was, then, the first of three innovations in state regulation that were ultimately carried over into national banking policy.

TO THE ASSEMBLY

Gentlemen,

In my communication to the Legislature at the opening of the session, I alluded briefly to the outlines of a plan suggested to me relative to the renewal of bank charters. Understanding that it was the general expectation, that a full development of its details would be laid before you by me, I have requested its author to furnish me with a more ample statement of his views; and have now the honor to transmit the communication which I have received from him.

Although this plan is of a character somewhat novel, yet as connected with the most important object of your present duties, it is at least worthy of your deliberate attention. The necessarily imperfect notice taken of the subject in my former communication, has called forth, as I anticipated, expressions of disapprobation from those whose opinions are entitled to much respect. Imperfect as that notice was, it has however been sufficient to excite inquiry into its merits, and lead to favorable views of it on the part of several well informed and capable judges. It was reasonable to expect objections from those who so much misapprehended the proposed measure, as to believe that it designed to cast on solvent banks an immediate and unqualified responsibility for all those that might become insolvent: It will now be seen that such is not the case—Instead of that immediate, undefined and unlimited responsibility, it is proposed to substitute for the payment of a gross sum to the state, which has sometimes been exacted as a consideration for the exclusive privilege granted, (and which

---

From New York *Assembly Journal,* 1829, pp. 172–182.

is still advocated by several,) the creation of a permanent fund, to be held as a security against all losses which our citizens may hereafter sustain through the failure of banks. That fund is to be raised gradually, and in a manner little burthensome to the banks; to be at all times kept good by them, and instead of going into the public treasury for the general benefit, is to be applied to the protection from actual loss of those of our constitutents who would otherwise suffer by the failure of banks improvidently chartered by the state, or unskilfully managed by those to whom they were so granted; and whose paper, in the unavoidable state of our currency, our citizens can hardly be said to have the option to take or refuse—To this is added a system of supervision, which if fairly carried into effect, cannot fail, it would seem, to protect the contributing banks against further calls, to preserve the fund, and to give our paper currency the utmost credit and stability. That the charters of the sound portion of the existing banks ought to be renewed, appears, so far as the feelings and wishes of our constituents can be ascertained, to be the prevailing opinion. If you should participate in that sentiment, the questions that will necessarily arise, will be, whether such extension should be without new conditions; and if not, then whether the plan now proposed, or some other and better one, shall be adopted—questions, which are properly, and may safely, be left to the wisdom and justice of the legislature. All that is asked for the plan now proposed, is your full and unbiassed consideration—If it should not be approved, the suggestion of it will not have been entirely useless: It has already assisted, and will probably further assist, to give a right direction to the public mind on a very important subject, by causing the establishment of banks and their regulation to be regarded as a matter of deep public concern, from their effects upon the great body of the people, and not merely as grants made for local accommodation, or to promote the individual interests of applicants and stockholders.

It will be seen that the author has added some reflections touching the propriety of an investment of their capital by the banks, and a change in the nature and form of their discounts. His views in that respect, have been now for the first time communicated to me, and were not referred to in my message at the commencement of the session. They are expressed with great force and perspicuity; and I lay them before you, in the belief that any thing calculated to throw light on a subject of such deep interest, is worthy of your consideration.

MARTIN VAN BUREN

Albany, January 26, 1829

To His Excellency Martin Van Buren,
Governor of the State of New York.
SIR,

In compliance with your request, I have prepared a more full exposition of the plan, of which I had the honor to submit to you the outlines, for placing the banking operations of the state under a system of regulations calculated to produce the good management of the banks, secure the public against loss by their failure, and furnish a sound and well regulated currency, adequate to the necessities of this great and highly commercial state. It is my decided opinion, supported by that of many gentlemen of intelligence and extensive experience, that the principles upon which it is founded, if judiciously applied and faithfully executed, cannot fail to remedy the evils growing out of the present system, and produce much good to the community. Conceived and matured in retirement, with the sole view to correct those evils of which I have long been conscious, this system interferes with the interests and policy of the existing banks, where they interfere with the public good, and appeals for support to the good sense and patriotism of an impartial and discerning public. It is offered,

in the hope that it may be the means of producing great and
lasting benefits to my native state.

Accept, Sir, my best wishes for your health and prosperity.

I remain, your most obedient servant,

JOSHUA FORMAN

Albany, January 24, 1829

PLAN, &c.

The convenience of bank notes as a circulating medium,
the facility and economy with which they may be increased
to answer the demands of business, with the fashion of the
age of extending business by credit, have rendered bank
accommodations necessary to every seat of commerce. Under
the influence of this necessity, our legislature has from time
to time incorporated banks, as the increase of business and
the advance of commerce required, until we have already
about forty banks in operation; and from the increasing commerce of New-York, and the new field of business opened
along the line of the canals, their number and amount of
capital must be essentially increased, before every place of
considerable trade shall be accommodated with bank facilities
proportioned to its business.

Each of these banks is invested with the right of making
bills to pass as money in the ordinary transaction of business,
with no other regulation than certain restrictions in its charter,
which may or may not be regarded, and no other security
for the payment of those bills, than the corporate property
of the company—each independent of, and sometimes in
hostility to, the others. The legislature could not foresee the
immense increase of business, and consequent multiplication
of banks: It is therefore nowise strange, that they did not
from the beginning adopt any system of regulations applicable
to the present state of things. It is from experience we have

been taught the result of such an organization—how banks could be got into operation with fictitious capitals, and flood the community with paper of no intrinsic value—how banks got up by well meaning men, could be bought in by knaves, who, after circulating three or four times the amount of paper they paid for them, could withdraw what capital there was, and leave the public to bear the loss—how, when most of the capital of a bank had been lost by its officers in wild speculations, its credit could be kept up by making the usual dividends, until the knowing ones had sold out, and nothing be left to pay its notes and deposits—and how, when banks had pushed their discounts and accommodations to a most unwarrantable length, from the desire of making large profits, they have, on a change of times, so suddenly and violently called in their demands, as to cause the ruin of multitudes of enterprising men, and furnished opportunities to dishonest ones, under cover of the general distress, to screen their property, and rid themselves of their debts; thus discouraging regular business, encouraging adventurous speculation, and corrupting the morals of the mercantile public to the very core: And great as has been the evil and loss from the *failure* of banks, they dwindle into insignificance, compared with the public injury occasioned by the *irregular and injudicious management* of the solvent banks.

It was early discovered by intelligent men, that this mode was defective; and about twenty years since, when the older banks were re-incorporated, they were all limited to about the same time, with a view, that at their re-incorporation, some general system of regulation might be adopted, which should afford a better security for the paper issued, and ensure a better management of their affairs. . . .

In this state of things, the time has arrived when the great body of the existing banks must be re-incorporated; or in calling in their demands, to be ready to close their concerns at the expiration of their charters, a very general and distressing embarrassment would be produced through all classes of the community. From this legislature we must therefore expect the final establishment of a banking system for many years to come, the effects of which will be felt by succeeding ages. The object to be attained, is of incalculable importance to the prosperity, happiness, and moral character of this highly commercial and growing state—to secure them a sound, well regulated currency, which shall not only be in the hands of the receiver of the value it purports to be, but shall be so adapted to the necessities of business, as to insure to regular, well directed business, the support and protection necessary to preserve its well earned profits, and depress and restrain that adventurous, speculating business, which causes those convulsions in the money market, baffling all calculation, and defeating the best arranged plans of business. The task is an arduous one. To have succeeded in accomplishing what so many legislatures have attempted, and been most wofully disappointed, would at once give to our state as high a credit and respectability in her monied concerns, as she stands pre-eminent in commercial rank among the states of the Union, and redound to the lasting honor of the men whose good sense had selected and adopted the system.

Presuming that various plans would be suggested, I was induced, from principles and opinions long since discerned and entertained, to digest a system for effecting this object, and communicated the outlines of it to His Excellency the Governor. As it has received his favorable consideration, and been noticed in his message to the Legislature, I am the more confirmed in the opinion I entertained of its utility, (before I had communicated with any one on the subject,) and shall with more confidence explain its leading features, with my views of their bearing and consequences. . . .

. . . As it is thus evident that banks have powers committed to them so deeply affecting the interest of community, they ought to be considered and treated as public institutions, intended as much for the public good, as the profit of the stockholders; and while they are allowed such latitude as may enable them, with good management, to make profits as good or better than any other business of equal risque, they ought to be put under such regulations as to prevent their injuring that community, for whose benefit they were instituted.

For this purpose, I propose,

1st. A set of regulations to insure a sound capital to each bank at starting; to keep it good and available; to limit their loans and discounts to an amount, to which it is safe for them to extend their credit; to prevent their issuing any bills payable otherwise than on demand, and in the lawful coin of the country, and compel their regular payment when demanded; to prevent the banks and their officers speculating upon the depreciation of their paper, and making transfers of their effects in anticipation of insolvency, to give a preference to their officers or their friends, or to defraud its creditors.

2d. As no mechanism can be so arranged as long to keep in order, without being occasionally adjusted; much less a moral machinery, in which human passions and frailties have so great an influence; I propose a board of commissioners, chosen by all the banks, voting according to capital, or appointed by the state, or part by the banks and part by the state, whose constant business it shall be, thoroughly, firmly, but confidentially, to inspect the concerns of all the banks; see that they are kept within the prescribed regulations; concert measures for the good of all; give such information to each, as shall be necessary to prevent extravagant issues at times when the monied operations of the country are like to be embarrassed—and thus, as far as possible, prevent their failure. And whenever they shall find any bank violating those essential provisions for public safety, or so embarrassed in their concerns as to require them to be closed for the security of the public, and the other banks interested, to be invested with extensive powers to secure the property of such bank from being wasted or embezzled. And on the rendering of a judgment of insolvency against it, by a chancellor or judge, to have its affairs settled by trustees under their direction— its effects collected and converted into money, and its debts ascertained and certified—and when so ascertained, paid by the commissioners from the effects of the bank, and the fund hereafter mentioned. The commissioners to be removable by the Governor, for neglect of duty, or misconduct, on the application of a majority of the banks in interest.

3d. As the banks have, by their charters, and the operation of the law to prevent private banking, the exclusive right of furnishing a paper currency for the citizens of the state, and thus exercise a quasi right of sovereignty, equivalent to coining, by which they derive profits beyond the interest of their capital, it is but a just consideration for the state to exact from them a guarantee for the goodness of that paper. I therefore propose a fund to be raised from an annual payment by all the banks according to capital, to be applied to the payment of the debts of such banks as shall fail, to go on accumulating until it shall amount to $500,000 or $1,000,000, when the annual payments are to be omitted, until it is reduced by the payment of the debts of insolvent banks, below that sum, when it is to be immediately replenished by calling in so many arrear instalments as shall raise it to that amount. . . .

4th. To render the system effectual, it ought, as far as possible, be made universal; and as the only mode to render it so, I propose, that *as a measure of state policy,* such of the charters of banks about to expire, now in good credit, as shall be thought expedient, be continued for a given period, say twenty years, subject to these regulations, and on condition that they shall consent to be subject to their operation from some early day, say the first Monday of May next. That all the charters in which the Legislature, with a wise forecast, have reserved the right to amend, shall be continued to the same time, and these regulations made amendments to their respective charters, to take effect from said first Monday of May next. . . .

6th. The wilful loaning or discounting beyond the limit set by law, the making false reports of the state of their concerns, neglecting for more than three months to pay their annual payment to said fund when required, having lost on the face of their books more than one half their capital according to the rules prescribed for estimating it, or suspending the payment of their bills in specie for more than sixty days, or either of them, to be adjudged an act of insolvency, and the affairs of such banks to be closed as before mentioned. An officer of a bank making false returns, false entries in the books of the bank, exhibiting false papers as evidence of indebtedness to the bank, for the purpose of deceiving the commissioners as to the true situation of the bank, to be guilty of felony, and punished as for forgery. . . .

By the application of these provisions, the whole body of banks would constitute a kind of community something after the model of our federal union, in which each in its proper sphere would have the same freedom of action, separate patronage and individual benefit or loss from good or bad management, they now possess—with a supervision over the whole, as perfect and more beneficial for the public than that of a general bank over its branches—and a common fund for the common security, which, under the operation of the principle of inspection to prevent mismanagement, and the power to secure the property of the failing banks before mismanagement has progressed to its consummation, total ruin, and the wreck of its property has been hypothecated and made way with for the benefit of the directors and their friends— is on the whole a more ample security to the public than that of a general bank with branches, where, in case the general direction misjudged, they might ruin the whole concern; but under this system, like the union of the states, the right of self government in each, constitutes the security of the whole. If occasionally a bank should make bad calculations, they would be kept in check by the others, now more interested in their welfare than before; and if they should succeed in breaking through all restraints, and consummate their ruin, the losses would be comparatively small, and within the means of the fund to meet them; and at all events, although not sufficient to cover every *possible* loss, it will be acknowledged on all hands, is not only more available, but of more intrinsic value than the personal responsibility of the directors and stockholders, for the double reason that the property of persons rendered liable for the defaults of others, is rarely found to answer the execution, and that few who had any thing would be found in situations to be made liable.

The propriety of making the banks liable for each other, was suggested by the regulations of the Hong merchants in Canton, where a number of men, each acting separately, have, by the grant of the government, the exclusive right of trading with foreigners, and are all made liable for the debts of each in case of failure. The case of our banks is very similar; they enjoy in common the exclusive right of making a paper currency for the people of the state, and by the same rule should in common be answerable for that paper. This abstractly just principle, which has stood the test of experience for seventy years, and under which the bond of a Hong merchant has acquired a credit over the whole world, not exceeded by that of any other security, modified and adapted to the milder features of our republican institutions, constitutes the basis of this system.

As there has grown up with the banks now in good standing, a body of men capable of managing their concerns, in whom the public have confidence, and who are conversant with the demands of the various subjects of industry and business in the state; this system, placing them under proper regulations in their present form, must not only have a preference over that of a general bank with branches, the success of which must depend upon the selection of suitable men not only for the principal bank, but for all its branches, because the experience of their present managers is a pledge to the public of their avoiding those shoals and quicksands upon which most new directions get stranded, and the institutions under their management injured—but also on account of the derangement of business which must be produced by the calling in the funds of the present banks, and placing them under new management, before they would find their way through new channels, again to set in motion the numerous wheels of business through the country.

The stipulations on the part of the state are a necessary guarantee to those banks which shall submit to these onerous provisions, that no old insolvent bank or new one with a fictitious capital shall be added to their fraternity to drain their fund—and the penalties on the banks are a just punishment upon the stockholders for employing unprincipled or incompetent men—and considering the progressive nature of vice, and that the men chosen to such offices are generally men of good habits and character at starting, it can scarcely happen but the penalties against the officers must prevent those first steps in error which lead to the gross villainy the acts mentioned imply. The superiority of this inspection over a return made on oath as a mean of ascertaining the state of a bank, or to prevent its mismanagement, will be readily preceived. . . .

Without attempting answers to all the objections which interest and ingenuity may devise to the plan proposed, I readily admit that I do not consider it perfect for all the purposes attainable by legal provision; but one calculated to put under regulation the existing institutions; as far as possible to secure the public from loss by their failure, and maintain a well regulated currency, compatible with the present state of things, and their established modes of business, and as favorable for the public as there is any reason to expect can now be enforced upon them.

To render the system perfect for both those purposes, two further regulations are necessary, interfering at once with the present modes of business, and the commonly received opinions on the subject of banking.

1st. To confine the banks to discounting business paper to fall due at short periods, to be paid at maturity, and without renewals promised or expected.

2nd. To compel them to invest their capital in safe public stocks, or put it out on bonds and mortgages upon productive real estate of double the value, for long periods on interest, and not to employ it in their ordinary business.

31. James K. Polk:
"A Fraud Upon Note-Holders"

After the charter of the Second Bank expired, there was a great increase in the number of banks operating under the authority of state governments. There were, however, particularly in the newer areas, great variations from state to state. Some prohibited banking altogether in the hope that their economies could operate entirely on a "hard money" basis. In Indiana, a single institution with branches, largely financed by the state, followed conservative principles of commercial banking. In other western states a profusion of private institutions operated under loose regulation, and their record includes the often-described excesses of "wildcat banking," as well as genuine contributions to economic development.[1]

Tennessee had both a state bank and state-chartered private institutions. The latter were sharply criticized by James K. Polk in his Governor's Message of 1841. The attack is made in

---

[1] Carter H. Golembe, "State Banks and the Economic Development of the West, 1830–1844," unpublished Ph.D. dissertation, Columbia University, 1952.

the name of a state that was mainly agricultural, but the charge is not that the banks have given too little credit to agriculture. The fault is a simpler one. The banks have suspended specie payment and will not redeem their notes in gold or silver, although some of them continue to pay dividends to eastern stockholders. Their notes have therefore depreciated in value, and "the heavy loss has fallen upon the people."

MESSAGE OF THE GOVERNOR OF TENNESSEE TO THE

TWENTY-FOURTH GENERAL ASSEMBLY OF THE STATE

Fellow-Citizens of the Senate,
and of the House of Representatives:
   In discharging the duty devolved upon me by the Constitution, by "giving to the General Assembly information of the State of the Government, and recommending to their consideration such measures" as are deemed to be "expedient," it is a source of satisfaction to believe that, within the last two years, nothing has occurred in the State Administration to diminish or impair the prosperity of our people, or the growing importance of the State as a member of the Union. Order has prevailed, and the laws, as far as I am informed, have been faithfully executed. All the elements of our accustomed prosperity, afforded by a genial climate and a fertile soil, the enjoyment of usual health, and the inestimable blessing of civil and religious liberty, continue to exist. A people thus favored over millions of the human race in other parts of the world, should be ever mindful of the high obligations they owe to the author of all good, in whose hands are the destinies of nations and of men, and upon whose wise councils they are

---

From Tennessee *Senate Journal,* 1841–1842, from the message of October 7, 1841.

dependant for the preservation and continuance of these blessings.

Whilst the products of the labor of the agriculturist have been rewarded with fair prices, habits of frugality and economy, within the last two years, have been in a great degree substituted for that spirit of extravagance and speculation which had for some years prevailed in every portion of the Union. Prudent men, with few exceptions, chiefly among the mercantile and trading classes, who had extended their business and speculations beyond their means, and become too deeply involved entirely to recover, have been enabled to relieve themselves from much of the pecuniary pressure and embarrassment under which they labored.

Ours is essentially an agricultural State. Nineteen-twentieths of her population are cultivators of the earth, and the protection of their interests therefore, at the same time that the just rights of others shall not be impaired, should at all times be an object of paramount consideration.

It has but too frequently happened that the course of legislation and the operation of Banks, in many of the States, have been made to take a direction to favor the supposed or real interests of large dealers and speculators, to the manifest prejudice of the farming and planting classes. What the farmer or planter should most desire is a regular course of policy, steadily pursued, by which prices may remain settled and not be subjected to great and sudden changes, often brought about by extended Bank credits to a small class who have overtraded or engaged in visionary or disastrous speculation.

There is reason to believe that it was by a course of favoritism of this kind, in extending enormous loans to a few large commission and trading-houses, to the almost total exclusion of smaller dealers and the body of the community that much of the embarrassments which fell upon our Banks a few years ago and through them upon the people, is mainly to be attributed.

The suspended debts of our Banks, it is believed, will be found to consist chiefly, in demands against a very few of the larger borrowers, with some of whom it is known they have been compelled for their own security to compound by the purchase of real estate and other property, which has become for a time dead in their hands, and is alike unavailable to themselves as Banking institutions, and to the community as affording to them the means of furnishing to the people a sound convertible currency. It is understood that our Banks are now rapidly converting these and other unavailable, into available means, thus placing themselves in a position of increased strength; and it is hoped they may, for the future, profit by the experience of the past.

Other causes which contributed to the embarrassment of our Banks in common with most of the Banks of other States, upon the occurrence of the general commercial revulsion which took place in May, 1837, were so fully presented in my message to the last General Assembly, that it is deemed unnecessary again to refer to them in this communication.

It was hoped and believed when the Banks of the State suspended the payment of specie a second time, near two years ago, that it would be of temporary duration. In the reports made to the General Assembly at its last session by the Boards of Directors of the Union and Planters' Banks, assurances were given that they were fully solvent, that they would be prepared to meet all their liabilities at an early day, and that they considered "their suspension as temporary." The General Assembly having adjourned without any legislative action on the subject, I regret to say that all the Banks of the State, except the Branch of the South Western Rail Road Bank at Knoxville, still continue in a suspended state. If the question of resumption be left to the voluntary action of the Banks, this state of things may continue for an indefinite period of time. And the question arises whether the duty does not devolve on the General Assembly, as the immediate guardian of the interests of the people, to adopt suitable measures, at their present session, requiring these institutions to return to cash payments. Whilst the suspension continues, the tax upon the active industry and labor of the State, imposed by the depreciation of their paper issues, must continue to be borne; and whilst the people are suffering the loss to the amount of this depreciation, as they have done for the last two years, it is understood that two of our principal stock Banks (the Union and Planters' Banks) have since your last adjournment declared a dividend of profits among their stockholders. This is so manifestly improper, that I am constrained by a sense of duty to bring the fact to your notice. Principles of common justice require that they should pay their debts to the community before they divide profits among their owners.

During periods of suspension, Banks, owned by individual stockholders, tempted by a desire to enlarge their profits, often unduly extend their business, and generally at the expense of the community in which they exist. There is no sound principle of ethics or of public policy which should exempt Banks from the moral and legal obligations which rest upon individuals to pay their debts. They are generally composed of wealthy capitalists who have thrown their joint funds together, and under a legislative charter of incorporation, engaged in the business of banking with a view to make profit. They are usually invested with exclusive rights and privileges which are withheld from the balance of the community; and in consideration of these, they contract certain duties and obligations to the public which they should be required strictly to perform. The most important of these, is to pay their liabilities in specie on demand, and I recommend to the consideration of the General Assembly the necessity of making suitable provision by law to enforce the faithful observance of this, as well as of all other obligations which they have contracted. Let a future day be fixed upon which they shall be required to resume, giving them reasonable and sufficient time to prepare to do so,

without oppressing their debtors. In fixing a future day for resumption, the occasion may be a fit one to impose such additional restrictions, liabilities and penalties, as experience may
have shown to be necessary to guard the public against future
suspensions. If the Banks have violated their charters, the
General Assembly possess the undoubted power to impose such
restrictions, liabilities and penalties, as conditions upon which
they may be permitted to continue the exercise of their corporate privileges. To ensure resumption on the day which may be
fixed, and a faithful observance of their obligations afterwards,
it must be made the interest, as well as the duty of the Banks,
to conform to the Legislative requirements, by keeping their
business in such condition as to avoid future suspensions. As
means likely to effect objects so desirable, I submit to the consideration of the General Assembly that they should not be permitted, during the period of their suspension, and for a limited
time after resumption, to declare any dividends of profits to
their stockholders, and that a general provision should be made
by law requiring any of the Stock Banks which shall, after the
day which may be fixed for their resumption, again suspend for
a greater period than a specified number of days in any one
year, to be placed in the hands of commissioners for liquidation
and final settlement of their affairs.

It is believed to be far better for the community that all the
Stock Banks, which may so manage their business as to be unable to pay promptly the demands upon them, should wind up
their affairs, and let their places be supplied, if the interests of
the State shall be found to demand it, by an enlargement of the
capital of the Bank of Tennessee, owned exclusively by the
people of the State, and under the sole control of their immediate Representatives. To sanction by the silence and aquiescence
of the public authorities repeated suspensions, and often for
long periods of time, is to tolerate a legalized fraud upon the
note-holders as impolitic as it is unjust. The loss sustained by
the people by the depreciation of Bank paper since the last

suspension of our Banks, has been far greater than the whole amount of the annual tax which they are required to pay for the support of the State Government, as will be manifest by adverting to a few facts. The average amount of Bank notes of all the Banks in the State in circulation during the last two years, it is estimated will not vary much from three millions of dollars. The average rate of depreciation of these notes during the same period below specie, has been about 8½ per cent., being sometimes at 6, and at others 11 per cent.—The heavy loss has fallen upon the people; every note-holder bearing his proportion, whilst the Bank-owners, as we have seen, have been dividing profits among themselves.

As far as my information enables me to judge, our Banks are believed to be in a solvent condition, and could, if reasonable time be given, be prepared to resume payment permanently, without inconvenience to themselves or oppression to their debtors. The interests of the public in my judgment demand it, whilst none of the rights of the Banks themselves will be infringed or impaired if they shall be required to do so. Unless efficient Legislative action be had on this subject, the public can have no guaranty at what period the principal Stock Banks may resume, for it is a fact worthy of observation, that much the larger portion of their capital stock, it is understood, is owned by citizens of the eastern cities and of other States; and however much the local stockholders may be disposed, from a sense of propriety and duty, to return to cash payments, they may, and probably will, be controlled in their policy by their nonresident co-partners, who have no interest in common with the community in which these institutions exist, and who may be contented that they shall remain in their present suspended condition so long as they can receive their accustomed dividend.

This is not the first time we have had a suspension by the Banks for a protracted period in this State. In 1819, the Banks, not only of this State, but generally throughout the Union, suspended payment. In 1821, and again in 1823, the General Assembly passed laws requiring them to resume, and in pursuance of these laws they did resume in 1824 and 1825. During this long suspension of five years or more, the depreciation of their paper was greater than it is at present, being at sometimes as great as 25 and 30 per cent. This heavy loss upon the community would doubtless have continued longer than it did at that time, but for effective Legislative interposition. At that time, as at the present, it was urged, chiefly by the banks themselves, their debtors, and those who hoped to obtain further loans, that it was against the public policy to force or require resumption, because it was said, the specie in their vaults would be taken from the State, and their immediate debtors, and through them the community oppressed.

The General Assembly thought otherwise. They passed laws requiring them to pay their debts, under pain of losing their charters. They did resume and no such consequences as had been predicted followed; and the opinion is confidently entertained that no such consequences as are now predicted would follow a resumption, especially if reasonable time be given to the Banks to prepare for the same; but on the contrary, that the public interest would be greatly promoted by it.

The evil consequences apprehended by many as likely to follow resumption by the Banks of one State whilst the Banks of other States remain suspended, it is believed are more imaginary than real. The banks of New York and of the States east of her, it is known, did not yield to the suspension which took place in Pennsylvania and other States in her neighborhood, in October, 1839; but have continued to pay specie and to maintain a sound convertible currency. The Bank of Missouri did not suspend at that time because those of the States adjacent to her territory did so, but continued to pay specie. In the specie paying States the money market is easy, and there is no pressure on the people. The Banks on returning to cash payments should be in a position of strength, and may for a time, and until general confidence is restored, deem it prudent somewhat to restrict their business; but this cannot operate as any general or permanent inconvenience to the public, and would be much more than counterbalanced by the sound state of currency which would be restored. To wait for the action of other States, is to make our policy dependant upon theirs, whilst they in turn may make theirs dependant on ours, and thus the suspension be continued much beyond the period when all solvent Banks could be in condition to pay. The General Assembly of 1821 and 1823, did not wait for the uncertain action of other States, but required our Banks to resume without reference to what their course might be. If this State leads off and manifests a fixed purpose to require her Banks to pay, there can be but little doubt that the other States in the south and south-west will soon follow her example.

The whole subject is submitted to your deliberate consideration, in the full confidence that you may adopt such measures as will protect the interests of our common constituents from the heavy losses which they have borne and still bear by the failure of the Banks to perform their chartered obligations.

In the Bank of Tennessee every citizen has a direct interest. Owned as it is exclusively by the State, it should receive the constant and fostering care and attention of the General Assembly. That institution, I am happy to state from information derived from its officers, is in a perfectly solvent condition, and can be prepared to resume payment permanently at the earliest future day which may be designated for resumption by the Stock Banks. Should that Bank be required to resume without the co-operation of the Stock Banks in its immediate neighborhood, it would probably be compelled for a time somewhat to restrict its business to avoid embarrassments from their operations. To avoid this, all the Banks of the State should be required to resume at the same time.

PART SIX

THE FACILITATION OF

CORPORATE ENTERPRISE

32. Control over Quality: "Cullers of Fish"

Economic life in the American colonies was carried on under a variety of governmental restrictions. Some activities were prohibited and others subsidized by British colonial policy. In addition, colonial and local regulations prescribed in detail the conditions of apprenticeship and indentured service and set the price and terms of sale of various commodities, as in the assize of bread. Taverns, turnpikes, bridges, and ferries were treated as what would now be called public utilities, and their operation and charges were closely controlled. For a number of commodities, quality was subjected to minute public inspection.

Most of these colonial regulations either continued in force or were reenacted in the early years of the Republic. The illustration given below is from a Massachusetts law of 1784 providing for inspection of the state's most characteristic exports by local officials chosen in town meeting, like the still earlier hog-reeves and fence-viewers. The purpose of the regulation is that stated in the preamble to an act of the preceding year:

> Whereas it is the wisdom of every commercial country to prevent an abuse in the manufacture of those articles intended for expor-

tation, in such a manner as that they may preserve their credit
with foreigners, and thereby render their exports as permanent
and beneficial as possible. . . .[1]

Yet if the Searchers of Beef and Pork and the Cullers of Fish
of the 1784 measure were charged only to maintain the quality
and the reputation of the state's exports, the elaborate specifications to be enforced by the Surveyors of Shingles under an
earlier act were intended to protect local customers as well.

Regulations of these traditional types remained in force in
most of the states for much of the period and were sometimes
made more comprehensive.[2] Yet their relative importance diminished as business enterprise grew and took on more modern
forms. As early as 1806, counsel in the Cordwainers' Case (as
Document 45 will show) were proud to claim that labor and
enterprise were less restricted in the United States than in
Great Britain. For the remainder of the period, the more
important issue of state policy becomes not the maintenance or
repeal of these traditional restrictions on individual enterprise
but that of the degree of freedom to be given to enterprise in
its developing corporate form.

Be it further enacted by the authority aforesaid, That the
selectmen, or the major part of them, in every town in the

From Massachusetts *Acts and Resolves,* 1784–1785, ch. 30, pp. 102–105;
from law of November 7, 1784.

---

[1] Massachusetts *Acts and Resolves,* 1783, ch. 54.

[2] Milton S. Heath, *Constructive Liberalism* (Cambridge: Harvard University Press, 1954), ch. XIV; Louis Hartz, *Economic Policy and Democratic Thought* (Cambridge: Harvard University Press, 1948), pp. 204–
219; Oscar Handlin, *Commonwealth* (New York: New York University
Press, 1948), pp. 220–225. James Neal Primm, *Economic Policy in a
Western State* (Cambridge: Harvard University Press, 1954), p. 116,
notes that Missouri adopted a law for the inspection of tobacco in its
first year as a state.

Commonwealth, where there may be occasion, be, and they are hereby empowered and directed, to choose and appoint annually a fit person or persons to be searchers and packers of barreled Beef, Pork and Fish, who shall be sworn to the faithful execution of their trust, by the town clerk of said town, and the said town clerk shall record the same in the town books; whose duty shall be to pack and search all the Fish, Beef and Pork which shall be packed in the same, designed for exportation out of this State, and they shall not pack any Fish, Beef or Pork, in any cask which shall be of unseasoned stuff, or which shall be under the assize established by law, under the penalty of ten shillings for every cask so packed.

And be it further enacted, That in every town where such commodities are packed up for sale, the searcher and packer of such town, or of the town where they are put to sale or shipped, shall, previously thereto, see that they be properly repacked, and that there be good salt in each cask, sufficient to preserve the Fish, Beef or Pork, from damage to any port or place to which they are designed to be shipped; and it shall be his business to see that the Beef and Pork in cask is of the whole, half and quarter and so proportionably, that the best be not left out; and that each barrel of Pork shall weigh two hundred pounds weight, and each barrel of Beef two hundred and twenty pounds weight, each cask to be well seasoned, and bound with not less than twelve sufficient hoops; and that Mackarel and other barreled Fish be packed all of one kind, and in cask well seasoned, containing not less than thirty gallons, and that all casks so packed be full, and the fish sound and well seasoned; on all which casks of Beef, Pork and Fish, so searched, examined and approved, the said packer shall brand or imprint, with a burning iron, the following brand or mark, *Mass. RPD.* with the initial letters of his christian name and his sirname at large, and the letter *P* at the end thereof, denoting that the same is merchantable, and in good order for exportation; and all such other provision as the packer shall find wholesome and useful, though for its quality it be not merchantable, he shall cause to be well packed, salted and filled, and the same mark with the word *Refuse;* for which he shall receive from the owner six pence for each barrel, and so in proportion for a large or smaller cask. . . .

And be it further enacted by the authority aforesaid, That no vessel on board of which any cask of Flax Seed, Pot Ash, Pearl Ash, barreled Pork, Beef, or Fish, is shipped for exportation, shall be cleared out by the naval officer until the master or owner thereof shall have produced a certificate or certificates from some person or persons duly appointed for the purpose of surveying, assaying, proving or packing the said articles, that the same have been surveyed, assayed, proved, packed or re-packed, as by this act is required, which certificate or certificates shall be granted free from any expense.

And whereas great inconvenience and damage to merchants, and much loss to the interests of the Commonwealth, arise for want of proper persons being appointed in the seaport towns to cull dry fish:

Be it therefore enacted by the authority aforesaid, That there shall be annually chosen in every seaport town within this Commonwealth, where Fish is made and cured or sold, at the annual *March* meeting, a suitable number of skilful and dis-interested persons, inhabitants of such town, to be cullers of Fish; and any person who shall cull fish without being chosen and sworn, shall forfeit the sum of five pounds for every quintal of Fish by him culled, and such cullers in culling Fish shall have regard to the contract between the buyer and seller, with respect to the season of the year wherein such Fish is cured.

And be it further enacted, That every master or commanding officer of any ship or other vessel, who shall take on board any Fish in order to transport the same beyond sea, without having the same first surveyed or culled by a person duly appointed and under oath, shall forfeit and pay a fine of six shillings for each and every quintal so received or taken on board; and every person chosen into the office of a culler of Fish, shall before he enter on the duties of his office, be sworn as other town officers are, to the faithful discharge of his trust, and shall be allowed and paid one penny half-penny for every quintal of Fish which he shall survey or cull, by the purchaser thereof. *Provided nevertheless,* When it shall so happen that the sworn cullers cannot be obtained, that then it shall and may be lawful for the buyer and seller to agree upon some meet person to be a culler in such case,—*Provided,* he be first sworn faithfully to discharge the trust. . . .

And be it further enacted, That penalties and forfeitures arising by force and virtue of this act, shall be one half to the use of the Commonwealth, and the other half to him or them who shall inform and sue for the same.

33. Pennsylvania: "The Effect of Incorporated Companies"

In March 1833, a committee of the Pennsylvania Senate was instructed to investigate the coal industry within the state and especially "to ascertain the effect of incorporated companies (with mining and trading privileges,) on the progress of the business, and the improvement and prosperity of the country."[1]

---

[1] Pennsylvania *Senate Journal,* 1833–1834, II, 497. The Report of the Committee is analyzed in Hartz, *Economic Policy and Democratic Thought.*

Its Report, presented a year later, contains a history of coal mining in the anthracite fields and the newer bituminous areas, and a prediction of the industry's future greatness. Its resources will be essential to the manufactures and commerce of the nation. "If ever that unhappy day should arrive when this Union shall be severed into fragments, (which may Providence in his wisdom avert,)" Pennsylvania will for this reason "have less cause than any other state to dread this separation."

The passages presented below are the introduction to the Report, the Committee's comments on the monopoly grant already held by the Lehigh Coal and Navigation Company, and its judgment with respect to the future organization of the industry. It sees the choice as one between individual and corporate enterprise. The Committee's view is clearly stated. Every corporate charter infringes to some degree on the rights of the people and tends naturally to monopoly. Yet corporate privileges may be justified in order to accomplish works of public utility that are beyond individual means. One such exceptional case was that of the Lehigh Company, which had had to make a costly river improvement before it could exploit its coalfield. Even here, however, there were abuses, and the state should purchase the Lehigh Navigation. In the rest of the industry, there was no need for corporate powers and the mining of coal should be left "to the free and untrammeled exercise of individual enterprise."

As later selections will show, pronouncements like this could not long delay the rise of the corporation. Yet the southern or Schuylkill coalfield, containing about half of the industry to which the report referred, remained throughout the period a stronghold of individual proprietors and partnerships. In this area "the collapse of individual enterprise" before the large corporation did not take place until after 1870.[2]

---

[2] C. K. Yearly, Jr., *Enterprise and Anthracite: Economics and Democracy in Schuylkill County, 1820–1875* (Baltimore: The Johns Hopkins Press, 1961), especially chs. 2 and 6.

MR. PACKER FROM THE COMMITTEE APPOINTED IN PURSUANCE

OF A RESOLUTION ADOPTED BY THE SENATE AT THE LAST

SESSION OF THE LEGISLATURE, UPON THE SUBJECT OF

THE COAL TRADE, AND TO WHOM WAS REFERRED

THE MEMORIAL OF SUNDRY COAL DEALERS

IN THE COUNTY OF SCHUYLKILL,

RESPECTFULLY SUBMIT THE

FOLLOWING REPORT:

The coal trade of Pennsylvania, recently and suddenly starting into existence, now constitutes one of the main branches of our domestic industry, and an important portion of the commerce of the State and the Union. It has given a new stimulus to individual as well as national enterprize, and affords active and profitable employment for numerous and various classes of the community. It has produced a spirit of improvement, interspersing the country with canals and railroads, which, by connecting the distant parts together, promote the convenience and prosperity of the people, while they add to the strength and elevate the character of the State. It has raised up in our formerly barren and uninhabited districts, an intelligent and permanent population, and converted the mountains into theatres of busy life, and our hitherto waste and valueless lands, into sites for flourishing and populous villages. It has opened a new field for the investment of capital, the expenditure of labour, and the pursuit of all the purposes of civilization and society. Its benefits are not alone confined to those engaged

From "Report of the committee of the Senate, upon the subject of the Coal Trade," Pennsylvania *Senate Journal,* 1833–1834, II, 449, 463–466, 490–494. The date is March 4, 1834.

immediately in the trade, but are becoming general and universal. Possessing all the varieties of their species, anthracite and bituminous; furnishing a cheap and preferable article of fuel; and affording new facilities to the manufacturer, whose products enter into all the ramifications of domestic as well as foreign consumption, the mineral coals of Pennsylvania now exert an influence upon every other branch of trade, and afford the means of rearing and permanently supporting, on this side of the Atlantic, all the mechanic arts and handicraft of the old world.

It will readily be admitted, that any legislation calculated to affect, either immediately or remotely, an interest thus important, and yet in its infancy, ought to be guarded with peculiar care; and that grants of perpetuity, or privileges having a tendency to a monopoly of an article that must soon become the staple product of the State, ought only to be conferred in obedience to the clearest and most irresistible demands of public policy and paramount necessity. Viewing the subject committed to them in this light, the committee have devoted a due share of attention to it, and now submit to the Senate the result of their best reflections: . . .

This grant (to the Lehigh Coal and Navigation Company) was an extensive one; and although at this day it may be viewed by some as an extraordinary relinquishment of sovereignty, and a singular encroachment upon the natural rights of our citizens; it was at that time regarded as an inducement scarcely commensurate with the magnitude and the hazard of an enterprise which had long been projected, and repeatedly attempted, but which had as long been delayed, or as frequently baffled. Few other men or other companies, it is presumed, could have been found willing to commence the work upon less favourable terms, and much more extensive privileges would no doubt have been conferred by the state, had they been deemed essential to the accomplishment of the object. It conferred upon the company, with certain limitations, the sole jurisdiction of the river Lehigh, for the distance of eighty-three miles, and the free and uncontrolled use of its waters. So dangerous and hazardous was the natural navigation of the river regarded at that day, and so difficult was it to transport coal over the mountain from the first coal field to the stream, that the Mauch Chunk coal lands, now so valuable, were leased by the company for a period of twenty years for the payment of the rent of *one ear of Indian corn* annually.

The company first improved the river by artificial locks and other devices, at an expense of one hundred fifty-five thousand four hundred and twenty dollars. This improvement, being greatly interrupted by freshets, and failing generally to answer the purpose, the present navigation, admitted to be the best in the United States, was constructed at an expense of one million five hundred forty-six thousand ninety-four dollars and ninety-six cents. The different rail-roads and other improvements made by the company to the mines, &c. cost the sum of three hundred twenty-three thousand five hundred eighty dollars and twenty-seven cents. Repairs and other expenses, one hundred seventy-one thousand ninety-five dollars and ninety-one cents: Whole original cost of improvement two millions one hundred ninety-six thousand one hundred ninety-one dollars and fourteen cents. From the limited examination of the subject by the committee, they have not been able to perceive, that in the expenditure of this large sum of money in the completion of their works, and in the expenditure of an additional sum of about one million of dollars in carrying on the coal trade, the company have violated the letter of their acts of incorporation, or committed any act which would be deemed to amount to a forfeiture of their charter. They completed the lower grand division from Nesquehoning to the mouth of the Lehigh, 48 miles, nine years before the time limited for its completion, and have commenced the upper division within the seven years prescribed by law for that purpose. Nor is it pretended they have imposed higher rates of toll than the law authorizes them to charge. It is argued, however, that they have laid exorbitant tolls for the purpose of prohibition, and that this amounts to such abuse and misuse of their charter, as would justify the Legislature in resuming the grant. The committee think otherwise. So long as the company keep within the provisions of the law, and do not assess a higher toll than the law permits them to receive, they may impose it either for the purpose of prohibition or for the purpose of remunerating the stockholders for their large expenditures. Their acts and not their motives must determine whether they have or have not forfeited their chartered privileges. Whether they have adopted a wise or erroneous policy, which, by grasping after large tolls, may prevent them from receiving any, is a question between them and the stockholders. And even if the grant, as is contended with ability by the convention were unconstitutional, still the Legislature, having conferred the power upon the company for the accomplishment of a great public object, and the individuals so authorised having in good faith executed the trust, and expended their substance in pursuance of the law, the state would be bound in equity to see them out, and to remunerate them for any loss which they might sustain by reason of a decision of the proper tribunal that the Legislature had exceeded its authority, and that the charter was of consequence null and void.

The company, therefore, having in nowise violated their chartered privileges, the issue is, in the opinion of the committee, not between them and the people, but between the people and the Legislature. We are thus led to inquire, how the people have been affected by this legislative grant, and what are the natural consequences resulting from it? That the people at large have enjoyed many benefits which they otherwise would not have enjoyed, cannot be denied. The country in consequence has been to some extent improved—large sums of money have been, and continue to be yearly expended, passing into the hands of the labourer and the mechanic, and a permanent market is created in the mountains for all the produce of the farmer. The river Lehigh, formerly a wild, rugged and dangerous stream, has been converted into a safe, permanent and excellent navigation. These are some of the many advantages conferred by the grant upon the public. Let us inquire whether it may not be turned to still greater advantage, and by subserving the views of the many, instead of those of the few, become productive of greater good—and whether instead of retarding, it may not become the means of improving and enriching the whole face of the northern territory of the state—of converting the wilderness and barren mountains into usefulness and value, and of augmenting the trade and strengthening the resources of our metropolis.

Every charter or act of incorporation, is to a greater or less extent, an infringement upon the natural rights and liberties of the people—and their natural tendency is to monopoly. As an auxiliary or additional stimulant to this inherent principle of corporate bodies, the Lehigh Coal and Navigation company possess, by express legislative grant, the privilege of mining and transporting coal—a power which, when connected with an improvement depending alike upon its tolls for support, must ultimately prove its own bane, and become injurious to the interests of the community:—and this, by the strong inducement that is presented to the company to monopolize the trade, and to keep down competition. Companies, like individuals, will endeavour always to pursue their own interests; and if they believe they can realize a greater profit by engaging themselves in a particular branch of trade than by relying upon tolls accruing from the produce of others engaged in the same business, they will of course embark in the trade, and endeavour to monopolize it. They will not be willing to furnish upon equal terms facilities to their competitors of the same trade, nor allow them upon even ground "to plough with their own oxen." They will, unless prevented by their charter, raise their tolls so high as to exclude him from market, and throw every other obstacle in the way. This is a state of things naturally resulting from the operations of incorporated companies possessing these powers; and the great and radical error of former legislatures in reference to this subject has been, in the opinion of the committee, the blending of traficing privileges with the authority to construct canals and rail-roads, which, instead of being great and free communications for the accommodation of the whole country, belong to private companies, with authority to use them for their own benefit, and to lock up or open at pleasure the resources of a whole valley or community. The Schuylkill navigation and the improvements at Pottsville, when contrasted with those now under consideration, abundantly demonstrate the correctness of this position. And yet, had similar privileges been considered necessary to ensure the completion of the work, they would no doubt have been conferred by the Legislature upon the Schuylkill Navigation company; and of course a policy similar to that pursued by the Lehigh company would have been adopted. But, coal was not then regarded as an object of much importance, the company, as appears from their memorial, having in view, primarily, the lumber and agricultural trade of the Schuylkill valley.

While the committee therefore deprecate the policy of uniting trading privileges with the authority to make public railroads and canals, (believing that this constitutes the strongest grounds of opposition to such companies,) and while they believe that the Lehigh company might have adopted a course of policy more conducive to the public prosperity and convenience, as well as to their own interests, they are of opinion that any other company might have pursued a similar policy under like circumstances; and that if the people on the Lehigh have been subjected to hardship or inconvenience, it has been done *according to law;* and perhaps few other companies, with powers and privileges of like extent, would have exercised them with greater lenity or with more advantage to the public. No complaints are known to exist, excepting in relation to the transportation of coal.—Indeed, if the public had any assurance that the policy of the company would remain as now established, there would be little necessity for legislative interference. They have reduced their tolls on coal for 1834, from one dollar and three cents to seventy-three cents a ton, for forty-six miles. They have thrown open to sale, lots in the town of Mauch Chunk, "free from any restrictions on the business or occupations of purchasers." Churches, store houses, and shops have recently been erected, and mechanics of all descriptions are now established in the town, and begin to breathe the air of liberty. But, the affairs of the company are managed by a board of directors. The present stockholders as well as the directors, may soon be succeeded by others with different views and different feelings. Those of the next year may reverse the proceedings of their predecessors; and it is not to be expected that individuals will this year engage in the coal trade in the second coal field, or construct railroads from the mines to the canal, when next year, by a single resolve of another board of directors, the policy may be changed, and upon a sudden rise in the coal market, or from any other cause, their coal be prohibited by high tolls from passing upon the canal. It is on account of this state of fluctuation and uncertainty that the country above Mauch Chunk, on the Lehigh, has thus long remained a howling wilderness without population; the second coal field without miners, and the contemplated improvements to connect the Lehigh with the north branch of the Susquehanna, so long delayed. These improvements, so vitally important to the northern section of the State will never, it is feared, be made, while the Lehigh navigation remains in the hands of an incorporated company, holding and exercising mining and trading privileges.

Then, is there any remedy—any healing in the law for this malady—any measure which, while it shall render full justice to those who have expended their money and their labour upon the faith of our laws, may restore the people to their natural rights, bring forth the mineral resources of another section of the state, increase our population, and open another avenue to the city of Philadelphia for a trade which has hitherto sought a different and a more distant market?

The committee therefore, without entering more minutely upon an investigation not immediately contemplated by their appointment, but viewing the subject as closely identified with the best interests of the Commonwealth, are led to the conclusion that the State ought to adopt the only alternative which appears to be free of difficulty or doubt:—the purchase of the Lehigh navigation. . . .

It only remains for the committee, in the language of the resolution referred to them, to speak of "the effect of incorporated companies, having mining and trading privileges, on the progress of the business, and the improvement and prosperity of the country." These may readily be discovered by an examination of the facts contained in this report. That they have generally been beneficial, is obvious. They have been mainly instrumental in introducing the use of anthracite coal; and in the "progress of the business," they have contributed largely to furnish a constant and regular supply, by which the demand for coal has been increased, and the community accommodated at a fair and reasonable price.

With the exception of the grants to the Delaware and North American coal companies, made by the last Legislature, under peculiar circumstances, mining privileges have never been granted where mining alone was the object of the association, but for considerations of a secondary nature, and as inducements to companies to accomplish what have been regarded as greater public objects. Neither the Lehigh navigation, by which coal was first introduced into Philadelphia, nor the Delaware and Hudson canal and rail-road, would have been made without this inducement; and it must be admitted that the "improvement and prosperity of the country" have been thereby greatly promoted, and to a much greater extent than if they never had been made. It does not follow, however, that if these improvements had been made, without those privileges, and as great public highways for the general accommodation of the country, they would not have been more useful, and more conducive to the public weal.

The principle upon which corporate powers are conferred appear to be well known, and the policy of the Legislature to have been long established. They have been conferred when deemed necessary to promote objects of a public nature, and for the purpose of developing new and untried enterprizes which may be supposed in their results to confer public benefits, but never where the object is exclusively private, and where individual means can be more appropriately applied. In 1806, application was made to the Legislature by the "Pittsburg Carpenter's Society", for an act of incorporation. The petition was referred to a committee of which Mr. *Lacock* was chairman, and whose report unfavourable to the object was adopted by a *unanimous vote* of the House of Representatives. It was then declared by the Legislature, that "whatever might tend in the remotest degree, to establish preferences among any class of citizens engaged in any art, trade, or manufacture, or to destroy a just competition; or which in any shape, might encourage the least kind of monopoly, should be carefully avoided in a republican government, having for one of its great leading principles, that of an equality of rights."

There is at this day no greater necessity for conferring corporate powers upon a class of men to mine coal, than there was at that day to enable a society of carpenters to plane boards, or of farmers to plough their lands. Canals and rail-roads are now completed to a sufficient extent, particularly in the first coal field, for present purposes, and every man of sufficient means to purchase a tract of coal land, may engage in the business and prosecute it with ample success, regardless alike of risk and uncertainty as of corporate privileges. The business can now be brought entirely within the controul of individual means, and individual enterprize. A large number of mines are worked by tenants, who send to market yearly from two to six thousand tons of coal, and employ a capital of less than fifteen hundred dollars. A "respectable colliery establishment," including the price of a tract of coal land, has been estimated at about ten thousand dollars.

Coal land,	$ 3,500
Opening mines, wagons, &c.	3,000
Boats,	2,500
Working capital,	1,000
Total	$10,000

Mines are now extensively opened, and the many difficulties and expenses incident to the business are overcome. All the coal dealers agree, that with the mines now opened and improvements made, double the quantity of coal could have been sent to market during the last year, had there been a demand for it.

But, notwithstanding individual means may be adequate to prosecute the coal trade, without charters of incorporation, it may be well doubted whether, if the demand for coal continue to increase in the same ratio for the next ten years, attempts may not be made here, as in England, to monopolize the business—and whether here as there, it may not ultimately pass into the hands of rich capitalists. A large business will of course require a large capital; and if, in the pursuit of honest industry one class of citizens should become wealthy and amass large fortunes we cannot and ought not to deprive them of the advantages of their wealth; but, the Legislature may and ought to prevent them from uniting with these advantages artificial powers and distinctions which may, if improperly exercised, make "the rich richer and the poor poorer." The more diffused and widely spread are the operations, the greater will be the advantages to the public, and the less the liability to a consolidation or monopoly of trade; and if ever this spirit should manifest itself by endeavouring to monopolize coal lands, it may become necessary for the purpose of preserving divisions of labour, and to keep down monopoly, for the Legislature to authorize limited partnerships, with limited capital, limited parcels of lands, and so restricted in other respects as to promote the very objects for which individual coal dealers now so laudably and legitimately contend. That even corporations could be erected, and with these advantages, cannot be doubted. A corporation in law is just what the incorporating act makes it. It is the creature of the law, and may be moulded to any shape or for any purpose that the Legislature may deem most conducive to the general good. It is hoped, however, that a necessity for such acts may not occur; nor should they ever be conferred as a matter of convenience or for private benefit, but as a matter of the direst necessity and for the common good of the community. Natural liberty and human action should be no farther restrained by legislative enactment than is consistent with, or indispensible to the purposes of civil society and republican government; and every citizen, suffering no greater restraints than it may be absolutely necessary for him to yield to these purposes, should be allowed freely to pursue his own true and substantial happiness. Too much legislation is more to be dreaded than the entire want of it. The maxim is true, that "the world is governed too much."

It has been said that charters were granted to the Delaware Coal Company, and the North American Coal Company, for the term of five years, by the last Legislature under peculiar circumstances. It was so. These companies had obtained charters originally from other states, and were composed of citizens who were among the first to enter the wilderness and the mountains of Schuylkill county, and to develope her mineral wealth. They were among the pioneers in the business, and expended very large sums in opening mines and in the general improvement of the country. They have pursued the legitimate objects of their creation, by yearly mining and sending to market large quantities of coal. It is not urged in the answers of the respectable coal dealers of Schuylkill county to the committee, that their corporate privileges should now be resumed. Individual operators are rather opposed to the principle of granting charters, and rather deprecate the policy, than fear any injury from the operations of these two companies. . . .

. . . The committee, after a full consideration of the case, have no reason to question the propriety of these grants, nor to urge their resumption. They are now actively and usefully engaged in the mining and transportation of coal. They possess no undue controul over rail-roads or canals, nor powers of exclusion. They are carefully restricted in their charters as to quantity of land, and the extent of their duration; and so long as they pursue the line of open and honorable competition, and honestly continue to rely upon the mining of coal to remunerate their stockholders, there would seem to exist little cause of complaint on the part of their individual competitors. If, however, they shall be found in the progress of their operations, to engage in any thing foreign to the purposes of their creation, or in any measures calculated to retard the public prosperity or to cripple individual enterprize, this would present a proper case for the interposition of the Legislature. So long as no charge of impropriety, or of injurious tendency to the public is preferred against them, it would in the opinion of the committee be unwise in the Legislature, and not desired by the intelligent citizens of Schuylkill county, at present, to resume their privileges and destroy their operations. They have yet four years to prosecute their business, in their corporate capacities, and to close their concerns. Their charters will then expire, and the individuals composing the companies be placed in possession of their lands and be allowed either to discontinue or pursue the business upon equal grounds with other operators.

The grand evil, in relation to the incorporation of companies, and against which the committee would most earnestly protest, is in giving them, in addition to their mining privileges, the controul of a canal or rail-road, with power to lock up at pleasure the resources of a whole valley or community. To this source may be traced many of the evils complained of by the public; and it is hoped, as at this day such inducements cannot be considered necessary to the construction of public improvements, they may in future be guarded against by the Legislature. For mining purposes alone, such powers would at present seem to be entirely unnecessary, unless in the cases already adverted to. Should they ever hereafter, under change of circumstances, be deemed necessary, the Legislature will then be competent to determine the question. Until that exigency arrive, it would, in the opinion of the committee, be the surest and safest policy to allow the business to remain open to the free and untrammelled exercise of individual enterprize, and individual controul.

The committee, therefore, having extended this report to a greater length, they fear, than may be acceptable to the Senate, will not stop to comment upon the many other points which the case would seem to present, nor to analyze, more in detail, the facts communicated by the Coal Dealers of the different districts. They conclude by expressing the opinion, that, with the exception of the measures already recommended, there is at present no "further Legislative provision necessary to protect, facilitate and encourage the coal trade."

34. Improvements vs. Privilege: The Charles River Bridge

Possessor of an eighteenth-century charter and successor to a ferry privilege granted to Harvard College in the seventeenth century, the Charles River Bridge occupied an advantageous position joining Cambridge and Boston. Acting, it was said, because of "a clamor about monopoly," the Massachusetts Legislature authorized the Warren Bridge Company to build and operate a parallel structure. By the time the case of the two bridges was decided by the United States Supreme Court in 1837, the Warren Bridge had become a toll-free property of the state, and the Charles River charter had completely lost its value.

The readings are taken from Daniel Webster's plea for the Charles River proprietors and from the opinion of the court delivered by Chief Justice Roger Taney, who had been Andrew Jackson's Attorney General. In Webster's argument, the case is a simple matter of private right. The charter is a valid contract, subject to constitutional protection, which the state has violated by destroying its value. The Court, however, brushes aside this argument. The Charles River Bridge, like other corporations, must face the consequences of competition. If charters had been construed as granting the right of property in lines of travel, railroads could not have superseded turnpikes without buying out their privileges, and the public would have been denied the advantages of technological progress.

The immediate issues of the case were confined to transportation, but the decision may be regarded as a step in the more general process by which the corporation lost its original character as an exceptional privilege and came to be regarded as a normal agency of competition.

DANIEL WEBSTER: THE DEFENSE
OF "A PRIVATE RIGHT"

WEBSTER, for the plaintiffs in error, stated, that the question before the court was one of a private right, and was to be

------

From *Charles River Bridge v. Warren Bridge,* United States Reports, 1837, 11 Peters, 419, at 514–536.

determined by the fair construction of a contract. Much had been said, to bring the claims of the plaintiffs in error into reproach. This course of remark does not affect their right to their property, if this court shall consider that property has been taken from them by proceedings which violate a contract; and in a case where this court has a constitutional right to interpose for its protection and restoration.

It is said, that the proprietors of Charles River bridge have been repaid for the advances made by them in building the bridge. But this is not the question upon which the court has to decide; it is a question of contract; and if so, where is the necessity to inquire whether the plaintiffs have laid out a million, or nothing? If there was a contract, the question is not, what was the amount of profit to be derived from it, but what were its provisions; however advantageous to those with whom it was made. It is a contract for the annual receipt of tolls, for a specified period of time; and it is said, the state, which, by its law, brought the company into existence, by allowing these tolls, may break the contract, because the amount of the tolls is large; and by a legislative act, say, that, for a portion of the time granted, the contract shall not be in force! . . .

The localities of the two bridges, the Charles River bridge, and the Warren bridge, are well understood by the court. They accommodate the same line of travel, and either of them furnishes all the convenience, and all the facilities the line of travel requires. That one is sufficient, is shown by the fact, which is not denied, that since the Warren bridge has become free, all travellers pass over it, and no tolls are received by the proprietors of the Charles River bridge. When the act authorizing the Warren bridge was passed, and the company was about to erect the bridge, the plaintiffs applied to the superior court of Massachusetts for an injunction to prevent the work going on. This was refused, on the ground that nothing had been done by the company which presented the question of the unconstitutionality of the law. Before the Warren bridge was in the actual receipt of tolls, the bill now before the court was filed; and afterwards, a supplement bill, the proprietors of the Warren bridge being in the actual receipt of tolls; claiming that the charter under which they acted was a violation of the contract of the state, with the proprietors of the Charles River bridge, and was, therefore, against the constitution of the United States. The case is now before this court, on this question.

It is said, that Boston has many of such bridges as that constructed by the plaintiffs. This must necessarily be so; Boston is an exception in the ocean; she is almost surrounded by the waters of the sea, and is approached everywhere, but in one part, by a bridge. It is said, that those numerous bridges have given rise to no litigation. This is so, but the just inference is, that by no one of these has a right been interfered with. In fact, in all the cases where rival bridges, or bridges affecting prior rights, have been put up, it is understood, that there have been agreements with those who were or might be affected by them. This was the case with West Boston bridge. It was purchased by those who sought to make a free bridge which would interfere with it. . . .

. . . The history of the Warren bridge exhibits an entirely different state of things. It was undertaken on different principles, and under a different temper. It began with a clamor about monopoly! It was asserted, that the public had a right to break up the monopoly which was held by the Charles River bridge company; that they had a right to have a free bridge. . . .

The counsel for the defendants have said, that the plaintiffs have sustained no loss but that of their golden prospects. They have lost all their property; a property worth $300,000 before the new bridge was built, and now not worth $30. The rights of the plaintiffs are no monopoly. They are the enjoyment of the property for which they had paid in advance; and which, by a contract made by the law, they were entitled to enjoy for twenty years yet to come. They are called rapacious monopolists, when they claim to hold what they have purchased. Those who have assailed this property, have taken it from them—have taken all from them, without compensation. Where, and with whom, is the rapacity to be found in the transaction? . . .

It is said, that the distinguished honor of maintaining principles which will arrest the progress of public improvements, is left to the plaintiffs in this case. This is not so. All that is asked, is, that the franchise shall be protected. Massachusetts has not made any improvement of her own, although she has subscribed liberally to those which have been undertaken by individuals and corporations. In all these cases, private rights have been respected; and except in the case now before the court, Massachusetts has kept her faith. Recent and previous acts by her legislature show this. In every case, but this, compensation has been made in the law, or provided for.

The plaintiffs do not seek to interrupt the progress of improvements, but they ask to stay revolution; a revolution against the foundations on which property rests; a revolution which is attempted on the allegation of monopoly: we resist the clamor against legislative acts which have vested rights in individuals, on principles of equal justice to the state, and to those who hold those rights under the provisions of the law. . . .

The erection of the bridge was an undertaking of great hazard, and the result of the effort to construct it, was considered exceedingly doubtful. It cannot, therefore, be supposed that the franchise was to be diminished, and its enjoyment to be limited. Nothing of this is expressed, and nothing so unreasonable can be implied. . . .

In conclusion, Mr. Webster said, the plaintiffs have placed their reliance upon the precedents and authority established by this honorable court, in the course of the last thirty years, in support of that construction which secured individual property against legislative assumption: and that they now asked the enlightened conscience of this tribunal, if they have not succeeded in sustaining their complaint, upon legal and constitutional grounds: if not, they must, as good citizens of this republic, remain satisfied with the decision of the court.

CHIEF JUSTICE ROGER B. TANEY:

THE DECISION OF THE SUPREME COURT

TANEY, CH. J., delivered the opinion of the court.—The questions involved in this case are of the gravest character, and the court have given to them the most anxious and deliberate consideration. The value of the right claimed by the plaintiffs is large in amount; and many persons may, no doubt, be seriously affected in their pecuniary interests, by any decision which the court may pronounce; and the questions which have been raised as to the power of the several states, in relation to the corporations they have chartered, are pregnant with important consequences; not only to the individuals who are concerned in the corporate franchises, but to the communities in which they exist. The court are fully sensible, that it is their duty, in exercising the high powers conferred on them by the constitution of the United States, to deal with these great and extensive interests, with the utmost caution; guarding, so far as they have the power to do so, the rights of property, and at the same time, carefully abstaining from any encroachment on the rights reserved to the states.

It appears, from the record, that in the year 1650, the legislature of Massachusetts granted to the president of Harvard College "the liberty and power," to dispose of the ferry from Charlestown to Boston, by lease or otherwise, in the behalf, and for the behoof, of the college; and that under that grant, the college continued to hold and keep the ferry, by its lessees or agents, and to receive the profits of it, until 1785. In the last-

From 11 Peters, 419, at 536–553.

mentioned year, a petition was presented to the legislature, by Thomas Russell and others, stating the inconvenience of the transportation by ferries, over Charles river, and the public advantages that would result from a bridge; and praying to be incorporated, for the purpose of erecting a bridge in the place where the ferry between Boston and Charlestown was then kept. Pursuant to this petition, the legislature, on the 9th of March 1785, passed an act incorporating a company, by the name of "The Proprietors of the Charles River Bridge," for the purposes mentioned in the petition. Under this charter, the company were empowered to erect a bridge, in "the place where the ferry was then kept;" certain tolls were granted, and the charter was limited to forty years from the first opening of the bridge for passengers; and from the time the toll commenced, until the expiration of this term, the company were to pay 200*l*., annually, to Harvard College; and at the expiration of the forty years, the bridge was to be the property of the commonwealth; "saving (as the law expresses it) to the said college or university, a reasonable annual compensation, for the annual income of the ferry, which they might have received, had not the said bridge been erected."

The bridge was accordingly built, and was opened for passengers on the 17th of June 1786. In 1792, the charter was extended to seventy years from the opening of the bridge; and at the expiration of that time, it was to belong to the commonwealth. The corporation have regularly paid to the college the annual sum of 200*l*. and have performed all of the duties imposed on them by the terms of their charter.

In 1828, the legislature of Massachusetts incorporated a company by the name of "The Proprietors of the Warren Bridge," for the purpose of erecting another bridge over Charles river. This bridge is only sixteen rods, at its commencement, on the Charlestown side, from the commencement of the bridge of the plaintiffs; and they are about fifty rods apart, at their termination on the Boston side. The travellers who pass over either bridge, proceed from Charlestown square, which receives the travel of many great public roads leading from the country; and the passengers and travellers who go to and from Boston, used to pass over the Charles River Bridge, from and through this square, before the erection of the Warren bridge.

The Warren bridge, by the terms of its charter, was to be surrendered to the state, as soon as the expenses of the proprietors in building and supporting it should be reimbursed; but this period was not, in any event, to exceed six years from the time the company commenced receiving toll. . . .

In the argument here, it was admitted, that since the filing of the supplemental bill, a sufficient amount of toll had been reserved by the proprietors of the Warren bridge to reimburse all their expenses, and that the bridge is now the property of the state, and has been made a free bridge; and that the value of the franchise granted to the proprietors of the Charles River bridge, has by this means been entirely destroyed. . . .

. . . The case most analogous to this . . . is the case of the *Providence Bank* v. *Billings,* 4 Pet. 514, which was decided in 1830. In that case, it appeared, that the legislature of Rhode Island had chartered the bank, in the usual form of such acts of incorporation. The charter contained no stipulation on the part of the state, that it would not impose a tax on the bank, nor any reservation of the right to do so. It was silent on this point. Afterwards, a law was passed, imposing a tax on all banks in the state; and the right to impose this tax was resisted by the Providence Bank, upon the ground, that if the state could impose a tax, it might tax so heavily as to render the franchise of no value, and destroy the institution; that the charter was a contract, and that a power which may in effect destroy the charter is inconsistent with it, and is impliedly renounced by granting it. But the court said, that the taxing power was of vital importance, and essential to the existence of government; and that the relinquishment of such a power is never to be assumed. And in delivering the opinion of the court, the late chief justice states the principle, in the following clear and emphatic language. Speaking of the taxing power, he says, "as the whole community is interested in retaining it undiminished, that community has a right to insist that its abandonment ought not to be presumed, in a case in which the deliberate purpose of the state to abandon it does not appear." The case now before the court is, in principle, precisely the same. It is a charter from a state; the act of incorporation is silent in relation to the contested power. The argument in favor of the proprietors of the Charles River bridge, is the same, almost in words, with that used by the Providence Bank; that is, that the power claimed by the state, if it exists, may be so used as to destroy the value of the franchise they have granted to the corporation. The argument must receive the same answer; and the fact that the power has been already exercised, so as to destroy the value of the franchise, cannot in any degree affect the principle. The existence of the power does not, and cannot, depend upon the circumstance of its having been exercised or not.

It may, perhaps, be said, that in the case of the Providence Bank, this court were speaking of the taxing power; which is of vital importance to the very existence of every government. But the object and end of all government is to promote the happiness and prosperity of the community by which it is established; and it can never be assumed, that the government intended to diminish its power of accomplishing the end for which it was created. And in a country like ours, free, active and enterprising, continually advancing in numbers and wealth, new channels of communication are daily found necessary, both for travel and trade, and are essential to the comfort, convenience and prosperity of the people. A state ought never to be presumed to surrender this power, because, like the taxing power, the whole community have an interest in preserving it undiminished. And when a corporation alleges, that a state has surrendered, for seventy years, its power of improvement and public accommodation, in a great and important line of travel, along which a vast number of its citizens must daily pass, the community have a right to insist, in the language of this court, above quoted, "that its abandonment ought not to be presumed, in a case, in which the deliberate purpose of the state to abandon it does not appear." The continued existence of a government would be of no great value, if, by implications and presumptions, it was disarmed of the powers necessary to accomplish the ends of its creation, and the functions it was designed to perform, transferred to the hands of privileged corporations. The rule of construction announced by the court, was not confined to the taxing power, nor is it so limited, in the opinion delivered. On the contrary, it was distinctly placed on the ground, that the interests of the community were concerned in preserving, undiminished, the power then in question; and whenever any power of the state is said to be surrendered or diminished, whether it be the taxing power, or any other affecting the public interest, the same principle applies, and the rule of construction must be the same. No one will question, that the interests of the great body of the people of the state, would, in this instance, be affected by the surrender of this great line of travel to a single corporation, with the right to exact toll, and exclude competition, for seventy years. While the rights of private property are sacredly guarded, we must not forget, that the community also have rights, and that the happiness and well-being of every citizen depends on their faithful preservation.

Adopting the rule of construction above stated as the settled one, we proceed to apply it to the charter of 1785, to the proprietors of the Charles River bridge. This act of incorporation is in the usual form, and the privileges such as are commonly given to corporations of that kind. It confers on them the ordinary faculties of a corporation, for the purpose of building the bridge; and establishes certain rates of toll, which the company are authorized to take: this is the whole grant. There is no exclusive privilege given to them over the waters of Charles River, above or below their bridge; no right to erect another bridge themselves, nor to prevent other persons from erecting one, no engagement from the state, that another shall not be erected; and no undertaking not to sanction competition, nor to make improvements that may diminish the amount of its income. Upon all these subjects, the charter is silent; and nothing is said in it about a line of travel, so much insisted on in the argument, in which they are to have exclusive privileges. No words are used, from which an intention to grant any of these rights can be inferred; if the plaintiff is entitled to them, it must be implied, simply, from the nature of the grant; and cannot be inferred, from the words by which the grant is made.

The relative position of the Warren bridge has already been described. It does not interrupt the passage over the Charles River bridge, nor make the way to it, or from it, less convenient. None of the faculties or franchises granted to that corporation, have been revoked by the legislature; and its right to take the tolls granted by the charter remains unaltered. In short, all the franchises and rights of property, enumerated in the charter, and there mentioned to have been granted to it, remain unimpaired. But its income is destroyed by the Warren bridge; which, being free, draws off the passengers and property which would have gone over it, and renders their franchise of no value. This is the gist of the complainant; for it is not pretended, that the erection of the Warren bridge would have done them any injury, or in any degree affected their right of property, if it had not diminished the amount of their tolls. In order, then, to entitle themselves to relief, it is necessary to show, that the legislature contracted not to do the act of which they complain; and that they impaired, or in other words, violated, that contract, by the erection of the Warren bridge. . . .

The act of 1792, which extends the charter of this [Charles River] bridge, incorporates another company, to build a bridge over Charles river; furnishing another communication with

Boston, and distant only between one and two miles from the old bridge. The first six sections of this act incorporate the proprietors of the West Boston bridge, and define the privileges, and describe the duties of that corporation. In the 7th section, there is the following recital: "And whereas, the erection of Charles River bridge was a work of hazard and public utility, and another bridge in the place of West Boston bridge may diminish the emoluments of Charles River bridge; therefore, for the encouragement of enterprise," they proceed to extend the charter of the Charles River bridge, and to continue it for the term of seventy years from the day the bridge was completed; subject to the conditions prescribed in the original act, and to be entitled to the same tolls. It appears, then, that by the same act that extended this charter, the legislature established another bridge, which they knew would lessen its profits; and this, too, before the expiration of the first charter, and only seven years after it was granted; thereby showing, that the state did not suppose, that, by the terms it had used in the first law, it had deprived itself of the power of making such public improvements as might impair the profits of the Charles River bridge; and from the language used in the clauses of the law by which the charter is extended, it would seem, that the legislature were especially careful to exclude any inference that the extension was made upon the ground of compromise with the bridge company, or as a compensation for rights impaired. On the contrary, words are cautiously employed to exclude that conclusion; and the extension is declared to be granted as a reward for the hazard they had run, and "for the encouragement of enterprise." The extension was given, because the company had undertaken and executed a work of doubtful success; and the improvements which the legislature then contemplated, might diminish the emoluments they had expected to receive from it. . . .

Indeed, the practice and usage of almost every state in the Union, old enough to have commenced the work of internal improvement, is opposed to the doctrine contended for on the part of the plaintiffs in error. Turnpike roads have been made in succession, on the same line of travel; the later ones interfering materially with the profits of the first. These corporations have, in some instances, been utterly ruined by the introduction of newer and better modes of transportation and travelling. In some cases, railroads have rendered the turnpike roads on the same line of travel so entirely useless, that the franchise of the turnpike corporation is not worth preserving. Yet in none of these cases have the corporations supposed that their privileges were invaded, or any contract violated on the part of the state. . . .

And what would be the fruits of this doctrine of implied contracts, on the part of the states, and of property in a line of travel, by a corporation, if it would now be sanctioned by this court? To what results would it lead us? If it is to be found in the charter to this bridge, the same process of reasoning must discover it, in the various acts which have been passed, within the last forty years, for turnpike companies. And what is to be the extent of the privileges of exclusion on the different sides of the road? The counsel who have so ably argued this case, have not attempted to define it by any certain boundaries. How far must the new improvement be distant from the old one? How near may you approach, without invading its rights in the privileged line? If this court should establish the principles now contended for, what is to become of the numerous railroads established on the same line of travel with turnpike companies; and which have rendered the franchises of the turnpike corporations of no value? Let it once be understood, that such charters carry with them these implied contracts, and give this unknown and undefined property in a line of travelling; and you will soon find the old turnpike corporations awakening from their sleep, and calling upon this court to put down the improvements which have taken their place. The millions of property which have been invested in railroads and canals,

upon lines of travel which had been before occupied by turnpike corporations, will be put in jeopardy. We shall be thrown
back to the improvements of the last century, and obliged to
stand still, until the claims of the old turnpike corporations
shall be satisfied; and they shall consent to permit these states
to avail themselves of the lights of modern science, and to partake of the benefit of those improvements which are now adding to the wealth and prosperity, and the convenience and
comfort, of every other part of the civilized world. Nor is this
all. This court will find itself compelled to fix, by some arbitrary rule, the width of this new kind of property in a line of
travel; for if such a right of property exists, we have no lights
to guide us in marking out its extent, unless, indeed, we resort
to the old feudal grants, and to the exclusive rights of ferries,
by prescription, between towns; and are prepared to decide
that when a turnpike road from one town to another, had been
made, no railroad or canal, between these two points, could
afterwards be established. This court are not prepared to sanction principles which must lead to such results.

35. Daniel Webster: "The Application of
Capital to the Benefit of All"

As a leading spokesman for the rising business interests of the
day, Daniel Webster undertook to assure a popular audience
that the corporation was no monster, but rather a useful instrument for the benefit of all. American factories producing for a
mass market were increasing the wealth and comfort of the
entire population. Their progress required the accumulation of
large amounts of resources; and corporations which, he said,
were nothing but "partnerships regulated by law," and pro-

vided a convenient means for accomplishing the essential "union of many to form capital."

Webster's argument ran in very general terms, as was natural in a public lecture, and made no attempt to explain how the corporation's advantages of limited liability and transferability of stock made easier the "union of capitals." He did, however, make two points applying specifically to American conditions. The corporation was particularly necessary in the United States because of its democratic institutions; there were few individuals wealthy enough to build factories with their own resources. Because of these same institutions, the corporation was less to be feared; "capital and labor (were) much less distinctly divided" than in other industrial countries.

The document is taken from an address before the Society for the Diffusion of Useful Knowledge, delivered in Boston on November 11, 1836.

———————

If these, and other considerations may suffice to satisfy us that the application of science to art is the main cause of the sudden augmentation of wealth and comfort in modern times, a truth remains to be stated of the greatest magnitude, and the highest practical importance, and that is, that this augmentation of wealth and comfort is general and diffusive, reaching to all classes, embracing all interests, and benefiting, not a part of society, but the whole. There is no monopoly in science. There are no exclusive privileges in the workings of automatic machinery, or the powers of natural bodies. The poorest, as well as the richest man in society, has a direct interest, and generally the poor a far greater interest than the rich, in the successful operation of these arts, which make the means of

From *The Writings and Speeches of Daniel Webster* (Boston: Little, Brown & Co., 1903), vol. XVIII, pp. 72–77.

living, clothing especially, abundant and cheap. The advantages conferred by knowledge in increasing our physical resources, from their very nature, cannot be enjoyed by a few only. They are all open to the many, and to be profitable, the many must enjoy it. The products of science applied to art in mechanical inventions, are made, not to be hoarded, but to be sold. Their successful operation requires a large market. It requires that the great mass of society should be able to buy and to consume. The improved condition of all classes, more ability to buy food and raiment, better modes of living, and increased comforts of every kind, are exactly what is necessary and indispensable in order that capital invested in automatic operations should be productive to the owners. Some establishments of this kind necessarily require large capital, such as the woollen and cotton factories. And in a country like ours, in which the spirit of our institutions, and all our laws, tend so much to the distribution and equalization of property, there are few individuals of sufficient wealth to build and carry on an establishment by their own means. This renders a union of capitals necessary, and this among us is conveniently effected by corporations which are but partnerships regulated by law. And this union of many to form capital for the purpose of carrying on those operations by which science is applied to art, and comes in aid of man's labor in the production of things essential to man's existence, constitutes that aggregated wealth of which complaint is sometimes heard. It would seem that nothing could be plainer than that whatever reduces the price, whether of food or of clothing, must be in the end beneficial to the laboring classes. Yet it has not unfrequently happened, that machinery has been broken and destroyed in England, by workmen, by open and lawless violence. Most persons in our country see the folly as well as the injustice and barbarism of such proceedings; but the ideas in which these violences originated are no more unfounded and scarcely more disreputable,

than those which would represent capital, collected, necessarily, in large sums, in order to carry on useful processes in
which science is applied to art, in the production of articles
useful to all, as being hostile to the common good, or having
an interest separate from that of the majority of the community. All such representations, if not springing from sinister
design, must be the result of great ignorance, or great prejudice. It has been found by long experience in England, that
large capitalists can produce cheaper than small ones, especially in the article of cotton. Greater savings can be made and
these savings enable the proprietor to go on, when he must
otherwise stop. There is no doubt that it is to her abundant
capital, England is now indebted for whatever power of competition with the United States she now sustains, in producing
cheap articles.

There are modes of applying wealth, useful principally to the
owner, and no otherwise beneficial to the community than as
they employ labor. Such are the erection of expensive houses,
the embellishment of ornamental grounds, the purchase of
costly furniture and equipages. These modes of expenditure,
although entirely lawful and sometimes very proper, are yet
not such as directly benefit the whole community. Not so with
aggregate wealth employed in producing articles of general
consumption. This mode of employment is, peculiarly and in an
emphatic sense, an application of capital to the benefit of all.
Any one who complains of it, or decries it, acts against the
greatest good of the greatest number. The factories, the steamboats, the railroads, and other similar establishments, although
they require capital, and aggregate capital, are yet general and
popular in all the good they produce.

The unquestionable operation of all these things has been
not only to increase property, but to equalize it, to diffuse it,
to scatter its advantages among the many, and to give content,
cheerfulness, and animation to all classes of the social system.
In New England, more particularly, has this been the result.

What has enabled us to be rich and prosperous, notwithstanding the barrenness of our soil and the rigor of our climate? What has diffused so much comfort, wealth, and happiness among all classes, but the diligent employment of our citizens, in these processes and mechanical operations in which science comes in aid of handicraft? Abolish the use of steam and the application of water power to machinery, and what would at this moment be the condition of New England? And yet steam and water power have been employed only, and can be employed only, by what is called aggregated wealth. Far distant be the day then, when the people of New England shall be deceived by the specious fallacy, that there are different and opposing interests in our community; that what is useful to one, is hurtful to the rest; that there is one interest for the rich, and another interest for the poor; that capital is the enemy of labor, or labor the foe of capital. And let every laboring man, on whose understanding such a fallacy is attempted to be imposed, stop the mouth of the false reasoner at once, by stating the plain and evident fact, that while aggregated wealth has for years, in Massachusetts, been most skilfully and steadily employed in the productions which result from the application of science to art; thereby reducing the cost of many of the articles most essential to human life in all conditions; labor, meantime, has been constantly rising, and is at this very moment, notwithstanding the present scarcity of money, and the constant pressure on capital, higher than it ever was before in the history of the country. These are, indeed, facts which baffle all former dogmas of political economy. . . .

The truth, in my opinion, rather is, that such is the enterprise of our people, such the astonishing amount of labor which they perform, and which they perform cheerfully because it is free and because it is profitable, and such the skill with which capital is used, that still more capital would be useful, and that its introduction would be advantageous, and most of all to the busy and industrious classes. And let it never be forgotten, that with us labor is free, intelligent, respecting itself, and respected by other interests; that it accumulates; that it is provident; that it lays up for itself; and that these savings become capital, and their owners in time capitalists.

I cannot omit to notice, here, another fact peculiar to this country, and which should cause us to hesitate in applying to ourselves, and our condition, European maxims respecting capital and labor. In Europe, generally speaking, the laborer is always a laborer. He is destined to no better condition on earth, ordinarily he rises no higher. We see proofs, melancholy proofs, of this truth often in the multitudes who come to our own shores from foreign countries for employment. It is not so with the people of New England. Capital and labor are much less distinctly divided with us. Few are they, on the one hand, who have need to perform no labor; few are they, on the other, who have no property or capital of their own. Or if there be those of the latter class among the industrious and the sober, they are young men who, though they are laborers to-day, will be capitalists to-morrow. A career of usefulness and enterprise is before them. If without moneyed capital, they have a capital in their intelligence, their knowledge, and their good habits. Around them are a thousand collections of automatic machinery, requiring the diligence of skilful and sober laborers; before them is the ocean, always inviting to deeds of hardihood and enterprise; behind them are the fertile prairies of the West, soliciting cultivation; and over them all is the broad banner of free institutions, of mild laws, and parental Government. Would an American young man of good health and good habits need say that he is without capital? Or why should he discredit his own understanding by listening to the absurdity, that they who have earned property, and they who have not yet lived long enough to earn it, must be enemies? The proportion of those who have not capital, such as to render them independent without personal labor, and who are yet not without some capital, is vastly larger in this community than any other. They form indeed the great mass of our society. They are its life and muscle; and long may they continue free, moral, intelligent, and prosperous as they now are.

36. A. B. Johnson: A Defense of the
Policy of Free Incorporation

At the beginning of the period, incorporation of a business enterprise was an exceptional privilege. It required the special act of a state legislature and a demonstration that the object, as in the case of the internal improvement companies, was of particular public utility. The privilege, moreover, was widely suspect and often the subject of "anti-charter" agitation,[1] inspired by "zeal for the disallowment of any corporate grants; no other remedy for the monopoly evil being apparent." As late as the 1830's, the legislative committee cited in Document 33 expressed the hope and belief that Pennsylvania's coal mines could be developed without further use of the corporate device. With industrial and financial growth, however, the corporation came into increasingly common use as the agency for carrying on any business that required considerable capital. A number of state legislatures responded to and facilitated this process by making it possible to organize corporations under the regulations of general rather than special legislation. Though promoters continued in many cases to seek and obtain exceptional privileges through special acts,[2] passage of the general laws represented both the acceptance of the corporate device and the belief that its use should be open to all on equal terms. This change in "the great exemplar state of New York" was

---

[1] The strength and the decline of anti-charter feeling are principal themes of Hartz, *Economic Policy and Democratic Thought.*

[2] See, for example, John W. Cadman, Jr., *The Corporation in New Jersey, Business and Politics, 1791–1875* (Cambridge: Harvard University Press, 1949), chs. 4 and 5.

described in an article in *Hunt's Merchant Magazine* written by A. B. Johnson, who was the president of a Utica bank and had been a determined opponent of the Bank of the United States.[3] A law permitting the incorporation of manufacturing enterprises under general regulations rather than under special acts was passed as early as 1811. In banking, where the struggle for lucrative special privileges had resulted in particularly flagrant lobbying and corruption, a Free Banking Act was adopted in 1838. The Convention that framed the Constitution of 1846 was, he says, "intent on removing from corporate agency its monopoly character."[4] Finally, the legislature of 1850 extended the privilege of general incorporation even to the railroad industry, which had been the subject of so much governmental promotion in the past and was to be the subject of so much governmental regulation in the future, in an act which Professor Benson describes as carrying "laissez-faire precepts to unprecedented lengths in New York and the country at large."[5]

Mr. Johnson's view of the process is expressed in the subtitle of his article, "The Progress of Liberal Sentiments." Legislation should not "unnecessarily" conflict with "the fruition of man's natural aspirations"; and the rape of the Sabine women was more the sin of the Sabine fathers than of the Romans themselves. The earlier restrictions on the formation of corporations were futile and unnecessary "attempts to restrain men . . . from promoting their own interests." The policy of free incorporation removed the monopoly feature and makes it possible to retain "corporate agency as an allowable and valuable facility of social progress."

[3] Joseph Dorfman, *The Economic Mind in American Civilization 1606–1865* (New York: The Viking Press, 1946), vol. II, p. 608.

[4] Selections from the relevant debate in the Convention are presented in Louis M. Hacker and Helene S. Zahler, eds., *The Shaping of the American Tradition* (New York: Columbia University Press, 1947), pp. 515–519.

[5] Lee Benson, *Merchants, Farmers & Railroads: Railroad Regulation and New York Politics* (Cambridge: Harvard University Press, 1955), ch. 1, especially p. 4. The author points out that even this measure contained provisions recognizing the public character of the railroad industry.

In accounting for this triumph of liberal sentiments, Mr. Johnson appears to lay more stress on "pressure from without the Legislature" than on "the progress of intelligence within." No American public authority in the 1850's was likely to take the initiative in urging its citizens to form corporations, as the government of Japan was to do later in the century.[6] What American legislators had done was to make adaptations in the institutional framework to the demands and requirements of business enterprise conducted on an increasing scale.

State Constitution of 1777.—The first constitution of New York contained no specific provision for the creation of corporations, and they came into existence as only an incident of the general powers of the Legislature. The Legislature, on being solicited to create them, came easily to deem them favors, which were to be dispensed sparingly, lest capitalists should refuse to invest money in corporate enterprises; a notion that was assiduously propagated by the few then existing corporations, who naturally loved the possession of special privileges, and, perhaps, honestly feared competition.

Banking came early to be deemed peculiarly within the province of corporate agency, and as the business was lucrative to capitalists, and to men void of capital, who desired to borrow, a sharp contest soon arose between applicants for new banking corporations, and the existing banks that resisted the creation of rival institutions. This resistance was deemed so effective, that in April, 1799, a bank was smuggled through the Legisla-

---

From A. B. Johnson, "The Legislative History of Corporations in the State of New York, or, The Progress of Liberal Sentiments," *Hunt's Merchants Magazine*, XXIII (December 1850), 610–614.

---

[6] Yasuzo Horie, "Modern Entrepreneurship in Meiji Japan," in William W. Lockwood, ed., *The State and Economic Enterprise in Japan* (Princeton: Princeton University Press, 1965), ch. 4, especially p. 201.

ture, under the guise of a charter, "to supply the city of New York with pure and wholesome water." Such an expedient could necessarily not be immediately repeated; hence, in the year 1803, some persons associated without a Legislative grant, and organized a joint stock bank in the city of New York, on a species of limited partnership; and another was formed, on the same principle, in Albany. But the influence which could prevent the creation of banking incorporations was sufficient to procure, when the Legislature assembled, the enactment, in the spring of 1804, of a law to prohibit unchartered banking; and under its very penal restraints, the joint stock associations were suppressed; and banking, which previously was a lawful business to any person who possessed the requisite means of conducting it, was made a franchise, to be exercised only under a special grant of the Legislature. It qualifiedly continues a franchise up to this day, except as to the reception of deposits, and making of discounts, which branches of banking were, in the year 1837, exempted from the restraining law, and made lawful to any person, or persons, except foreign banks, and officers of the chartered banks of the State.

Lobby Members.—To resist the creation of new banks, or to assist in procuring them, came, at length, to be a regular mercenary employment, by men, who, like the straw bail in courts of law, attended the halls of legislation, to be hired, and were sarcastically called lobby members. They disguised their venality by feigning to possess a reputable interest in the projects they undertook to support; or to be patriotic promoters of the measures for merely an alleged public benefit; or if they were hired to oppose the measures, they feigned to be disinterested exponents of an alleged hostile public sentiment. Some of the persons thus engaged, were otherwise respectable; and some were even distinguished as men of station, talent, and wealth. But the practices to which they resorted in secret, were worse than their open acts, and became so threatening to public virtue, that on the 27th March, 1812, the then Governor of the

State, Daniel D. Tompkins, terminated abruptly the Legislature, by prorogation, that the members might have time for reflection, on the appliances to which they were ostensibly yielding. He declared, in a public message, "that beyond any reason of doubt, corrupting inducements were some years since held out to the members of the Legislature, to obtain their votes for the incorporation of a banking institution in the city of New York, and very strong and general suspicion existed, that the emoluments then tendered, were, in certain instances, accepted; thereby inflicting a deep wound upon the honor of the State, and upon the purity and independence of legislation. At the last session, an act was passed incorporating the late Jersey bank, and a very general public opinion exists, that unwarrantable attempts were resorted to, on that occasion, to influence unduly the then Legislature. The journals of the Assembly show that attempts have been made to corrupt, by bribes, four members of that body, in relation to the bank now under consideration; and that improper influences have been employed on, at least, one member of the Senate. I entertain, therefore, the most fearful apprehensions that the confidence of the people, in the purity and independence of the Legislature, will be fatally impaired."

Legislation against the tendency of Nature.—But the evil reprobated by the Governor was not curable by prorogation, and when the Legislature re-assembled on the 21st of the following May, the bank, which had caused the prorogation, was triumphantly incorporated. The evil of the times consisted, not in the susceptibility to bribery of the Legislature, nor in the existence of corrupt corporation procurers, but in the attempt to restrain the creation of corporations, that were lucrative to the corporators, and beneficial to the public. We might well dispair of the purity of legislation, at any time, if its security consisted in the absence of bribes. Providence has so organized man that he can rarely be bribed to perpetrate actions that will affect, injuriously, private persons or the public; but he can be easily bribed to perform actions which he deems beneficial, how much soever any erroneous laws may interdict them. Beneficial laws are rarely violated, and the violation of them is always disreputable; but laws of an opposite character are everywhere violated systematically, and the violation of them is hardly disreputable. Men will endeavor to circumvent unjust restraints; hence, in the year 1816, another attempt to smuggle through the Legislature a bank charter, was again successful in an act to incorporate an insurance company, though it was met by a new restraining law on the 21st of April, 1818, which, under very penal enactments, stopped the newly discovered leak in the existing prohibitions. The above examples show the demoralizing effect of legislative attempts to restrain men unnecessarily from promoting their own interests. The rape perpetrated on the Sabine women by the Romans, was more a sin of the Sabines, who refused their daughters in marriage to the Romans, than of the Romans, who were destitute of women. In a recent publication of Carlyle, he reprobates legislation that is counter to the laws of God, and he probably alludes to legislation like the foregoing, which unnecessarily conflicts with the fruition of man's natural aspirations.

The Constitution of 1777 superceded by the Constitution of 1821.—When our State adopted a new constitution in 1821, corporations were for the first time recognized as one of the great interests which the organic law should regulate. The legislation which we have described had long caused corporations to be deemed odious monopolies; and partisan agitators designated bankers as "rag barrons," and manufacturers as "cotton lords." The new constitution, in attempting to remedy the existing evil, prohibited the creation of any new corporation, except by the affirmative vote of two-thirds of the members elected to each branch of the Legislature. This alteration was either a political blunder of men who wished to remedy an existing evil without knowing how, or it was a stratagem of interested men to perpetuate existing monopolies, by rendering the creation almost hopeless of competing new institutions. But contrary to every reasonable expectation, the restraints imposed by the new constitution, facilitated the creation of corporations, by reason that a negative vote came to be deemed a harsh exercise of an unreasonable power; while an affirmative vote came to be deemed a common courtesy, which every member of the Legislature ought to grant to a fellow member, whose constituents desired to participate in corporate privileges. So numerous, by these means, became banking corporations, that except in some few inland localities, no pecuniary interest existed to resist the further creation of those institutions. Hence, in the year 1838, a law was enacted by which banks could be instituted by voluntary associations, under prescribed general forms and regulations. The Legislature was unable to accord to the associations a complete corporate organization, by reason that the constitution had been construed as prohibiting the creation of more than a single corporation in any one bill. The associations are, however, essentially corporations though not endued with the usually prescribed machinery of a corporate seal, a board of directors, and a right to sue and be sued, under a corporate name; and without the usually prescribed limitation to the number of the directors, the duration of their office, and the mode of their election. The associations have remedied such of these omissions as are remediable; but some of the associations have adopted few directors, and some many. Some are governed by directors, who are chosen annually, while others are governed by directors who are never elected by the stockholders, but continue in the office for life; with a power in the survivors of the board to supply all vacancies that may happen therein by death or resignation. Such an organization seems almost irreconcilable with honest intentions on the part of the originators, and is certainly capable of great perversion against stockholders, who happen not to be directors; but we have heard of no fraudulent result, a fact which shows remarkably that the absence of dishonest practices depends but little on legislative precautions; and that honest practices depend as little on legislative furtherance.

The Constitution of 1846.—Thus existed corporate agency, and banking corporations in particular, when the constitution of 1821 was superceded, in 1846, by our present constitution. The old argument, that corporations could not sustain unrestricted competition, had been disproved by eight years of prosperous experience in banking, under the above system of voluntary associations; and of several laws for the creation, at will, in 1811, of manufacturing corporations; in 1813, of religious corporations, medical corporations, and colleges; and, as early as in 1796, of corporate libraries; besides the daily experience, in his private concerns, of every man, that "competition is the life of business,"—not its death. The convention that formed the constitution of 1846, became, therefore, intent on removing from corporate agency its monopoly character, which was so generally odious as to excite, at one time, an ill-directed zeal for the disallowment of any corporate grants; no other remedy for the monopoly evil being apparent. But the new constitution devised a better remedy. It retained corporate agency as an allowable and valuable facility of social progress, but removed its monopoly feature, by permitting, under general laws, every person to obtain a corporate organization who desired the facility; and by interdicting only special grants of corporate powers. And thus was consummated the greatest triumph that our American experiment of equal rights has ever achieved in practical results. And when we reflect that this triumph was not achieved till sixty years after the theoretic legal equality of our citizens had been a fundamental axiom of our government, we can see how slowly the human intellect comprehends new truths; and how long men bear patiently, and almost unconsciously, accustomed abuses. We can see, also, the fallacy of the belief that property is not strong enough to protect itself against numerical personal preponderance, when it was able, from 1777 to 1846, to engross for itself, in our State, privileges that could always have been advantageously shared in common by all persons. Unfortunately, however, the makers of the constitution of 1846 were not wholly untrammeled from old prejudices, or, perhaps, from sinister influences; for, to the above prohibition against special privileges, they added an exception in favor of cases; "where, in the judgment of the Legislature, the objects of the corporation cannot be obtained under general laws"—an exception which enables the timid, and the interested, to still make a logical fight to shield, under various pretexts, some few remaining objects of corporate enterprise; as, for instance, the business of insurance, till the winter of 1849; of railroads, till the winter of 1850; of savings banks, that are not yet extricated from the grasp of special philanthropists; the care of the poor not being so wholly destitute of resulting private gains as it would seem to be. But as the reserved branches are annually diminishing in number, by reason of the pressure from without the Legislature, and the progress of intelligence within, we may well felicitate the world on the hopeful prospect, that after a few more struggles against both the letter and the spirit of our new constitution, special acts of incorporation will be wholly discontinued in the great exemplar State of New York. When any man shall find that no general law is adapted to his wants, he will be compelled to obtain some salutary enlargement of an existing general law, or the enactment of some new general law to suit all class of cases like his own; and thus each man's interest will tend to the promotion of the interests of all men similarly situated;[7] and

---

[7] The bank-notes in circulation belonging to one of the banks of this State, were, some years since, constantly mutilated by some secret enemy. The bank did not apply to the Legislature for a special law to meet its own case only, but it applied for a general law to punish such conduct, against whomsoever it might be perpetrated. So when a man wishes an inland stream navigation company, like the one incorporated last winter, or any other new application of corporate agency, he should be compelled to obtain some general law, under which all persons who shall desire, may obtain the same corporate organization; and our progress in useful enterprises would thereby be greatly accelerated.

all our citizens will enjoy the legal facilities in enterprise that are accorded to any citizen—an extent of privilege never before enjoyed by any people. Then, also, the time of our law makers will no longer be dissipated in private legislation; and the morals of our Senators and Assemblymen no longer be subjected to the corrupting influences of private solicitation, for the consummation of personal advantages. In the language of the Bible, "these were offences which heretofore, through ignorance, the law winked at, but against which every man is now called to repentance."

PART SEVEN

THE DEVELOPMENT OF

HUMAN CAPACITIES

37. George Washington: "The Expediency of a National University"

To George Washington, the development of human capacities through education was a proper and important function for the national government to undertake. The principal means he proposed was the creation of a national university. This he urged in two of his annual messages; and his Last Will and Testament, which included a bequest for this purpose, is proof of his continuing devotion to the idea.

Washington's pleas for the establishment of a national university are, as will be noted, embedded in arguments for the encouragement of agriculture and manufactures; and the specific bequest made, that of his shares of stock in the Potomac Company, illustrates his interest in another means of promoting the country's economic development, "the extension of its Inland Navigation, under Legislative patronage."

FIRST ANNUAL MESSAGE

The advancement of agriculture, commerce, and manufactures by all proper means will not, I trust, need recommendation; but I can not forbear intimating to you the expediency of giving effectual encouragement as well to the introduction of new and useful inventions from abroad as to the exertions of skill and genius in producing them at home, and of facilitating the intercourse between the distant parts of our country by a due attention to the post-office and post-roads.

Nor am I less persuaded that you will agree with me in opinion that there is nothing which can better deserve your patronage than the promotion of science and literature. Knowledge is in every country the surest basis of public happiness. In one in which the measures of government receive their impressions so immediately from the sense of the community as in ours it is proportionably essential. To the security of a free constitution it contributes in various ways—by convincing those who are intrusted with the public administration that every valuable end of government is best answered by the enlightened confidence of the people, and by teaching the people themselves to know and to value their own rights; to discern and provide against invasions of them; to distinguish between oppression and the necessary exercise of lawful authority; between burthens proceeding from a disregard to their convenience and those resulting from the inevitable exigencies of society; to discriminate the spirit of liberty from that of licentiousness—cherishing the first, avoiding the last—and uniting a speedy but temperate vigilance against encroachments, with an inviolable respect to the laws.

From James D. Richardson, *A Compilation of the Messages and Papers of the Presidents* (New York: Bureau of National Literature and Art, 1897–1920), vol. I, p. 66. The date is January 8, 1790.

Whether this desirable object will be best promoted by affording aids to seminaries of learning already established, by the institution of a national university, or by any other expedients will be well worthy of a place in the deliberations of the Legislature.

EIGHTH ANNUAL MESSAGE

Congress have repeatedly, and not without success, directed their attention to the encouragement of manufactures. The object is of too much consequence not to insure a continuance of their efforts in every way which shall appear eligible. As a general rule, manufactures on public account are inexpedient; but where the state of things in a country leaves little hope that certain branches of manufacture will for a great length of time obtain, when these are of a nature essential to the furnishing and equipping of the public force in time of war, are not establishments for procuring them on public account to the extent of the ordinary demand for the public service recommended by strong considerations of national policy as an exception to the general rule? Ought our country to remain in such cases dependent on foreign supply, precarious because liable to be interrupted? If the necessary article should in this mode cost more in time of peace, will not the security and independence thence arising form an ample compensation? Establishments of this sort, commensurate only with the calls of the public service in time of peace, will in time of war easily be extended in proportion to the exigencies of the Government, and may even perhaps be made to yield a surplus for the supply of our citizens at large, so as to mitigate the privations from the interruption of their trade. If adopted, the plan ought to exclude all those branches which are already, or likely soon to be, estab-

From Richardson, *Messages and Papers of the Presidents,* vol. I, pp. 201–203. The date is December 7, 1796.

lished in the country, in order that there may be no danger of interference with pursuits of individual industry.

It will not be doubted that with reference either to individual or national welfare agriculture is of primary importance. In proportion as nations advance in population and other circumstances of maturity this truth becomes more apparent, and renders the cultivation of the soil more and more an object of public patronage. Institutions for promoting it grow up, supported by the public purse; and to what object can it be dedicated with greater propriety? Among the means which have been employed to this end none have been attended with greater success than the establishment of boards (composed of proper characters) charged with collecting and diffusing information, and enabled by premiums and small pecuniary aids to encourage and assist a spirit of discovery and improvement. This species of establishment contributes doubly to the increase of improvement by stimulating to enterprise and experiment, and by drawing to a common center the results everywhere of individual skill and observation, and spreading them thence over the whole nation. Experience accordingly has shown that they are very cheap instruments of immense national benefits.

I have heretofore proposed to the consideration of Congress the expediency of establishing a national university and also a military academy. The desirableness of both these institutions has so constantly increased with every new view I have taken of the subject that I can not omit the opportunity of once for all recalling your attention to them.

The assembly to which I address myself is too enlightened not to be fully sensible how much a flourishing state of the arts and sciences contributes to national prosperity and reputation.

True it is that our country, much to its honor, contains many seminaries of learning highly respectable and useful; but the funds upon which they rest are too narrow to command the ablest professors in the different departments of liberal knowledge for the institution contemplated, though they would be excellent auxiliaries.

Amongst the motives to such an institution, the assimilation of the principles, opinions, and manners of our countrymen by the common education of a portion of our youth from every quarter well deserves attention. The more homogeneous our citizens can be made in these particulars the greater will be our prospect of permanent union; and a primary object of such a national institution should be the education of our youth in the science of *government*. In a republic what species of knowledge can be equally important and what duty more pressing on its legislature than to patronize a plan for communicating it to those who are to be the future guardians of the liberties of the country?

The institution of a military academy is also recommended by cogent reasons. However pacific the general policy of a nation may be, it ought never to be without an adequate stock of military knowledge for emergencies. The first would impair the energy of its character, and both would hazard its safety or expose it to greater evils when war could not be avoided; besides that, war might often not depend upon its own choice. In proportion as the observance of pacific maxims might exempt a nation from the necessity of practicing the rules of the military art ought to be its care in preserving and transmitting, by proper establishments, the knowledge of that art. Whatever argument may be drawn from particular examples superficially viewed, a thorough examination of the subject will evince that the art of war is at once comprehensive and complicated, that it demands much previous study, and that the possession of it in its most improved and perfect state is always of great moment to the security of a nation. This, therefore, ought to be a serious care of every government, and for this purpose an academy where a regular course of instruction is given is an obvious expedient which different nations have successfully employed.

LAST WILL AND TESTAMENT

Item Whereas by a Law of the Commonwealth of Virginia, enacted in the year 1785, the Legislature thereof was pleased (as an evidence of Its approbation of the services I had rendered the Public during the Revolution; and partly, I believe, in consideration of my having suggested the vast advantages which the Community would derive from the extension of its Inland Navigation, under Legislative patronage) to present me with one hundred shares of one hundred dollars each, in the incorporated company established for the purpose of extending the navigation of James River from tide water to the Mountains: and also with fifty shares of one hundred pounds Sterling each, in the Corporation of another company, likewise established for the similar purpose of opening the Navigation of the River Potomac from tide water to Fort Cumberland; the acceptance of which, although the offer was highly honorable, and grateful to my feelings, was refused, as inconsistent with a principle which I had adopted, and had never departed from, namely, not to receive pecuniary compensation for any services I could render my country in its arduous struggle with great Britain, for its Rights; and because I had evaded similar propositions from other States in the Union; adding to this refusal, however, an intimation that, if it should be the pleasure of the Legislature to permit me to appropriate the said shares to public uses, I would receive them on those terms with due sensibility; and this it having consented to, in flattering terms, as will appear by a subsequent Law, and sundry resolutions, in the most ample and honourable manner, I proceed after this recital, for the more correct understanding of the case, to declare:

From "Last Will and Testament of George Washington of Mount Vernon," 62nd Congress, 1st Session, Senate *Document No. 86*, pp. 6–10. The will was recorded on July 9, 1799. Also reproduced in Saxe Commins, ed., *Basic Writings of George Washington* (New York: Random House, 1948), pp. 657–659.

That as it has always been a source of serious regret with me, to see the youth of these United States sent to foreign Countries for the purpose of Education, often before their minds were formed, or they had imbibed any adequate ideas of the happiness of their own; contracting, too frequently, not only habits of dissipation and extravagence, but principles unfriendly to Republican Governmt. and to the true and genuine liberties of mankind; which, thereafter are rarely overcome. For these reasons, it has been my ardent wish to see a plan devised on a liberal scale which would have a tendency to sprd. systematic ideas through all parts of this rising Empire, thereby to do away local attachments and State prejudices, as far as the nature of things would, or indeed ought to admit, from our National Councils. Looking anxiously forward to the accomplishment of so desirable an object as this is (in my estimation) my mind has not been able to contemplate any plan more likely to effect the measure than the establishment of a *university* in a central part of the United States, to which the youth of fortune and talents from all parts thereof might be sent for the completion of their Education in all the branches of polite literature; in arts and Sciences, in acquiring knowledge in the principles of Politics and good Government; and (as a matter of infinite Importance in my judgment) by associating with each other, and forming friendships in Juvenile years, be enabled to free themselves in a proper degree from those local prejudices and habitual jealousies which have just been mentioned; and which, when carried to excess, are never failing sources of disquietude to the Public mind, and pregnant of mischievous consequences to this Country: Under these impressions, so fully dilated,

Item I give and bequeath in perpetuity the fifty shares which I hold in the Potomac Company (under the aforesaid Acts of the Legislature of Virginia) towards the endowment of a *university* to be established within the limits of the District of Columbia, under the auspices of the General Government, if that government should incline to extend a fostering hand towards it; and until such Seminary is established, and the funds arising on these shares shall be required for its support, my further WILL and desire is that the profit accruing therefrom shall, whenever the dividends are made, be laid out in purchasing Stock in the Bank of Columbia, or some other Bank, at the discretion of my Executors; or by the Treasurer of the United States for the time being under the direction of Congress; provided that Honourable body should Patronize the measure, and the Dividends proceeding from the purchase of such Stock is to be vested in more stock, and so on, until a sum adequate to the accomplishment of the object is obtained, of which I have not the smallest doubt, before many years passes away; even if no aid or encouraged is given by Legislative authority, or from any other source.

38. The Debate over Federal Grants to Agricultural Colleges

Washington's proposal for a National University, though later supported by Jefferson and Madison and several times considered by Congress, was never carried out. However, the Military Academy he proposed played a significant role in the economic development of the young nation as well as in its military preparedness. It was in effect the country's first engineering school; and its graduates, both in the Army Corps of Engineers and in private capacities, provided much of the direction for the nation's canals and early railroads.[1]

Other federal aid took the indirect form of grants of land to

---

[1] Forest G. Hill, *Roads, Rails and Waterways: The Army Engineers and Early Transportation* (Norman, Oklahoma: University of Oklahoma Press, 1957.)

the states. Beginning with the Ordinance of 1787, which declared that "religion and the means of education should be forever encouraged," it was the practice to give a small fraction of the public lands to each new state on admission to be used at its discretion for general educational purposes. Toward the end of the period, sharp controversy was aroused by a proposal for grants of public land to all the states for a more specific purpose, the support of colleges devoted primarily to agriculture and the mechanic arts. Proponents of the measure argued for it as an act of justice to the otherwise neglected agricultural interest and as a way of improving the performance of the nation's agriculture. In arguments foreshadowing the Conservation Movement of a half century later, they pointed to soil erosion as one of the evils to be overcome. Opponents of the measure denied that it was desired by "the honest tillers of soil"; instead, it was a "scheme of peculation and plunder," pressed by capitalists who wished to speculate in the sale of land warrants, and an invitation to the people to "surrender the supervision, control, and direction of their education to the Federal Government." A Senator from Alabama expressed the fervent hope that his state would not "abase herself at the footstool of Federal power" and give up "her original and reserved power to manage her own domestic and internal affairs in her own way."[2]

The selections below include parts of a speech by one of the bill's principal sponsors, Representative Justin Smith Morrill of Vermont; the veto message of President James Buchanan, omitting the greater part of its argument on constitutional grounds; and a brief passage from Morrill's reply. The President's veto prevailed, since the motion for repassage obtained only 105 votes against 96. But three years later, with the states of the Confederacy unrepresented in Congress, substantially the same measure was adopted, and Congressman Morrill gave his name to the Act which established the system of land-grant colleges.

---

[2] *Congressional Globe,* 35th Congress, 2nd Session, February 7, 1858, Part I, p. 852.

JUSTIN SMITH MORRILL: SPEECH ON THE
AGRICULTURAL COLLEGES BILL

. . . Mr. Speaker, I know very well that when there is a lack of arguments to be brought against the merits of a measure, the Constitution is fled to as an inexhaustible arsenal of supply. From thence all sorts of missiles may be hurled, and though they "bear wide" of the mark, they do not "kick the owner over." I have also noticed that lions accustomed to roar around the Constitution are quite disposed to slumber whenever it is desirable for certain gentlemen, who carry extra baggage, to leap over the impediment. But, while I do not propose to consider the constitutional argument at any great length, I shall not wholly blink it out of sight; and all the favor asked is, that the Constitution may not be strained and perverted to defeat a measure no less of public good than of public justice—just politically, just to all the States, and just, above all, to the manhood of our country.

We exert our power and expend millions to protect and promote commerce through lighthouses, coast surveys, improvement of harbors, and through our Navy and Naval Academy. Our military "crown-jewels" are manufactured at West Point on Government account. We make immense grants of lands to railroads to open new fields of internal trade. We secure to literary labor the protection of copy-right. We encourage the growth and discipline of hardy seamen by eking out their scanty rewards through governmental bounties. We secure to ingenious mechanics high profits by our system of patent-rights. We make munificent grants to secure general education in all the new States. But all direct encouragement to agriculture has been rigidly withheld.

From *Congressional Globe,* 35th Congress, 1st Session, April 20, 1858, Part II, pp. 1692, 1696, 1697.

When Commerce comes to our doors, gay in its attire and lavish in its promises, we "hand and deliver" at once our gold. When Manufactures appears, with a needy and downcast look, we tender, at worst, a "compromise." And then the fiery little god of war bristles up and makes havoc of all we have left. So that, when Agriculture appears,

> A creature not too wise or good
> For human nature's daily food

though taxed to support all her sisters and idle brothers, and to espouse their quarrels—we coldly plead there is nothing left for her, and even spurn the admission of her affinity to the family by omitting all mention of her on the records of our statutes. Ceres does not appear among the gods of Olympus— only appears in a picture on one of our Treasury notes!

It is our province, as a nation and as individuals, to do *well* whatever we undertake. The genius and skill of our artists and artisans have been universally commended. Our naval architecture is a subject of national pride. Our engineers are doomed to no merely local fame. Our agricultural implements are beyond the reach of competition. Yet, while we may be in advance of the civilized world in many of the useful arts, it is a humiliating fact that we are far in the rear of the best husbandry in Europe; and, notwithstanding here and there an elevated spot, our tendency is still downward. Does not our general system of agriculture foreshadow ultimate decay? If so, is it beyond our constitutional power and duty to provide an incidental remedy?

The prosperity and happiness of a large and populous nation depend:

1. Upon the division of the land into small parcels.

2. Upon the education of the proprietors of the soil.

Our agriculturists, as a whole, instead of seeking a higher cultivation, are extending their boundaries; and their education, on the contrary, is limited to the metes and bounds of their forefathers.

If it be true that the common mode of cultivating the soil in all parts of our country is so defective as to make the soil poorer year by year, it is a most deplorable fact, and a fact of national concern. If we are steadily impairing the natural productiveness of the soil, it is a national waste, compensated only by private robbery. . . .

Grants of lands during and since 1850 have been made to ten States and one Territory, to aid in the construction of more than fifty railroads, of an extent of about nine thousand miles, amounting to 25,403,993 acres. These grants were made on the argument of "prudent proprietorship," and alternate sections were given away to double the price of the remainder. Whether the policy will result in any loss to the Government or not, these States were treated with a liberality they will never forget. As a prudent proprietor, may we not do that which will not only tend to raise the value of all land, whether owned by individuals or by Government, but make agricultural labor more profitable and more desirable as a pursuit in life?

Up to the 30th of June, 1857, we had ungrudgingly donated to different States and Territories sixty-seven million seven hundred and thirty-six thousand five hundred and seventy-two acres of land for schools and universities. No one shall be twitted for such acts by me; but, if the purpose be a noble one as applied to a Territory sparsely populated, it is certainly not less so to States thickly peopled. If such donations are constitutional to inchoate States, can they be unconstitutional when proposed to the Old Dominion, the Empire, Keystone, and Little Rhody? Is there a more urgent demand for such aid in behalf of the people of a Territory free of debt, whose frame of government is supported by the nation, than in behalf of States bearing all the debt and burdens of the national Government, and bending under $245,211,259 of present State indebtedness? Surely the endowment of agricultural colleges ought not to depend upon the resources of States already so oppressively laden, nor upon the come-by-chance charities of individuals, but upon the liberal administration of the Government which has been expressly constituted the trustee of an ample store for the common benefit of all the States?

The executive and legislative precedents which can be arrayed to sustain the principles embodied in this measure are of great weight and authority. . . .

Washington brought the subject of agriculture before Congress in his first message. He thought it a subject within the constitutional jurisdiction, and his experience increased that conviction; for in his last message, December 7, 1796, he recurs to it with elaborate argument. He says:

> It will not be doubted that, with reference either to individual or national welfare, agriculture is of primary importance. In proportion as nations advance in population and other circumstances of maturity, this task becomes more apparent, and renders the cultivation of the soil more and more an object of public patronage. Institutions for promoting it grow up, supported by the public purse; and to what object can it be dedicated with greater propriety?

Thus we have the very germ of the whole project. "The cultivation of the soil," *institutions* "supported by the public purse," he exclaims, "to what object can it be dedicated with greater propriety?" It cannot be doubted that donations of land for agricultural colleges would have received the approval of Washington. . . .

While agriculture has been a neglected field of legislation, it does not now call for the exercise of novel constitutional power. Congress has long asserted the right to dispose of the public lands to establish school funds and universities, and no one now questions the soundness of such a policy. This measure is but an extension of the same principle over a wider field—wider in its applications, but not wider in its amount, for the number of acres now proposed for all the States is scarcely larger than have been donated to individual States. It is general and not local in its reach. If we have the power to make special grants, in particular and individual cases, we certainly have the power, and it would be far more just and expedient to exercise it, in its general application. Pass this measure and we shall have done—

Something to enable the farmer to raise two blades of grass instead of one;

Something for every owner of land;

Something for all who desire to own land;

Something for cheap scientific education;

Something for every man who loves intelligence and not ignorance;

Something to induce the father's sons and daughters to settle and cluster around the old homesteads;

Something to remove the last vestige of pauperism from our land;

Something for peace, good order, and the better support of Christian churches and common schools;

Something to enable sterile railroads to pay dividends;

Something to enable the people to bear the enormous expenditures of the national Government;

Something to check the passion of individuals, and of the nation, for indefinite territorial expansion and ultimate decrepitude;

Something to prevent the dispersion of our poulation, and to concentrate it around the best lands of our country—places hallowed by church spires, and mellowed by all the influences of time—where the consumer will be placed at the door of the producer; and thereby

Something to obtain higher prices for all sorts of agricultural productions; and

Something to increase the loveliness of the American landscape. Scientific culture is the sure precursor of order and beauty. Our esthetic Diedrich Knickerbockers, who have no land, will have a fairer opportunity to become great admirers of land that belongs to others.

Many of our wisest statesmen have denounced our general land system as a prolific source of corruption; but what corruption can flow from endowing agricultural colleges? Here is neither profligacy nor waste, but a measure of justice and beneficence. Without meaning to express my opinion for or against the homestead policy, I ask, in all candor, what man is there in the whole length and breadth of our country, who would not prefer, if he could have his choice, such an education as might be obtained at one of these colleges to a warrant for one hundred and sixty acres of land?

The persuasive arguments of precedents; the example of our worthiest rivals in Europe; the rejuvenation of worn-out lands, which bring forth taxes only; the petitions of farmers everywhere, yearning for "a more excellent way;" philanthropy, supported by our own highest interests—all these considerations impell us for once to do something for agriculture worthy of its national importance.

By the recent statement of the Land Office, we have 1,088,-792,498 acres of land to dispose of; and when this bill shall have passed, there will then remain about one thousand and eighty-three millions of acres. We shall still be the largest landholder in the world, while confessedly we are not the best farmers. Let it never be said we are "the greatest and the meanest of mankind.". . .

JAMES BUCHANAN: VETO MESSAGE

Washington City, February 24, 1859

To the House of Representatives of the United States:
I return with my objections to the House of Representatives, in which it originated, the bill entitled "An act donating public

From Richardson, *Messages and Papers of the Presidents,* vol. V, pp. 543–546, 549–550.

lands to the several States and Territories which may provide colleges for the benefit of agriculture and the mechanic arts," presented to me in the 18th instant.

This bill makes a donation to the several States of 20,000 acres of the public lands for each Senator and Representative in the present Congress, and also an additional donation of 20,000 acres for each additional Representative to which any State may be entitled under the census of 1860.

According to a report from the Interior Department, based upon the present number of Senators and Representatives, the lands given to the States amount to 6,060,000 acres, and their value, at the minimum Government price of $1.25 per acre, to $7,575,000.

The object of this gift, as stated by the bill, is "the endowment, support, and maintenance of at least one college [in each State] where the leading object shall be, without excluding other scientific or classical studies, to teach such branches of learning as are related to agriculture and the mechanic arts, as the legislatures of the States may respectively prescribe, in order to promote the liberal and practical education of the industrial classes in the several pursuits and professions in life."

As there does not appear from the bill to be any beneficiaries in existence to which this endowment can be applied, each State is required "to provide, within five years at least, not less than one college, or the grant to said State shall cease." In that event the "said State shall be bound to pay the United States the amount received of any lands previously sold, and that the title to purchasers under the State shall be valid."

The grant in land itself is confined to such States as have public lands within their limits worth $1.25 per acre in the opinion of the governor. For the remaining States the Secretary of the Interior is directed to issue "land scrip to the amount of their distributive shares in acres under the provisions of this act, said scrip to be sold by said States, and the proceeds thereof applied to the uses and purposes prescribed in this act, and for no other use or purpose whatsoever." The lands are granted and the scrip is to be issued "in sections or subdivisions of sections of not less than one-quarter of a section."

According to an estimate from the Interior Department, the number of acres which will probably be accepted by States having public lands within their own limits will not exceed 580,000 acres (and it may be much less), leaving a balance of 5,480,000 acres to be provided for by scrip. These grants of land and land scrip to each of the thirty-three States are made upon certain conditions, the principal of which is that if the fund shall be lost or diminished on account of unfortunate investments or otherwise the deficiency shall be replaced and made good by the respective States.

I shall now proceed to state my objections to this bill. I deem it to be both inexpedient and unconstitutional.

1. This bill has been passed at a period when we can with great difficulty raise sufficient revenue to sustain the expenses of the Government. Should it become a law the Treasury will be deprived of the whole, or nearly the whole, of our income from the sale of public lands, which for the next fiscal year has been estimated at $5,000,000.

A bare statement of the case will make this evident. The minimum price at which we dispose of our lands is $1.25 per acre. At the present moment, however, the price has been reduced to those who purchase the bounty-land warrants of the old soldiers to 85 cents per acre, and of these warrants there are still outstanding and unlocated, as appears by a report (February 12, 1859) from the General Land Office, the amount of 11,990,391 acres. This has already greatly reduced the current sales by the Government and diminished the revenue from this source. If in addition thirty-three States shall enter the market with their land scrip, the price must be greatly reduced below even 85 cents per acre, as much to the prejudice of the old soldiers who have not already parted with their land warrants as to Government. It is easy to perceive that with this glut of the market Government can sell little or no lands at $1.25 per acre, when the price of bounty-land warrants and scrip shall be reduced to half this sum. This source of revenue will be almost entirely dried up. Under the bill the States may sell their land scrip at any price it may bring. There is no limitation whatever in this respect. Indeed, they must sell for what the scrip will bring, for without this fund they can not proceed to establish their colleges within the five years to which they are limited. It is manifest, there-fore, that to the extent to which this bill will prevent the sale of public lands at $1.25 per acre, to that amount it will have precisely the same effect upon the Treasury as if we should impose a tax to create a loan to endow these State colleges.

Surely the present is the most unpropitious moment which could have been selected for the passage of this bill.

2. Waiving for the present the question of constitutional power, what effect will this bill have on the relations estab-lished between the Federal and State Governments? The Constitution is a grant to Congress of a few enumerated but most important powers, relating chiefly to war, peace, foreign and domestic commerce, negotiation, and other subjects which can be best or alone exercised beneficially by the common Government. All other powers are reserved to the States and to the people. For the efficient and harmonious working of both, it is necessary that their several spheres of action should be kept distinct from each other. This alone can prevent con-flict and mutual injury. Should the time ever arrive when the State governments shall look to the Federal Treasury for the means of supporting themselves and maintaining their systems of education and internal policy, the character of both Gov-ernments will be greatly deteriorated. The representatives of the States and of the people, feeling a more immediate in-

terest in obtaining money to lighten the burdens of their constituents than for the promotion of the more distant objects
intrusted to the Federal Government, will naturally incline to
obtain means from the Federal Government for State purposes.
If a question shall arise between an appropriation of land or
money to carry into effect the objects of the Federal Government and those of the States, their feelings will be enlisted
in favor of the latter. This is human nature; and hence the
necessity of keeping the two Governments entirely distinct.
The preponderance of this home feeling has been manifested
by the passage of the present bill. The establishment of these
colleges has prevailed over the pressing wants of the common
Treasury. No nation ever had such an inheritance as we possess
in the public lands. These ought to be managed with the
utmost care, but at the same time with a liberal spirit toward
actual settlers.

In the first year of a war with a powerful naval nation the
revenue from customs must in a great degree cease. A resort
to loans will then become necessary, and these can always be
obtained, as our fathers obtained them, on advantageous terms
by pledging the public lands as security. In this view of the
subject it would be wiser to grant money to the States for
domestic purposes than to squander away the public lands
and transfer them in large bodies into the hands of speculators.

A successful struggle on the part of the State governments
with the General Government for the public lands would deprive the latter of the means of performing its high duties,
especially at critical and dangerous periods. Besides, it would
operate with equal detriment to the best interests of the States.
It would remove the most wholesome of all restraints on legislative bodies—that of being obliged to raise money by
taxation from their constituents—and would lead to extravagance, if not to corruption. What is obtained easily and without
responsibility will be lavishly expended.

3. This bill, should it become a law, will operate greatly

to the injury of the new States. The progress of settlements and the increase of an industrious population owning an interest in the soil they cultivate are the causes which will build them up into great and flourishing commonwealths. Nothing could be more prejudicial to their interests than for wealthy individuals to acquire large tracts of the public land and hold them for speculative purposes. The low price to which this land scrip will probably be reduced will tempt speculators to buy it in large amounts and locate it on the best lands belonging to the Government. The eventual consequence must be that the men who desire to cultivate the soil will be compelled to purchase these very lands at rates much higher than the price at which they could be obtained from the Government.

4. It is extremely doubtful, to say the least, whether this bill would contribute to the advancement of agriculture and the mechanic arts—objects the dignity and value of which can not be too highly appreciated.

The Federal Government, which makes the donation, has confessedly no constitutional power to follow it into the States and enforce the application of the fund to the intended objects. As donors we shall possess no control over our own gift after it shall have passed from our hands. It is true that the State legislatures are required to stipulate that they will faithfully execute the trust in the manner prescribed by the bill. But should they fail to do this, what would be the consequence? The Federal Government has no power, and ought to have no power, to compel the execution of the trust. It would be in as helpless a condition as if, even in this, the time of great need, we were to demand any portion of the many millions of surplus revenue deposited with the States for safekeeping under the act of 1836.

5. This bill will injuriously interfere with existing colleges in the different States, in many of which agriculture is taught as a science and in all of which it ought to be so taught.

These institutions of learning have grown up with the growth
of the country, under the fostering care of the States and the
munificence of individuals, to meet the advancing demands
for education. They have proved great blessings to the people.
Many, indeed most, of them are poor and sustain themselves
with difficulty. What the effect will be on these institutions of
creating an indefinite number of rival colleges sustained by
the endowment of the Federal Government it is not difficult to
determine. . . .

It has been asserted truly that Congress in numerous instances have granted lands for the purposes of education.
These grants have been chiefly, if not exclusively, made to the
new States as they successively entered the Union, and consisted at the first of one section and afterwards of two sections
of the public land in each township for the use of schools,
as well as of additional sections for a State university. Such
grants are not, in my opinion, a violation of the Constitution.
The United States is a great landed proprietor, and from the
very nature of this relation it is both the right and the duty
of Congress as their trustee to manage these lands as any
other prudent proprietor would manage them for his own
best advantage. Now no consideration could be presented of
a stronger character to induce the American people to brave
the difficulties and hardships of frontier life and to settle upon
these lands and to purchase them at a fair price than to give
to them and to their children an assurance of the means of
education. If any prudent individual had held these lands, he
could not have adopted a wiser course to bring them into
market and enhance their value than to give a portion of
them for the purposes of education. As a mere speculation
he would pursue this course. No person will contend that donations of land to all the States of the Union for the erection
of colleges within the limits of each can be embraced by this
principle. It can not be pretended that an agricultural college
in New York or Virginia would aid the settlement or facilitate

the sale of public lands in Minnesota or California. This can not possibly be embraced within the authority which a prudent proprietor of land would exercise over his own possessions. I purposely avoid any attempt to define what portions of land may be granted, and for what purposes, to improve the value and promote the settlement and sale of the remainder without violating the Constitution. In this case I adopt the rule that "sufficient unto the day is the evil thereof."

JAMES BUCHANAN

JUSTIN SMITH MORRILL:

SPEECH ON THE VETO, 1859

The measure was not introduced here as a party measure, nor was it advocated as a party measure. It has received the cordial support of members of both sides of this House. It fought its way on its own merits. It has been pressed here by petitions and resolutions from the Legislatures of at least thirteen States, and by an indefinite number of memorials from private citizens of the highest character. It is a measure which has been indorsed by agricultural societies and agricultural men throughout the whole country, with unprecedented unanimity. It is a measure dear to the hearts of all farmers, young and old. It would have been approved by all the earlier Presidents, and was especially dear to the heart of Washington, and occupied his last thought. . . .

The President objects to this bill because he wants to keep the State governments and the General Government separate. Well, sir, this measure by no means combines the State gov-

From *Congressional Globe*, 35th Congress, 2nd Session, Part II, p. 1414. The date is February 26, 1859.

ernments and the General Government. It especially leaves
the whole matter to the entire control of the several States
to arrange, manage, and control, as they may see fit. The States
were to be trustees merely for a certain and specific object. . . .

Mr. Speaker, the Constitution gives to Congress the unre-
served and unrestricted power to "dispose of" the public lands;
but the President says this does not grant the power to *give
them away.* Sir, I contend that this provision does give to
Congress the power to dispose of them in any way not prohibited by the Constitution. It is absolute and unqualified. If
there is any limitation in the deeds of cession, which provides
that they shall be disposed of for the common benefit of all
the States, this bill is in strict conformity thereto. Nor does
this bill propose to *give* them away at all. Like a prudent
proprietor, we adopt a policy to increase the value of the whole
landed property of the country. The bill expressly demands
a full and proper consideration. That consideration is, that the
several States shall establish these colleges, "where the leading
object shall be, without excluding other scientific or classical
studies, to teach such branches of learning as are related to
agriculture and the mechanic arts." If this were done, there
can be no doubt the interests of the country, the benefits to
accrue, would be fifty-fold greater than any sum which would
be abstracted from the Treasury. If we cannot give away the
lands we already possess, under what clause of the Constitution are we to pour out millions for the purchase of Cuba, only
for the purpose of giving it back again to the Spanish slave-
holders?

We have heretofore very properly, in our legislation pertaining to new States and Territories, granted one or two sections of land, in each township, for the especial purpose of
establishing schools. This bill is nothing more than a pursuance of the same policy, and was a fit complement of the
system. Many literary universities had already been established
with the approval of James Buchanan, who, with many other dis-

tinguished Democrats, voted for the deaf and dumb school, endowed by Congress, in Kentucky, in 1827. If we can legislate for the deaf and dumb, may we not legislate for those who can hear and speak? If we can legislate for the insane, may we not legislate for the sane? We have granted lands for railroad purposes, for military services and we have granted lands to the several states for the purposes of health; that is, we have granted to the States the swamp and overflowed lands within their limits. Now, sir, if we can grant lands for the promotion of physical health, can we not grant them for the purpose of promoting the moral health and education of the people? We granted seven hundred and fifty thousand acres for the benefit of the Sault St. Marie canal and also other large grants for canals. Well, sir, if we can grant lands for the benefit of commerce, trade, military service, and health, cannot we grant them for other purposes? Cannot we grant them for education, and for the education of the great mass of the country; and a class, too, which has received no special benefit from any act of Congress? . . .

39. Horace Mann: "The Effect of Education on Worldly Fortunes"

The major public efforts for the promotion of education were those of state and local governments rather than of the nation. States north and south gave aid to privately initiated colleges and academies. By the end of the period, seventeen state universities were in operation, and a start had been made in the establishment of agricultural colleges that were to flourish after the final passage of the Morrill Act.

The most celebrated educational achievement of the period

was the establishment in parts of the country of a system of free public schools. In this, the responsibility for support and administration rested mainly with the local government; but state governments took part in the process through laws requiring the establishment of schools, by financial aid through their "common school funds," and sometimes through the guidance and leadership of special state agencies. One such body was the Massachusetts State Board of Education. Its Secretary, Horace Mann, was an active leader of the movement and its indefatigable propagandist; and the Board's Annual Reports from 1837 through 1848 served as vehicles for the expression of his philosophy.

The Report for 1841 contains as one of its headings, "The effect of education upon the worldly fortunes of men." This, Mann hastened to explain, was not the highest view that could be taken of "the beneficent influence of education"; it might, "perhaps, be justly regarded as the lowest."[1] Education as a bulwark of republican government and as a foundation of religion and morality were for him nobler and more congenial themes. Yet few writers have ever insisted more forcefully that intelligence is "a primary ingredient in the wealth of nations." When Mann wrote of the folly of a political economy that leaves out of account "the element of a widespread mental development," he was making a point that struck many present-day economists as a novel one when it was restated a few years ago in a Presidential Address before the American Economic Association.[2]

In addition to their emphasis on the economic consequences of education, the documents below contain Horace Mann's claims for the primacy of Massachusetts Bay and New England and a report on the enforcement of legislation requiring schooling for children employed in factories. Further reference to the latter issue will be made in Documents 40 and 44.

---

[1] *Life and Works of Horace Mann,* 2nd ed. (Boston: Lee & Shepard, 1891), vol. III, p. 92.

[2] Theodore W. Schultz, "Investment in Human Capital," *American Economic Review,* LI (1961), 1–17.

ANNUAL. REPORT FOR 1839

Another subject, respecting which I have sought for information from all authentic sources, and to which I have given especial attention in my circuit through the State, is the observance or non-observance of the law "for the better instruction of youth employed in manufacturing establishments." This law was enacted in April, 1836, and was to take effect on the first day of April, 1837. The substance of its provisions is, that no owner, agent, or superintendent of any manufacturing establishment shall employ any child, under the age of fifteen years, to labor in such establishment, unless such child shall have attended some public or private day school, where instruction is given by a legally qualified teacher, at least three months of the twelve months next preceding any and every year in which such child shall be so employed. The penalty for each violation is fifty dollars. The law has now been in operation sufficiently long to make manifest the intentions of those to whom its provisions apply, and whether those humane provisions are likely to be observed or defeated. From the information obtained, I feel fully authorized to say, that, in the great majority of cases, the law is obeyed. But it is my painful duty also to say, that, in some places, it has been uniformly and systematically disregarded. The law is best observed in the largest manufacturing places. In several of the most extensive manufacturing villages and districts, all practical measures are taken to prevent a single instance of violation. Some establishments have conducted most generously towards the schools; and, in one case (at Waltham), a corporation, besides paying its proportion of taxes for the support of the public schools in the town, has gratuitously erected three

From *Life and Works of Horace Mann*, 2nd ed., vol. III, pp. 4–6.

schoolhouses, the last in 1837, a neat, handsome, modern stone building, two stories in height,—and maintained schools therein, at a charge, in the whole, upon the corporate funds, of a *principal* sum of more than seven thousand dollars. It would be improper for me here to be more particular than to say, that these generous acts have been done by the "*Boston Manufacturing Company;*" though all will regret that the identity of the individual members who have performed these praiseworthy deeds, should be lost in the generality of the corporate name.

Comparatively speaking, there seems to have been far greater disregard of the law by private individuals and by small corporations, especially where the premises are rented from year to year, or from term to term, than by the owners or agencies of large establishments. Private individuals, renting an establishment for one or for a few years,—intending to realize from it what profits they can and then to abandon it, and remove from the neighborhood or town where it is situated,—may be supposed to feel less permanent interest in the condition of the people who are growing up around them; and they are less under the control of public opinion in the vicinity. But, without seeking an explanation of the cause, there cannot be a doubt as to the fact.

It is obvious that the consent of two parties is necessary to the infraction of this law, and to the infliction of this highest species of injustice upon the children whom it was designed to protect. Not only must the employer pursue a course of action by which the godlike powers and capacities of the human soul are wrought into thorough-made products of ignorance and misery and vice with as much certainty and celerity as his raw materials of wool or cotton are wrought into fabrics for the market by his own machinery, but the parent also must be willing to convert the holy relation of parent and child into the unholy one of master and slave, and to sell his child into ransomless bondage for the pittance of money he can earn. Yet, strange to say, there are many parents, not only of our immigrant, but of our native population, so lost to the sacred nature of the relation they sustain towards the children whom they have brought into all the solemn realities of existence, that they go from town to town, seeking opportunities to consign them to unbroken, bodily toil, although it involves the deprivation of all the means of intellectual and moral growth; thus pandering to their own vicious appetites by adopting the most efficient measures to make their offspring as vicious as themselves. . . .

ANNUAL REPORT FOR 1846

The institution of a free-school system on so broad a basis, and of such ample proportions, appears still more remarkable when we consider the period in the world's history at which it was originated, and the fewness and poverty of the people by whom it was maintained. In 1647, the entire population of the colony of Massachusetts Bay is supposed to have amounted only to twenty-one thousand souls. The scattered and feeble settlements were almost buried in the depths of the forest. The external resources of the people were small, their dwellings humble, and their raiment and subsistence scanty and homely. They had no enriching commerce; and the wonderful forces of Nature had not then, as now, become gratuitous producers of every human comfort and luxury. The whole valuation of all the colonial estates, both public and private, would hardly have been equal to the inventory of many a private citizen of the present day. The fierce eye of the savage was nightly seen glaring from the edge of the surrounding wilderness; and no defence or succor, save in their own brave natures, was at hand. Yet it was then, amid all these privations

---

From *Life and Works of Horace Mann*, 2nd ed., vol. IV, pp. 110–112, 114.

and dangers, that the Pilgrim Fathers conceived the magnificent idea, not only of a universal, but of a free education, for the whole people. To find the time and the means to reduce this grand conception to practice, they stinted themselves, amid all their poverty, to a still scantier pittance; amid all their toils, they imposed upon themselves still more burdensome labors; and, amid all their perils, they braved still greater dangers. Two divine ideas filled their great hearts,—their duty to God and to posterity. For the one, they built the church; for the other, they opened the school. Religion and knowledge,—two attributes of the same glorious and eternal truth, and that truth the only one on which immortal or mortal happiness can be securely founded!

It is impossible for us adequately to conceive the boldness of the measure which aimed at universal education through the establishment of free schools. As a fact, it had no precedent in the world's history; and, as a theory, it could have been refuted and silenced by a more formidable array of argument and experience than was ever marshalled against any other institution of human origin. But time has ratified its soundness. Two centuries of successful operation now proclaim it to be as wise as it was courageous, and as beneficent as it was disinterested. Every community in the civilized world awards it the meed of praise; and states at home, and nations abroad, in the order of their intelligence, are copying the bright example. What we call the enlightened nations of Christendom are approaching, by slow degrees, to the moral elevation which our ancestors reached at a single bound; and the tardy convictions of the one have been assimilating, through a period of two centuries, to the intuitions of the other.

Again: the expediency of free schools is sometimes advocated on grounds of political economy. An educated people is always a more industrious and productive people. Knowledge and abundance sustain to each other the relation of cause and effect. Intelligence is a primary ingredient in the wealth of nations. Where this does not stand at the head of the inventory, the items in a nation's valuation will be few, and the sum at the foot of the column insignificant. The moralist, too, takes up the argument of the economist. He demonstrates that vice and crime are not only prodigals and spendthrifts of their own, but defrauders and plunderers of the means of others; that they would seize upon all the gains of honest industry, and exhaust the bounties of Heaven itself, without satiating their rapacity for new means of indulgence; and that often, in the history of the world, whole generations might have been trained to industry and virtue by the wealth which one enemy to his race has destroyed.

And yet, notwithstanding these views have been presented a thousand times with irrefutable logic, and with a divine eloquence of truth which it would seem that nothing but combined stolidity and depravity could resist, there is not at the present time, with the exception of the States of New England and a few small communities elsewhere, a country or a state in Christendom which maintains a system of free schools for the education of its children. Even in the State of New York, with all its noble endowments, the schools are not free. . . .

ANNUAL REPORT FOR 1848

. . . The reason why the mechanical and useful arts,— those arts which have done so much to civilize mankind, and which have given comforts and luxuries to the common laborer of the present day, such as kings and queens could not command three centuries ago,—the reason why these arts made no progress, and until recently, indeed, can hardly be said to have had any thing more than a beginning, is, that the labor

From *Life and Works of Horace Mann,* 2nd ed., vol. IV, pp. 258–260.

of the world was performed by ignorant men. As soon as some degree of intelligence dawned upon the workman, then a corresponding degree of improvement in his work followed. At first, this intelligence was confined to a very small number, and therefore improvements were few; and they followed each other only after long intervals. They uniformly began in the nations and among the classes where there was most intelligence. The middle classes of England, and the people of Holland and Scotland, have done a hundred times more than all the Eastern hemisphere besides. What single improvement in art, or discovery in science, has ever originated in Spain, or throughout the vast empire of the Russias? But just in proportion as intelligence—that is, education—has quickened and stimulated a greater and a greater number of minds, just in the same proportion have inventions and discoveries increased in their wonderfulness, and in the rapidity of their succession. The progression has been rather geometrical than arithmetical. By the laws of Nature, it must be so. If, among ten well-educated children, the chance is that at least one of them will originate some new and useful process in the arts, or will discover some new scientific principle, or some new application of one, then, among a hundred such well-educated children, there is a moral certainty that there will be more than ten such originators or discoverers of new utilities; for the action of the mind is like the action of fire. One billet of wood will hardly burn alone, though dry as suns and northwest winds can make it, and though placed in the range of a current of air; ten such billets will burn well together; but a hundred will create a heat fifty times as intense as ten, will make a current of air to fan their own flame, and consume even greenness itself.

For the creation of wealth, then,—for the existence of a wealthy people and a wealthy nation,—intelligence is the grand condition. The number of improvers will increase as the intellectual constituency, if I may so call it, increases. In former times, and in most parts of the world even at the present day, not one man in a million has ever had such a development of mind as made it possible for him to become a contributor to art or science. Let this development precede, and contributions, numberless, and of inestimable value, will be sure to follow. That political economy, therefore, which busies itself about capital and labor, supply and demand, interest and rents, favorable and unfavorable balances of trade, but leaves out of account the element of a widespread mental development, is nought but stupendous folly. . . .

40. George Wallis: "The Versatility of an Educated People"

The claims of Horace Mann for the economic benefits of education and the retrospective analyses of twentieth-century economists receive significant confirmation in the opinions of British observers who visited the United States in 1853. The British Government sent an official commission to the New York Industrial Exhibition, and the reports of its members were published as Parliamentary Papers. Two of them included comments on American education. The "Special Report of Mr. Dilke" spoke of the great efforts made in every township and declared that "The United States takes rank above all other nations in its exertions for the education of the people."[1]

His colleague, George Wallis, an official of a technical school in Birmingham, relates education directly to economic development. In the selection given below, he attributes the progress of the Northeast, as a Governor of Louisiana had done nearly

---

[1] "Special Report of Mr. Dilke," New York Industrial Exhibition, Great Britain, *Parliamentary Papers*, 1854, p. 85. Dilke also quoted a speech made by Horace Mann.

thirty years before,[2] in considerable part to the public school system. The remarkable growth of American manufactures, he argues, is largely due to "the adaptive versatility of an educated people."

REPORT ON THE NEW YORK
INDUSTRIAL EXHIBITION

The successful application of mechanical means to one manufacture has been, as a matter of course, stimulative of their application to another, however different, and the adaptative versatility of an educated people was never more fully displayed than in the constant effort to supply their greatest want—that of skilled labour—by applications of mechanical powers to that object. Nor can the most superficial observer fail to be impressed with the advantages thus derived from the long and well-directed attention paid to the education of the whole people by the public school systems of the New England States and of the State of Pennsylvania. Here, where sound and systematic education has been longest and, in all probability, most perfectly carried out, the greatest manufacturing developments are to be found, and here it is also where the greatest portion of the skilled workmen of the United States are educated, alike in the simplest elements of knowledge, as in the most skilful application of their ingenuity to the useful arts and the manufacturing industry of their country, and from whence they are spread over the vast territories of the Union, becoming the originators, direc-

From "Special Report of Mr. George Wallis," New York Industrial Exhibition, Great Britain, *Parliamentary Papers*, 1854, pp. 3, 67–68.

[2] H. Johnson, Louisiana *House Journal*, December 13, 1824.

tors, and, ultimately, the proprietors of establishments which would do no discredit to the manufacturing States of Europe.

As there is no apprenticeship system, properly so called, the more useful the youth engaged in any industrial pursuit becomes to his employer, the more profitable it is for himself. Bringing a mind prepared by thorough school discipline, and educated up to a far higher standard than those of a much superior social grade in society in the Old World, the American working boy developes rapidly into the skilled artizan, and having once mastered one part of his business, he is never content until he has mastered all. Doing *one* mechanical operation well, and only that one, does not satisfy him or his employer. He is ambitious to do something more than a set task, and, therefore, he must learn all. The second part of his trade he is allowed to learn as a reward for becoming master of the first, and so on to the end, if he may be said ever to arrive at *that*. The restless activity of mind and body—the anxiety to improve his own department of industry—the facts constantly before him of ingenious men who have solved economic and mechanical problems to their own profit and elevation, are all stimulative and encouraging; and it may be said that there is not a working boy of average ability in the New England States, at least, who has not an idea of some mechanical invention or improvement in manufactures, by which, in good time, he hopes to better his position, or rise to fortune and social distinction. . . .

The compulsory educational clauses adopted in the laws of most of the States, and especially those of New England, by which some three months of every year must be spent at school by the young factory operative under 14 or 15 years of age, secures every child from the cupidity of the parent, or the neglect of the manufacturer; since to profit by the child's labour during *three-fourths* of the year, he or she must be regularly in attendance in some public or private school conducted by some authorised teacher during the other fourth.

This lays the foundation for that wide-spread intelligence which prevails amongst the factory operatives of the United States, and though at first sight the manufacturer may appear to be restricted in the free use of the labour offered to him, the system re-acts to the permanent advantage of both employer and employed.

The skill of hand which comes of experience is, notwithstanding present defects, rapidly following the perceptive power so keenly awakened by early intellectual training. Quickly learning from the skilful European artizans thrown amongst them by emigration, or imported as instructors, with minds, as already stated, prepared by sound practical education, the Americans have laid the foundation of a wide-spread system of manufacturing operations, the influence of which cannot be calculated upon, and are daily improving upon the lessons obtained from their older and more experienced compeers of Europe.

Commercially, advantages of no ordinary kind are presented to the manufacturing States of the American Union. The immense development of its resources in the West, the demands of a population increasing daily by emigration from Europe, as also by the results of a healthy natural process of inter-emigration, which tends to spread over an enlarged surface the population of the Atlantic States; the facilities of communication by lakes, rivers, and railways; and the cultivation of European tastes, and consequently of European wants; all tend to the encouragement of those arts and manufactures which it is the interest of the citizens of the older States to cultivate, and in which they have so far succeeded that their markets may be said to be secured to them as much as manufacturers, as they have hitherto been, and will doubtless continue to be, as merchants. For whether the supply is derived from the home or foreign manufacturer, the demand cannot fail to be greater than the industry of both can supply. This once fairly recognised, those jealousies which have ever tended to retard the progress of nations in the peaceful arts, will be no longer suffered to interfere by taking the form of restrictions on commerce and the free intercourse of peoples.

The extent to which the people of the United States have as yet succeeded in manufactures may be attributed to indomitable energy and an educated intelligence, as also to the ready welcome accorded to the skilled workmen of Europe, rather than to any peculiar native advantages; since these latter have only developed themselves as manufacturing skill and industry have progressed. Only one obstacle of any importance stands in the way of constant advance towards greater perfection, and that is the conviction that perfection is already attained. This opinion, which prevails to a larger extent than it would be worth noting here, is unworthy of that intelligence which has overcome so many difficulties, and which can only be prevented from achieving all it aspires to, by a vain-glorious conviction that it has nothing more to do.

In concluding this report I cannot do so without expressing my obligations, as an individual member of the Commission, for the courtesy, attention, and ever-ready kindness with which all my inquiries were responded to by all classes of Americans with whom my duties brought me in contact in the United States.

I have, &c.

(Signed)   GEORGE WALLIS

Society of Arts and Government School of Art
Birmingham, December 31st, 1853

PART EIGHT

THE UTILIZATION

OF THE WORKING FORCE

SLAVERY

41. Georgia: The Slave Code, 1860

The institution of Negro slavery provided the social structure for a large part of the country and the economic basis for the production of its leading exports. Its bearing on the development, or nondevelopment, of human capacities is an obvious one; its political consequences were even more conspicuous. At the close of our period the tensions between free and slave states broke out in the Civil War; and of that conflict the most definite outcome, aside from the preservation of the union, was the emancipation of the slaves. A century later, no one needs a reminder of the degree to which the heritage of slavery continues to affect American life and politics.

Yet in spite of all this, the issue of slavery provides surprisingly little documentation of direct use for a volume on the relation between government and the economy. Federal decisions during the period, as subsequent selections will show, dealt with the periphery rather than the core of the system.

Within the states, slavery was treated largely as the private business of the individual owner. Under the protection of the legal system, the planter was free to manage his working force, like his other property, at his own discretion, subject to a minimum of governmental control. These elements of protection and control were embodied in the "slave codes" of the several states. Their provisions are not to be read as a complete description of life under slavery. Precisely because the plantation was so much a private affair, neither the harshest nor the more humanitarian clauses were universally applied in practice. What the codes do represent are the underlying and little-debated assumptions regarding the nature of the system and the limits of state responsibility.

The selection below gives the principal features of the slave code of the state of Georgia. It is taken from the laws in effect at the outbreak of the Civil War, but it had remained in force without major change throughout the history of the state.[1] A provision against teaching slaves to read or write, sometimes thought of as a countermeasure against the propaganda of the Abolitionists, was already included in a colonial act of 1770; and the preamble to the same measure could still have served to express the principal purposes of the code of 1860:

> Whereas from the increasing number of slaves in this province, it is necessary as well to make proper regulations for the future ordering and governing such slaves, and to ascertain and prescribe the punishment of crimes by them committed, as to settle and limit, by positive laws, the extent of the power of the owners of such slaves over them so that they may be kept in due subjection and obedience, and owners or persons having the care and management of such slaves, may be restrained from exercising unnecessary rigour or wanton cruelty over them.[2]

---

[1] Milton S. Heath, *Constructive Liberalism* (Cambridge: Harvard University Press, 1954), pp. 350–356. In this book, devoted to the relations between the state government and the economy, Professor Heath finds it necessary to devote only these seven pages to the question of slavery.

[2] Oliver H. Prince, *Digest of the Laws of the State of Georgia* (Milledgeville: Grantland & Orme, 1822), pp. 446, 455. The date is May 10, 1770.

OF SLAVES

§ 1599. A slave is one over whose person, liberty, labor and property another has legal control.

§ 1600. All negroes and mulattoes are deemed, and are hereby declared to be *"prima facie"* slaves, and it rests upon those alleging freedom to prove it.

§ 1601. A mulatto is one in whose veins there is at least one-eighth of negro blood.

§ 1602. All slaves are chattels personal, and to be governed by the same laws, except in cases expressly provided by statute, or where the nature of the property requires a modification of the ordinary rule.

§ 1603. The laws of nature guarantee to every man the right to his life and his limbs, unless forfeited for crime. The state of slavery debars no one of this right.

§ 1604. While the slave is under the dominion of his master, third persons have no right of dominion over him, farther than the laws give such right for police purposes.

§ 1605. A slave cannot acquire or hold property. All his acquisitions belong to his master. Gifts to him accompanied by delivery, accrue to the benefit of the master; without delivery they cannot be enforced by law.

§ 1606. All property held by a slave, with the consent of the master, is subject to the will of the master at any time.

§ 1607. The children of all female slaves shall follow the condition of their mother, and shall belong to the person holding title to the mother at the time of their birth. If there be several estates in the mother, the same shall attach to the offspring.

§ 1608. A free person of color, over twenty years of age,

From R. H. Clark, T. R. R. Cobb, and D. Irwin, *The Code of the State of Georgia* (Atlanta: John H. Seals, 1861), pp. 319–320, 367–371, 876–877, 266–277.

may voluntarily sell him or herself into slavery. In all such cases the sale must be made openly at a regular term of the Inferior Court of the county, when the Justices of said court shall privately examine such free persons of color to satisfy themselves of his or her free consent. A record shall be made of such sale in the minutes of said term, and also in the book of registry of free persons of color in said county.

§ 1609. Slaves may be brought into this State from any other slaveholding State of this Confederacy; but no negroes, or other slaves, shall be imported into this State either as slaves or apprentices, from their native land, or any foreign country; and all such negroes, so illegally imported into this State and placed under the control of the Executive of this State, shall be sold by his order under such regulations as he may prescribe; one-fourth of the proceeds of such sale shall be given to the person or persons instrumental in causing the said negroes to be seized under the Acts of Congress, and the remainder shall be paid into the treasury of this State.

§ 1610. If prior to said sale the American Colonization Society shall voluntarily propose to take possession of such negroes, and at their own expense colonize the same in Africa, the Governor is authorized to deliver the same to them. . . .

OF THE RELATIVE DUTIES OF MASTER AND SLAVE

§ 1849. The master is entitled to the time, labor and services of the slave, and to a prompt obedience to all his lawful commands. The master may enforce his rights by corporal punishment, not extending to life or limb or cruel treatment.

§ 1850. Cruel treatment may consist of withholding necessary food or clothing from the slave, inflicting cruel punishment or doing any act, the necessary consequence of which is to impair the health or endanger the life or limb of the slave.

§ 1851. The master is bound to treat his slave with humanity, to furnish him a sufficiency of nutritious and healthy food and proper clothing, to provide him lodging and fuel, to furnish him medical attendance and nursing during sickness, and to provide for all his necessary wants when infirmity or old age renders him incapable of service.

§ 1852. It is the duty of the Inferior Court in every county on receiving information, on oath, that any infirm slave is suffering from the neglect of the owner, to investigate as to the fact, and render such relief to such slave as his condition may require.

§ 1853. The said court shall cite the owner or overseer of such slave, if resident in the county, to show cause why a *fi.fa.* should not issue against him for the amount so expended by the court from the county funds, and if no sufficient cause is shown, may cause the same to be issued. If the owner or overseer does not reside in the county, the said court may sue for and recover the amount so expended in any court having jurisdiction.

§ 1854. The LORD's day—called Sunday—is a day of rest of Divine appointment. No master or hirer shall employ any slave in any work or labor on that day—work of absolute necessity and the necessary occasions of the family only excepted. Any master, overseer, or employer, violating this provision of this Code, shall forfeit for each violation the sum of one hundred dollars, to be recovered in the name of the Inferior Court—one half to be paid to the informer, and the other half to the Educational Fund of the county.

§ 1855. The owner should keep his slave on his own premises, or within his control. He must not permit him to labor or transact business for himself, except during holidays, or upon his own premises. Nor shall any slave be permitted to hire or rent any house, room, store or land, on his own account or that of another slave.

§ 1856. Slaves shall not be permitted to traffic on their own account, except in articles of their own manufacture, or agricultural products of their own raising, or poultry raised by their master's permission, or articles of the like character usually permitted to slaves. And even in these articles a traffic by and with the slave is prohibited, except by the written permission of the master specifying the particular articles to be sold.

§ 1857. Slaves shall not be employed in any apothecary shop or drug store in putting up or dispensing, purchasing or selling medicines of any description, nor where they can, by reason of their employment, have access unaccompanied by a white person, to poisonous drugs. For every violation of this clause, the master allowing it, and the employer consenting to it, shall forfeit the sum of one hundred dollars, to be recovered and paid— one half to the informer and the other half to the Educational Fund of the county.

§ 1858. The relation of master and slave, in an especial manner and to the fullest extent, authorizes and justifies the mutual protection of each other.

§ 1859. A master convicted twice, criminally, of cruel treatment to his slave, shall on the second conviction be declared by the Superior Court incapable of holding title to slave property within this State. And the same court shall appoint a receiver to take possession of, and sell under its order, all the slaves then belonging to such master, for his benefit. Any conveyance of slave property thereafter to such person shall be null and void, except so far as to convey the title to the informer, who may sue for and recover the same. . . .

OF THE RIGHTS AND LIABILITIES OF THE MASTER

TO THIRD PERSONS

§ 1860. Masters are bound by all the acts of their slaves done by their command, and also by their transactions and dealings in respect to the business in which they are employed, and also by all transactions which by receiving the profits the master has tacitly ratified.

§ 1861. The master may constitute his slave his agent, and in such case is bound by his acts, as of any other agent. A presumption of agency arises in all matters where the slave has acted without complaint by the master.

§ 1862. During the usual hours of labor the master or employer is presumed to be cognizant of the business of the slave, and in such business he is presumed to be acting under the master's or employer's command. On Sabbaths, holidays, or during the hours of rest, no such presumption arises.

§ 1863. The master is responsible for all damages arising from the negligence of his slave while engaged in his business.

§ 1864. Except so far as authorized by the patrol and police regulations of this State, and is necessary for the preservation of public order, third persons have no right to interfere with, control, coerce or correct a slave, and for all such acts the master may recover damages.

§ 1865. Any person harboring or concealing a runaway or fugitive slave, shall be liable to the master in damages, and the jury in every such case shall give exemplary damages, according to the circumstances of each case. If the person harboring or concealing is a free person of color the owner shall have his remedy against the guardian, and for the payment of the recovery such free person of color shall be hired out as prescribed for other debts. . . .

§ 1867. Every master or employer having on a plantation more than ten slaves, over the age of sixteen years, shall have a white man as overseer, manager or superintendent, residing on or near said plantation. For a violation of this clause such master or employer shall forfeit the sum of one hundred dollars, one-half to be paid to the informer. . . .

§ 1870. The master shall not furnish to his slave any poisonous drug or medicine, or spirituous liquors, except as administered medicinally or used in his presence. And any person whose slave or other property has been injured by such poison or liquors received from the slave of another having possession of the same by his master's consent, shall recover from such master the full amount of the damage so sustained and the reasonable expense of his litigation.

§ 1871. No slave shall keep any fire-arms in his own possession, nor carry or make use of them or any weapon of offence, except upon the plantation of the master or employer, or accompanied by a white person at least sixteen years of age; and any white person finding a slave violating this section may seize such weapons, and having notified the owner or employer of the slave of the fact, and the time of his application, he may apply to a Justice of the Peace of the district to hear the facts upon his own affidavit and the testimony of others, and to grant a certificate of forfeiture declaring the said weapons to belong to such informer. . . .

OFFENSES RELATIVE TO SLAVES

§ 4488. Sec. II. Any person who shall remove or carry, or cause to be removed or carried away out of this State, or any county thereof, any slave being the property of another person, without the consent of the owner or other person having authority to give such consent, either with or without any intention or design on the part of the offender to sell or otherwise appropriate the said slave to his own use; or shall, by bribery, promises of freedom, or any other enticement, induce any slave in this State to leave the services of his owner, or who shall attempt, by any of these means, to induce the slave of another to run away or leave the service of his owner, such person so offending shall be guilty of a misdemeanor, and be punished by imprisonment in the penitentiary not less than seven nor more than ten years.

§ 4489. Sec. III. Any person, except the owner, overseer, or employer of a slave, who shall beat, whip, or wound such slave; or any person who shall beat, whip, or wound a free person of color, without sufficient cause or provocation being first given by such slave or free person of color, such person so offending may be indicted for a misdemeanor, and, on conviction, shall be punished by fine or imprisonment in the common jail of the county, or both, at the discretion of the court; and the owner of such slave, or guardian of such free person of color, may, notwithstanding such conviction, recover in a civil suit damage for the injury done to such slave or free person of color.

§ 4490. Sec. IV. Any owner, overseer, or employer of a slave or slaves, who shall cruelly treat such slave or slaves, by unnecessary and excessive whipping, beating, cutting or wounding, or by cruelly and unnecessarily tearing or biting with dogs, by withholding proper food and sustenance, by requiring greater labor from such slave or slaves than he, she or they are able to perform, or by not affording proper clothing, or cause or permit the same to be done; every such owner, overseer, or employer, shall be guilty of a misdemeanor, and, on conviction, shall be punished by fine or imprisonment in the common jail of the county, or both, at the discretion of the court. On second conviction, such person shall be declared incapable of holding slave property in the State. See section 1859. . . .

POLICE REGULATIONS

§ 1369. No congregation or company of slaves, exceeding seven males in number, shall, under any pretence, except for Divine worship, assemble themselves outside of any incorporated town, and then they must be under the control and presence of as many as five citizens of the neighborhood, except slaves who may assemble on their masters' premises when he or his overseer is present. Other slaves, by their masters' permission in writing, may also join in such assemblies.

§ 1370. Every Justice of the Peace, upon his knowledge or

information from others, may go in person, or by warrant, directed to any officer or private person, or both, and command the assistance of other persons to disperse any assembly of negroes which may disturb, endanger the safety, or excite the apprehension of the community. Every negro taken at such assemblages may, by special order of said Justices, be corrected, without trial, by receiving, on the bare back, not more than twenty lashes, with the instrument allowed to be used by the patrols, and in the same manner. . . .

§ 1374. Any person may take up any negroes that shall be found out of the plantation or place where they belong, or incorporated town where they reside, acting unlawfully, or under suspicious circumstances, and if found with an offensive weapon shall take the same away, and if the negro is insolent, or refuses to answer, may whip said negro as the patrol may.

§ 1375. If any master, overseer, or employer shall permit his slave to carry arms contrary to law, or shall suffer any illegal public meeting, or unlawful feasting of slaves, not his own, without the permission of their owners, or under his charge, on his plantation, or other home, he shall forfeit for each offence five hundred dollars, one half to the informer the other half to the Educational Fund of the county.

§ 1376. It shall be unlawful for any church, society, or other body, or any persons to grant any license or other authority to any slave or free person of color to preach, or exhort, or otherwise officiate in church matters.

42. The Constitutional Safeguards of Slavery

John C. Calhoun, the great leader of the proslavery forces, and William Lloyd Garrison, the great leader of the abolitionists, were in full agreement on one point. That is that the Constitution provided guarantees for the protection of slavery. In an Address to the Friends of Freedom and Emancipation, the Garrisonian wing of the anti-slavery movement made the following statement:

> To the argument that the words "slaves" and "slaveholders" are not to be found in the Constitution, and therefore that it was never intended to give any protection or countenance to the slave system, it is sufficient to reply, that though no such words are contained in that instrument, other words were used, intelligently and specifically, *to meet the necessities of slavery.*[1]

From this premise the two leaders drew opposite conclusions. Garrison believed that the North should repudiate this covenant with sin and withdraw from the Union. Calhoun, who regarded abolitionism as a mortal disease threatening the life of the nation, insisted that the constitutional guarantees of slavery should be maintained in full force and that the interests of the slaveholding states, which were now in a permanent minority, should be given additional protection.

The Constitution's recognition of slavery and the slave question was in three parts: the familiar compromise under which slaves were counted on a three-fifths ratio for representation and direct taxation; the obligation to return fugitive slaves; and the provision that the importation of slaves from abroad could not be prohibited for the next twenty years.[2] The maritime slave trade was prohibited with little opposition just as soon as the Constitution permitted, though there was later agitation in some parts of the South for its revival. The fugitive slave clause was a recurring subject of controversy. Throughout the period, however, the major decisions made by the federal government concerning slavery dealt with the question of its extension to new areas. The first of these was taken even before the framing of the Constitution when the Ordinance of 1787 prohibited slavery in the Northwest Territory. The Com-

---

[1] *William Lloyd Garrison, 1805–1879: The Story of His Life Told by His Children* (New York: The Century Co., 1889), vol. III, pp. 107–108.

[2] See Document 43 below.

promise of 1820 provided for the admission of Missouri as a slave state but on condition that slavery should not be allowed in the rest of the Louisiana Purchase north of 36° 30′, the latitude of Missouri's southern border. The annexation of Texas, on the other hand, added to the slave area; and the proposed purchase of Cuba, referred to in the headnote to Document 13, would have resulted in its further extension.

The selections from Calhoun are taken from his speeches in the debate over the bill to admit Oregon to the Union as a free state. In these, he expresses his indignation over the failure of the North to carry out in good faith the "solemn guaranty" of the Constitution for the return of fugitive slaves. On the extension of slavery he takes an uncompromising position. All restrictions on its spread, from the Ordinance of 1787 on, have been misguided. The territories belong to the southern states as much as to the northern, and the North with its numerical majority has no right to "exclude the South" from any of them. Yet, somewhat unexpectedly, he also attempts to assure the northerners that slavery is not in any case likely to establish itself much to the north of the line of the Missouri Compromise.

The selections from Garrison come from the resolutions he drafted for adoption by the anti-slavery societies. The most famous of these, which used the words of the prophet Isaiah to describe the Union as "a covenant with death and an agreement with hell," became the masthead of Garrison's abolitionist paper, the *Liberator*. The other resolutions emphasize the repugnance to the return of runaway slaves as a basis of abolitionist feeling. When in the next decade Garrison made the gesture of burning the Constitution in a public meeting, he burned with it a copy of the strengthened Fugitive Slave Act of 1850 and of the order by a Boston judge for the imprisonment of a runaway Negro.[3]

The fugitive slave issue could hardly have had a major effect on the economics of slavery, but the selections suggest that it did much to intensify the dissension between North and South.

---

[3] *William Lloyd Garrison*, vol. III, p. 412; July 4, 1854.

JOHN C. CALHOUN: "A SOLEMN GUARANTY"

SPEECH ON THE OREGON BILL, JUNE 27, 1848

There is a very striking difference between the position on which the slaveholding and non-slaveholding States stand, in reference to the subject under consideration. The former desire no action of the Government; demand no law to give them any advantage in the territory about to be established; are willing to leave it, and other territories belonging to the United States, open to all their citizens, so long as they continue to be territories,—and when they cease to be so, to leave it to their inhabitants to form such governments as may suit them, without restriction or condition,—except that imposed by the constitution, as a prerequisite for admission into the Union. In short, they are willing to leave the whole subject where the constitution and the great and fundamental principles of self-government place it. On the contrary, the non-slaveholding States, instead of being willing to leave it on this broad and equal foundation, demand the interposition of the Government, and the passage of an act to prevent the citizens of the slaveholding States from emigrating with their property into the territory, in order to give their citizens and those they may permit, the exclusive right of settling it, while it remains in that condition, preparatory to subjecting it to like restrictions and conditions when it becomes a State. The 12th section of this bill is intended to assert and maintain this demand of the non-slaveholding States, while it remains a territory. . . .

The first question which offers itself for consideration is— Have the Northern States the power which they claim, to

From Richard K. Crallé, ed., *The Works of John C. Calhoun* (New York: D. Appleton & Co., 1854), vol. IV, pp. 479–483, 504–506, 528–529.

prevent the Southern people from emigrating freely, with their property, into territories belonging to the United States, and to monopolize them for their exclusive benefit? . . .

I ask, at the outset, where is the power to be found. Not, certainly in the relation in which the Northern and Southern States stand to each other. They are the constituent parts or members of a common Federal Union; and, as such, are equals in all respects, both in dignity and rights, as is declared by all writers on governments founded on such union, and as may be inferred from arguments deduced from their nature and character. Instead, then, of affording any countenance or authority in favor of the power, the relation in which they stand to each other furnishes a strong presumption against it. Nor can it be found in the fact that the South holds property in slaves. That, too, fairly considered, instead of affording any authority for the power, furnishes a strong presumption against it. Slavery existed in the South when the constitution was framed, fully to the extent, in proportion to the population, that it does at this time. It is the only property recognized by it; the only one that entered into its formation as a political element, both in the adjustment of the relative weight of the States in the Government, and the apportionment of direct taxes; and the only one that is put under the express guaranty of the constitution. It is well known to all conversant with the history of the formation and adoption of the constitution, that the South was very jealous in reference to this property; that it constituted one of the difficulties both to its formation and adoption; and that it would not have assented to either, had the convention refused to allow to it its due weight in the Government, or to place it under the guaranty of the constitution. Nor can it be found in the way that the territories have been acquired. I will not go into particulars, in this respect, at this stage of the discussion. Suffice it to say, the whole was acquired either by purchase, out of the common funds of all the States,—the South as well as the North,—or by arms and mutual sacrifice of men and money;—which, instead of giving any countenance in favor of the power claimed by the North, on every principle of right and justice, furnishes strong additional presumption against it.

But, if it cannot be found in either,—if it exists at all,—the power must be looked for in the constitutional compact, which binds these States together in a Federal Union; and I now ask, can it be found there? Does that instrument contain any provision which gives the North the power to exclude the South from a free admission into the territories of the United States with its peculiar property, and to monopolize them for its own exclusive use? . . .

How can the question be settled? It can, in my opinion, be finally and permanently adjusted but one way,—and that is on the high principles of justice and constitution. Fear not to leave it to them. The less you do the better. If the North and South cannot stand together on their broad and solid foundation, there is none other on which they can. If the obligations of the constitution and justice be too feeble to command the respect of the North, how can the South expect that she will regard the far more feeble obligations of an act of Congress? Nor should the North fear that, by leaving it where justice and the constitution leave it, she would be excluded from her full share of the territories. In my opinion, if it be left there, climate, soil, and other circumstances would fix the line between the slave-holding and non-slaveholding States in about 36° 30′. It may zigzag a little, to accommodate itself to circumstances—sometimes passing to the north, and at others passing to the south of it; but that would matter little, and would be more satisfactory to all, and tend less to alienation between the two great sections, than a rigid, straight, artificial line, prescribed by an act of Congress.

And here, let me say to Senators from the North;—you make a great mistake in supposing that the portion which might fall to the south of whatever line might be drawn, if left to soil, and climate, and circumstances to determine, would be closed to the white labor of the North, because it could not mingle with slave labor without degradation. The fact is not so. There is no part of the world where agricultural, mechanical, and other descriptions of labor are more respected than in the South, with the exception of two descriptions of employment—that of menial and body servants. No Southern man—not the poorest or the lowest—will, under any circumstance, submit to perform either of them. He has too much pride for that, and I rejoice that he has. They are unsuited to the spirit of a freeman. But the man who would spurn them feels not the least degradation to work in the same field with his slave; or to be employed to work with them in the same field or in any mechanical operation; and, when so employed, they claim the right—and are admitted, in the country portion of the South—of sitting at the table of their employers. Can as much, on the score of equality, be said of the North? With us the two great divisions of society are not the rich and poor, but white and black; and all the former, the poor as well as the rich, belong to the upper class, and are respected and treated as equals, if honest and industrious; and hence have a position and pride of character of which neither poverty nor misfortune can deprive them.

SPEECH ON AN AMENDMENT TO THE OREGON BILL,

AUGUST 12, 1849

It is not only through Congress, but also through the legislation of the Northern States, and the acts of their public functionaries, that we have been assailed. It is well known, that one of the strong objections which the South had to entering into a more intimate union with the North, was the danger to which we would be thereby exposed in reference to our slaves. To guard against it, and to reconcile us to the constitution, the Northern States entered into a solemn guaranty, to deliver up fugitive slaves on the demand of their owners. Instead of complying with this solemn stipulation, by passing laws to carry it into execution, and making it the duty of their public functionaries and citizens to co-operate in seizing and delivering them up, as they were in duty bound to do, there is scarcely a single Northern State that has not passed laws, which, in effect, have annulled the stipulation. They, indeed, have practically expunged it from the constitution. And we on our part have permitted this flagrant violation of the constitution and our rights under it to be perpetrated without effort to resist, rather than party associations should be disturbed. They have gone further. They have permitted societies to be organized, not only to assault and disturb the relation between master and slave, but to seduce them from their masters, and pass them secretly and rapidly into Canada, and there to place them beyond the reach of recovery, and the stipulations of the constitution. Such outrages would, between independent States, be sufficient cause to justify war; and will, if we permit them to be continued, end in abolitionism, by rendering slave property worthless.

WILLIAM LLOYD GARRISON:

"AN AGREEMENT WITH HELL"

RESOLUTIONS PREPARED FOR ESSEX COUNTY
ANTI-SLAVERY SOCIETY, FEBRUARY 1842

"WHEREAS, the existence of slavery is incompatible with the enjoyment of liberty in any country;

From *William Lloyd Garrison*, vol. III, pp. 58–60, 88, 96. The case cited in the 1842 resolutions is Prigg *v.* Commonwealth of Pennsylvania, 16 Peters, 539, 1842, in which the Supreme Court held that obligations under the federal fugitive slave law took precedence over state legislation.

"And WHEREAS, it is morally and politically impossible for a just or equal union to exist between Liberty and Slavery;

"And WHEREAS, in the adoption of the American Constitution and in the formation of the Federal Government, a guilty and fatal compromise was made between the North and the South, by which slavery has been nourished, protected, and enlarged up to the present hour, to the impoverishment and disgrace of the nation, the sacrifice of civil and religious freedom, and the crucifixion of humanity;

"And WHEREAS, the South makes even moral opposition to her slave system a heinous crime, and avows her determination to perpetuate that system at all hazards, and under all circumstances; . . .

"And WHEREAS, by a recent decision of the Supreme Court of the United States, the right of trial by jury is denied to such of the people of the free States as shall be claimed as goods and chattels by Southern taskmasters, and slavery is declared to be the supreme law of the land; from which decision there is no appeal to any higher judicatory, except to the people on the ground of revolutionary necessity;

"And WHEREAS, to reverence justice, to cherish liberty, and to promote righteousness, are the primary duties of every people, from the performance of which they cannot innocently escape by any compact or form of government; therefore,

"1. *Resolved,* That the consequences of doing right must ever be more safe and beneficial than those of doing wrong; and that the worst thing Liberty can do is to unite with Slavery, and the best thing is to withdraw from the embraces of the monster.

"2. *Resolved,* That the American Union is, and ever has been since the adoption of the Constitution, a rope of sand (so far as the North is concerned), and a concentration of the physical force of the nation to destroy liberty and to uphold slavery.

"3. *Resolved,* That the safety, prosperity, and perpetuity of the non-slaveholding States require that their connexion be immediately dissolved with the slave States in form, as it is now in fact."

RESOLUTION ADOPTED BY MASSACHUSETTS
ANTI-SLAVERY SOCIETY, JANUARY 1844

Resolved, That the compact which exists between the North and the South is "a covenant with death and an agreement with hell"—involving both parties in atrocious criminality—and should be immediately annulled.

RESOLUTION PREPARED FOR MASSACHUSETTS
ANTI-SLAVERY SOCIETY, JANUARY 1844

. . . The ballot-box is not an anti-slavery, but a pro-slavery argument, so long as it is surrounded by the U.S. Constitution, which forbids all approach to it except on condition that the voter shall surrender fugitive slaves—suppress negro insurrections—sustain a piratical representation in Congress, and regard man-stealers as equally eligible with the truest friends of human freedom and equality to any or all offices under the United States Government.

43. Abraham Lincoln: The Territories as Homes "For Free White People"

The extension of slavery was again a bitterly contested issue in the 1850's. The Kansas-Nebraska Act of 1854, introduced by Senator Stephen Douglas of Illinois, set aside the Missouri

Compromise and left the decision on slavery to the inhabitants
of the territories in the name of "popular" or "squatter sovereignty." Three years later, in the Dred Scott case, the Supreme
Court in effect adopted Senator Calhoun's position and held
that Congress had never had the right to prevent a slaveholder
from taking his property into the territories.

Abraham Lincoln's position was stated in the speeches
quoted below, one of which formed part of the historic debate
with Senator Douglas. The Republican Party, says Lincoln,
insists that slavery be "treated as a wrong" and contained
firmly within its present boundaries. This will tend to place
the institution "in the course of ultimate extinction" and on its
way to a "peaceful end" at some undetermined time. Unlike
both Calhoun and Garrison, Lincoln argues that the framers
of the Constitution had this in mind. On the other hand, he
acknowledges, though with distaste, that the people of the
South are constitutionally "entitled to a congressional fugitive-
slave law,"[1] and he is as explicit as Calhoun in declaring that
the federal government has no power "to disturb slavery in the
States where it exists."

Lincoln differed from Calhoun on a point of practical consequences. The latter had thought that plantation slavery was
unlikely to flourish in much of the area north of the line of
the Missouri Compromise. Lincoln on the other hand argues
that climate will not "keep slavery out of these Territories,"
and that legislation is needed in order to make them available
as homes for "free white people," Americans and immigrants.
Calhoun's point was stated more forcefully in 1860 by David
Cristy in the pro-slavery tract, *Cotton is King!* Since "white
free labor is doubly productive over slave labor in grain-grow-
ing," Kansas and Nebraska would probably be settled by free
farmers. They would, however, contribute to the strength of
the plantation system by growing food for the South; and
slavery would not be overthrown because neither the Northeast nor the Middle West could risk the disruption of the great

---

[1] John G. Nicolay and John Hay, *Abraham Lincoln: Complete Works*,
2nd ed. (New York: The Century Co., 1915), vol. I, pp. 509, 512.

system of economic exchanges that rested on the export of cotton.[2] In retrospect, there can be little doubt that Calhoun and Cristy had a more realistic view of the economic prospects of Kansas and Nebraska than that expressed by Lincoln; as grain states they would hardly have provided fertile ground for the plantation. Cristy's political prediction, however, would soon be confuted by the great events of War and Emancipation.

SPEECH AT PEORIA, ILLINOIS

Let me here drop the main argument, to notice what I consider rather an inferior matter. It is argued that slavery will not go to Kansas and Nebraska, in any event. This is a palliation—a lullaby. I have some hope that it will not; but let us not be too confident. As to climate, a glance at the map shows that there are five slave states—Delaware, Maryland, Virginia, Kentucky, and Missouri—and also the District of Columbia, all north of the Missouri compromise line. The census returns of 1850 show that, within these, there are 867,276 slaves, being more than one fourth of all the slaves in the nation.

It is not climate, then, that will keep slavery out of these Territories. Is there anything in the peculiar nature of the country? Missouri adjoins these Territories by her entire

From *Abraham Lincoln: Complete Works*, vol. I, pp. 192, 197, 204. The date is October 16, 1854.

[2] David Cristy, *Cotton is King, or Slavery in the Light of Political Economy*, 3rd ed., reprinted in E. N. Elliott, *Cotton is King and Pro-Slavery Arguments* (Augusta, Ga.: Pritchard, Abbot & Loomis, 1860), pp. 123–127, 219–221. Cristy's argument on "the energizing influence" of slavery and the cotton trade might be compared with the passages indexed under "Cotton—as Expansive Force" in Douglass C. North, *Economic Growth in the United States* (Englewood Cliffs, N. J.: Prentice-Hall, 1961).

western boundary, and slavery is already within every one of her western counties. I have even heard it said that there are more slaves in proportion to whites in the northwestern county of Missouri, than within any county in the State. Slavery pressed entirely up to the old western boundary of the State, and when rather recently a part of that boundary at the northwest was moved out a little farther west, slavery followed on quite up to the new line. Now when the restriction is removed, what is to prevent it from going still farther? Climate will not, no peculiarity of the country will, nothing in nature will. Will the disposition of the people prevent it? Those nearest the scene are all in favor of the extension. The Yankees who are opposed to it may be most numerous; but, in military phrase, the battle-field is too far from their base of operations. . . .

Whether slavery shall go into Nebraska, or other new Territories, is not a matter of exclusive concern to the people who may go there. The whole nation is interested that the best use shall be made of these Territories. We want them for homes of free white people. This they cannot be, to any considerable extent, if slavery shall be planted within them. Slave States are places for poor white people to remove from, not to remove to. New free States are the places for poor people to go to, and better their condition. For this use the nation needs these Territories. . . .

If the ordinance of '87 did not keep slavery out of the Northwest Territory, how happens it that the northwest shore of the Ohio River is entirely free from it, while the southeast shore, less than a mile distant, along nearly the whole length of the river, is entirely covered with it?

If that ordinance did not keep it out of Illinois, what was it that made the difference between Illinois and Missouri? They lie side by side, the Mississippi River only dividing them while their early settlements were within the same latitude. Between 1810 and 1820, the number of slaves in Missouri increased

7211, while in Illinois in the same years they decreased 51. This appears by the census returns. During nearly all that ten years both were Territories, not States. During this time the ordinance forbade slavery to go into Illinois, and nothing forbade it to go into Missouri. It did go into Missouri, and did not go into Illinois. That is the fact. Can any one doubt as to the reason of it?

THE LAST LINCOLN-DOUGLAS DEBATE

In every speech you heard Judge Douglas make . . . every speech on that Nebraska bill was full of his felicitations that we were just at the end of the slavery agitation. The last tip of the last joint of the old serpent's tail was just drawing out of view. But has it proved so? . . . When was there ever a greater agitation in Congress than last winter? When was it as great in the country as to-day? . . .

I have intimated that I thought the agitation would not cease until a crisis should have been reached and passed. I have stated in what way I thought it would be reached and passed. I have said that it might go one way or the other. We might, by arresting the further spread of it and placing it where the fathers originally placed it, put it where the public mind should rest in the belief that it was in the course of ultimate extinction. Thus the agitation may cease. It may be pushed forward until it shall become alike lawful in all the States, old as well as new, North as well as South. I have said, and I repeat, my wish is that the further spread of it may be arrested, and that it may be placed where the public mind shall rest in the belief

From *Abraham Lincoln: Complete Works,* vol. I, pp. 502–504, 507–509. The date is October 15, 1858.

that it is in the course of ultimate extinction. I have expressed that as my wish. I entertain the opinion, upon evidence sufficient to my mind, that the fathers of this government placed that institution where the public mind did rest in the belief that it was in the course of ultimate extinction. Let me ask why they made provision that the source of slavery—the African slave-trade—should be cut off at the end of twenty years? Why did they make provision that in all the new territory we owned at that time slavery should be forever inhibited? Why stop its spread in one direction and cut off its source in another, if they did not look to its being placed in the course of ultimate extinction?

Again, the institution of slavery is only mentioned in the Constitution of the United States two or three times, and in neither of these cases does the word "slavery" or "negro race" occur; but covert language is used each time, and for a purpose full of significance. What is the language in regard to the prohibition of the African slave trade? It runs in about this way: "The migration or importation of such persons as any of the States now existing shall think proper to admit, shall not be prohibited by the Congress prior to the year one thousand eight hundred and eight."

The next allusion in the Constitution to the question of slavery and the black race, is on the subject of the basis of representation, and there the language used is, "Representatives and direct taxes shall be apportioned among the several States which may be included within this Union, according to their respective numbers, which shall be determined by adding to the whole number of free persons, including those bound to service for a term of years, and excluding Indians not taxed, three fifths of all other persons."

It says "persons," not slaves, not negroes; but this "three fifths" can be applied to no other class among us than the negroes.

Lastly, in the provision for the reclamation of fugitive slaves it is said: "No person held to service or labor in one State under the laws thereof, escaping into another, shall in consequence of any law or regulation therein, be discharged from such service or labor, but shall be delivered up, on claim of the party to whom such service or labor may be due." There again there is no mention of the word "negro," or of slavery. In all three of these places, being the only allusions to slavery in the instrument, covert language is used. Language is used not suggesting that slavery existed or that the black race were among us. And I understand the contemporaneous history of those times to be that covert language was used with a purpose, and that purpose was that in our Constitution, which it was hoped, and is still hoped, will endure forever,—when it should be read by intelligent and patriotic men, after the institution of slavery had passed from among us,—there should be nothing on the face of the great charter of liberty suggesting that such a thing as negro slavery had ever existed among us. This is part of the evidence that the fathers of the Government expected and intended the institution of slavery to come to an end. They expected and intended that it should be in the course of ultimate extinction. . . .

The judge alludes very often in the course of his remarks to the exclusive right which the States have to decide the whole thing for themselves. I agree with him very readily that the different States have that right. He is but fighting a man of straw when he assumes that I am contending against the right of the States to do as they please about it. Our controversy with him is in regard to the new Territories. We agree that when the States come in as States they have the right and the power to do as they please. We have no power as citizens of the free States or in our federal capacity as members of the Federal Union through the General Government, to disturb slavery in the States where it exists. We profess constantly that we have no more inclination than belief in the power of the Government to disturb it; yet we are driven constantly to defend ourselves from the assumption that we are warring upon the rights of the States. What I insist upon is, that the new Territories shall be kept free from it while in the territorial condition. Judge Douglas assumes that we have no interest in them—that we have no right whatever to interfere. I think we have some interest. I think that as white men we have. Do we not wish for an outlet for our surplus population, if I may so express myself? Do we not feel an interest in getting to that outlet with such institutions as we would like to have prevail there? If you go to the Territory opposed to slavery and another man comes upon the same ground with his slave, upon the assumption that the things are equal, it turns out that he has the equal right all his way, and you have no part of it your way. If he goes in and makes it a slave Territory, and by consequence a slave State, is it not time that those who desire to have it a free State were on equal ground? Let me suggest it in a different way. How many Democrats are there about here ["a thousand"] who have left slave States and come into the free State of Illinois to get rid of the institution of slavery? [Another voice—"a thousand and one."] I reckon there are a thousand and one. I will ask you, if the policy you are now advocating had prevailed when this country was in a Territorial condition, where would you have gone to get rid of it? Where would you have found your free State or Territory to go to? And when hereafter, for any cause, the people in this place shall desire to find new homes, if they wish to be rid of the institution, where will they find the place to go to?

Now, irrespective of the moral aspect of this question as to whether there is a right or wrong in enslaving a negro, I am still in favor of our new Territories being in such a condition that white men may find a home—may find some spot where they can better their condition—where they can settle upon new soil, and better their condition in life. I am in favor of this not merely (I must say it here as I have elsewhere) for our own people who are born amongst us, but as an outlet for free white people everywhere—in which Hans, and Baptiste, and Patrick, and all other men from all the world, may find new homes and better their condition in life.

I have stated upon former occasions, and I may as well state again, what I understand to be the real issue in this controversy between Judge Douglas and myself. On the point of my wanting to make war between the free and the slave States, there has been no issue between us. So, too, when he assumes that I am in favor of introducing a perfect social and political equality between the white and black races. These are false issues, upon which Judge Douglas has tried to force the controversy. There is no foundation in truth for the charge that I maintain either of these propositions. The real issue in this controversy—the one pressing upon every mind—is the sentiment on the part of one class that looks upon the institution of slavery as a wrong, and of another class that does not look upon it as a wrong. The sentiment that contemplates the institution of slavery in this country as a wrong is the sentiment of the Republican party. It is the sentiment around which all their actions, all their arguments, circle; from which all their propositions radiate. They look upon it as being a moral, social, and political wrong; and while they contemplate it as such, they nevertheless have due regard for its actual existence among us, and the difficulties of getting rid of it in any satisfactory way, and to all the constitutional obligations thrown about it. Yet having a due regard for these, they desire a policy in regard to it that looks to its not creating any more danger. They insist that it, as far as may be, be treated as a wrong, and one of the methods of treating it as a wrong is to make provision that it shall grow no larger. . . .

FREE   LABOR

44. Child Labor: The Demand for Regulation

In the first American factories, the rights of the employer to manage his working force of free labor were hardly less complete than those of the planter to manage his working force of slaves. At least this was true with respect to direct interference from public authorities, however great the practical differences resulting from the fact that in a new country free labor was often difficult to obtain and to hold. As the period advanced, some encroachments on the employer's authority were made by the beginnings of factory legislation and by the rise of trade unions, although it must be emphasized that neither of these movements became of major national importance until long after the Civil War.

The issue of child labor was one of the earliest to arouse the attention of reformers. It was, for example, considered by a committee which reported to the Pennsylvania Senate in 1838. The selection below reproduces the report in full and parts of the extensive testimony which the committee collected. Among the committee's recommendations is a requirement for schooling of child workers similar to the requirements referred to in Documents 39 and 40. Among the witnesses quoted, two were men who had worked in both British and American factories. Both considered American conditions on the whole less onerous, but one declared that the children in the Scottish factories were better educated than those in Pennsylvania. The third witness cited was an employer who considered that the entire agitation was unfounded and had originated in what he called an "agrarian" spirit.[1]

---

[1] The same epithet was still current more than two decades later when President Buchanan vetoed the Homestead Bill. See above, Document 13.

MR. PELTZ, FROM THE SELECT COMMITTEE APPOINTED AT THE LAST
SESSION OF THE LEGISLATURE, UNDER THE FOLLOWING RESOLU-
TION OF THE SENATE—"RESOLVED, THAT THE COMMITTEE BE
AUTHORIZED TO VISIT THE CITIES OF PITTSBURG AND PHILA-
DELPHIA, AND SUCH OTHER MANUFACTURING DISTRICTS OF
THE STATE AS THEY MAY THINK NECESSARY, DURING THE
RECESS OF THE LEGISLATURE, FOR THE PURPOSE OF
INVESTIGATING AND INQUIRING INTO THE SYSTEM
OF LABOR ADOPTED IN COTTON AND OTHER FAC-
TORIES, AND PARTICULARLY WITH REFERENCE
TO CHILDREN EMPLOYED IN SUCH MANU-
FACTORIES, AND TO REPORT THEREON, AT
AN EARLY PERIOD OF THE NEXT SES-
SION OF THE LEGISLATURE,"
REPORTED:

That, in pursuance of this resolution of Senate, the committee met, in the city of Philadelphia, on the 9th of May last,
and proceeded to investigate the subject, in the following
manner: Subpœnas were issued, directed to operatives, ma-
chinists, foremen or bosses, owners of factories, and, in some
instances, to the parents of children employed, to physicians,
teachers, and citizens residing in the vicinity of manufactories,

From "Report of the Committee on the Employment of Children in Manufactories," Pennsylvania *Senate Journal,* 1837–1838; I, 322–327; II,
319–320, 344–345, 354–356.

and in manufacturing towns. In some instances, a list of queries were forwarded to persons at a distance, and written answers requested. These queries being, in substance, the same as those put to witnesses who were examined before the committee, embrace points relating to the business of manufacturing in Pennsylvania and other States; and, particularly, to the system of labor adopted in different manufactories; the number, ages, and sexes of the hands; hours of labor; the effect of labor on operatives, particularly on children; the character of children, their treatment, and the effect of factory employment on their health and morals. Also, to the discipline of factories and modes of government, and the manner of heating and ventilating the rooms, &c.

Questions, on the statistics of the business; on its rise and progress in this country; on the subject of competition with other States, and with Europe; on the effect of the tariff and compromise acts, were proposed; and much testimony, of an interesting and valuable character, obtained.

Aware that legislation on the subject, even of the labor of children in factories, must produce some effect on the business, the committee held it to be their duty to gather all the information bearing on the point, that could be readily obtained, and to arrange the most important part of the testimony for publication. It will be valuable for future reference, if no other benefit should immediately result from the labors of the committee.

There is nothing which deserves the name of a system in the time of labor, in the factories in Pennsylvania, so far as the investigation of the committee extended. In the vicinity of Philadelphia, for instance, where the cotton mills are numerous, eleven hours of labor, per day, are exacted in some establishments; twelve in others, and in one, at least, it has exceeded fourteen hours per day; the humanity, or cupidity of employers, being the only motive by which it is regulated.

The operations of the mills are such, that the children are

necessarily compelled to remain at their labor as long as the adults. That these long periods of labor operate injuriously on the health of children of a tender age, the committee conceive to be a well-established fact, notwithstanding some of the testimony on this point is contradictory.

The testimony, in almost every instance, has been given on oath or affirmation; and shows—

That no particular attention is paid to the education or morals of the children, by the employers, or those having charge of them in mills:

That, of the hands employed in cotton mills, as far as the information possessed by the committee will show, the proportion, as to age and sex, will stand thus: males, one-third; females, two-thirds; under the age of twelve years, one-fifth; and that, of all those under eighteen years of age, employed in these mills, not more than one-third can either read or write; and that this is an effect of their early employment in factories, and the total neglect of their education afterwards.

The apprehension, that the abridgment of the hours of the labor of children employed in factories, by enactments which will make the system uniform in this respect, would affect, injuriously, the manufacturing interests of Pennsylvania, the committee conceive is exaggerated. It is true, that our manufacturers have to compete with those in other States, engaged in the same business, where, perhaps, no such system may be adopted; but, if such enactments here, are associated with enactments to secure the benefits of education in the elementary branches, essential to make good citizens, while they will guard against what may become revolting tyranny, they will secure the benevolent, employed against competition of men in the same business in this State, of less humanity, who are restrained by no feeling, from requiring excessive labor from the children employed; and, besides, although the time of labor may be restricted, the operatives, who are not overworked, will work with greater activity and zeal, and, being in a degree educated, with greater intelligence and cheerfulness; circumstances will counterbalance the effect of the restriction, and perhaps fully compensate for it.

But, at all events, the committee are satisfied that, in a republic, where so much depends upon the virtue and intelligence of the people, it is far better that we should forego pecuniary advantages, rather than permit large masses of children to become the miserable victims of an oppressive system, and to grow up in ignorance and vice, alike disgraceful to themselves and dangerous to the community.

The results which have followed the reduction of the hours of labor in England, support, in some degree, these views; for it seems to be a settled matter in the history of manufacturing, that a reduction of hours is not attended wih a proportionate reduction of wages. The various reports which have been made, from time to time, to the British House of Commons, by committees of that body, and commissioners appointed at different times by the King, show, conclusively, that the reduction of hours of labor in England, has not carried with it a concomitant reduction of wages, and that it has not had the effect of lessening the quantity of production. The number of hands employed, has, invariably, increased with each successive reduction of hours; and the products of the country have steadily increased, notwithstanding the operation of this law, which it was contended by many would produce the reverse effect.

The committee are decidedly of opinion, that a reduction of the hours of labor in factories, in every State of the Union, would be attended with the most happy effects.

The testimony further shows, that the labor of children under twelve years of age, in factories, is not desirable or profitable; and that no injury would result to employers, by the enactment of a law to prohibit the employment of all children under that age. The reasons alleged by them, for the employment of younger children, is, that they are forced on them by poor and, in many instances, by worthless parents. Instances are related, of parents who have taken little children, under seven years of age, from factory to factory, and begged for employment for them. Sometimes they have obtained it; and the children are then compelled, in some instances, by the laws of the mill, to labor, without supper, until eight o'clock in the evening; and are left to find their way home at that hour, no matter how inclement the weather, sometimes the distance being little less than a mile. Children have sometimes been kept in the factories, without ever having been sent to school for a single hour, and their hard earnings appropriated by their unnatural parents, as long as they can legally control them.

By reference to the government and regulations adopted in factories, the advantages and disadvantages of the children will more clearly appear. Most of the mills are propelled by steam, and are warmed by the same means; the engineer is required to run the machinery so many hours per day; to stop his thirty, forty-five minutes, or an hour, as the case may be, at meal times. He also regulates the speed of the machinery, and all the operatives; adults and children, must keep pace with it. The factory bell is rung five minutes before the period of quitting work for the day, or of quitting to go to meals; and the same is done on returning to work. The time is kept at the factory, and those who are not up in time, are sometimes punished, by reduction of wages; sometimes for a repetition of the offence, by dismissal.

These regulations are usually enforced by employers, without consulting workmen. Engaging to work in a factory, is considered as yielding assent to the laws. Another regulation and practice prevails, particularly in the vicinity of Pittsburg, where the committee commenced their labors on the twentieth of June, and closed on the thirtieth of the same month, of informing all the employers in the vicinity, whenever a hand has been discharged. These regulations, taken together, leave scarcely an alternative to the operative, but unconditional submission.

The owners of mills are not always the employers of the children. The mule spinners are frequently paid by the piece, for their work, and are required to continue at it while the machinery runs, and to furnish their own assistants, who are called piecers. The labor of piecing is not severe, but the children are kept on their feet during the whole time, and are actively engaged. Whether employed by master or journeyman, the only interest felt for the child is, to get its labor—between parent and employer, the child can have no indulgence—the rules of the factory must be obeyed. Reference is made to these regulations for the better understanding of the subject, and not with a view to comment on their propriety or impropriety, which, so far as they affect adults, is a subject for the consideration of the parties only.

It may be asked, why confine this inquiry exclusively to manufactories, and not extend it to business of other kinds? The answer is, that in most occupations the apprenticing system prevails. In our factories, there is no such thing; no indenture is executed to secure to the child its trade; no provision is made for its education. This deficiency is peculiar to the factory system alone; and here is the point where legislative interposition seems to be necessary.

No particular guardianship being exercised over the morals of the children, the effect of associating them in such numbers in the factory, without proper restraint, is generally shown in the manufacturing districts. The teachers who have been examined, say that they find that the few that have been placed under them, are less tractable in their dispositions, and possess less regard for character, than other children; and they attribute this to their early servitude, and the consequent absence of parental care.

The injurious effect of factory labor on the health, has for its causes the long hours of labor, close confinement, and a vitiated atmosphere. Improvements in machinery, have done much towards mitigating the latter cause. The quality of the cotton also makes an important difference, and mills engaged in the manufacture of coarse material, are more subject to this inconvenience than others.

The improvements in labor-saving machinery, great as they have been, have not yet had the effect of lessening the number of hands employed in manufacturing, and cannot be expected to produce that effect in any reasonable length of time to come. The gradual increase of the business affords employment for all who may be displaced by the introduction of new and improved machinery. These improvements have not had the effect of lessening the number of children employed in factories in proportion to an increase of business. The labor of females has been increased, and that of males lessened. In most manufactories, the weavers are exclusively females, and some are employed at piecing. It is not likely, that any future improvements will greatly lessen the amount of female labor; whether that of children will be reduced, it is impossible to say. Ten years ago, it was generally supposed, that few improvements in machinery could take place. The machinery of that day, is now useless; and another period of ten years, may make the same difference; manufacturers are subject, in this particular, to a heavy tax. He who advances with the times, must incur the cost of continual improvement; he who lags behind, must lose in the cost of his productions.

The committee, in making this investigation, have extended their inquiries into many branches of the business, and have gathered, as before stated, testimony of an interesting and valuable character, calculated to throw much light upon the business of manufacturing and its history, and to furnish data, upon which, calculations may be founded, in matters of political economy. The statistical information, as far as it goes, will be found to possess much interest. The testimony of one of the witnesses, furnishes a most interesting history of one of the principal manufacturing towns of the State; of the rise, progress and failure, or success of its manufacturers; of the systems of government in manufactories; the character of the inmates, and of the population generally, and other information which the committee deem worthy of preservation.

The committee have already submitted a bill, containing such provisions as they think may be adopted, without serious injury to any one, and with essential benefit to the health and morals of children, whose misfortune it is, to be compelled to labor at an early age in manufactories. The provision, that no child, of a less age than ten years, shall be so employed, with the provision, that children in factories who are not sufficiently well-educated, to be able to read and write, and keep an account, shall be sent to school at least three months, in each and every year, while they are so employed, it is obvious, will operate advantageously. The fact of uneducated children being taken three months in the year from their labor, will form an inducement for parents and guardians, to send their children and wards to school before they are ten years old; at which age, any child may possess the rudiments of an English educa-tion, and the moral instruction that may constitute a good basis for his character and principles in after life.

The last provision, that children of a less age than sixteen years, shall not be allowed to labor more than ten hours per day, the committee deem to be essentially necessary for the preservation of their health. The witnesses nearly all concur in the opinion, that ten hours of labor per day, is as much as the majority of adults can perform without ultimate injury to their health. It is reasonable, then, to suppose, that a greater propor-tion of time than this, must prove very injurious to children of a less age than sixteen years. This provision may subject em-ployers to some inconvenience, it is true. It may induce them, if the ten hour system should not come into general operation, to dispense with the labor of children altogether, or to employ double sets, and let them labor six hours each, per day, or as many hours as may be necessary to make up, in two sets, the number of hours in which adults may be engaged.

In either case, it must ultimately become beneficial to the

children, whatever inconvenience it may occasion elsewhere, for a time. The committee deem it altogether better, that counties should become, in some cases, chargeable with indigent parents, than that the health, morals, and future prospects of their offspring should be sacrificed, or even jeopardized, for the precarious maintenance that is earned by their toil.

They, therefore, offer the following resolution:

Resolved, That they be discharged from the further consideration of the subject.

On motion of Mr. Peltz and Mr. Darragh,

The resolution attached to said report was read the second time, considered and adopted; and

On motion of Mr. James and Mr. Kelly,

Ordered, That two thousand copies in the English and five hundred in the German language, of said report, together with the accompanying documents, be printed for the use of the Senate.

TESTIMONY OF JEREMIAH WILKINSON

JEREMIAH WILKINSON sworn,

Says that he has been employed in the cotton factories about twenty-five years; when he was first employed, he was about thirteen years of age; he is now superintendent of the throstle room, in Mr. Ripka's mill, at Manayunk; when this mill is in full operation, about four hundred persons would be employed; probably more than three-fourths of these persons are females; about thirty or forty of these persons are children, under the age of twelve years; he considers the employment of children under the age of twelve, as one of the prominent evils of the factory system; another is, the long hours for work. The hours of work are, in summer, from sunrise to sunset—half an hour being allowed for breakfast and one hour for dinner; in winter, we work from sunrise to half-past seven or eight o'clock, P. M.

Children under the age of twelve, look in ill health, after

being in the factories some time; sickness in factories is more frequent among children than others; no attention is bestowed upon the education, nor in regard to the morals; profane or obscene language is not of frequent occurrence; the lowest wages I have known paid to children, is one dollar and a-quarter per week. Deponent has known deformities among children from early and over work in England—but has not seen such cases here; the children in factories, have no time to acquire an education; if the hours were restricted, it would certainly be advantageous to their health, and would likewise afford time for schooling. He has not heard parents of children complain of their children being over worked. Generally, employers would rather not take children under twelve years; they are in this country generally taken as a matter of charity.

Deponent is lame himself, and is stunted in his growth, from early labor in the cotton factories of England; he was at the age of seventeen, put to mule spinning, and from this work, became lame, and was stunted in his growth; he thinks that seventeen years of age is too young for spinning at mules. The boys and girls work together and use the same water closets. At present, there are not fifty persons employed at Mr. Ripka's mills.

Deponent thinks that ten hours per day of labor, is as much as children should work. This would be serviceable to the children; and were the matter general throughout the country, would be of no loss to employers; but if introduced in Pennsylvania and not in other States, our manufacturers could not compete with the manufacturers of other States.

TESTIMONY OF DANIEL HOUSTON

Daniel Houston sworn,

Says that he has been engaged in the cotton manufacturing business about fifteen years; all that time except three or four months in Scotland; those three or four months in this country. I am now employed in the iron works of Bissell, Morrison, Stelle & Co. in Alleghenytown; the three or four months he was engaged in the cotton manufacturing business, he was employed at the factory of Blackstock, Bell & Co. The system among cotton factories in Scotland is now for children, under twelve years of age, eight hours labor per day, and four hours for schooling; this is day schooling; and for this, and their doctor or medical treatment, they pay a penny out of each shilling earned by them; in addition to this, they get two hours schooling each night, gratis, which is paid for by the employers. From the age of twelve to fifteen years, they labor ten hours each day, and the schooling is the same. This change in the factory system in Scotland, has resulted in eminent advantage to the children employed, as regards health, education and morals.

Witness has been in the United States three years; he regards the factory system as practised in this country, as prejudicial to the health, morals and education of the children employed; he regards the great evil to be, the long hours of labor, wearying out the children, and unfitting them for to receive any education; the atmosphere of the cotton factories is also injurious to health. The children in this country are kindly treated; witness has seen many children in Scotland, who were deformed by early employment in the cotton factories; he has not seen any such in this country; he attended last fall a meeting of the operatives, having reference to lessening the hours of labor in cotton factories; he was appointed one of a committee to inform the owners that the hands desired the ten hour system; he did so inform the proprietors; Mr. Blackstock spoke to witness about the application, and observed that he and Mr. Briggs had taken rather too efficient a part in the business, and without further notice he was discharged a few days afterwards; Mr. Blackstock paid both Mr. Briggs and myself, on our discharge, a week's wages more than we worked, because he had discharged us without notice; he did not give me a certificate when I was discharged, because I did not ask him for one; I did not apply to any other cotton factory for employment—I went immediately to the iron works.

I can state that all the children employed in factories in Scotland, who are of the age of ten years, can read and write; such, I know, is not the case in this country. It is of a rare occurrence to find a child in this country of the age of ten years, that is employed in factories, that can both read and write.

TESTIMONY OF CHARLES AVERY[2]

Question 2.—Have you any knowledge of any evil existing as it [the factory system] is practised in Pennsylvania; if yea, state what that evil is, and what in your opinion is the appropriate remedy.

Answer.—I know of no evil worth notice, except that which arises from the refractory, factious spirit of some of the men, and they are mostly foreigners. . . .

Question 5.—What are your hours of work?

Answer.—From eleven and a-half to twelve hours.

Question 6.—What time is allowed for meals?

Answer.—From one-half to three-quarters of an hour.

Question 7.—Is the labor for children excessive?

Answer.—Far from it—it approaches nearer to amusement.

Question 8.—Is that labor done sitting or standing?

Answer.—Chiefly standing and walking.

Question 9.—Do they appear tired when they leave work, or complain of pain from over work?

Answer.—I have heard of no complaint whatever, and am certain there is no cause. . . .

I cannot close these remarks without adding, that, in my

---

[2] This contains the notation, "Furnished by Himself." The testimony has been rearranged in order to juxtapose the Committee's questions and the witness's answers. [ED.]

opinion, the memorial against the cotton factories, got up in this city, originated in an erroneous, factious, agrarian spirit— that it is full of misrepresentation and falsehood. I could add much more, but forbear.

45. Trade Unions and the Law of Conspiracy

The Wagner Act of 1935 established the encouragement of union organization and collective bargaining as an objective of national policy. In the early part of the nineteenth century, the issue took a very different form. Some trade unions did exist, though more in the old established urban crafts than in the newly erected factories, and there were the rudiments of collective bargaining. The question, however, was not whether such union activities should be encouraged but whether or not they should be prohibited as conspiracies in restraint of trade. The principal declarations of government policy on this question were made not by Congress nor by the state legislatures but by the courts.

The first of a notable series of labor conspiracy cases was that of the Philadelphia Cordwainers in 1806 and the last was the Massachusetts case of *Commonwealth* v. *Hunt* in 1842. The record of the former was printed in colorful detail in a contemporary pamphlet.[1] Both masters and journeymen had organizations in the boot and shoe trade of Philadelphia and several "turn-outs" or strikes had occurred. The practice of the union was to refuse to work with men who refused to join it or to take part in its strikes. A "tramping committee" checked on enforcement, and testimony was introduced to show the

---

[1] John R. Commons *et al.*, eds., *The Documentary History of American Industrial Society* (Cleveland: The Arthur H. Clark Co., 1910), vol. III, pp. 59–248. The two volumes on "The Labor Conspiracy Cases" were edited by John R. Commons and Eugene A. Gilmore. *The Documentary History,* long out of print, was republished in 1958 by Russell and Russell, New York.

consequences to the employer when his "shop was scabbed," and the coercion of men who wished to work in defiance of the union. "The name of a scab is very dangerous; men of this description have been hurt when out of nights."[2]

The indictment in the case charged that the defendant members of the Journeymen's Association were guilty of a conspiracy "to exact and procure great sums of money, for their work and labour" and to prevent, "by threats and menaces and other injuries," the employment of workmen not members of their "club and combination."[3] The passages below are taken from arguments for the prosecution by Jared Ingersoll, a former Attorney-General of the state, and for the defense by Caesar A. Rodney, who was speaking thirty years after his famous vote for the Declaration of Independence. Ingersoll's case rests on two principal grounds. One is that of general policy. Excessive wages will threaten Philadelphia's export trade and endanger the flourishing manufactures. The other is "the liberty of individuals." Individuals are of course free to set whatever price they like on their own labor, but they are not free to coerce anyone else to demand the same price. The state legislature would have no right to pass a law "that a man should not work under a certain sum." It is even more unthinkable that such a right should be claimed by a private club or combination.

Rodney's plea for the defendants expresses more sympathy for the "humble, but honest circle of journeymen" than for the opulent manufacturers, some of whom, he said, had landed as poor immigrants and acquired fortunes with extraordinary rapidity. His principal argument, however, places the defense of the collective activities of the union on grounds that are as completely individualistic as Ingersoll's argument against them. Wages, like other prices, should find their "natural level" in the "open market," but the workers have as much right to act together in the market as to act separately. They are, moreover, as much entitled to refuse to associate with non-union men as a literary society at Princeton University would be to expel a

---

[2] *Ibid.*, p. 93.

[3] *Ibid.*, pp. 62–67.

member. Discrimination is a universal right; "you must permit every body to choose their associates."

The jury held the defendants guilty and they were fined eight dollars each and costs. Similar verdicts were handed down in a number of other conspiracy trials; but the case of the Boston Journeymen Bootmakers' Society *(Commonwealth* v. *Hunt)* reached a different conclusion. It was decided on appeal by the Supreme Judicial Court of Massachusetts in 1842, and the opinion by Chief Justice Lemuel Shaw has been often cited. Though the jurist's style is very different from that of the Revolutionary patriot, the basic argument, as will be seen, is the same as Rodney's. If the defendants did in fact "compel one Wait to turn out of his employ one Jonathan Horne," they did so only by exercizing their right not to work for a particular employer. If this tended to "impoverish" a particular person, so do many other acts of legitimate competition, and this consequence should not limit the journeymen's "acknowledged right to contract with others for their labor."

Adverse findings in the early conspiracy trials did not prevent, though they may have somewhat impeded, the growth of trade unionism. On the other hand, Justice Shaw's opinion in the Massachusetts case was not always followed in other jurisdictions. Yet the arguments and the decisions are significant indications of what were felt to be the nature and the limits of government responsibility in the field of industrial relations.

THE PHILADELPHIA CORDWAINERS

JARED INGERSOLL FOR THE PROSECUTION

The witnesses, both on the part of the prosecution and defendants, concur in stating the material facts on which the prose-

---

cution rests, and which are prohibited by the laws of the country; and which the court are bound to punish upon conviction.

When I use the word punish, I would not be understood that it is intended to do any personal injury to the defendants; nor that they should come under any severe penalty. . . All I wish is to establish the principle by the decision of the court, and the correspondent verdict of a jury. We have no wish to injure these men, but we trust you will decide as the law decides; and after establishing the illegality of the measures pursued by the defendants, no men will be more ready than the prosecutors to shield the journeymen from any disagreeable consequences from a conviction.

The cause is an important one. . . It is said on the one side to involve an important principle of civil liberty, that men in their transactions with others, have a right to judge in their own behalf, and value their labour as they please: on the contrary, we shall shew that the claims and conduct of the defendants are contrary to just government, equal laws, and that due subordination to which every member of the community is bound to submit . . . all these are essentially connected with the present prosecution.

Almost two days have been consumed in the examination of witnesses, and much of that time has been spent by the defendants, in enquiring into points not relating to the issue. It has been attempted to be shewn, that the master workmen, associated and formed themselves into similar societies, and this they say constitutes a defence for the defendants, if the fact be so . . . two wrongs never make a right. If the masters have associated in the manner stated, they are amenable to the law in the same manner as the associated journeymen. But you cannot say, that one crime shall merge the other: yet in justice to them, I must say, that all proof of this sort has failed; there has been no proof shewn, that the masters associated for unlawful, or oppressive purposes; or that when associated, they ever attempted to controul the journeymen. There is nothing like it in the constitution and minutes, that were read from the book produced. They say they associated for the convenience of the trade; nothing is said of raising or decreasing wages; nothing relative to any provision or declaration, as to the price of workmanship, &c. . . .

Without recurring particularly to the evidence, I venture to state, without any apprehension of contradiction, it has been proved, a certain number of persons, among whom are the present defendants, associated for several distinct and criminal purposes. This is the gi[s]t of the prosecution, it is not for what any one man of them has done, that the state prosecutes: the offence is in the combination.

Why a combination in such case is criminal, will not be difficult to explain: we live under a government composed of a constitution and laws . . . and every man is obliged to obey the constitution, and the laws made under it. When I say he is bound to obey these, I mean to state the whole extent of his obedience. Do you feel yourselves bound to obey any other laws, enacted by any other legislature, than that of your own choice? Shall these, or any other body of men, associate for the purpose of making new laws, laws not made under the constitutional authority, and compel their fellow citizens to obey them, under the penalty of their existence? This prosecution contravenes no man's right, it is to prevent an infringement of right; it is in favour of the equal liberty of all men, this is the policy of our laws; but if private associations and clubs, can make constitutions and laws for us . . . if they can associate and make bye-laws paramount, or inconsistent with the state laws; What, I ask, becomes of the liberty of the people, about which so much is prated; about which the opening counsel made such a flourish!

There is evidence before you that shews, this secret association, this private club, composed of men who have been only a little time in your country, (not that they are the worse for that,) but they ought to submit to the laws of the country, and not attempt to alter them according to their own whim or caprice.

It is in proof, that they combined together; for what?— to say what each man shall have for his labour: no. . . . It is not intended to take away the right of any man to put his own price upon his own labour; they may ask what they please, individually. But when they associate, combine and conspire, to prevent others from taking what they deem a sufficient compensation for their labour . . . and where they undertake to regulate the trade of the city, they undertake to regulate what interferes with your rights and mine. I now am to speak to the policy of permitting such associations. This is a large, encreasing, manufacturing city. Those best acquainted with our situation, believe that manufactures will, bye and by, become one of its chief means of support. A vast quantity of manufactured articles are already exported to the West Indies, and the southern states; we rival the supplies from England in many things, and great sums are annually received in returns. It is then proper to support this manufacture. Will you permit men to destroy it, who have no permanent stake in the city; men who can pack up their all in a knapsack, or carry them in their pockets to New-York or Baltimore? . . .

. . . A few more things of this sort, and you will break up the manufactories; the masters will be afraid to make a contract, therefore he must relinquish the export trade, and depend altogether upon the profits of the work of Philadelphia, and confine his supplies altogether to the city. The last turnout had liked to have produced that effect. . . .

It must be plain to you, that the master employers have no particular interest in the thing . . . if they pay higher wages, you must pay higher for the articles. They, in truth, are protecting the community. . . .

If this conspiracy was to be confined to the persons themselves, it would not be an offence against the law; but they go further. There are two counts in the indictment; you are to consider each, and to give your verdict on each. The first is for contriving, and intending, unjustly, and oppressively, to encrease and augment the wages usually allowed them. The other for endeavouring to prevent, by threats, menaces, and other unlawful means, other journeymen from working at the usual prices, and that they compelled others to join them.

If these persons claim the right to put the price on their own work, if they say their labour is their own, and they are the judges of its value, why not admit the same right to others? If it is the right of Dubois, and the other defendants, is it not equally the right of Harrison and Cummings? We stand up for the right of the journeymen, as well as of the masters. The last turn-out was carried by a small majority . . . 60 against 50, or thereabout: shall 60 unreasonable men, perhaps single men, having no one to provide for but themselves, distress and bring to destruction, 50 married men with their families? Let the 60 put what price they please on their own work; but the others are free agents also: leave them free, or talk no more of equal rights, of independence, or of liberty.

. . . By their constitution you find, and from their own lips I must take the words, that though a man wants no more wages than he gets, he must join in a turn-out. The man who seeks an asylum in this country, from the arbitrary laws of other nations, is coerced into this society, though he does not work in the article intended to be raised; he must leave his seat and join the turn-out. This was Harrison's case . . . he worked exclusively in shoes, they in boots; he was a stranger, he was a married man, with a large family; he represented his distressed condition; they entangle him, but shew no mercy. . . .

He trusted the jury would see the present cause in this double point of view; the general policy, as it relates to the good of the community, and the flourishing state of our manufactures: the liberty of individuals, and the enjoyment of common and equal rights, secured by the constitution and laws. This case has exhibited such a tissue of infractions of personal rights by the club of journeymen shoemakers, that was our state legislature to dare to pass such laws as these men have passed, it would be a just cause of rebellion. I will go further, and say, it would produce rebellion if the legislature should say, that a man should not work under a certain sum . . . it would lead to beggary, and no man would submit to it. Then, shall a secret body exercise a power over our fellow-citizens, which the legislature itself is not invested with? The fact is, they do exercise a sort of authority the legislature dare not assume.

It now rests with the jury, under the direction of the court to say, whether we shall in future be governed by secret clubs, instead of the constitution and laws of the state; a verdict of not guilty, will sanction combinations of the most dangerous kind; a contrary verdict will give the victory to the known and established laws of the commonwealth.

CAESAR A. RODNEY FOR THE DEFENSE

. . . The true and only question in this cause . . . is whether the wealthy master shoemakers of this populous and flourishing city, shall charge you and me what price they please for our boots and shoes, and at the same time have the privilege of fixing the wages of the poor journeymen they happen to employ. . . .

You are called to decide for the first time, in this free country, and to fix the precedent, in favour of the doctrine contained in this indictment. The prosecutors, not content with building costly mansions, rapidly amassing fortunes, aspire to lay up their plums annually, and they will do it, if you once

---

From Commons, *Documentary History,* vol. III, pp. 162–202.

give them the privilege of fixing the prices of those who are to work for them; to discover all this does not require day light; a candle, wax taper, or a lanthern will be sufficient for the purpose. . . .

When you look at the mass of testimony adduced on this occasion, you will find as long ago as 1789, the masters had a society for the management of their concerns . . . that the journeymen instituted a society in 1794, for the benefit of the individuals who composed it; in 1798 you hear of a turn-out; in 1799 you hear the same; and notwithstanding all this, you hear of no prosecutions by way of indictment. Were the prosecuting officers of the state, asleep all this time? Have they and the grand juries been slumbering at their posts, and suffered a flagitious, a notorious offence to be repeated with impunity, and to continue its operation without notice or check? . . .

. . . Was there not another body of men, who combined together to raise their wages; who would not move a rope or start tack or sheet till their terms were complied with? I am instructed to say, that the pilots of this port, did a few years ago, refuse to conduct a vessel to or from the ocean, agreeable to the rates of pilotage, before usually received. This circumstance must have been a matter universally known through the city at the time; the interest of the port, the value of the property afloat, was all placed in jeopardy. . . . If that combination had been a criminal offence, it would undoubtedly have been prosecuted. Their conduct was productive of serious inconvenience, I admit; but they had the right to say, at what price they would perform the service; and it was apparent, that if you did not give the wages, you could not compel them to pilot your vessels. . . .

We are told that this prosecution is brought forward from public motives, and not from personal views; when you see a formidable band of masters attending on the trial of this cause, and some of the most eminent counsel in the city employed to prosecute it; and when you see, further, that it is not taken up by any of their customers, it will require strong arguments to convince you, it is done out of pure patriotic motives. . . .

To stiffen the heel of their case, as you would a child's shoe, they tell a pitiable tale of Mr. Bedford, who lost a profitable job by the perverseness of the journeymen, who abandoned his shop because he would not pay sixteen or twenty dollars to the society to readmit Harrison and the other man. I appeal to the testimony, whether a few dollars would not have removed the scab from his blighted shop, and yet we are gravely informed, that rather than pay a paltry sum, he declined a lucrative contract to the amount of four thousand dollars! If he did, who is to blame for this? Is it our fault, or his own? The journeymen ask a certain price for their labour, Mr. Bedford does the same for his work. . . Nobody disputes his right to do so; but he refuses to give the journeymen the wages they demand. This also he has an undoubted right to do. Well, they decline working for him, and he cannot get his boots made in time to catch the bargain. This is the sum and substance of the lamentable story, which we have heard so affectingly told. . . .

Suppose I were to ask Mr. Bedford what was his situation when he first landed on our free shores; and how much he has made, since he came into this country? Whether he bro't with him the capital he now possesses? And whether he then belonged to the class of master cordwainers, or to the more humble, but honest circle of journeymen? I believe, if we were to make out a complete account current, or post the profit and loss fairly up in the ledger, we should find a balance in round numbers in his favour, so large, that the net proceeds of the 4,000 dollar job would not sensibly affect the calculation. In fact, we should discover that he has amassed an ample fortune since he sought an asylum in this new country (where the poorest individual can claim the full price of his labour) from the oppressions of the old world, where statutable provisions fix and regulate the price of every thing almost; here honesty and industry are sure to meet a due reward, and days of labour and fatigue are crowned with years of ease and competence. . . .

No person is compelled to join the society, and it would be as novel a definition of the term, compulsion, as it would be preposterous in an individual, to contend that he was compelled to join a society, because, otherwise the members would not associate with him. . . .

They assert, as soon as an emigrant journeyman arrives in this city, he is asked to join the society. What then? He has the right to accept or decline the offer; the thing is perfectly optional. If he declines, we only say, we will not work or board with you. This is no force: if he comes, it is his voluntary act. When you become a member of any institution, you engage to obey its rules. This complaint ought to be made of sterner stuff, it is too flimsey to shelter the prosecution. Those who are declared against by the present body, may form a new one, and enter into similar regulations; the masters may join them, and when a journeyman asks for work, they may enquire to which society he belongs? If to the old, they may answer, we will not employ you; if to the new, we will give you work; you shall be supported. There would be nothing criminal in this conduct, they neither offend the law or the commandments. So the body-men have a right to say, we will work only where we please, and at what price we please; and we know that no earthly power can in this free country compel us. But give a verdict against the defendants, and farewell to the dearest privilege which they enjoy! The masters may then dictate where they shall work, with whom, and at what prices.

Much has been said of the importance of manufactures to this city, and the injury manufacturing interest would sustain, if journeymen were permitted to regulate the price of their own labour. The gentleman has shewn you one side of the picture; I wish to call your attention to the other. The great advantage possessed by Philadelphia over New-York and Baltimore, in the extent of her monied capital. Those cities give more wages. . . .

The gentleman calls out, why do they not go there? Suppose they should at his bidding take wing and fly away, how would Mr. Bedford and Mr. Ryan make their boots, and what is to become of their export trade? Do you wish to banish them? the verdict called for by the prosecutors, will effectually answer the purpose. . . . New-York and Baltimore will gladly receive them, as they take care to profit by every other advantage which our inattention or narrow policy throws into their way. You are not ignorant of the rapid strides they have made to engross your commerce; drive away your artists, and mechanics, and your manufactures will in like manner dwindle.

. . . To make myself perfectly understood, I presume it is admitted that a single journeyman shoemaker, may as lawfully ask any price for his work, as he may do the most meritorious act; this being understood let us proceed to investigate the principle which renders the joint act of two, criminal, though the same act would be lawful for either of them separately to perform.

One method of reasoning, is by analogy. In natural philosophy, this mode is frequently relied upon. We will, therefore, adopt it. . . .

Mr. Hopkinson[1] and myself, were once members of a law society, intended to prepare us, like the manœuvres of a parade day, to discipline the military, for the real action of the war. It was a very lawful object in any individual to fit himself for the active sciences of his profession, but for such a number to associate, was absolutely incompatible with his present principles. We could expel any member who violated our rules,

---

[1] Of counsel for the prosecution. [ED.]

this would have excluded him from the society. Was this criminal in us? If not, why is it charged as a crime against the defendants?

The Cliosophic and whig societies of Princeton college (the school in which many of the first characters of our country have received their education) are founded on the same laudable principles. Would the members of either of those bodies be considered amenable in a court of criminal justice, for uniting in an act of expulsion or refusing to associate with the member when expelled? . . .

The determination of any number, not to lodge in the same boarding house with particular individuals, surely cannot be considered as a confederation wrongfully to injure them, let it proceed from whim, caprice, or any other motive. The old proverb says, a man is known by the company he keeps; and you must permit every body to choose their associates. . . .

. . . My learned friend has said, he was advocating the interests of the journeymen, I assert, that when rationally understood, I am pleading the cause of the masters. Remember I now tell you, that if you convict the defendants, for asking the same wages which are received in New-York and Baltimore; not a month will elapse, before the present prosecutors will gladly offer them the same terms, and they will entreat those they have driven away, to return and work for them. If you will take my advice, you will leave the regulation of these things to the open market. There every article, like water, acquires its natural level: adopt this rule, and you will be more likely to get your boots much cheaper. . . .

In this last contest between the journeymen and the masters, the weaker power against the stronger, (for whilst the masters may lose the profits on a good job, the journeymen may want bread) we have been unsuccessful, after a struggle to obtain the same wages with our fellow labourers in New-York and Baltimore: we have been compelled to yield and submit to the former reduced prices for our work. The masters have been completely triumphant, and victorious as they are, they persist in this cruel prosecution! They have already accomplished all they asked, what can they desire more? Is it their wish to alarm, terrify, and persecute us; until they reduce us to the servile state of vassels? You have all heard, gentlemen, of the fable of the hen and golden egg. I fear it will be verified in the conduct of the masters. They grasp at too much! They are not satisfied, with the rapid rate at which they are at present amassing wealth. They wish to make their fortunes by a single turn of the wheel. They may destroy the source from whence the golden streams flow. They may, and I believe, will banish every good workman from this city, if they continue this system of persecution with success. You, gentlemen, may stop their career. For your own interests, for theirs, and for the sake of the community, I beg and entreat you to arrest the arm of vengeance.

COMMONWEALTH *vs.* HUNT,

MASSACHUSETTS, 1842

CHIEF JUSTICE LEMUEL SHAW:

DECISION OF THE SUPREME JUDICIAL COURT

SHAW, C. J. Considerable time has elapsed since the argument of this case. It has been retained long under advisement, partly because we were desirous of examining, with some attention, the great number of cases cited at the argument, and others which have presented themselves in course, and partly because we considered it a question of great importance to the

---

From Chief Justice Shaw, in *Commonwealth v. Hunt*, 1842, *Massachusetts Reports*, 4 Metcalf, 111, at 121–135.

Commonwealth, and one which had been much examined and considered by the learned judge of the municipal court.

We have no doubt, that by the operation of the constitution of this Commonwealth, the general rules of the common law, making conspiracy an indictable offence, are in force here, and that this is included in the description of laws which had, before the adoption of the constitution, been used and approved in the Province, Colony, or State of Massachusetts Bay, and usually practised in the courts of law. . . .

The first count set forth, that the defendants, with divers others unknown, on the day and at the place named, being workmen, and journeymen, in the art and occupation of boot-makers, unlawfully, perniciously and deceitfully designing and intending to continue, keep up, form, and unite themselves, into an unlawful club, society and combination, and make unlawful by-laws, rules and orders among themselves, and thereby govern themselves and other workmen, in the said art, and unlawfully and unjustly to extort great sums of money by means thereof, did unlawfully assemble and meet together, and being so assembled, did unjustly and corruptly conspire, combine, confederate and agree together, that none of them should thereafter, and that none of them would, work for any master or person whatsoever, in the said art, mystery and occupation, who should employ any workman or journeyman, or other person, in the said art, who was not a member of said club, society or combination, after notice given him to discharge such workman, from the employ of such master; to the great damage and oppression, &c.

Now it is to be considered, that the preamble and introductory matter in the indictment—such as unlawfully and deceitfully designing and intending unjustly to extort great sums, &c.—is mere recital, and not traversable, and therefore cannot aid an imperfect averment of the facts constituting the description of the offence. The same may be said of the concluding matter, which follows the averment, as to the great damage and oppression not only of their said masters, employing them in said art and occupation, but also of divers other workmen in the same art, mystery and occupation, to the evil example, &c. If the facts averred constitute the crime, these are properly stated as the legal inferences to be drawn from them. If they do not constitute the charge of such an offence, they cannot be aided by these alleged consequences.

Stripped then of these introductory recitals and alleged injurious consequences, and of the qualifying epithets attached to the facts, the averment is this; that the defendants and others formed themselves into a society, and agreed not to work for any person, who should employ any journeyman or other person, not a member of such society, after notice given him to discharge such workman.

The manifest intent of the association is, to induce all those engaged in the same occupation to become members of it. Such a purpose is not unlawful. It would give them a power which might be exerted for useful and honorable purposes, or for dangerous and pernicious ones. If the latter were the real and actual object, and susceptible of proof, it should have been specially charged. Such an association might be used to afford each other assistance in times of poverty, sickness and distress; or to raise their intellectual, moral and social condition; or to make improvement in their art; or for other proper purposes. Or the association might be designed for purposes of oppression and injustice. But in order to charge all those, who become members of an association, with the guilt of a criminal conspiracy, it must be averred and proved that the actual, if not the avowed object of the association, was criminal. An association may be formed, the declared objects of which are innocent and laudable, and yet they may have secret articles, or an agreement communicated only to the members, by which they are banded together for purposes injurious to the peace of society or the rights of its members. Such would undoubtedly be a criminal conspiracy, on proof of the fact, however meritorious and praiseworthy the declared objects might be. The law is not to be hoodwinked by colorable pretences. It looks at truth and reality, through whatever disguise it may assume. But to make such an association, ostensibly innocent, the subject of prosecution as a criminal conspiracy, the secret agreement, which makes it so, is to be averred and proved as the gist of the offence. But when an association is formed for purposes actually innocent, and afterwards its powers are abused, by those who have the control and management of it, to purposes of oppression and injustice, it will be criminal in those who thus misuse it, or give consent thereto, but not in the other members of the association. In this case, no such secret agreement, varying the objects of the association from those avowed, is set forth in this count of the indictment.

Nor can we perceive that the objects of this association, whatever they may have been, were to be attained by criminal means. The means which they proposed to employ, as averred in this count, and which, as we are now to presume, were established by the proof, were, that they would not work for a person, who, after due notice, should employ a journeyman not a member of their society. Supposing the object of the association to be laudable and lawful, or at least not unlawful, are these means criminal? The case supposes that these persons are not bound by contract, but free to work for whom they please, or not to work, if they so prefer. In this state of things, we cannot perceive, that it is criminal for men to agree together to exercise their own acknowledged rights, in such a manner as best to subserve their own interests. One way to test this is, to consider the effect of such an agreement, where the object of the association is acknowledged on all hands to be a laudable one. Suppose a class of workmen, impressed with the manifold evils of intemperance, should agree with each other not to work in a shop in which ardent spirit was furnished, or not to work in a shop with any one who used it, or not to work for an employer, who should, after notice, employ a journeyman who habitually used it. The consequences might be the same. A workman, who should still persist in the use of ardent spirit, would find it more difficult to get employment; a master employing such an one might, at times, experience inconvenience in his work, in losing the services of a skilful but intemperate workman. Still it seems to us, that as the object would be lawful, and the means not unlawful, such an agreement could not be pronounced a criminal conspiracy. . . .

The second count, omitting the recital of unlawful intent and evil disposition, and omitting the direct averment of an unlawful club or society, alleges that the defendants, with others unknown, did assemble, conspire, confederate and agree together, not to work for any master or person who should employ any workman not being a member of a certain club, society or combination, called the Boston Journeymen Bootmaker's Society, or who should break any of their by-laws, unless such workmen should pay to said club, such sum as should be agreed upon as a penalty for the breach of such unlawful rules, &c; and that by means of said conspiracy they did compel one Isaac B. Wait, a master cordwainer, to turn out of his employ one Jeremiah Horne, a journeyman bootmaker, &c. in evil example, &c. So far as the averment of a conspiracy is concerned, all the remarks made in reference to the first count are equally applicable to this. It is simply an averment of an agreement amongst themselves not to work for a person, who should employ any person not a member of a certain association. It sets forth no illegal or criminal purpose to be accomplished, nor any illegal or criminal means to be adopted for the accomplishment of any purpose. It was an agreement, as to the manner in which they would exercise an acknowledged right to contract with others for their labor. It does not aver a conspiracy or even an intention to raise their wages; and it appears by the bill of exceptions, that the case was not put upon the footing of a conspiracy to raise their wages. Such an agreement, as set forth in this count, would be perfectly justifiable under the recent English statute, by which this subject is regulated. . . .

As to the latter part of this count, which avers that by means of said conspiracy, the defendants did compel one Wait to turn out of his employ one Jeremiah Horne, we remark, in the first place, that as the acts done in pursuance of a conspiracy, as we have before seen, are stated by way of aggravation, and not as a substantive charge; if no criminal or unlawful conspiracy is stated, it cannot be aided and made good by mere matter of aggravation. . . .

But further; if this is to be considered as a substantive charge, it would depend altogether upon the force of the word "compel," which may be used in the sense of coercion, or duress, by force or fraud. It would therefore depend upon the context and the connexion with other words, to determine the sense in which it was used in the indictment. If, for instance, the indictment had averred a conspiracy, by the defendants, to compel Wait to turn Horne out of his employment, and to accomplish that object by the use of force or fraud, it would have been a very different case; especially if it might be fairly construed, as perhaps in that case it might have been, that Wait was under obligation, by contract, for an unexpired term of time, to employ and pay Horne. . . .

. . . To mark the difference between the case of a journeyman or a servant and master, mutually bound by contract, and the same parties when free to engage anew, I should have before sited the case of the *Boston Glass Co.* v. *Binney,* 4 Pick. 425. . . .

. . . It acknowledges the established principle, that every free man, whether skilled laborer, mechanic, farmer or domestic servant, may work or not work, or work or refuse to work with any company or individual, at his own option, except so far as he is bound by contract. But whatever might

be the force of the word "compel," unexplained by its connexion, it is disarmed and rendered harmless by the precise
statement of the means, by which such compulsion was to be
effected. It was the agreement not to work for him, by which
they compelled Wait to decline employing Horne longer. . . .

The third count, reciting a wicked and unlawful intent to
impoverish one Jeremiah Horne, and hinder him from following his trade as a boot-maker, charges the defendants, with
others unknown, with an unlawful conspiracy, by wrongful
and indirect means, to impoverish said Horne and to deprive
and hinder him, from his said art and trade and getting his
support thereby, and that, in pursuance of said unlawful combination, they did unlawfully and indirectly hinder and prevent, &c. and greatly impoverish him.

If the fact of depriving Jeremiah Horne of the profits of his
business, by whatever means it might be done, would be unlawful and criminal, a combination to compass that object
would be an unlawful conspiracy, and it would be unnecessary
to state the means. . . .

Suppose a baker in a small village had the exclusive custom
of his neighborhood, and was making large profits by the sale
of his bread. Supposing a number of those neighbors, believing
the price of his bread too high, should propose to him to reduce his prices, or if he did not, that they would introduce
another baker; and on his refusal, such other baker should,
under their encouragement, set up a rival establishment, and
sell his bread at lower prices; the effect would be to diminish
the profit of the former baker, and to the same extent to impoverish him. And it might be said and proved, that the purpose of the associates was to diminish his profits, and thus
impoverish him, though the ultimate and laudable object of the
combination was to reduce the cost of bread to themselves
and their neighbors. The same thing may be said of all competition in every branch of trade and industry; and yet it is
through that competition, that the best interests of trade and

industry are promoted. It is scarcely necessary to allude to the familiar instances of opposition lines of conveyance, rival hotels, and the thousand other instances, where each strives to gain custom to himself, by ingenious improvements, by increased industry, and by all the means by which he may lessen the price of commodities, and thereby diminish the profits of others.

We think, therefore, that associations may be entered into, the object of which is to adopt measures that may have a tendency to impoverish another, that is, to diminish his gains and profits, and yet so far from being criminal or unlawful, the object may be highly meritorious and public spirited. The legality of such an association will therefore depend upon the means to be used for its accomplishment. If it is to be carried into effect by fair or honorable and lawful means, it is, to say the least, innocent; if by falsehood or force, it may be stamped with the character of conspiracy. . . .

IMMIGRATION

46. Wisconsin: The Competition for Immigrants

Five million immigrants entered the United States between 1820 and 1860, most of them from 1845 on. The newcomers provided skilled and unskilled labor for the factories and mines, dug canals and built railroads, and took a large part in the agricultural settlement in the West. Their coming had profound effects on the economy and on the society. Yet

American governments took almost no direct measures either to promote or to impede this great movement of people.

On the part of the federal government, inclusion of immigrants in the benefits of the liberal land laws may well have been an important stimulus to migration; and debate over the issue brought out, as has been seen,[1] vigorous statements of the immigrants' contribution to American expansion. Abraham Lincoln had a warm welcome for "Hans and Baptiste and Patrick," (Document 43) although Olav came more often than Baptiste. Andrew Johnson referred to immigration as "one of the great secrets" of American success.[2] Acting on a similar belief, Australia, New Zealand, and Canada have all at various times offered direct financial assistance to induce immigrants to come to them. This the United States never did, either for western settlers or for the "artists" and skilled workmen whom Hamilton wished to attract.

The only fully Hamiltonian program of encouragement ever carried on in the United States was that of the church-state of the Mormons, which recruited immigrants from Great Britain for their industrial skills as well as for their religious convictions and subsidized their transportation to the Great Basin frontier.[3] The first of the land-grant railroads, the Illinois Central, also set a precedent of organized colonization.[4] Among state governments, Wisconsin made a deliberate attempt to attract settlers. For two years in the 1850's it maintained the office of an Emigrant Commissioner in the port of New York and circulated pamphlets in Europe advertising the state's attractions. This was a modest program—in comparison not only with Brigham Young but also with William Penn, whose

---

1 Document 12.

2 *Congressional Globe,* 36th Congress, 1st Session, p. 1799.

3 Leonard J. Arrington, *Great Basin Kingdom: An Economic History of the Latter-Day Saints, 1830–1900* (Cambridge: Harvard University Press, 1958), pp. 97–108. Jonathan Hughes, *The Vital Few: American Economic Progress and Its Protagonists* (Boston: Houghton Mifflin Co., 1966), ch. 3.

4 Paul Wallace Gates, *The Illinois Central and Its Colonization Work* (Cambridge: Harvard University Press, 1934).

agents in colonial Pennsylvania had sent recruiters to Europe as well as pamphlets—but it was more than was done at the time by any other state.

The readings are the report of one of the Commissioners and the recommendations of two legislative committees. The former describes the activities of the New York office, and the three documents reflect the beliefs on which the program was based. There should be no doubt "of the policy of encouraging immigration," and Wisconsin must not fall behind other states. Immigrants are needed, as settlers and buyers of state land and as workers on the railroads. They bring not only "intelligence and physical strength" but also "capital," in some cases averaging nearly five hundred dollars per family. Wisconsin wants them and can attract them if it succeeds in making known its advantages over other states.

The Commissioner's Report and that of his predecessor, G. Van Steenwijk, both emphasize the abuses inflicted upon immigrants by unprincipled travel agents and "runners" in New York City. The earlier document suggests a petition to Washington on the subject. Perhaps the federal government has no power to intervene directly but it could at least call the problem to the attention of the seaboard states. "A memorial to Congress by our Legislature . . . would at any rate, show an honorable sympathy with our future citizens of foreign birth."[5]

In spite of the favorable report of the Select Committee, the Legislature abandoned the program at the end of its second year. In 1860, however, California decided to station a similar Commissioner of Emigrants in New York City[6]; and after the war Wisconsin and a number of other midwestern states were to engage in further competitive efforts to attract immigration.[7]

---

[5] Wisconsin *Senate Journal*, 1853, Appendix L, "First Annual Report of the Commissioner of Emigration," especially pp. 15–16.

[6] Gerald D. Nash, *State Government and Economic Development* (Berkeley and Los Angeles: University of California Press, 1964), p. 66.

[7] Theodore C. Blegen, "The Competition of the Northwestern States for Immigrants," *Wisconsin Magazine of History*, III (1919–1920), 3–29.

REPORT ON THE EMIGRANT AGENCY

THE COMMITTEE ON STATE AFFAIRS, TO WHOM THAT PORTION
OF THE GOVERNOR'S MESSAGE RELATING TO THE "EMIGRANT
AGENCY" AND THE "REPORT OF THE COMMISSIONER OF
EMIGRATION" WERE REFERRED, HAVING HAD THE SUB-
JECT UNDER CONSIDERATION, HAVE DIRECTED ME TO
SUBMIT THE FOLLOWING REPORT

From the first a wide difference of opinion has prevailed as
to the propriety and policy of establishing and maintaining a
State Emigrant Agency. Some have urged its propriety
strongly, and others have opposed it decidedly in different
parts of the State, and it is due to your committee to remark
that they are not fully agreed upon the subject in all its details;
yet all concur in recommending its continuance for another
year, in order that it may have a fair trial, and that our State,
if possible, may reap the benefits of the exertions of its commissioner and of the outlay of the past year, and not by abandoning it, thus early, allow other States (which have imitated
our example in establishing similar commissions) to reap the
entire reward of our expenditure and exertion. It can hardly
be successfully denied that one year affords too little time to
enable us to calculate the practical good which may result to
the State, and to discover and remove the causes that have
operated against us, and to put affairs in a train, and give
the establishment a character in Europe, in order that its continuance may be rendered, subsequently, more advantageous.

From Wisconsin *Senate Journal,* 1853, Appendix, "Report of the Committee on State Affairs on Matters Relating to the Emigrant Agency," pp. 3–5.

Of the policy of encouraging immigration, there ought not to be a doubt, since the present prosperous condition of the United States affords so striking and forcible an illustration of its practical results, and the rapid growth and prosperity of our State is no less demonstrative of the same fact.

It is true, that without a State Agency, Wisconsin, as in years past, might continue to receive a very considerable immigration, composed mostly of the friends and connexions of persons already here; but it is to be feared, should no effort be made by the State, that much of the immigration which might be attracted to it would be directed to other parts, and the benefits to flow from it be enjoyed by other States as a reward of their exertion.

There are large quantities of school land yet unsold, in the sale and occupancy of which the State has a deep and double interest, as well as in the sale of the vast tracts of congress lands now in market within our limits. Could all such lands as those above referred to, together with land held on speculation within this State, once pass into the hands of actual settlers, the benefits to be derived by Wisconsin from such a condition of things are hardly susceptible of calculation.

To induce emigrants to prefer Wisconsin, it seems only necessary that the advantages offered by her be fairly understood.

She offers the inducement of cheap and fertile land, consisting of prairie, opening, and timber, in large quantities—a healthy and salubrious climate—abundance of good water, and water-power—rich and productive mines of lead, iron and copper—good market facilities—magnificent forests, composed of nearly every variety of timber—rare opportunities for the investment of capital—an excellent school system, and the basis of the most magnificent school fund in the whole universe.

The appropriation of a few thousand dollars by the State, when compared with all the benefits to flow to it from large accessions to its population, and the capital thereby added, and the increased amount of taxable property, dwindles into insignificance.

It is estimated that the immigration to the State during the past year amounted to more than 20,000, which number would make about 4,000 families, and that the average amount of ready cash brought in by them was not less than one hundred dollars per capite, which estimate, if correct, shows an addition to the cash capital of the State of two millions of dollars. . . .

HERMAN HAERTEL: REPORT OF THE
EMIGRANT COMMISSIONER

To His Excellency William A. Barstow,
Governor of the State of Wisconsin:

Sir:—At the close of a period of eight months, during which I have discharged the duties of the office of Emigrant Commissioner, conferred upon me by the State of Wisconsin, I deem it a pleasant task herewith to present to your favorable notice a concise report of what I have done, its result, and my observations hitherto. . . .

As for many years past I had been accustomed regularly to visit New York, and neglected no opportunity to acquire information upon the condition of Emigration, it could not be difficult for me soon to become acquainted with the main influences that cause the newly arrived emigrant to direct his steps to this or that State.

One of the most prominent aids, I unquestionably found in the Press, which by means of books and newspaper reports

From Wisconsin Legislature: Public Documents, 1859, *Document C*, pp. 3–15. The spelling of the names of foreign journals has not been altered.

upon single States, or the United States in general, of statistical information upon particular branches of industry—as agriculture, trade, mining, &c.—not only excites attention, but especially gives a determinate direction to the steps of the emigrant, as to the State in which to fix his residence.

This opinion thus formed, my now daily intercourse with emigrants fully confirmed. Although I omitted no opportunity that presented itself to labor for the good of our State in New York itself, I yet directed my chief aim to the press here and in Europe, and in a long series of articles, presented Wisconsin in general; its advantages above other States; descriptions of particular localities; its commerce; the wealth of its mineral, timber and agricultural districts; its climate, public institutions, political privileges, means of education, &c., before the eyes of all those, who for whatever cause, were determined to change their residence.

I also sent copies of the pamphlets, which in the meantime I had received, to the editors of a large number of newspapers in the United States, Germany, Ireland, England, Scotland, Norway, Sweden, Holland and Switzerland, with the request to insert extracts therefrom in their respective journals.

The journals which I selected for advertisement and correspondence are, especially, the New York Tribune, Herald, Staats Zeitung, Irish American, Abend Zeitung, New York Democrat, Daily Wisconsin, Sentinel, Wisconsin Banner, Volksfreund, Niewsbode, Newarker Zeitung, Phoenix and Anzeiger des Nordwestens, and Republicaner in America, and the Times, Tablet and Tipperary Free Press, in England and Ireland, in the Leipziger Allgemeine Zeitung, Schwabaebise Hercur, Casselsche Zeitung, Allgemeine Auswanderungs Zeitung in Rudolstadt, Nuernberger Correspondent, Eeipiger Zeitung, Bremer Auswanderungs Zeitung, in Germany, and Baseler Zeitung, in Switzerland.

. . . The results thus accomplished exhibited themselves in a surprising degree in a very short time, in written and personal inquiries from nearly every State in the Union and from many parts of Europe, and in the daily increasing number of inquiries at my office. From the first of May to the present time, a period of eight months, I received the really considerable number of 317 letters from Europe and America in reference alone to my official position, of which a large majority contained particular inquiries about Wisconsin, to which I made it my business to give faithful and detailed answers.

Over three thousand persons visited my office, during the same period, of whom nearly four hundred were from New York and vicinity, two or three hundred from other States and Wisconsin, and over two thousand came direct from Europe,— many of whom again, of course, often represented one or more families. Besides these, many emigrants were spoken with on the arrival of the ships in port.

The visitors were two-thirds Germans, a small number Americans, and the remainder Irish, Norwegians, Swedes, English, Scotch, and Hollanders.

If it be true that the Irish emigration is near as extensive as the German, the reason why comparatively so few of them appeared at the office is, as Mr. Byrne, an Irishman by birth, and who had the most intercourse with them, can confirm, that the greater portion arrive with but limited means, and are therefore induced to seize upon the first work offered them for subsistence, which, indeed, is abundantly furnished by railroads and other important enterprises. Competition among employers is at present so great that, for example, the contractors upon the Illinois Central, and many other roads, have established agencies in New York, where not only are high wages offered to those seeking employment, but they are also transported, free of cost, or, at least, at much reduced rates of fare, to the place of their labor. The Irishman, also, is more inclined than the German to a residence in large cities.

I have received, mainly from Wisconsin, remittances of money, in sums of from $5 to $20, amounting to more than

$3,000, with the request to pay them to relatives, children, sisters, brothers, and parents, who were expected, but had not sufficient means to complete their journey.

There were also many minor children and aged persons referred to me, that on their arrival they might be protected against impositions, which humane requests I always willingly and cheerfully complied with.

Of the descriptions of the State placed at my disposal I have made the most liberal use, and have circulated them not only among the emigrants on the arrival of the ships, but have sent them off by mail, especially to Europe. In this, Dr. W. Hildebrandt, U. S. Consul at Bremen, and his Secretary, Mr. Whittlesey, (both from Wisconsin,) afforded me the most cheerful aid, for which I owe them my acknowledgments.

During the first two months, it was often difficult to gain a personal interview with those newly arrived, as they knew neither my name nor office, and therefore appeared very distrustful; but from the month of July, a ship rarely entered the harbor with emigrants, some of whom were not already in possession of my pamphlets, or had read some of my notices and communications: often, indeed, my address had been given them by emigrant societies or ship-owners, with the advice to follow my directions before all others. By living together during a long sea voyage, utter strangers often became strongly attached to each other, and thus it frequently happened that my station on the arrival of a ship was known to nearly all on board, when at the departure from the foreign port, usually but a few individuals had any knowledge of me, thereby often one-half met me with confidence, which was again the occasion that those who were yet undecided about their destination in America, generally chose Wisconsin as their new fatherland.

The number of pamphlets distributed and sent abroad is nearly 30,000, of which one-half found their way to Europe; I also seldom failed to give descriptions of Wisconsin, even to those who influenced by relatives and friends intended to settle in other States; and I have found this practical result, that more than one, discontented with the conditions of things which they there found, at once removed to Wisconsin, where some have since written to me, and expressed their acknowledgment for the counsel given them. . . .

After the most careful inquiries respecting the Emigration from Europe to Wisconsin during the year just past, I am able to give only the following approximate numbers:

From Germany, including the adjoining countries where the prevailing language is German	16 to 18,000
Ireland	4 — 5,000
Norway (mostly by way of Ruebeck,) perhaps	3 — 4,000
Holland, England, Scotland, Sweden and other European countries	2 — 3,000

• • •

My efforts to bring the State of Wisconsin, with its healthful climate, and its rich and boundless resources and advantages, to the notice of the inhabitants of Europe, by means of the press, and the result of those efforts cannot exhibit themselves at once, as every one knows who is partially acquainted with such affairs, but their effects will more evidently appear in the coming season of 1854, for such are the circumstances in Europe, that it often requires a year or more of preparation before the emigrant can leave his old home. Not only was I inclined to activity by the duties directly imposed upon me, but by the certain consciousness that if I should succeed in directing the long trains of emigrants to Wisconsin, I could confer no greater kindness, and could in no way better promote the further prosperity of these weary wanderers from Europe.

Every unprejudiced citizen and observer of our State must confess and acknowledge that the continued prosperity of its inhabitants, is in a great degree dependent upon further accessions to its population from abroad. If they are large, the prosperity and power of Wisconsin will increase in an equal degree; if not large, they will suffer many reverses. Whether he comes from other States of the Union, or from Europe, each individual contributes some thing to the general wealth and expansion, whether in physical strength, knowledge or capital. It may be asserted that a large number of enterprises of greater or less importance, have been undertaken upon the assumption of the most rapid possible increase of our population; and should such increase be cut off, or in a great degree lessened, many disastrous failures would be the certain result. Wisconsin, with the other western States, ought therefore earnestly to oppose all those measures which have been adopted either by the general government, or from selfishness by certain eastern States, for the sake of temporary profit, to undermine the established reputation and good name of the United States.

For years past, emigrants, especially those landing in New York, have been systematically plundered, for which shameless wrong not only the hireling sub-agent, runners, &c., are responsible, but especially those who retain these unprincipled subjects in their employ.

The eager desire for money, induces the various forwarding lines leading to the West, or their agents, to resort to the most shameless means; and the profit that is made thereby, of which frequently the larger portion goes to the agents and the hirelings of those lines, is the chief cause that many laws designed expressly to check this crying injustice, are not only not executed, but are daily, and even hourly, most grossly violated with impunity, in the very presence and under the eyes of the public authorities. If, indeed, one of the victims attempts to bring the swindler to punishment, the venal tool is pushed forward, and every possible assistance afforded him, so that the unfortunate friendless foreigner, a stranger to the customs and laws, and often speaking a strange language, seldom succeeds in finding justice, and he suffers, in addition to his severe loss, the bitter experience of being compelled to find much in his new father-land quite different from the expectations he had indulged in. With bitter curses and complaints such incidents are reported to the home he left, and are by no means the least important reason that of late thousands of emigrants have emigrated to other countries. . . .

The capital which, besides intelligence and physical strength, is brought hither by European emigrants, is much larger than is usually supposed. To give an example only, I state that 120 persons, including women and children, who landed from a single ship from Germany, in August last, and were nearly all induced by me to locate in Wisconsin, had in their possession nearly sixty thousand dollars. It is a well-known fact that in the new states the value of imports greatly exceeds that of exports, often, indeed by one half, and yet the condition of those States improves, and their wealth increases year by year. Who supplies the deficit but the immigrant? Perhaps one quarter of the present inhabitants of Wisconsin from the middle and eastern States of the Union, would to this day never have seen the shores of Lake Michigan if they had not found purchasers for their property in the immigrants from Europe, who by their settlement in the eastern and middle States still contribute to the prosperity of the West.

If it be statistically proven that the population of Ireland during the last ten years has suffered serious diminution in consequence of emigration, this has and can have no application to Germany. While the population of Ireland never exceeded ten millions, on the other hand, the German language is still at this moment by more than fifty millions spoken upon the Continent; and it is further settled, that an annual emigration of half a million, if uniformly distributed, would occasion no perceptible decrease. If it be considered that in the United States, and therefore proportionately in Wisconsin, magnificent enterprises are daily begun, with which lesser undertakings are connected, which can only realize their anticipated profits through the most rapid possible growth and prosperity of the State, to which immigration must contribute the highest aid. It must be a most narrow-minded policy to neglect not only to favor and encourage immigration, but also to use every exertion to direct it more and more to our own State.

In my daily intercourse with the emigrant, I directed the attention of those who intended to purchase land, to the school lands of our State, showing to those of limited means, that they could at once plant themselves in an entirely independent situation, as it could not be difficult for them, with industry and patience, and the long term allowed for payment, to meet their obligation. Upon inquiry, I have had the satisfaction to learn, that during the past year large quantities of these lands, largely exceeding the sales of the previous year, have been sold, and chiefly to actual settlers. The interest and taxes paid upon the lands thus sold, will not only swell the resources of our free school system, but also will aid in the support of the burdens of the State.

It is also gratifying to direct your attention to the fact, that though the entire immigration to the United States during the year 1853, has little, if at all, exceeded that of the year preceding—Wisconsin has received, at least, 15 per cent. more than in 1852.

I have not the least doubt, that it can be yet greatly increased, if in connection with the glorious year of prosperity just past, which affords the best evidence of the fertility of the soil of Wisconsin, the State will, by the enactment of liberal laws suited to the times, and conservative of the personal freedom of each of its citizens, draw upon itself more and more the eyes of the world of progress. . . .

Respectfully submitted,
Yours, &c.,

HERMAN HAERTEL

Milwaukee, Wisconsin
Dec. 30, 1853

REPORT OF THE SELECT COMMITTEE

THE SELECT COMMITTEE TO WHOM HAD BEEN REFERRED SO

MUCH OF THE MESSAGE OF HIS EXCELLENCY THE GOVERNOR,

AS RELATES TO THE SUBJECT OF THE COMMISSIONER OF

EMIGRATION, AND ALSO THE REPORT OF SAID OFFICER,

HAVE HAD THE SAME UNDER CONSIDERATION, AND

BEG LEAVE TO REPORT:

That from the report of the Commissioner and other sources of information which your committee have obtained, they fully concur with the Governor, in his views as expressed in his message, as to the usefulness of the Agency and its importance to the State.

Among the many reasons which have been presented in its examination of the subject, and which induce them to regard the continuance of this Agency as important, your committee would briefly allude to the following:

1. The operation of the Agency thus far, although in the incipiency, has been manifestly advantageous, as emigrants have been induced, through the instrumentality of the Commissioner, to locate in Wisconsin, bringing with them a large amount of capital, which together with the known frugality, industry and economy which characterizes a great portion of our immigration, will add to our annual revenue more than the amount expended annually in keeping up in its activity and usefulness, our Agency in New York.

2. The course adopted by the Commissioner, of writing and placing himself in communication with agents in the various shipping ports of Europe, will, in the opinion of your commit-

---

From Wisconsin *Senate Journal,* 1854, Appendix, "Report of the Select Committee . . . [on] the Subject of the Commissioner of Emigration," pp. 3–7.

of our institutions. It has accordingly received that careful consideration by the committee which its importance seemed to demand. It may be safely assumed that the national prosperity of a community, no matter what the character or form of its government, mainly depends on the morals, industry, and frugality of its people, and that the weakest and least permanent of all governments is that in which indolence and vice are allowed to flourish under the name of liberty. A nation of freemen, no matter how great or powerful, cannot long continue as such without religion and morality, industry and frugality; for these are indispensable supports of popular government. Crime and pauperism are the bane of a republic, and they cannot be too carefully considered, nor too stringently guarded against, if those in authority would be true to the trust reposed in them by their fellow-citizens. That these evils have, of late years, grown far beyond the ratio of the increase of our population, and have alarmed the considerate and reflecting portion of all classes of the American people, is an admitted fact. That this increase is traceable to the immense influx of foreigners within the last ten years past, no one who examines the subject can deny. Thousands have come hither within that period to fill our streets as beggars, or to become the inmates of our alms-houses, and other charitable institutions. Undesirable as such a population may be, we are yet afflicted with one of a still worse character, derived from the same source. Our country has been converted into a sort of penal colony, to which foreign governments ship their criminals. It is not only the thriftless poor who come hither, spending their last cent in crossing the Atlantic to add to the burden of our poor laws, and to stand between native misfortune and the relief provided for it by charity, but inmates of the prisons of Europe are sent hither by their governments to prey upon society and to contaminate our people with their vices. Of the truth of this, there is ample proof. The evil complained of, and asked to be remedied, exists in a most fearful reality; and such powers as are conferred upon the government by the Constitution to protect and guard the people against it, should be promptly employed in their behalf. Already the fountains of public morality have been corrupted and the public safety compromised. Our commercial cities have become filled with these foreign felons, deep dyed in crime, who themselves constituting a powerful class, are not only constantly engaged in committing crimes, but conspiring against the public peace. They are the stuff that mobs are made of in those cities, who invade the sanctity and purity of the ballot-box, and destroy the freedom of the elective franchise.

FOREIGNERS CROWDED IN THE CITIES

That a large part of the foreign born population resides in the cities and towns may readily be perceived by examining the following table, showing the number of inhabitants, native and foreign, of the cities therein named:

Free States	Native	Foreign	Slave States	Native	Foreign
New York	277,752	235,733	Baltimore	130,491	35,492
Philadelphia	286,246	121,699	New Orleans	50,470	48,601
Boston	88,948	46,677	St. Louis	36,529	38,397
Cincinnati	60,558	54,541	Washington	33,530	4,282
Albany	31,162	16,591	Louisville	25,079	12,461
Providence	31,755	9,679	Charleston	17,809	4,643
Chicago	13,693	15,682	Richmond	15,441	2,102
Newark	26,561	12,322	Mobile	9,565	4,086
Detroit	11,055	9,927			
Portland	17,265	3,512			
New Haven	16,641	3,697			
Milwaukie	7,181	12,782			
Total	868,917	542,832	Total	318,914	150,064

Aggregate of free States	1,411,749
Aggregate of slave States	468,978
Aggregate population	1,880,727
Native	1,187,831
Foreign	692,896

It will thus be seen that almost one-third of the entire foreign population in the country reside in the twenty cities named in the foregoing table, while they contain but about the fifteenth part of the native population of the United States. . . .

These facts clearly show that a very large portion of the immigrant population is in the cities and towns, and though we are without statistics on the subject, we may fairly draw the inference that the major part of the worthless portion of it may be found in the cities and towns. It is there where the outcasts, mendicants, and convicts, disgorged from the jails and workhouses of Europe, are mostly exercising their corrupting influence upon public morals, and oppressing the honest and virtuous citizen with heavy taxation. Need it then be wondered at that both national and State interference are now demanded? . . .

INCREASE OF INTEMPERANCE, AND ITS CAUSE

Intemperance is undoubtedly one of the great causes of pauperism and crime. The progress of intemperance can, to a very great extent, be traced to the immense influx of foreigners of these classes. Especially true is this in regard to all our commercial cities. As already shown, they love the haunts of cities, and do not spread themselves over the country and cultivate our soil. Coming generally without means, trades or professions, they are compelled to remain at the port at which they land upon our shore, and seek refuge in our public institutions for the poor, or engage in some business requiring little or no capital. The first step of hundreds and thousands of them consequently is, to open a grog shop, and thus aid to promote vice. The natural result is, that irreligion, immorality, pauperism and crime radiate from the cities, and spread over the land their demoralizing influence. . . .

FOREIGN PAUPERISM

The census returns of 1850 show that the amount of public means expended during the preceding year, for the support of paupers, is $2,954,806, and the number of paupers supported during the same period, in whole or part, was 134,972. They show further that, of the number thus supported, there were 68,538 of foreign birth, *being over one half of the whole number.* Those of foreign birth then in the country numbered 2,244,625, and one out of every *thirty-three* of that number was, therefore, a pauper; while the native born, including the free colored, and those whose birth was unknown, numbered 19,979,563, of whom *only one* out of every *three hundred* was a charge on the public. . . .

. . . During the year 1852 . . . the number of immigrants arrived at New York was 300,992, and the number supported or pecuniarily assisted by the commission[1] was 141,992! . . .

FOREIGN CRIMINALS

The census of 1850 shows that the whole number of criminals within the year preceeding, in all the States, except California, was 26,679; of which number 12,988 were natives, and 13,691 foreigners, being *one* conviction out of every *fifteen hundred and eighty* of the natives, and *one* out of every *one hundred and sixty-five* of the foreign population of the United States at that time. The proportion of native and foreign crime, it thus appears, was as one to ten—one American to ten foreigners. . . .

NEGLECT OF EDUCATION

If it be true, and no rational mind will doubt it, as we are told by Washington, in his farewell address, that "in proportion

---

[1] The New York State Commissioners of Emigration. [ED.]

as the structure of a government gives force to public opinion, it is essential that public opinion should be enlightened;" then we have another serious cause of alarm in the deleterious influences the immense influx of vicious foreigners must exercise upon our free institution. Ignorance is the parent of vice; and it is a lamentable fact, that a large portion of the immigrant population are not only ignorant themselves, and wholly incapable of communing with either the school book or the Bible, but, what is yet worse, permit their offspring to grow up in the same ignorance. Though our schools are open to all, it is nevertheless true that thousands of the children of this class of our population do not attend the schools, but grow up in ignorance, idleness, vagrancy and vice. . . .

IMPORTATION OF FOREIGN INFIDELITY

Another serious evil resulting from the unguarded admission of vicious foreigners, is the flood of infidelity which has been brought along with them, and is now being attempted to be popularized by them in this country. A large portion of them are atheists, deeply imbued with feelings of hostility both to religion and social order. . . .

HAS CONGRESS POWER OVER IMMIGRATION?

It is the inherent right of every community to protect itself against all public evils; and why has it not also the power to close our ports against convicts and paupers, sent here by foreign governments, and whose corrupt public morality disseminate and popularize infidelity, disturb the public peace, degrade our character as a nation, fill our prisons and almshouses, and seriously impair the stability of our free institutions? The power exists somewhere, either in the States, or in the general government, or in both of them. . . .

WHO SHALL REMEDY THE EVIL?

Both the general and State governments can do much to stay the tide of immigration of this undesirable population, and to protect society against its pernicious influences, and the injuries it threatens, not only to the prosperity and welfare of the country, but the perpetuity of our republican institutions. Each can, within its own sphere and the limits of its constitutional power, not only adopt measures which will contribute greatly to prevent and put an end to the introduction of foreign convicts and paupers, but to save our country from the further increase of the evils resulting from such an accession to our population. Both the national and State governments having ample power, what is to prevent the adoption of measures by Congress and by the State legislatures to guard against this gigantic evil? It is known, felt, and acknowledged to exist; and the most indifferent to the subject cannot but appreciate the imminence of the danger alike to the public prosperity and the public morals, as well as the oppressive character of the public burdens it imposes upon our countrymen. The necessity for prompt and energetic measures to arrest its further progress must be evident to every sagacious statesman. Let us then have legislative action, State and national, on the subject. Meet it we must, and it is the duty of those in power to meet it at once, or in a little while longer it will prove irremedial. . . .

The only deductions fairly to be drawn from the facts adduced in regard to the immigration of foreign paupers and criminals are plainly and unmistakeably these:

First. That it is the chief source of intemperance, and the main cause of the alarming increase of that great public evil in our country.

Second. That it has filled our commercial cities with a foreign convict and pauper population, the material of which mobs are made to such an extent as to endanger the public peace and the public morals, and to be generally regarded as a frightful evil.

Third. That it is a fruitful source of pauperism, and the chief cause of its fearful increase within the last few years.

Fourth. That it is a prolific source of crime, and that to it the enormous increase of crime may almost wholly be attributed.

Fifth. That it has brought upon the country a large juvenile vagrant population, now growing up to prey upon society, which is fearfully on the increase, and almost entirely of foreign origin.

Sixth. That it is the source of ignorance, the mother of crime, filling our country with a people whose vicious propensities predominate over both the moral and intellectual faculties, and who, urged on by ungoverned appetites and passions, with fancied or superstitious objects in view, constitute a population from which the country has nothing to expect but evil to its free institutions.

Seventh. That it has brought into the country a large body of men who are inimical to our free institutions and our social organization, and who are devoted to dogmas and creeds, which experience as well as all past history have shown to be not only incompatible with republican institutions, or a well regulated constitutional liberty, but antagonistic to the welfare and happiness of mankind; and which, if carried out here, would make this country a pandemonium on earth.

Eighth. That it has flooded our country with irreligion, immorality, and licentiousness, and is the source from whence infidelity comes. State legislation can reach many of these evils, and it behooves the State legislatures to institute the necessary measures of reform on the subject. Among those which commend themselves as most likely to be effective are:

First. The adoption of a State policy which will discountenance the *esprit du corps,* now so studiously cultivated among foreigners in our large cities, which is calculated, if not designed, to keep them foreigners in feelings, sentiments, and habits, though they enjoy the benefits of our institutions and owe allegiance to our laws. Let their separate and distinctive civil and military organizations, wherever they exist, be frowned down, and a policy be pursued which will break up and destroy those foreign organizations, and oblige those belonging to them to identify themselves with the country of their adoption, and to be naught else than what they ought to be—Americans, and *only* Americans.

Second. The rigid enforcement of all license laws authorizing the sale of liquor, promptly punishing those who violate them, and the adoption of a provision in all those laws, like that passed by the recent legislature of Pennsylvania, prohibiting a license to be granted for the sale of liquor to any other than a citizen of the United States. Experience demonstrates that most of the grog shops in cities are kept by unnaturalized foreigners, who will thus be excluded from pursuing a business fraught with misery and crime.

Third. The adoption of measures, as far as is practicable, to indemnify the State in case those landed upon its shores shall become paupers, and to compel those maintained by the public to earn their support, if possessed of sufficient health and strength to do so, and thus present to them the alternative of honest industry or starvation. A rigid enforcement of such a policy would soon rid the public of the body of mendicants who, too indolent to work, though abundantly able to do so, now crowd our thoroughfares and fill our poor-houses.

Fourth. The more prompt conviction and more certain punishment of all offenders, and the abandonment of that mistaken zeal of philanthropy which now steps in so often between the outraged laws and their violators.

Fifth. The establishment of institutions so as to take charge and provide for all that class of juveniles known as delinquents or vagrants. Though our common schools are in a more advanced state than those in any other part of the world, our reformatory efforts to save neglected and forsaken children have not kept pace with our progress of common school education, and hence our country is now cursed with so large a juvenile population growing up in vice and crime. This is an alarming evil, and demands prompt legislative attention. In a government like ours, where all power is derived from the people, they should be wise, virtuous, and enlightened, lest they abuse it. How can we expect the next generation to be so, if a large portion of it is permitted to grow up in sottish ignorance and brutal sensuality, and sure of becoming adept in crime long before arriving at manhood? Not only have we been remiss in establishing and maintaining a sufficient number of these juvenile reformatory institutions, but, good as our common schools are, much too is yet required of us in regard to them. Thousands of children, especially those of foreigners, do not enjoy their benefits, though open to them. Thus far no legal measures have been taken to ensure all the advantages of a common school education. Is it not a grave question, whether the time is not at hand when the gross neglect of parents to send their children to schools should receive some attention, and steps be taken to guard the public from the evil resulting therefrom?

Sixth. Lastly, and most important of all at the present juncture, is the adoption and enforcement of a truly American policy on all subjects—one which will tend to cultivate and develop an undying attachment to our country, its history, and its institutions, and to inspire a profound veneration and respect for the examples of our patriotic revolutionary ancestors. One of the first acts of the Continental Congress was to order an edition of God's Holy Book; and it is not too much to say, perhaps, that beyond all other causes combined which enabled our forefathers to achieve independence, was the deep and universal acquaintance with that Holy Book, scattered among the children of a former generation, and the training of mind and heart and spirit which they received. Nor is it more than the truth, perhaps, to say now that is the remnant of that spirit which has maintained our republic up to the present time. Is it not then of the first and highest importance, now that the land is flooded with foreign infidels, who, taught at home to repudiate everything to be revered in human institutions, have already here raised the black standard of atheism, and declared a war of extermination against the faith which supported our ancestors in establishing the republic, and the hope which animates us for the future—is it not, in view of all this, the sacred duty of all Americans who love their country, and mean to perpetuate its institutions, to imitate the illustrious example of their sires, and to *insist* upon having their children taught in our schools the lessons of wisdom to be found only in the Bible, and thus have that Holy Book as one of the text books of our public schools?

Let a policy like this be adopted by the States, and let Congress exercise the powers conferred upon it to arrest the evils so justly complained of, and the public good, the peace and prosperity of the country, and the welfare and happiness of the people, will be thereby promoted.

INDEX

THE AMERICAN HERITAGE SERIES

THE COLONIAL PERIOD

THE REVOLUTIONARY ERA

THE YOUNG NATION

TOPICAL VOLUMES